AL QAEDA IN ITS OWN WORDS

AL QAEDA
IN ITS
OWN
WORDS

EDITED BY

GILLES KEPEL AND
JEAN-PIERRE MILELLI

TRANSLATED BY

PASCALE GHAZALEH

THE BELKNAP PRESS OF HARVARD UNIVERSITY PRESS

Cambridge, Massachusetts · London, England · 2008

Originally published as *Al-Qaida dans le texte*
présenté par Gilles Kepel
© Presses Universitaires de France, 2005

LIBRARY OF CONGRESS CATALOGING-IN-PUBLICATION DATA
Al-Qaida dans le texte. English
Al Qaeda in its own words / edited by Giles Kepel and Jean-Pierre Milelli.
p.   cm.
Includes bibliographical references and index.
ISBN-13: 978-0-674-02804-3
1. Qaida (Organization)   2. Terroism.   3. Jihad.   4. Islamic fundamentalism.
5. Islam and politics.   I. Kepel, Gilles.   II. Milelli, Jean-Pierre.   III. Title.
HV6431.A4613 2008
363.325—dc22   2007040883

In memory of Rémy Leveau
(July 6, 1932–March 2, 2005)

Contents

ANNOTATION

CONTRIBUTORS

Thomas Hegghammer, a scholar at the Institute for Political Studies in Paris and a researcher at the Norwegian Defence Research Establishment, is an expert on Islamism.

Gilles Kepel, professor at the Institute for Political Studies in Paris, is a specialist in contemporary Islam. Among his other published works are *Muslim Extremism in Egypt: The Prophet and Pharaoh,* 2nd ed. (Berkeley: University of California Press, 2003), originally published as *Le Prophète et le Pharaon: Aux sources des mouvements islamistes* (Paris: Seuil, 1993), *Jihad: The Trail of Political Islam,* trans. Anthony F. Roberts (Cambridge, Mass.: Harvard University Press, 2002), originally published as *Jihad: Expansion et déclin de l'islamisme* (Paris: Gallimard, 2000), and *The War for Muslim Minds: Islam and the West,* trans. Pascale Ghazaleh (Cambridge, Mass.: Harvard University Press, 2004), also published as published as *Fitna: Guerre au coeur de l'islam* (Paris: Gallimard, 2004).

Stéphane Lacroix, a scholar at the Institute for Political Studies in Paris, is an expert on political movements in Saudi Arabia.

Jean-Pierre Milelli holds an advanced degree in Arabic and teaches at the Institute for Political Studies in Paris. He has translated several books into French, among them Peter L. Bergen's *Holy War, Inc.: Inside the Secret World of Osama Bin Laden* (New York: Free Press, 2001; London: Weidenfield and Nicolson, 2001).

Omar Saghi, a scholar at the Institute for Political Studies in Paris, is an expert on Saudi Arabia and contemporary Arabic literature. He is also the author of *Figures de l'engagement* (Figures of Commitment), (Paris: L'Harmattan, 2003).

NOTE ON THE TRANSLATION

Note to the French Edition

Any anthology entails choices, and we tried to make them here in a way that would give a fair idea of the work of each author, while also taking up as many questions as possible through the texts.

An introduction by one of the contributors precedes the texts by each author, and the excerpts are annotated, not only to make them more intelligible, but also to shed light on the shared culture that inspires them and the ideology they reflect and express.

All these texts from various sources were translated from the Arabic. The most common source, however, is the Web sites of the radical Islamist movement.

We have used ellipses in the translation to indicate omitted passages and have left the numerous bibliographical references as we found them, even though the reader may discover that the editions cited are inaccessible or out of print. Transliteration of many Arabic words has been simplified, and the numerous citations from the Quran [in the French edition] were taken from the translation by Denise Masson, published in the Pléiade edition (Paris: Gallimard, 1967).

—JEAN-PIERRE MILELLI, translator of the French edition

Note to the English Edition

For Quranic citations, I have relied on the highly respected English-language interpretation by Abdullah Yusuf Ali, *The Holy Quran* (Beirut: Dar al Arabia, 1968). In the interests of familiarity for the English reader, however, I have rendered the verbs and pronouns in a modern form ("you" instead of "ye," "takes" instead of "taketh," and so on), and replaced references to "Allah" with the word "God." Other translations of some texts presented here are available online; I have consulted these where appropriate and cited them in the notes.

I also took the liberty of removing many of the repeated pious invocations (for instance, "May he be exalted," used in reference to God, and "Blessings and peace upon him," in reference to the Prophet Muhammad. These purely formulaic expressions, while common in Arabic, would merely distance the reader from the English text, by creating an exotic and alien effect that would detract from the content of the book.

—PASCALE GHAZALEH, translator of the English edition

AL QAEDA IN ITS OWN WORDS

General Introduction

AL QAEDA, THE ESSENTIALS

GILLES KEPEL

Although the events of September 11, 2001, have left the realm of current affairs and entered history, Al Qaeda remains an elusive phenomenon. As of this writing, the hunt for its leaders has led nowhere; Bin Laden and Zawahiri still show themselves with impunity on television screens worldwide, as people everywhere hold their breath in anticipation of another spectacular, devastating attack. The very nature of Al Qaeda as an entity remains unclear, even when the metaphors drawn from astronomy have been exhausted: whether one calls it a terrorist nebula or a galaxy, the terms point to the vastness of infinite, frightening space, but they also underscore our inability to conceive of this unidentified object. Al Qaeda challenges the categories through which we were accustomed to understand political or religious organizations and international relations at the time when the cold war between Moscow and Washington was unfolding, according to a certain number of clearly defined codes, norms, and rules. By violating them, Al Qaeda—one meaning of the Arabic phrase is "the rule"— has revealed in the breach, although not clearly established, new rules of relations among states, nations, and societies, between violence and media spectacle; it has revealed new modes of militant mobilization, while apparently reviving ancient codes that were believed to have become obsolete: the quest for martyrdom and the process of religious indoctrination spontaneously evoke the Middle Ages more readily than they do the age of information technology.

We have dressed up this inability to conceive of the phenomenon in the name "terrorism," a name acceptable to all those who see Bin Laden and his acolytes as monsters, and rejected, of course, by those who for various reasons take them to be heroes. Whether or not one sympathizes with such value judgments and condemns terror from a moral point of view, however, leaves us none the wiser about Al Qaeda's nature. To the contrary, perhaps; as is demonstrated by the logic of the "war on terror," which confuses matters by justifying in a single breath the unsuccessful hunt for Bin Laden, the eradication of the Taliban regime, and the elimination of Saddam Hussein's dictatorship, the term "terrorism" represents an intellectual shortcut that is content to conflate, as objects of reproof, phenomena whose dynamics we must strive to distinguish from one another. This is what Durkheim called a prenotion, which he defined as a sort of concept, roughly based on common sense, that presents itself as capable of clarifying a social phenomenon, although what it really does is to hinder its elucidation. In the United States today, the production of books on terrorism has become a veritable industry: they do little to advance knowledge, but they provide a sort of transition between a reading of the world structured by the cold war, in which the study of the Soviet Union constituted the principal discipline, and our present difficulty in apprehending the multipolar world that followed the collapse of communism—dominated by a single superpower opposed by complicated, confused modes of resistance, insurrection, and violence. The supposed "science of terrorism" (served up by instant experts who crowd the television studios and bookstore displays) props up wobbly theories of the "end of history" and the "clash of civilizations." It offers precious little help, however, in grappling with the changes the world is undergoing at the beginning of the third millennium. The phrase, which belongs to the register of rhetoric, flatters anguished public opinion, but fails to enlighten.

Going against the grain of such globalizing methodologies, this book has the more modest aim of analyzing—of exposing—the doctrinal system produced by what we call Al Qaeda, on the basis of what is out there to read. Everyone who watches television has easy access to the register of images that satellite channels broadcast: attacks, declarations made by turban-wearing ideologues posing in front of a cave, hostages reading a statement to beg for their lives—all in an untidy sequence that plays on fear and voyeurism, as any good spectacle does. Those who surf the Web find more extreme images, of hostages being beheaded, for instance—not unlike the violent sensations provoked by the display of various perversions on specialized sites. These images make up the most accessible spectrum of Al Qaeda's propaganda, but it is difficult to decipher them, for they function most readily in the register of emotion. They target a very wide audience and do barely anything to mobilize rational argument—except when declarations are read in Arabic. Even then, the complexity of discourse incites Western channels to reduce the images to brief, spectacular sequences, accompanied by translated quotations formulating specific threats or presenting some immediately comprehensible idea.

Beyond these televised declarations, however, the principal ideologues who have spoken in the name of Al Qaeda, or about it, have published on the Internet—and sometimes also in print form—an abundant literature that mainly, it would seem, targets circles of militants and potential sympathizers. In substance, it provides the rationale for action and stamps mobilization for political ends with spectacular violence, through the use of religious, historical, or even nationalist arguments. In the absence of any organizational chart for a hypothetical organization named Al Qaeda, this written body of work remains the most tangible element in the identity of such a phenomenon. It follows a rational, discursive mode, designed to convince and to justify an all-out jihadist warrior's investing the universe with Islamic meaning; it allows its readers to enter into a way of thinking, to get to the very heart of a specific worldview. This worldview is what makes up Al Qaeda's essence, whatever the subsequent ups and downs in the actions undertaken by jihad militants who identify with it. To elucidate this ideology, without simply calling it terrorism, is to enable ourselves to understand its modus operandi and define it by *comprehension*, rather than by extension.

Instead of giving a preliminary definition of Al Qaeda, cobbled together from various symptoms—attacks, murders, or hostage taking, audiovisually produced—this book gathers internal documents that allow us to build an elusive object up from the inside, beyond the manifestations that turn it into a spectacle and thereby disguise its identity. We have chosen texts attributed to four authors that have resulted in the production of Al Qaeda as a worldview and as a movement. After Bin Laden—the best point of entry to this universe and its most media-friendly incarnation, but one whose positions, as we shall see, have little theoretical depth—come two ideologues. The first, Abdallah Azzam, a Palestinian Muslim Brother, herald of jihad in Afghanistan, and theoretician of contemporary jihad worldwide, is known only to specialists. His thought, which is rooted in Islamic theology, is often abstruse, but it constitutes the key without which it is impossible to understand the central place of armed struggle in radical contemporary Islamism. The second, Ayman al-Zawahiri, besides being a media figure, provided the point of connection between the work of Azzam, assassinated in 1989, and the Islamist guerrillas of the 1990s, then theorized the shift toward "martyrdom operations," of which 9/11 was the apogee. He is undeniably the main thinker for this movement, having been nourished on the militant literature of Egyptian Islamists, whose course of action he radicalized, and occasionally evoking the messianic tones of Protestant millenarians, the Baader group, the Italian Red Brigades, or the French group Direct Action. Al Qaeda's mental landscape ends with Abu Musab al-Zarqawi, the activist who took over the Iraqi battlefield at the cost of the atrocities attributed to him, meanwhile pledging allegiance to Bin Laden and Zawahiri. His contribution is important less for its doctrinal value than for its anti-Shiite violence—an innovation in comparison to the other texts.

One of the characteristics of these online texts—their digital form is constitutive of the networking that makes up Al Qaeda's very substance—is our inability to identify their authors with any degree of certainty. In a universe where copyright does not exist, we cannot be sure that Bin Laden, Zawahiri, or Zarqawi really wrote everything that is attributed to them. (The probability is higher for Azzam, who lived before the Internet generation, and most of whose texts were printed on paper before being put online—even if copyright has always been a relatively fluid notion in the Arab world.) Paradoxically, the information age telescopes here into the bygone era of manuscript production, before the printing press was invented. Just as an expert on Aristotle establishes a definitive version of a text by collating various known manuscripts, eliminating the interpolations of medieval copyists, and restoring forgotten or omitted material, anyone who ventures into the jungle of online Islamist propaganda is never certain that a text should be definitively attributed to a given author or that an author wrote the whole of a given text. It becomes necessary to impute authenticity—while integrating an element of doubt nevertheless—depending on whether the text appears on one of the most notorious Islamist sites or another. Some of these, like the one set up by Abu Muhammad al-Maqdisi, a Jordanian militant who will be dealt with in more detail later, are veritable "collections" that serve as references for the movement. Here are echoes of that traditional art of Islamic theology, the authentification of hadith (the Prophet's words and deeds), which requires the elimination of dubious material. The difference is that the Islamist Webmaster, in the third millennium c.e., takes the place of yesteryear's people of the pen.

The very content of the pamphlets and tracts published electronically is another factor in the telescoping of time between the Middle Ages and today. These texts are full of references to the epic tales of the Prophet's companions and the history of the Arab caliphs—inexhaustible sources for a founding myth that seeks to edify by establishing the criteria by which to judge contemporary events and determine the principles of political action. In this literature, history is simply the infinite repetition of a single narrative: the arrival of the Prophet, the rise of Islam, the struggles to extend its dominion, and its expansion throughout the world. Each generation must apply itself anew to the task of this incomplete proselytism, taking up the original jihad to this end, against a multifarious enemy that Al Qaeda's discourse reduces to the characteristics of the initial, timeless enemy as stigmatized by the classical authors: the unbeliever, the infidel (*kafir*), the apostate (*murtadd*), and so on. Abdallah Azzam's contribution has a cardinal place in this demonstration: during the jihad against the Red Army in Afghanistan in the 1980s he situated the struggle within the missionary and messianic meaning of Islamic history as he interpreted it, thus transcending the role of pawn that the United States, in its endgame against the Soviet Union, sought to impose on the Afghan and Arab mujahedeen. The authors of the following decade—especially Bin Laden and Zawahiri—situated their worldview and their actions within the approach originated by Azzam. In their turn, they mobilized the forebears to describe and justify their own struggle, stigmatize the enemy, and finally draw lessons from the failure of guerrilla warfare in the 1990s, thereby establishing the legitimacy of the "martyrdom operations" that became Al Qaeda's signature and placed it at the center of global upheavals. The goal of this demonstration was to ensconce their actions at the heart of Islam and claim impeccable religious legitimacy—contested, of course, by all Muslims who oppose them. On the doctrinal level, this was a show of strength comparable to the 9/11 attacks, the goal being to take over Islamic terms of reference and terrorize the jihadists' adversaries within the contemporary Islamic religious arena. The space in which this struggle is unfolding, significantly, is the Internet, overwhelmingly occupied by a movement that has structured itself like the Web and shaped itself according the same model: the term *al qaeda*, in Arabic, also suggests a database or reservoir, for example, of information (*qaedat al-ma'lumat*).

For this set of reasons, we thought it necessary to provide readers who do not know Arabic with selected extracts from Al Qaeda's discourse, making up a sort of jihadist primer. But they would have made no sense had they not been relocated within the intellectual and doctrinal context where they operate, and through which they seek to gain adherents to win the war at the heart of Islam—a war of references, sources, and authority, which determines the real war. This large-scale project could only be a collective work, one that mobilized the shared energies and knowledge of teachers and young researchers in Department for Middle Eastern and Mediterranean Studies at the Institute for Political Studies. All of them placed their familiarity with the topic, their linguistic skills, their intellectual curiosity, and their intuition in the service of this common enterprise.

We decided to pair introductions with commentaries on the texts: after an introduction dealing with one of the four authors (Bin Laden, Azzam, Zawahiri, or Zarqawi), appears the text of one of his documents, annotated and glossed by Thomas Hegghammer, Stéphane Lacroix, Omar Saghi, and Jean-Pierre Milelli. For readers who do not know Arabic and have little knowledge of Islamic culture, the commentary clarifies references to history and Muslim traditions, identifies the authors cited, explains the implications of Arabic terms when they have specific connotations, places the work of each author within the mental universe of the contemporary Islamist movement, and explains the recent events, debates, excommunications, and alliances that make up the everyday life of the movement but are sufficiently complex to be inaccessible to novices. Thomas Hegghammer, Stéphane Lacroix, and Omar Saghi applied to this collective project the considerable erudition and knowledge they had displayed in preparing their doctoral dissertations. Jean-Pierre Milelli drew on his deep, nuanced knowledge of Arabic language and culture. In this multifaceted work we attempt to make Al Qaeda's doctrine and ideology accessible, and thus to help clear up one of the modern world's principal blind spots.

PART I

OSAMA BIN LADEN

INTRODUCTION

OSAMA BIN LADEN, THE ICONIC ORATOR

OMAR SAGHI

On the morning of September 11, 2001, a quadruple attack marked the beginning of the new century, and the continuation of the discords and demons of the preceding one. Many wanted to see the event as part of a linear progression leading directly from the young zealot in Jidda to the media icon of today: from that perspective, a mechanical sequence made up of fundamentalism, political crises, and criminal character fatally produced the various massacres attributed to Osama Bin Laden. Still, if one is to understand the man and the movement, it is necessary to reintroduce the peripheral strategies of various actors over the past quarter century and remember the role of chance and vicissitude in constructing this emblematic figure.

Growing up Saudi

Osama Bin Laden was born in Riyadh in 1957.[1] His father was a Yemeni immigrant who followed an exemplary path. Muhammad Bin Awad Bin Laden was originally from Hadramawt, a region of Yemen that has traditionally exported its inhabitants, as peaceful laborers or as conquering warriors, according to circumstances. Known for their hard work and frugality, the Hadramis make excellent masons and reliable financiers, both of which were necessary to the young kingdom of Abdul Aziz Ibn Saud, founded anew in 1932, an avatar of several earlier attempts.

Bin Laden's father left Husn Bahishn, the fortress town in the Wadi Dawan Valley where he was born, and went to seek his fortune in Mecca in the 1930s. He was lucky enough to gain access to King Saud's court, and the king, trusting his very reliable instincts, made this rough yet imposing man responsible for constructing a number of the buildings with which he filled his domain. Muhammad was a tall, bony, unattractive man, with a gaunt face and only one good eye; he never learned to read or write, but he was universally respected for his irrepressible energy.[2] This portrait of Osama's father irresistibly evokes that of the kingdom's founder: the two men resembled each other, even in their respective career paths. Both were self-made men who made an impact, the first on the technicians and businessmen who surrounded him, and the second on other heads of state.

This resemblance is the first that ties Osama Bin Laden's destiny, in a certain sense, to that of Saudi Arabia. It sheds a new light on the trajectory of Osama.

His father evolved with the kingdom; Muhammad Bin Laden quickly laid claim to a large share of the Saudi market in construction and public works, a sector that by tradition flourishes especially in countries transformed by sudden wealth. His marriages and offspring proliferated. A friend introduced him to a young Syrian woman from Lattakia, Alia Ghanem, whom he took as his companion. She may have been of Alawite stock: Lattakia is the capital of Alawite country, although the city's population has historically been Sunni, and if her family name is very common in the Levant, her first name—an homage to Ali, and one given especially among Muslims of various Shiite persuasions—sparked and perpetuated rumors about her heretical origin. A year after she met Muhammad, Alia Ghanem gave the Yemeni tycoon a son, who was named Osama, a fairly common name in Syria. Osama was the billionaire's seventeenth son (he had twenty-four, and thirty daughters). Paradoxically, Osama lived out his first years in the new neighborhood of Malazz, a modern sector of the capital where Arab immigrants settled, one of which the punctilious Saudi sheikhs did not always approve, some going so far as to publish a fatwa condemning the residents of this quarter, who were suspected of impious behavior.

When he was still a child, Osama Bin Laden left Riyadh for Jidda, the kingdom's western metropolis, where his mother, now a divorcée, married Muhammad al-Attas, another Yemeni immigrant, who had worked with Muhammad Bin Laden. Al-Attas married Alia Ghanem on the recommendation of his colleague, who was accustomed to providing a marital and economic future for the wives he cast off, and for their children. According to another rumor—one that young Osama himself seems to have fueled—his mother was only a sort of courtesan, whom Muhammad Bin Laden never actually married.[3] These two shadows cast on his origins (the possibility that his mother belonged to a sect that Sunni historiography condemns, and his parents' potentially adulterous relationship, which would have made him a bastard) probably played a role in shaping his identity as well as his desire for revenge and recognition.

Osama, lost among his many siblings, had the same kind of childhood as many Hadramis: he frequently accompanied his father, and then his stepfather, on their visits to construction sites, and received a strict education. In 1967 his father, who had never been very present in his life, died in a plane crash while he was inspecting a site. Osama spent his lackluster adolescence in Jidda. He lived in Musharrifa, then a very new neighborhood, where princes and the local social elite lived. He frequented the children of that elite at school, where he went unnoticed, save for a certain introversion that seemed to conceal a tenacious stubbornness: for instance, he opposed his schoolmates on certain points that he considered anti-Islamic and even at that early stage showed an uncommon interest in religion. The only vice he showed was his passion for cars and speed, and for football, which he played along with his schoolmates.

In 1973, after the October War, which pitted Israel against a Syrian-Egyptian coalition once again, an oil embargo was declared at the initiative of Saudi Arabia. The kingdom's revenues skyrocketed as a result. In a short time, it was not only the government's coffers that were overflowing; all society was also flooded with petrodollars. Osama was sixteen. He was one of the hundreds of thousands of teenagers born in the Saudi baby boom that modern medical advances made possible in the aftermath of World War II. His generation—unlike the one that preceded it—did not experience a gradual improvement in living standards after years of traditional life. It was born into relative prosperity, and, as it reached adolescence, on the threshold of manhood, it was stunned by massive amounts of money.

The effects were felt very quickly, first in the representations and then in the behavior of this age group. The richest had easy access to the rest of the world, where they discovered and experienced lifestyles that ran completely counter to the kingdom's culture and ideology. But increasing openness toward Western lifestyles echoed throughout Saudi society. Osama soon expressed his concern about the deleterious effects this could have on the faith and religious practices of his schoolmates; then he extended his analysis (and his fears) to encompass all society. In 1974 he married one of his cousins; the couple lived in his mother's house.

After September 11, an Augustinian image of Bin Laden was constructed that was intended to devalue him in the eyes of his friends, relatives, and adversaries: a returning sybarite, who after experiencing the heady pleasures of Western society, went to repent in the caves of Afghanistan, to his own misery and that of the world at large. This same image was supposed to reflect the experience of a whole generation in Saudi Arabia, and more generally in the Gulf: it was false, however, and neither Osama Bin Laden nor most of his comrades had to undergo such a painful conversion.

First of all, their education had already distanced them from the Western dolce vita. The Saudis who led such a charmed life with much pomp and ostentation after the oil boom were a relative minority, and a very highly placed one. The real shock that determined subsequent political engagement for Osama Bin Laden and others was the imagined possibility that this lifestyle was accessible and had been somehow democratized: the effective realization of the dissolution of traditional society promised or made possible by easy money in the late 1970s.

Osama Bin Laden's generation—the offspring of the kingdom's political or material founders—received the poisoned gift of a purist education and prosperity that infallibly caused it to break with the country. This generational factor, far more than Bin Laden's individual family circumstances or psychological idiosyncrasies, explains how easy it was for Osama to become an icon for many postboom Saudis who had grown up under Abdel Aziz and knew nothing of the epic founding years but the legend, now slowly decomposing in a web of wealth and frustration.

The Formative Years

Osama Bin Laden's founding myth, carefully rewritten under his supervision, portrayed the Afghan adventure as the revelation of his exception destiny as a savior. This reworked autobiography is not completely false, but it glosses over Bin Laden's modest but significant earlier career, making his first success seem like his first activity. In 1976 the Syrian Muslim Brothers launched a series of actions aimed at overthrowing President Hafez al-Assad, and culminating in a series of urban uprisings in the early 1980s. Although this opposition was linked to Syria's domestic situation, it benefited from a degree of support from activists in neighboring countries. Osama, who was interested in his mother's native country, financed the Syrian opposition in 1979. This was probably his first significant engagement, although it remained limited.

At the same time, he was lackadaisically studying management at King Abdul Aziz University in Jidda, although he did not complete his coursework. At the end of the decade, Abdallah Azzam, a Palestinian-Jordanian theologian who was very involved in the Muslim Brotherhood's political sphere, arrived in Jidda, where he obtained a teaching post at the university. The two men played an important role together, first in Afghanistan and then in structuring the jihadist movements of the 1990s, but although it has been said that they met in Saudi Arabia, nothing proves that this was indeed the case.

At the time, in fact, Osama may have been interested in the regional situation and seemed concerned with helping Islamist movements against a secular regime, but he was still undertaking action as a simple believer, with no particular structure or organized ideology. It is unlikely that he drew close to the high-flying theoreticians who had begun pouring into the kingdom a decade earlier, with the triumph of Arab nationalist regimes. His "autodidactic" approach, which rejected complexity in favor of an assertion that engagement was somehow self-evident—not as a political struggle but as the simple practice of true religion—later became one of the specific characteristics of his movement. At the time, this simplistic vision of militancy led him away from the embryonic movements that were beginning to appear in the kingdom itself. Another reason also for this somnambulism, this nonchalant way of intervening at the highest political levels without bothering to support his position with an apparatus and an ideology, is his social background. Osama Bin Laden may have had an austere upbringing, but he is still a millionaire's son. He knows how to talk to the wealthy, attract the poor, and, to make up for the lack of any compelling discourse, use his financial clout to convince the reticent. He thus situated himself at the intersection of several social categories.

When the Soviets intervened in Afghanistan in late 1979, he saw it as an opportunity to repeat his Syrian experience, but more openly this time: Saudi Arabia supported the resistance from the beginning, and the country's notables took it upon themselves to participate in the war effort. Osama became the Bin Laden family's representative in the Afghan jihad. For the regime, it was also necessary to purge the country of some of its negative fundamentalist elements, especially because in November of the same year some of those elements had taken hostages in a spectacular operation within the sanctuary at Mecca itself. The central characters in this undertaking (which ended tragically) were the same age as Osama, and this was another expression of the noxious effects that the oil boom and corrosive modernization were producing on this generation.

Although he has claimed that he went to Afghanistan as early as 1979, it is more likely that he arrived there for the first time in early 1980, when he began to seek out contacts and find local partners to finance them. Throughout the decade, he traveled back and forth between the Arabian Peninsula, Pakistan, and Afghanistan, collecting funds and distributing them to people who thus became his clients or his mentors. He fought in very few battles, perhaps only one armed engagement: the battle of Jaji in 1986, where, according to him, he was almost killed. His role was elsewhere: he had intimate access to the highest ranks of the Saudi royal family, collected money, and began to be known among young Saudis by intervening in public or in the media to encourage private donations to the mujahedeen. Between 1983 and the end of the decade, he became a public personality, admired and respected. At the time, everyone was happy with this equation: the Saudis preferred to give money to someone who was one of their own, rather than to Pakistani intelligence agents, and Bin Laden's celebrity restored some luster to a country buffeted by the Islamic revolution in Iran and the Mecca hostage crisis. Thanks to this young enthusiast, who looked dimwitted and harmless, Saudi Arabia was also able to restore some of its religious credit on the domestic scene. The Bin Laden myth was already being established—although it was restricted to the Saudi media at the time, and targeted an exclusively national audience.

Far from the conferences being held to encourage the resistance, and far from the television cameras that showed young Saudis gathered around Bin Laden, representing the Saudi kingdom in the international jihad, another story was unfolding. The decade Bin Laden had spent playing hooky was the opportunity—for him and more generally for the kingdom—for a violent, disconcerting encounter between, on one hand, a country whose oil resources seemed to place it beyond the reach of history's laws and, on the other, history's sordid, inspiring incarnation in the Arab volunteers. These volunteers had different tales to tell Osama. They were marked by exile, coups d'état, torture, and the supreme ambiguity—which Osama had not experienced at the time—of being at the front without really having any rear guard. Azzam was a Palestinian who had fled from Jordan; many of the Egyptians were fresh out of the jails where they had been incarcerated by Sadat or Mubarak; and the Algerians were either veterans of Bouyali's underground resistance or, more frequently, young men who came straight from the poverty of the Algiers outskirts to the high plateaus of Afghanistan.

In this cauldron, Bin Laden was revealed to himself. His collaboration with Abdallah Azzam, who had been welcoming volunteers to Peshawar since 1981, led to the creation of the Maktab al-Khadamat (Service Bureau) in the mid-1980s. At the beginning of the decade, the two men collaborated closely and had clearly defined roles: Osama financed the movement and may have served as a communications liaison; Azzam was the ideologue and party man. The events that took place in the middle of the decade upset the balance, however, precipitating divergence and therefore the creation of what later became Al Qaeda.

The U.S. strategy for Afghanistan, as defined by Zbigniew Brzezinski and other advisers as early as the Carter presidency, was to exhaust the Soviet Union by sinking it in an Afghan quagmire, but without dealing the USSR the final blow that might incite it to pull out. The goal was to make the war drag on. In this perspective, the point, for the United States, was not so much to liberate Afghanistan as to make its occupation a costly endeavor for the Soviets; and, by 1986, it was becoming increasingly clear that the Soviets intended to pull out as soon as possible. The United States then decided to inflict maximum losses before the final withdrawal. This was a real turning point. Logistically, the first Stinger missiles began pouring in; orders were to destroy the enemy's air defenses, and no one worried much about leaving weapons that were highly perfected by the standards of the day in many different hands. Financing standards also grew less stringent, and transactions between drug traffickers and mujahedeen increased. The feverish atmosphere that preceded the Soviet empire's now predictable, almost palpable collapse also had effects on the Arab volunteers. They began to expel Western humanitarian workers, and the first disagreements between Afghans and Arabs on questions of religious ritual (funerals, and so on) broke out. The Soviets' anticipated withdrawal, combined with the quantitative and qualitative increase in assistance, sharpened appetites and bids for power. Most particularly, these converging processes propelled individual potential to the fore: around 1987, Osama moved away from Azzam's organization and met Egyptians close to al-Zawahiri. In 1989 he set up his "database" (Qaedat al-Ma'lumat).[4] This was an insubstantial structure, which probably centralized information about the Arab volunteers with the intention of bringing them together under a more unified command.

The antagonism between Azzam and Bin Laden was not merely a question of ambition: Azzam, as a member of the Muslim Brotherhood, had inherited an eminently political vision of collective action. The movement was a tightly structured apparatus, seeking power by various means, which ranged from negotiation and power sharing to the violent capture of institutions; in its various national avatars, the Brotherhood based itself on elites. This particular ethos had given Azzam an instinctive wariness of hotheaded intervention and of speeches or attitudes promoting unconsidered action; he also made very sure that the people close to him followed coherent paths. Osama Bin Laden, during the first half of the 1980s, when their collaboration was closest and smoothest, was probably perturbed by the "human resource management" approach, which belonged to a tradition he did not know. As his former mentor grew increasingly distant, he was able to give his own instincts free range, recruiting individuals who had taken more chaotic paths. The first significant characteristic of the organism that later evolved into Al Qaeda was its acceptance within its midst of people from very different backgrounds, with obscure or frankly shady pasts. With a structure that resembled a sect more closely than it did a political party, Al Qaeda brought together many repentant born-again Muslims, militants who had broken with their former organizations, but also men who had been close to Azzam and now threw in their lot with this group and its lax, even soft, ideology and its far greater clout. Osama Bin Laden may have known how to speak to the wealthy, but he also knew how to address volunteers whose religious education was more primitive, if indeed they had received any: men who were disinclined to follow Azzam's demonstrations, but were dazzled by the luminous pedantries put forth by this autodidact. The first to join him, it would seem, were Egyptians, but these were men who had never been through the ranks of the Muslim Brotherhood.

At the end of the decade the Soviets withdrew, and clashes among Afghans broke out. Azzam died in Pakistan in a booby-trapped car (the perpetrator was never identified), and many volunteers began to return to their countries of origin. In this pernicious climate, Osama Bin Laden decided to leave Afghanistan and return to Saudi Arabia.

The Return of the Veteran

The 1990s, in many Arab countries and especially in Saudi Arabia, may be seen as the decade of failed veterans who would remain unable to reintegrate into civilian life. Bin Laden had gone to Afghanistan to carry out his "duty" as a Muslim. He came back a convinced militant, dissatisfied with living "hidden" behind the front lines. By 1989, he was already looking for a cause that would mobilize anew the formidable network built in Afghanistan.

Two potential causes interested him. The first was Iraq, which had emerged depleted but victorious from its war against Iran. Making demands pell-mell—for cancellation of its debts, modified borders with its neighbors, and a position of a great power in the region—it once again posed a threat to its neighbors. Strangely enough, the wounded country, another "veteran" that felt betrayed by neighbors it believed it had protected and which had "stabbed it in the back," provoked Bin Laden's anger: he declared to all and sundry that it was necessary to eliminate the atheist regime in Baghdad.[5] What started out as mere bravado became serious after the invasion of Kuwait, but things did not go as Bin Laden might have wished. Prince Sultan, the minister of defense, refused to assign him the mission of liberating Kuwait, although Bin Laden claimed he could provide a hundred thousand men—a much exaggerated figure. Saudi Arabia chose instead to call on Western armed forces under U.S. leadership. This decision, a difficult one for Saudi authorities to make, triggered a process of radicalization that affected many embryonic opposition movements.

This period is not key to understanding Bin Laden's trajectory, but it probably determined his choice of Saudi Arabia as the chief enemy: by considering that his country was occupied by foreign, non-Muslim forces, Osama Bin Laden was able to undergo the mental shift that occurred among all the Afghan veterans, and more generally in Al Qaeda's discourse: a shift that consisted of "Afghanizing" their countries of origin, making these countries a battleground in the struggle against an unbelieving enemy. The analogy between the front lines and civilian life resembles that drawn by European political movements born of massive, frustrating demobilization.

Osama Bin Laden then turned to Yemen, his father's country,

then still divided between communists in the south and a pro-Western regime in the north. He thought it could also be "liberated" with the help of his brothers in arms. But the ruling family considered Yemen to be its personal affair. Bin Laden, initially just a troublemaker, became a real concern when he began to put out manifestos condemning the Saudi authorities. In 1994, after having frozen his financial assets, the regime stripped him of his Saudi nationality, an exceptional measure that indicated he was really beginning to be taken seriously.

Bin Laden went into exile in Sudan, where Hassan al-Turabi, the Sudanese Islamist ideologue who was then the strongman of the Khartoum regime, welcomed him: al-Turabi was contemptuous of Bin Laden but interested in his money. Bin Laden set up camps where he hosted Afghan veterans and financed a few construction sites. He was indirectly implicated in the 1993 events in Mogadishu, but the Americans forced him to leave the region only in 1996, after the failed attempt to assassinate Egypt's president, Hosni Mubarak, in Addis Ababa. Bin Laden was probably involved via his Egyptian entourage, which saw the president as the man to eliminate, in order to topple the regime in Cairo and ensure the triumph of Islamist groups made up of numerous Afghan veterans.

Bin Laden returned once again to Afghanistan. This was the last trip he made openly.

His break with his former high-ranking connections and the absence in Afghanistan of a strong, restrictive power—as had been the case, relatively speaking, in Sudan—allowed the Bin Laden "system" to work at full throttle. When he attempted to create an ephemeral, labile World Islamic Front for Jihad against Jews and Crusaders on February 23, 1998, Bin Laden sought first and foremost to incarnate this new situation and to bring together dispersed members, scattered by local tactics, in a single coalition. The Bin Laden movement then aimed to crown these efforts: six months later, on August 7, 1998, the U.S. embassies in Nairobi (Kenya) and Dar es Salaam (Tanzania) were targeted in a deadly attack that left over two hundred dead. Al Qaeda's goal—representation through action—had been launched.

The 1998 attacks on the American embassies in Tanzania and Kenya revealed this system to the world. It was based on two specifics: the primacy of spectacular action, to the detriment of the elements that traditionally build a movement (like mobilization or organization), and a wide, decentralized recruitment program, combined with typically messianic characteristics. The choice of target was consubstantial with this nascent system. The two target countries brought his actions closer to the Arabian Peninsula, while the date (August 7) marked the eighth anniversary of U.S. troops' arrival in Saudi Arabia (on August 7, 1990). The movement led by Bin Laden henceforth chose its targets, and sometimes also the dates of the attacks it carried out, as one would move a cursor along a scale of meaning. After he left Saudi Arabia for good, he had sworn to bring down the Saudi regime, which, having traced its flaws back to the beginning of the twentieth century, he held responsible for the tragedies besetting the Muslim world. According to him, the House of Saud had rebelled against the Ottoman caliph in Istanbul with British help, and was therefore responsible for the collapse of the caliphate and the Muslim world's submission to the West. From that point onward, he established a series of analogies with the previous period. God's unified authority was to be reestablished over all Muslims by abandoning specific struggles and concentrating action against the two parties responsible for the system of shameful domination: America and Saudi Arabia.

The attacks also introduced another characteristic of Al Qaeda's modus operandi, which it is difficult to attribute to a particular mastermind, so closely does this singularity fit in with the zeitgeist: Al Qaeda, and any other, related group, now began to operate by staging a series of simultaneous attacks: from New York to London, via Casablanca, Istanbul, and Madrid, the organization brought terrorism into the era of technical reproduction. This eliminates the hypothesis of an accident in the case of simultaneous attacks, of course, but also in that of single events. One attack could be the result of favorable chance circumstances; two or three, and even four, simultaneous attacks—as in the case of Madrid—brought into play an assembly-line process that was controlled from start to finish and could be both predicted and reproduced. To the media amplification of the attack, Al Qaeda added the possibility that it could be perpetuated ad infinitum. The first occurrence of an attack, furthermore, signaled to the media that more were on their way. During the 1990s cyclical attacks proliferated (as was the case in France in the summer of 1995 and in Spain with the attacks carried out by ETA); as for Al Qaeda, it carried out an atemporal concentration of several attacks. These were the loudly proclaimed symbol of the group's ubiquity and omnipotence.

During one of the appearances he made on special occasions, in late October 2004, a few days before the U.S. presidential elections, Bin Laden traced his initial recognition of American imperialist hegemony back to the events of the Lebanese civil war, in 1982. Those, he suggested, had led to the idea of 9/11: an attack, he proclaimed, is the conjunction of history and will. The reconstruction was apocryphal, of course; it mainly served to reveal, in counterpoint, that the struggle against America as a priority was relatively recent, indeed almost concomitant with the early stages of its implementation.

Without a program or a structured ideology, it was difficult for Bin Laden's movement to let time elapse between the elaboration of a strategy and its execution. As a child of the television era, Bin Laden was the first to try out a televised strategy of subversion, live and in real time. Al Qaeda's strength would lie in its soft structuring and omnivorous ideology, molded entirely to media events.

Terrorism, Martyrdom, and Videotape

Al Qaeda only exists in cathodic mode. Its vast mobilization capabilities and the influence of the orders it emits depend on the media space, and television in particular, that it occupied in the late

1990s. Bin Laden's emergence as an orator was concomitant with a group of factors that made this emblematic mode of operation possible.

In the early 1990s, in a large part of the Arab world, regimes began to undergo fossilization, a process that reached its culmination as caricature at the beginning of the twenty-first century. As large swaths of the rest of the world were forced to liberalize politically, the region's regimes searched for new means to justify their increasingly anachronistic authoritarianism. They remained out of sync with global dynamics because the Palestinian problem was still unresolved, and because it was impossible to bypass an Islamist phase of government. To break Islamist opposition movements, whether self-designated or defined externally as such, various regimes resorted to shows of strength and seduction. The aim was to break the Islamist opposition's conciliatory façade and bring it back to its sociology, so to speak: to draw the timorous middle classes toward the regime, while marginalizing the most radical opposition movements, which based themselves on the younger generations sacrificed on the altar of 1980s austerity programs, the better to denigrate them in the eyes of the world. The textbook case was Algeria, where the regime gave Belhaj a wider media surface than his real position warranted in relation to Madani. The generals knew that competition within the various currents of Islamist opposition would lead to deadly escalation and delegitimate these movements.[6] In other systems there were attempts to monopolize legal political space for the benefit of the ruling group and its allies and to push movements that presented a real alternative toward a bloody periphery. The ideological output of opposition movements expresses this chronology whereby regimes exclude the opposition before it turns to radicalism: the rise in radicalism parallels the shrinking of free political space.

In tandem with this process, however, another began to unfold in the 1990s: the unification of Arab media space. Several factors brought this about. First was the media event of the 1991 Gulf War.

A great demand from large portions of the Arab middle classes for information coincided with the first stages of entry by Western news networks via satellite. Furthermore, many important Arab newspapers moved from Beirut, where they had initially been published, to London in the 1980s. Their geographical remoteness, combined with a proximity to their audience, made them a dangerous weapon for the Arab regimes. In sum, during these years the media interrogated the ruling establishment, which especially in the Arabian Peninsula had been hit hard by the Gulf War.

Saudi Arabia's response to these challenges was to attempt to control the press. Through the intermediary of various princes, Riyadh began a series of buyouts that led during the second half of the 1990s to virtually full control over most independent Arab newspapers (except for *Al-Quds al-Arabi*). Its bid for control of audiovisual media was less successful, mainly owing to a certain cowardice when it came to images, as well as a lack of audacity. The Saudi channel MBC was acclaimed by critics at the beginning of the decade, before Al-Jazeera appeared. The latter, created by the emirate of Qatar, began broadcasting in 1996. From the start, its provocative, liberated style stood out; it benefited from highly qualified and underpaid Arab journalists, initially from the Levant and then from the rest of the Arab world. Al-Jazeera imposed a new way of covering the news, which broke radically with the old generation of Arab political-media bosses. The situation of the donor state, Qatar, allowed for a great deal of daring. Qatar, like Saudi Arabia, wanted one or several media forums at its disposal, to protect itself from intrusion from the media or politics. Qatar had several advantages over Saudi Arabia, however—principally, the absence of a numerous population and an obtrusive, constricting ideology. In short, Saudi Arabia wanted to control the media to protect itself from a possible internal threat, whereas Qatar wanted to control the media, or at least a key source, to make itself disappear—to make the outside world forget it. The result was that Al-Jazeera became the first Arab media vehicle to introduce hypermodern methods: real-time coverage, brash images, attractive young journalists, talk shows with controversial guests, and so on. Al-Jazeera offered a type of media production that one could describe as liberal-populist, and which the other channels had to imitate in order to avoid being eliminated. With the last Gulf War, Saudi Arabia attempted to seize control of audiovisual media (Al Arabiya, Al-Ikhbariya) once again by using Al-Jazeera's methods.

This new technique was led by private channels, whose principal and perhaps only goal was to boost ratings. Such channels have therefore become increasingly populist. Channels like Al-Jazeera serve as the subconscious of the Arab world, without distance or detachment. Because they are private, highly dependent on private or institutional sponsors, and often rooted in domains (like Qatar, Lebanon, or London) that are "extraterritorial" relative to the rest of the Arab world, they are free from the Weberian imperative of controlling a territory and a population; these channels can therefore give free rein to Arab frustration. As the new avatar of impotent Arab populism, which was embodied initially in post-1967 nationalist discourse and then in radical Islamism, the transnational Arab media are an explosive mix of ultracapitalism (fluid, satellite-based, brilliant, and utterly devoid of any political perspective) and of radical discourse "plucked" by journalists from the social chaos of Arab "reality."

This grammar of the media and politics can no longer be controlled by state actors, but various protagonists on the regional scene, Al Qaeda among them, have integrated it perfectly. Al Qaeda's rise took place at the same time as these many processes. An objective alliance was created between a movement whose only material reality is provided by images, and peripheral satellite media that are concerned essentially with ratings, and therefore seek to cover anything that will boost them. Bin Laden did better than others at assimilating these new rules: the brief shelf life of media icons imposed a precise schedule of appropriate appearances, without which he ran the risk of being replaced by new figures.[7] An elusive, unpredictable star, Bin Laden invented a policy tailored to video clips and ads: brief speeches that were easily incorporated into prime-time news; carefully designed, simple settings; and straightforward speeches, devoid of affectation or sophistication.

For the Arab regimes, however, he posed no great threat. They could even get along with him, since Al Qaeda, by taking over the obligation of resistance that public opinion demanded, had rearranged the political architecture of the Middle East and had set itself up as a sort of pressure valve.

The movement led by Bin Laden, in fact, does not constitute an extension of those movements which were called terrorist or which described themselves as such. The various uses of the term "terrorist" in recent history have given it a full, effective meaning; whether the ruling French revolutionaries called themselves terrorists to distinguish themselves from the "enemies of the people" or whether the term was taken on by Russian revolutionary groups fighting tsarist authority, the reality of terror had to be superimposed on the image it projected. There was nothing metaphorical about the classic perception of that image of terror: targets were interchangeable and could be judged according to their inherent value, which might be that of exchange: in the 1970s, militant groups in the West and in the Middle East made terrorism the means of beginning a conversation with their adversaries. Terrorist acts could constitute an established dialogue, a medium of exchange, or a means of blackmail. When this version of terrorist attacks was transcended, it was in order to trigger the mechanical cause-and-effect cycle of attack, repression, and uprising, conceptualized by a Brazilian, Carlos Marighella. Bin Laden's movement used some of these themes, but did not make them its main motive. It was based not on a particular strategy that adherents worked hard to follow, but on a specific relationship with the media. This was imposed in part by its way of functioning, its targets, and its scope.

A Grammar of Al Qaeda

The particular regimen inherent in the relationship between terrorism and the media has established a specific style manual for attacks: they are no longer efficient in the classical manner, and they no longer have positivist goals. Targets are rarely economic, and indeed they have no intrinsic importance. Their essential value is to emphasize an image. The means employed are those of metonymy (a synagogue to designate Israel); synecdoche (demands made in the name of Islam); symbolism (an American killed, to represent the United States). This modus operandi suits the media, which format it in real time as a message magnified to a global scale.

For Arab audiences, things work in the same way, but rhetoric is preferably based on the narrative itself, and the syntax takes its themes from the most popular public causes: the Palestinian issue, for instance. Paradoxically, the way in which that issue is structured owes a lot to the media. Al Qaeda therefore functions by drawing upon them to integrate itself more fully into the media circuit: Bin Laden has used abundant audiovisual, as opposed to ideological, references, which have an impact on a young Arab audience that owes its education to television rather than to the crumbling educational system.

Another example is provided by Bin Laden's first appearance after 9/11, which he made on October 7, 2001, dressed in Afghan garb and sitting cross-legged at the mouth of a cave. He began his speech with a sermon peppered with Quranic citations, as if to set himself up as the opposite term of an oxymoron, part of which was then going up in flames in New York. The challenge he posed to America as an ascetic stripped of all worldly goods and hiding out in Afghanistan's miserable mountains was multiplied by the gaping breach that—as he delighted in emphasizing—separated him from the United States' predatory opulence.

The disparity between the sets of references he used was explicit.

Bin Laden, for instance, is an adamant opponent of Arab nationalism in its socialist variant. His discourse is replete with unconditional condemnations of nationalist aspirations, which fragment the compact and homogenous nature of the *umma*, the Muslim community. These condemnations, furthermore, are strengthened by the tendency to combine religious arguments (according to which ethnic and linguistic distinctions constitute a resurgence of the *jahiliyya*, or pre-Islamic period) with political and strategic arguments (according to which Arab nationalism was one of the main causes for the downfall of the last Muslim caliphate).

His discourse, however, is marked by contradictions that make Arab linguistic and geographical identity the essence of Islam, or at least one of its necessary, central components. Twice, he referred to the *jahiliyya* to illustrate the qualities necessary in contemporary militants. In his *Tactical Recommendations,* he employed a tone of romantic nostalgia to evoke the bellicose *jahiliyya*, before invoking strength and loyalty—the virtues characteristic of Arab men in the pre-Islamic period. These two references, furthermore, were not shocking in the context of his speech, but they caused a shift in register and anchored it in another tradition. Positive references to *jahiliyya* were common in classical literature and became common once again in political literature and essays during the Nahda, the nineteenth-century Arab renaissance. By using two citations in the sense given to them during a period that the Islamist movement condemns and despises, Bin Laden plugged his words into Arab nationalist discourse.

Arab identity, furthermore, seems to be the only "particularistic" character of one's identity as a Muslim. In reference to the war in Afghanistan, Bin Laden mentioned the "Arab lions of Islam," who fought valiantly side by side with their "brothers." Elsewhere, he might mention the "sons of Kurds" and their struggle, for instance, but mainly because of his concern with precision. In fact, no adjective indicating national or linguistic identity poses any competition to membership in the irenic Muslim community—apart, that is, from Arab identity, which in Bin Laden's discourse seems to confirm and strengthen membership in the *umma*.

This Arabocentrism occasionally allows him to expand on the Arabian Peninsula's "magical" virtues. In that light, the Sykes-Picot agreement, concluded during World War I and dividing up the Ottoman Empire's Arab provinces in the Levant between Britain and France, constituted a successful attempt to fragment the Muslim world, and it is prolonged today by an agreement between then British prime minister Tony Blair and U.S. president George W. Bush, whose desire to break up the Middle East thus becomes an attempt to break up the *umma* as a whole. Such connections show the flabby thought process working at full speed, indiscriminately absorbing any ideological components capable of mobilizing the masses. The lack of ideological depth, and of the methodological constraints and choices that a "hard" ideology would imply, goes hand in hand with the breadth that allows Bin Laden to cast as wide a net as possible.

Inconsistencies are therefore integrated into Bin Laden's discursive system in a systematic way: the heterogeneous references emerge from texts that claim to follow a strict dogmatic line. Even more than is the case for Zawahiri, one can observe Bin Laden's autodidacticism at work, free of any tinge of guilt and entirely subjected to the imperative of efficiency and the impact of the speech on the media.

In *What Is the French Communist Party For?* Georges Lavau proposes a historical metaphor that allows him to explain heterodoxy in relation to the expected goals of political parties, and in particular of the Communist Party in France. Lavau suggests that the party's function within the French political system of the 1970s be described as "tribunitial": in other words, the party, which was representative of a certain social fringe, legal but located outside the government, was satisfied with its position, which allowed it to express itself without ever facing sanction from the reality of effective power. For this reason, it did not want to "assume power"—for do-

ing so would have forced it to suggest actual policies—but preferred to consolidate its position as a legitimate mouthpiece. This
function had two other characteristics: if the Roman populace,
during a revolt, threatened to leave Rome and establish a rival city,
and if one of the popular tribune's fundamental roles was to keep
the populace in the city, the French Communist Party, in turn, had
the Soviet Union and the International as rival cities, which it used
as bogeymen in keeping the "populace" loyal to the republican
city.[8] The tribunitial function also made the struggle "a means of
avoidance and delay," a means of mobilization whose effectiveness
was more symbolic than concrete; in particular, it sought to avoid
provoking a change in the situation that legitimated the struggle,
as long as it remained in the cozy niche of contestation.

Whether they are organized in groups, result from individual
trajectories, or (as is most frequently the case) confined to the level
of discourse, jihadist movements in the contemporary Arab world
serve a new tribunitial function.

This function is expressed through jihadist groups (and especially discourse) via the formation of several concentric circles,
where the three conditions of the tribunitial function are progressively fulfilled: the expression of protest (which can be
maximalist); agitation for secession, alternative loyalties, a rival
city; and finally "the struggle as means of avoidance and delay."[9]
Bin Laden's movement successfully sought to bring together under
its banner the energy that such demands required, and which remained unfulfilled by impotent states. As a tribune or iconic orator, Bin Laden used his cathodic appearances to irradiate the entirety of Arab political space, emptied by three decades of political
stagnation.

Arab public space as a whole—including the media as well as
political and cultural groups—has been deeply destabilized by the
advertising results of Bin Laden's movement, at least when that
movement's actions are linked to Palestine or Iraq. Here, we are in
the widest circle, where the entire Arab world functions as the populace vis-à-vis the Western senate, supporting its collective tri-

bune—the martyrs—and its indestructible pretext and cause—Palestine. The goal, for regimes, is to obviate "the active ability to accomplish," which is costly, by glorifying martyrdom, as long as it remains outside their national territory. Bin Laden, however, has posed an increasing challenge to the "collective political good" that the irenic, consensual causes constituted, by directly denying them the right to use it without paying the entry cost represented by opposition to the American hegemon.

Still, broad social strata have established continuity between the actions of Palestinian martyrs and domestic problems, whereby martyrdom bears witness to an alternative city, opposed to existing iniquity. In so doing, they have begun to repatriate martyrdom toward the local, and to integrate its motives into a national perspective, thereby partially integrating violence into the strategies of those who claim it as a means of opposing the ruling authorities. This could imply the threat of action just as well as it could activism by proxy, and this explains Al Qaeda's various metastases in different Arab Muslim countries.

Miracle-Working Elites

How does Bin Laden justify his claim to being the exclusive representative of the Muslim world? First of all, by imposing multiple distinctions. Far from insisting on a monolithic form of dogmatism that should apply to all Muslims, he does not shy away from issuing parallel injunctions. Besides the five pillars of Islam, which form the unquestionable axis of all the legal schools, he also calls on Muslims to respect five others, citing the following hadith: "I [the Prophet] declare obligatory upon you five things; God has commanded me to do so. They are: organization [*jama'a*], and listening, and obeying, and making *hijra* and making jihad for God."[10] In Bin Laden's interpretation of the hadith, five hidden obligations therefore accompany the recognized pillars of the faith.[11] Furthermore, only an elite can apply these "extra-strength" divine prescriptions, by acting as a backup to the *umma*, in a sense.

This sophist's view of the law as a dual entity, with an easy exoteric aspect to which the *umma* as a whole must obey, and esoteric, or at least forgotten and marginalized, prescriptions that only a community of superior beings can carry out, has made it possible for Bin Laden to resolve the logical contradiction inherent in applying the injunction relating to jihad.

Fighting along God's path is sometimes seen as an individual obligation (*fard 'ayn*), which each Muslim of sound mind and body must carry out, and sometimes as a collective duty (*fard kifaya*), which some fighters can accomplish, thereby relieving other Muslims of the necessity. For some Sunni legal schools, and for all jihadists, jihad is, of course, a *fard 'ayn*, and neglecting it is as grave a transgression as breaking one's fast, for example. Bin Laden has also outlined a third principle, however, which allows him to remain in an irenic realm, while feeding his "dual" worldview: any jihad requires a certain number of fighters, because, as he has pointed out, it is unnecessary for several people to do the work that a few can accomplish. As long as the requisite number of combatants has not been reached, jihad is thus still a *fard 'ayn*. Once the quorum of warriors has been filled, according to him, jihad becomes a *fard kifaya*. Bin Laden has also made it clear that the first men to answer the call to arms, leaving behind them worldly preoccupations to undertake jihad, make up the community elite. His subtle argument allows him to maintain the general value of a divine law while reserving a certain cachet for the elite that is ready to sacrifice itself: "We can carry out the mission, and the rest of the *umma* is thereby absolved."[12]

In this respect, Al Qaeda also serves as a thaumaturgical elite that takes upon itself the duty of applying God's law and preserving the Muslim community from sin.

Because his aim is to represent all Muslims, Bin Laden builds a theory that can establish a distinction between the majority of Muslims and a handful of superior creatures. Unlike other minority groups that preceded his, like the Egyptian Gama'a, he avoids *takfir* (pronouncing the apostasy) of "worldly" behavior. Only the distinction between good Muslims behind the front lines and a vanguard elite could then justify his pretension to lead and represent Islam as a whole.

A "Base" to Impose the "Rule"

In September 1992 a man close to Bin Laden was arrested at John F. Kennedy International Airport in New York. He had with him an instruction manual detailing the use of explosives. Its title was mistakenly translated as *The Basic Rule* at the time of the World Trade Center bombing trial, in which the work was presented as evidence. The *New York Times* translated it correctly: *Al Qaeda*, meaning the base.[13]

The justice official who committed the translation error was not wrong, however: his mistake revealed the ambiguity in the name of Bin Laden's movement, and the project itself. *Qaeda*, in Arabic, means both "base" and "rule." The two terms share a set of obvious semantic implications. Their equivocal sense is full of meaning: the militant base, created in the wake of the Afghan war, presented itself (perhaps from the earliest stages of its existence) as the main axiological locus of the contemporary Muslim world. It sought to issue rules that would reestablish the forgotten Rule. Bin Laden's *Tactical Recommendations*, dictated in two parts, were a sort of Islamist *What Is To Be Done?* aimed at basing the movement's actions on a structured worldview.

This worldview revolves around the notion of the Law or Norm, which, although omnipresent, is hidden, and not addressed directly: it has been lost, forgotten, frayed. Bin Laden, who always placed himself under a mentor's dogmatic aegis—Azzam being his best-known inspiration—seemed obsessed by the loss of normative meaning, which he reformulated as obliviousness to the divine law. Al Qaeda, as a militant database, was first and foremost a grammar with the project of restructuring a damaged world.

Bin Laden is the ultimate avatar of the rampant modernization that besets the Arab political sphere: like its television channels and its cities, that sphere is striated, permeated, crisscrossed by contradictory signals, all of them orgasmic, calling for uninhibited consumerism, which cannot draw upon prosperous economies and therefore turns inward to devour itself. Al Qaeda is the first political machine devoid of any depth beyond its tautological legitimacy of representation. "A primary group is a number of individuals who have put one and the same object in the place of their ego ideal and have consequently identified themselves with one another in their ego."[14] Haunted by a past he wished to redeem or dissimulate through a life of blazing glory, devoured by the desire for recognition or searching for a mentor, Bin Laden was an empty character that other people's strategies and calculations fleshed out, before he devoted himself to the supreme vacuity of terrorism and the media. This character trait, paradoxically, gave him a head start on other radical actors: because his various partners and sponsors showed contempt for him—overlooking his secret, introverted tenacity and his painstakingly acquired knowledge of religious matters—and because of the shyness that made of him a nervous, flaccid, eternal adolescent, he ultimately became easy to identify with for generations of young people seeking signposts along the way, and sensitive to what one observer described as Bin Laden's "very strong, quiet, confident and effective charisma."[15]

Providing a distraught take on the spectacular, populist policy found in Western democracies, Osama Bin Laden claims to monopolize, by proxy, all the frustration and legitimate anger that legal institutions cannot, or can no longer, express. This is why, in order to fight his movement effectively, it would be necessary to solve the problems of the Middle East, or unplug the television—both equally improbable and costly solutions for American democracy.

The War in Iraq: A Countertrauma to September 11?

A third solution, with tragic but crystal-clear consequences, is unfolding before our eyes. Has the war in Iraq achieved its goals, or some of them? Set against the trauma of 9/11, the Iraqi countertrauma restored a territorial dimension to spectacular attacks: the attacks on London and Madrid were *local* actions, carried out by immigrants or naturalized citizens, even if they had long since acquired their passports. Henceforth, in a general state of stupor and uncertainty, the Middle East is going through a period of close-range attacks pitting one neighborhood against another, neighbor against neighbor. There are many reasons for this state of affairs; one important one is the neocons' stated desire to bring the conflict back toward the countries that are seen as exporters of terrorism. It is in the light of this new situation, which places renewed emphasis on the "nearby enemy," that Bin Laden's most recent statements must be read. His awareness of a new regional geopolitics is the reason he called on the Saudis in December 2004 to rise up against their regime, as he recited the litany of that regime's vices and faults; it is also why in April 2006 he condemned a number of Saudi writers and called for their murder. The fossilization of regional relations was seen as a solution in the 1990s, but that stagnation exploded in the dual undertakings of 9/11 and the American attack on Iraq in April 2003, which mirrored each other. These events made local affairs important once again, along with their sociology and their infinitesimal calculations.

From Icon to Voice

Another dimension, which is less spectacular but just as significant, must also be taken into account. Bin Laden no longer addresses his vast, inchoate audience via videotapes broadcast on major satellite television channels. The reasons for this may be immediate and accidental: the war wounds he may have sustained, or simple fatigue, may have diminished his charisma; technical means may be lacking . . . Whatever the reason, Bin Laden is now a voice, he has entered a "psycho-acoustic bubble," in the words of the German philosopher Peter Sloterdijk, and is floating like gas through cyberspace. His very image, which only yesterday took different forms—now a doll or a poster, in one case graffiti, in another a war cry—is no more than an static photo, which jihadist sites post to accompany his voice—the ultimate stamp of authenticity conferred on speech in the age of the videosphere.

But the essential reason the icon has been reduced to a disembodied voice must be sought in the phenomenology of spectacular violence that the alliance between Al Qaeda and the media has promoted and transmitted for the past decade: Bin Laden fell victim to his own success, producing in his wake a galaxy of wannabes. An Egyptian television channel broadcast a series of reports on terrorists, asking the audience to vote at the end for the terrorist of the century. The show was taken off the air, but who would have voted for Bin Laden, when so many imitators were vying with him for first place?

And yet no one ever again will take his place: What worth can the violence of a single attack have, the violence committed against the image and the imagined significance of the adversary, as opposed to the symbolic violence of the fall of Baghdad and the U.S. occupation of Iraq? By reducing terrorist actions to craftsmanship, history—bloody, metallic, amoral history—has returned to the region with a vengeance, making petty death industries even more banal. Homemade terrorism will exhaust itself in its bid to catch up with the large-scale war unleashed in 2003.

Attacks in the Age of Technical Reproduction

Walter Benjamin wrote about the possibility that reproducing works of art contributed in an essential way to the loss of their "aura." The same has been said of pornography. The mechanical transmission of a sacred, flamboyant, and at any rate scandalous image undermines its violent, subversive character, to the benefit of its serialization. Bloody, spectacular attacks are now reaching this asymptomatic limit: the compulsive repetition of attacks, the supply of volunteers—often exceeding demand—for this type of operation, the saturation of television screens with these images

. . . These phenomena do not make the attacks any less horrifying, but they make terrorism banal by industrializing it. It is precisely at this point that the media take control of exhibiting bleeding corpses, which had been carefully kept out of the public space, by detaching them from their obscenity and turning them into a spectacle. Contemporary terrorism is the exact opposite of fin de siècle terrorism, which first appeared in tsarist Russia and was then propagated by anarchist movements in several European countries. At the time, terrorist attacks aimed to disrupt the ordinary flow of social life, to provoke an "event" that was intended to suspend the repressive order of industrial society. By contrast, large-scale, spectacular terrorism of the sort introduced by Al Qaeda industrializes such events and subjects unexpected violence to the standards of prime-time television. Before our eyes, this type of terrorism lends reality to its own borders and limits: it is a product of media consumption; it is still a crime, but less and less effective as a political or military tool.

From Symbol to Reality

What narrative can be spun, in retrospect, from the gory asteroid called Bin Laden? The media icon that haunted the screens for a few years and then, like the Cheshire Cat, withdrew, leaving only the bloody trace of his smile, will probably be the last manifestation of a deadly course the Middle East has followed for the past few decades. Jacques Lacan mapped out our relation to the world according to a tripartite classification: symbolic, imaginary, real. These categories are revealed to perfection in the region: political space (a shared symbolic sphere, marked by common law) was curtailed, and then stifled completely, between the 1970s and the aftermath of the Gulf War, a situation that led to an inflationary, phantasmagorical media bubble (the private, narcissistic imaginary sphere of the 1990s, for which Al-Jazeera served as spokesman in its early years). That bubble then led (logically?) to the plunge taken on 9/11 (the trauma of reality).

As for the possibility of hyperterrorism put forward after 9/11, it splintered into multiple undertakings, captured and devitalized by the media apparatus. Strangely, that apparatus is not (or not yet) capable of reifying an older phenomenon, which is once again current: war.

The return of strategy, interstate relations, the game of superpowers and medium-sized states in the region will not push Al Qaeda or the media bubble to the side, but it will detach the postmodern nebula that has occupied center stage in the Middle East, and occasionally the world, for the past few years. Instead, we will witness the return of local ideologues, short-term socioeconomic stakes, as well as negotiations and confrontations in the wings.

The texts translated here seek to establish as complete a political and mental diagram as possible of the two-dimensional militancy instituted by Bin Laden's movement: as declarations or historical reconstructions or sketches of more theoretical political thought, they remain above all eminently media-friendly actions. Like all the actions transmitted through our television screens, they are inhabited by the paradoxical contingency of individual events, which in their very evanescence seem to promise the greatest proximity to the society of the spectacle and its atemporal truth.

THE COMPANIONS' DEN

(EXCERPTS)

The Service Office was an experience that had both positive and negative aspects.[1] The first person responsible for heading the office was a young man, Abu Akram al-Urduni, who worked there for several months and then left for Jordan, having complained continually of the lack of organization[2] . . . All those who took on the job complained that there were no clearly defined tasks. But despite these negative aspects, there were positive ones as well, because the office allowed the Arab mujahedeen to increase their ranks and participate actively in combat.

It was a sort of big boarding house, a large villa we had rented, where the young Arabs were housed.[3] Its administration was made up of several sections: military, administration, training, departures (which took care of convoys leaving for Afghanistan). Osama Bin Laden spent about half a million rupees a month just on running costs: around twenty-five thousand dollars. And when the office was under a lot of pressure, in 1985 and 1986, Osama Bin Laden decided to go and live there himself . . . but, at the same time, he was thinking about a better way to contribute to the Afghan jihad. Instead of spending money and paying to support the jihad, he decided to implement projects that would be useful to the Afghans: to build mountain roads, dig tunnels and shelters to protect the Afghan mujahedeen from air bombardments. This took place in agreement with the brothers who owned the enormous Bin Laden corporation and who helped a good deal by sending earthmovers, bulldozers, and power generators to Afghanistan.

The Afghans liked us as long as they saw us as guests.[4] They did not give the Arabs any military missions in combat, which bothered the young Arabs because they wanted to participate as mujahedeen. This is why I thought of setting up a training structure for combatants. In 1404 A.H. [1984 C.E.], I asked the emir of the Union of Mujahedeen in Afghanistan for permission to create a camp in the region near the border, so that the Arab brothers could train there.[5] At the time, a hundred brothers or so had joined the camp. This was a small number because in their countries young Arabs are brought up far from any taste for jihad or for the defense of religion, and so some of them considered jihad to be an elective action, which could be delegated.[6] It was summer, but when classes started again, most of the young men went back to their countries to start university again, although they were the best of the brothers. Only a small number remained: fewer than ten. Still, God was kind to us and we found a camp in Jaji, in Afghanistan[7] . . .

We trained alone, with the little experience we had. There were about fifty of us, but the same thing happened again. In winter, most of the fighters went home. Total awareness of the need to support this religion, and to fight the unbelievers, so that religion as a whole could be God's, was therefore absent. Then, God was kind to us in late 1406, early 1407 [October 1986], and encouraged us to stay in the region of Jaji, although there were only a dozen of us, most from Medina, the city of the Prophet (God's peace and blessings be upon him)[8] . . .

We were eleven brothers, working on digging out a road, tunnels, and shelters for the Afghan mujahedeen. But we made Shafiq (may God have mercy on him) and Osama Haydar responsible for following military developments in the region. It is important to remember that all these brothers were in their early twenties (may God honor them). They had left school to fight along God's path. Things went on in this way. But Shafiq and Osama told us that there was a high mountain range overlooking enemy positions, where there were no mujahedeen. I went there and found that it was indeed a remarkable, and highly sensitive, position. So when I asked why there were no mujahedeen there, despite its importance, I was told that the roads were snowed in and reinforcements had been halted because the region was being pummeled by artillery.

Because we wanted to have a center for us, the Arabs, among the sites on which construction was under way, we decided to set it up there. But when we started work, there were only three of us left: Brother Shafiq, Brother Osama, and myself. As for the other brothers, they were on holiday, or busy elsewhere.[9] At the time, we desperately needed any brother who was able to join us, given the harsh climate, our distance from the Afghan mujahedeen, and our proximity to the enemy. With just the three of us, we could not work and stand watch at the same time.

A brother who was visiting us even tried to dissuade us from working; he also tried with Brother Shafiq and Osama, but God sent us to other brothers, one of whom was named Abul-Dahab, an Egyptian of Sudanese origin who, before he left, came to see me and said: "We wish we could stay with you," at which I was overjoyed. While we were working in the spot we had chosen, the road was open and exposed, and when the enemy started firing on us, we would go down and hide behind the trees, before starting work once again.

This is how we chose the site that was later called the companions' den.[10] This was a magnificent time: we camped near the enemy, and at the same time we were building roads and trenches, sleeping in a single tent . . . We prayed together, made decisions together, and ate in the same place.[11] We would wake up at night to stand guard, fearfully, because the place was frightening, for the enemy and for us too. No one could go too far from the tent, because the place was covered with bushes, not to mention that the enemy was so close . . . Then Muhammad al-Sakhri, who had not hesitated for a second [to join us], arrived. I had met him in the Prophet's sanctuary, after I had decided to leave;[12] this was just after dawn prayers, and Abu Hanifa had told me about a brother who wanted to go to Afghanistan, but who wanted to finish his studies first and then leave the following summer. I met al-Sakhri and spoke with him for a few seconds; he was very enthusiastic, and he decided to leave with us the following day. He had understood where his duty lay, and he gave up school, diplomas . . . the whole world. He stayed with us for almost four years, until God granted him martyrdom in Jalalabad.[13]

We wondered what to call the place; the brothers suggested several names, and we liked the "companions' den." We found it in a verse by one of the companions (may they find favor with God),[14] praising the Prophet (God's peace and blessings upon him):

> Whoever wants to be eviscerated in a scrimmage, crackling
>   like a field of reeds aflame,
> Let him approach the den; our swords are sharpened, between
>   the prairie and the trench.[15]

We had reached an important phase and were well on our way to establishing the "den," when we heard about the enemy's movements during Ramadan 1407 [May 1987], but the information we had was incomplete. Determined to carry out an operation against the enemy around the 14th of the month [May 12], we started digging trenches. The Afghan chief Gulbuddin Hekmatyar was in the region, as was Sheikh Sayyaf, who encouraged us to attack the enemy on the 26th [May 24].[16] We started to bomb the enemy positions beneath us, and the response came from BM-21 rocket launchers situated very far away. This was the start of a very long battle, which lasted three weeks, and which the enemy had planned for, while we had planned only for a daylong battle. The goal of the offensive was to destroy these positions and to close off the road to Jaji, which was one of the main routes along which reinforcements arrived in Afghanistan. The 29th [May 27] was the most violent day of the battle. In the meantime, we had learned that the forces approaching included ten thousand men, among them three Russian brigades and a commando unit[17] . . .

During this battle, Ahmad al-Zahrani was martyred; he was carrying a heavy machine gun and was struck by a mortar. May God accept his soul—he was an excellent young man, the den's first martyr. He was twenty, and he came from Taif[18] . . . Operations continued, under the leadership of Abu Ubayda al-Misri[19] . . .

Jalalabad was the first and most important battle in which the Arabs participated. What was new about it was that previous battles had taken place around positions and fortresses, whereas Jalalabad is one of the principal cities of Afghanistan, and even the one closest to Kabul. During the battle of Jalalabad, we had no choice. After many positions around the city had fallen, and the Afghan mujahedeen had taken its fortresses, arriving at the Jalalabad airport, the enemy showed it was ready to defend the city by any means possible . . . This is how several months of exceptionally violent battles began, during which the brothers acquired the great experience they did not have previously. We had around eighteen Arab positions (trained in the "companions' den") around Jalalabad, but it was difficult to organize the battle for months on end, during which our forces had to be in action all the time. We constantly needed arms and reinforcements; the arms, among them rockets and rocket launchers, had to be ready when we wanted them. We had to organize evacuation services for the wounded and the dead, and we hope that God will accept them as martyrs.[20] We also needed brothers to observe the enemy's movements, and direct fire towards him. This is how the brothers learned to use missiles, mortars, and artillery in general, using maps to determine the coordinates of a target, in military parlance, and then to take aim. In this new experience, the resources of the Arab brothers became manifest, because they showed resolve and endurance. Staying on alert for months of uninterrupted combat is not easy, but our brothers, thank God, made up the most mobile group in terms of transport, weaponry, and ammunition. We had split up the cars among the different commandos, as we had done with the combat units. There was an assault unit headed by commander Khalil, one of the most famous Afghan military chiefs in Jalalabad. This leader took many positions, and the Arab brothers were one of the most remarkable units. During certain assaults, most of the men were Arabs, and he was the only Afghan, because most of the men who had been under his orders had been martyred in previous battles[21] . . .

On 10 Dhul-Hijja 1409 [July 3, 1989], we were subjected to a massive attack that sought to destroy the Arab brothers' positions, to encircle them, and to capture them, because we had a lot of ammunition, which we had bought on the Pakistani arms market.[22] That, incidentally, is what allowed us to subject the Afghan army units concentrated around Jalalabad, where we learned that troops had been massed heavily, to heavy, regular fire. We bombarded them for three days nonstop, killing eighty Indians, because the Kabul government had brought in Indian troops to make up for the shortfall in Afghan soldiers after the withdrawal of the Russian army—even though there were about twenty thousand Russians left after the army pulled out . . .

Enemy losses were substantial: forty-two tanks, of which we captured over twenty, and we inherited five tanks, among them two T-62s. These battles ended in Jalalabad, where more Arab martyrs fell than during the entire war in Afghanistan. We beg God to accept them as martyrs!

and the source of the divine message—the site of the holy Kaaba, to which all Muslims pray.[4] And who is occupying it? The armies of the American Christians and their allies. There is no power or strength save in God.

In light of this reality, but also in light of the blessed, ardent awakening of all regions of the world, and especially of the Muslim world, I am coming back to you after a long absence, imposed by the coalition led by the Americans against the ulema and preachers of Islam, for fear that they might incite the Muslim nation to rise against its enemies. I have sought consolation in the example of past ulema (may God receive their souls), like Ibn Taymiyya and Abd al-Aziz Ibn Abd al-Salam.[5]

Furthermore, the Judeo-Christian coalition assassinated or jailed the most sincere ulema and the most active preachers (who without God's grace would not have been so pure);[6] they killed Abdallah Azzam, the sheikh and mujahid, and jailed Ahmad Yassin, the sheikh and mujahid, on the path of the Prophet's "nocturnal voyage" (may blessings and peace be upon him).[7] They jailed Sheikh Omar Abdel Rahman in America;[8] and, on American orders, they jailed a large number of ulema, preachers, and young men from the land of the two sanctuaries, notably, Sheikh Salman al-Awda and Sheikh al-Hawali, along with their brothers.[9] There is no power or strength save in God.

Next, we bear the injustice of being unable to address the Muslim peoples: we have been expelled from Pakistan, Sudan, and Afghanistan, and that was the cause of this long absence.[10] But thank God, we found a safe base in Khorāsān, on the peaks of the Hindu Kush[11]—the same peaks against which the greatest atheist military power of the world collided, and on which the myth of the superpower died amid the cries of the mujahedeen: God is greater![12] Today, from these mountaintops where we work to erase the injustice committed against the Muslim nation by the Judeo-crusader coalition, especially after the path of the Prophet (blessings and peace be upon him) was occupied and the land of the two sanctuaries

Declaration of Jihad
Against the Americans
Occupying the Land of the
Two Holy Sanctuaries

(excerpts)

Each of you knows the injustice, oppression, and aggression the Muslims are suffering from the Judeo-crusading alliance and its lackeys.[1] The blood of Muslims no longer has a price; their goods and money are offered up for their enemies to pillage. Their blood is flowing in Palestine, Iraq, and Lebanon (the awful images of the Qana massacre are still present in everyone's mind),[2] not to mention the massacres in Tajikistan, Burma, Kashmir, Assam, the Philippines, Pattani, Ogaden, Somalia, Eritrea, Chechnya, and Bosnia-Herzegovina, where Muslims have been the victims of atrocious acts of butchery.[3] These things took place in full view of the entire world—not to say because of the conspiracy between the Americans and their allies, behind the smoke screen of the Unjust United Nations. But the Muslims realized that they were the main target of the Judeo-crusading alliance; all the false propaganda about human rights faded away behind the blows dealt to Muslims and the massacres perpetrated against them in every part of the world.

The most recent calamity to have struck Muslims is the occupation of the land of the two sanctuaries, the hearth of the abode of Islam and the cradle of prophecy, since the death of the Prophet was pillaged, we hope that God will grant us victory, for he is its master and possessor[13] . . .

When duties accumulate, it is necessary to begin with the most important one: to push back this enemy, the Americans who are occupying our territory. This, after belief, is the most important duty, and nothing can take precedence over it, as the ulemas have asserted. Thus, the sheikh of Islam, Ibn Taymiyya, wrote: "As for defensive warfare, it entails defending what is most sacred through religion, at any cost. This is a collective duty. There is nothing more imperative, after faith, than to repel the aggressor who corrupts religion and life, unconditionally, as far as possible" ("Scientific Excerpts," appendix to the *Great Fatwas*, 4/608).[14]

The only way of repelling the invasion is through the combined efforts of all Muslims, and so the Muslims must ignore what divides them, temporarily, since closing their eyes to their differences cannot be worse than ignoring the capital sin that menaces Muslims[15] . . .

A few days ago, the news agencies communicated a declaration issued by the American secretary of defense, a crusader and an occupier, in which he said he had learned only one lesson from the bombings in Riyadh and Khobar:[16] not to retreat before the cowardly terrorists. Well, we would like to tell the secretary that his words are funny enough to make even a mother grieving for the loss of her child burst out laughing, because they show only the fear that grips him. Where was this supposed bravery in Beirut, after the attack of 1403 [1983], which turned your 241 Marines into scattered fragments and torn limbs?[17] Where was this bravery in Aden, which you fled twenty-four hours after the two attacks had taken place?[18]

I'm telling you, William: these young men love death as much as you love life.[19] They have inherited honor, pride, bravery, generosity, sincerity, courage, and a spirit of sacrifice. These things are handed down from father to son, and their steadfastness in combat will show when the confrontation comes, because they inherited these qualities from their ancestors since the pre-Islamic period, before Islam took root in them.[20]

You claim that these young men are cowards . . . , but they bore arms for ten years in Afghanistan, and swore to carry on the struggle against you until you were gone, beaten, defeated, and shamed, if God wills it, as long as the blood flowed in their veins and tears streamed from their eyes.

O God, bolster your nation by honoring those who obey you and abasing those who disobey you. Bolster it by ordering good and forbidding evil.

May praise and salvation be upon Muhammad, who worshipped you and bore your message, and on his family and companions. Our last prayer will be: Praise to God, lord of the worlds!

Interview with CNN

(EXCERPTS)

Q. Mr. Bin Laden, could you give us your main criticism of the Saudi royal family that is ruling Saudi Arabia today?[1]

A. Regarding the criticisms of the ruling regime in Saudi Arabia and the Arabian Peninsula, the first one is their subordination to the US. So, our main problem is the US government while the Saudi regime is but a branch or an agent of the US. By being loyal to the US regime, the Saudi regime has committed an act against Islam. And this, based on the ruling of Shari'a, casts the regime outside the religious community. Subsequently, the regime has stopped ruling people according to what God revealed, praise and glory be to Him, not to mention many other contradictory acts. When this main foundation was violated, other corrupt acts followed in every aspect of the country, the economic, the social, government services and so on . . .

Q. Have Saudi agents attempted to assassinate you?[2] . . .

A. . . . Being killed for God's cause is a great honor achieved by only those who are the elite of the nation. We love this kind of death for God's cause as much as you like to live. We have nothing to fear . . . It is something we wish for.[3]

Q. What are your future plans?

A. You'll see them and hear about them in the media, God willing.[4]

Q. If you had an opportunity to give a message to President Clinton, what would that message be?

A. Mentioning the name of Clinton or that of the American government provokes disgust and revulsion. This is because the name of the American government and the names of Clinton and Bush directly bring to our minds the pictures of one-year-old children with their heads cut off. It reflects the picture of children whose members have been amputated, the picture of the children who died in Iraq, the hands of the Israelis carrying weapons that destroy our children.[5] The hearts of Muslims are filled with hatred towards the United States of America and the American president, [whose] heart [is immune to these images] . . . Our people in the Arabian Peninsula will sen[d] him messages with no words because he does not understand them.[6] If there is a message that I may send through you, then it is a message I address to the mothers of the American troops who came here willingly in their military uniforms, and who walk proudly up and down our land while the [religious] scholars of our country are thrown in prison.[7] I say that this represents a blatant provocation to one billion, two hundred and fifty thousand Muslims. To these mothers I say if they are concerned for their sons, then let them object to the American government's policy and to the American president. Do not let themselves be cheated by his standing before the bodies of the killed soldiers describing the freedom fighters in Saudi Arabia as terrorists. It is he who is a terrorist who pushed their sons into this for the sake of the Isr[ae]li interest. We believe that the American army in Saudi Arabia came to separate between the Muslims and the people for not ruling in accordance with God's wish. They came to be in support of the Israeli forces in occupied Palestine, the land of our Prophet's night journey.[8]

WORLD ISLAMIC FRONT STATEMENT
URGING JIHAD AGAINST
JEWS AND CRUSADERS

Praise be to God, who revealed the Book, controls the clouds, defeats factionalism, and says in his Book: "But when the forbidden months are past, then fight and slay the pagans wherever you find them, seize them, beleaguer them, and lie in wait for them in every stratagem (of war)";[1] and peace be upon our Prophet, Muhammad Ibn Abdallah, who said: "I have been sent with the sword in my hands to ensure that no one but God is worshipped, God who put my livelihood under the shadow of my spear and who inflicts humiliation and scorn on those who disobey my orders."[2]

Never since God made it, created its desert, and encircled it with seas has the Arabian Peninsula been invaded by such forces as the crusader armies that have swarmed across it like locusts, devouring its plantations and growing fat off its riches.[3] All this is happening at a time when nations are attacking Muslims like leeches. In light of increasing dangers and the lack of support, we must face what current events conceal, before agreeing on how to settle the matter.

Today, there is abundant proof of three indisputable facts, on which all just men agree. We will mention these facts for those who can hear, whether it kills them or allows them to live. They are:

First, for over seven years the United States has been occupying the most sacred of the Islamic lands, the Arabian Peninsula, plun-

dering its riches, dictating to its rulers, humiliating its people, ter-
rorizing its neighbors, and turning its bases in the peninsula into a
spearhead with which to fight the neighboring Muslim peoples.
Some may have contested this assertion in the past, but today all
the peninsula's inhabitants acknowledge it. The best proof of this is
the Americans' continuing aggression against the Iraqi people, using the peninsula as a launching pad, even though all its rulers are
against their territories' being used to that end but are nevertheless
helpless to prevent it.[4]

Second, despite the great devastation inflicted on the Iraqi people by the crusader-Zionist alliance, and despite the huge number
of those killed, which is approaching a million, the Americans are
once again trying to repeat the horrific massacres.[5] As though
they are not content with the protracted blockade imposed after
the ferocious war, or the fragmentation and devastation, here they
come to annihilate what is left of this people and to humiliate their
Muslim neighbors.

Third, if the war aims of the Americans are religious and economic, they also have the effect of serving the Jews' petty state and
diverting attention from its occupation of Jerusalem and murder
of Muslims there. Nothing shows this more clearly than their ea-
gerness to destroy Iraq, the strongest Arab state in the region, and
their attempts to fragment all the states of the region, such as Iraq,
Saudi Arabia, Egypt, and Sudan, into paper statelets, whose dis-
unity and weakness guarantees Israel's survival and perpetuates the
brutal crusader occupation of the peninsula.[6]

All these crimes and sins committed by the Americans are a
clear declaration of war on God, his messenger, and Muslims. And
the ulema throughout Islamic history have agreed unanimously
that jihad is an individual duty [fard 'ayn] if the enemy is destroying Muslim territory. This was revealed by Imam Ibn Qadama in
Al-Mughni (Indispensable), Imam al-Kasani in Al-Bada'i' (Wonders), al-Qurtubi in his "Commentary," and the Sheikh al-Islam in
his selected works, where he said: "As for defensive warfare, it is

aimed at defending sanctity and religion, and it is a duty as agreed unanimously [by the ulema].[7] Therefore, repel the aggressor, who corrupts religion and life." Nothing, other than belief, is more sacred.

On that basis, and in compliance with God's command, we issue the following fatwa [religious opinion] to all Muslims:

Killing the Americans and their allies—civilians and military— is an individual duty for every Muslim who can carry it out in any country where it proves possible, in order to liberate Al-Aqsa Mosque and the holy sanctuary [Mecca] from their grip, and to the point that their armies leave all Muslim territory, defeated and unable to threaten any Muslim.[8] This is in accordance with the words of God Almighty, "And fight the pagans all together as they fight you all together," and "fight them until there is no more tumult or oppression, and justice and faith in God prevail."[9]

Likewise with the words of the Almighty God: "And why should you not fight in the cause of God and of those who, being weak, are ill treated (and oppressed)?—women and children, whose cry is: 'Our Lord, rescue us from this town, whose people are oppressors; and raise for us from thee one who will help!'"[10]

We—with God's help—call on every Muslim who believes in God and wishes to be rewarded to comply with God's order to kill the Americans and plunder them of their possessions wherever and whenever they find them.[11] We also call on Muslim ulema, leaders, youth, and soldiers to launch the raid on Satan's U.S. troops and the devil's supporters allied with them and to displace those who are behind them, so that they may learn a lesson.[12] God Almighty said: "O you who believe, give your response to God and His Apostle, when He calleth you to that which will give you life. And know that God cometh between a man and his heart, and that it is he to whom you shall all be gathered."[13]

Almighty God also says: "O you who believe, what is the matter with you, that when you are asked to go forth in the cause of God, you cling so heavily to the earth! Do you prefer the life of this world to the hereafter? But little is the comfort of this life, as compared with the hereafter. Unless you go forth, He will punish you with a grievous penalty, and put others in your place; but Him you would not harm in the least. For God hath power over all things."[14]

Almighty God also says: "So lose no heart, nor fall into despair. For you must gain mastery if you are true in faith."[15]

SHEIKH OSAMA BIN MUHAMMAD BIN LADEN,
leader of Al Qaeda organization

AYMAN AL-ZAWAHIRI,
emir of the Jihad Group in Egypt

SHEIKH MIR HAMZAH,
secretary of the Jamiat-ul-Ulema-e-Pakistan[16]

FAZLUR RAHMAN KHALIL,
emir of Harakat al-Ansar, Pakistan[17]

SHEIKH ABD AL-SALAM MUHAMMAD KHAN,
emir of Harakat al-Jihad, Bangladesh[18]

ABU YASIR RIFA'i Ahmad Taha,
council member, Egyptian Islamic Group[19]

February 23, 1998

INTERVIEW WITH AL-JAZEERA

(EXCERPTS)

Q. What is your history?[1]

A. I am Osama Ibn Muhammad Bin Laden. By God's grace, I was born to Muslim parents in the Arabian Peninsula in the Malazz neighborhood of Riyadh, in 1377 A.H. [March 10, 1957], and then, by God's grace, we went to Medina six months after my birth.[2] We lived in the Hejaz, in the towns of Mecca, Jidda, and Medina.[3]

My father, Sheikh Muhammad Bin Awad Bin Laden, was born in Hadramawt, and came from there to the Hejaz for work, some time ago—more than seventy years ago.[4] God honored him as he had no builder before him, by giving him the bid to expand the great mosque at Mecca, where the Kaaba is.[5] At the same time, he also worked on expanding the Prophet's mosque (the best of prayers and salvation upon him).[6]

When my father found out that the Jordanian government had submitted a bid to renovate the Dome of the Rock [in Jerusalem], he gathered all the engineers and asked them to submit a bid at cost only.[7] They told him they could guarantee his winning the bid even if they added on a percentage for profit, but he insisted: "Establish a bid without interest."[8]

When they submitted their total figure to him, they were surprised that he (God rest his soul) had then gone ahead and reduced the total figure they had submitted for the project even further, in an attempt to guarantee that their company would win the bid for the renovation of God's houses, and of this one in particular.[9]

He won the bids and began the work. And on some days he was able to perform three of his daily prayers in three of the holiest sites.[10] He was one of those who founded the infrastructure of the Kingdom of Saudi Arabia.[11]

I studied economics in the Hejaz, at Jidda University, also called King Abdul Aziz University, but from a very early age I worked on the roads, in my father's company, even though when my father passed away I was only ten.[12] This is the brief history of Osama bin Laden.

Q. What do you seek?

A. What I seek is what is a right for any living being: that our land be liberated from enemies, liberated from the Americans.[13] God gave every living being the instinct to reject invasion by outsiders. Take the example—I apologize for its mundane nature—of domestic animals. Let us look at a chicken, for example. If an armed person were to enter a chicken's home turf with the aim of inflicting harm on it, the chicken would automatically fight back, even if it is only a chicken. So we are demanding a right shared by all living creatures, all human beings, not to mention all Muslims.[14] Given the kind of aggression to which Muslim countries have been subjected—especially the holy sites, starting with Al-Aqsa, the Prophet's first qibla—and the ongoing aggression of the Judeo-crusader alliance, led by America and Israel, which has taken the land of the two sanctuaries, we are trying to incite the world Muslim community to free our land and undertake a jihad for God.[15] Then revealed law will reign and God's word will be law.[16]

Q. What are your ultimate objectives, and what message would you like to convey to the Islamic world in general?

A. We believe very strongly—and I say this despite the pressures imposed on us by regimes and the media—that they want to deprive us of our manhood.[17] We see ourselves as men, Muslim men, committed to defend the greatest house in the universe, the holy Kaaba, which it is an honor to die for and defend.[18] We do not want to abandon the defense of the descendants of Saad and al-Muthanna, of Abu Bakr and Omar, to American women soldiers, whether Jewish or Christian.[19] Even if God had not given us Islam, our pagan ancestors would have rejected the presence of these red mules under a pretext one would be ashamed to give a child.[20] The governments of the region said: "The Americans came for only a few months," and they lied from start to finish.[21] Our Prophet said that on Judgment Day God would not accept three sorts of men, and he cited among them a lying king.[22] A few months passed; a year passed, and then another: nine years have passed, and the Americans are lying to everyone, saying: "We have interests in the region, and we will not move as long as we have not secured them." An enemy breaks into your house to steal your money. You ask him: "Are you robbing me?" He replies: "No . . . I am defending my interests." They are tricking us, and the governments of this region fell into the trap. Perhaps they have lost their manhood, and consider that men are women. But by God, free Muslim women refuse to be defended by these Jewish and American whores.[23] Our aim is therefore to apply the revealed law and to defend the sacred Kaaba, the great Kaaba, that venerable monument. God created men upon this earth to unify them in practice, and the most important practice, after faith and prayer, is jihad, as the *Sahih* of al-Bukhari says.[24] So God Almighty will not accept our prayers if we do not turn toward this venerable monument, and he chose the best of men, Abraham, the ancestor of the prophets— to establish it, along with Isma'il.[25] Our goal, therefore, is to free the land of Islam from unbelief, and to apply the law of God there.[26]

Tactical Recommendations

(EXCERPTS)

Historians tells us how al-Muthanna al-Shaybani came to Medina to ask the caliph for reinforcements to combat the Persians.[1] Omar tried for three whole days to mobilize the men for battle, but no one showed up. He understood what the men thought of going to war against a superpower and ordered al-Muthanna to speak to them and tell them what God had allowed him to achieve against the Persians, so that he could allay all their fears.[2] So al-Muthanna got up, spoke to them, and called them to battle: "O men, do not let this face frighten you, because we have penetrated Persia and defeated its soldiers by entering through two places in the south of Iraq. Then we shared fine spoils, grew bolder toward them, and, God willing, it is not over." So all the men became enthusiastic, Abu Obayd al-Thaqafi got up, the caliph gave him the banner, and they marched into battle.[3]

Don't let this face, that of America and its army, frighten you: we have struck America and its army many times, and we have beaten them over and over again. These are cowardly men. When we confronted the American enemies, we realized that their main recourse is psychological warfare, thanks to their enormous propaganda machine, and the massive air bombardments that serve to mask their weakest points: U.S. soldiers' fear, cowardice, and lack of any fighting spirit. If I had the luxury, I would tell you almost unbelievable things about the combats in Tora Bora, in Afghanistan, but I hope God will let me do so later.[4]

First, let me recall a few of the defeats inflicted on the great powers by the fighters in the holy war.

1. The defeat of the former Soviet Union, which is nothing but a memory, after ten years of ferocious combat against the Afghans and the Muslims who helped them, thank God.[5]

2. The defeat of the Russians in Chechnya by the fighters in the holy war, who offered the most remarkable examples of sacrifice. During this first war, the Chechen combatants, along with their Arab brothers and companions, broke the Russians' arrogance and inflicted heavy losses on them, causing them to withdraw, utterly defeated.[6] Then the Russians came back, with American support, and Russia is still suffering enormous losses inflicted by a small group of believers. We hope that God will strengthen and support them.[7]

3. I will also remind you of how the American forces were defeated in 1402 A.H., when the Tribe of Israel invaded Lebanon, and the resistance sent a truck packed with explosives into the center of the U.S. forces (Marines) in Beirut, killing over two hundred and fifty, who went to meet an unhappy fate in hell.[8]

4. Then, after the second Gulf War, America sent its army into Somalia, and thirteen thousand Muslims were killed there. But when the Muslim lions among the Afghan Arabs leaped forth by the side of their brothers in that land and opposed the Americans, they were able to grind America's pride into the dust.[9] They killed its soldiers, destroyed their tanks, and shot down their helicopters. One dark night, America and its allies fled in panic, God be praised.[10]

5. At the time, the young jihadists were preparing an attack against the Americans in Yemen, but they were forced to flee—not out of cowardice—in the space of twenty-four hours.

6. In the year 1415 A.H., an attack occurred in Riyadh that killed four Americans. This was a message showing the inhabitants' opposition to the American pro-Jewish policy, and to the occupation of the land of the two sanctuaries.

7. The following year in Khobar another explosion took place, which killed nineteen people and wounded over four hundred. It forced the Americans to transfer their main military bases from the cities to the desert.[11]

8. Then, in 1418 A.H., holy war combatants publicly warned America to stop supporting the Jews and to withdraw from the land of the two sanctuaries. But the enemy refused to heed this warning. Thank God, the fighters were able to inflict two enormous blows on him in East Africa.[12]

9. America was warned again but did not listen, so God granted success to a great suicide attack on the U.S. destroyer *Cole* in Aden. This was a stinging blow to the American army and also showed the treachery of the Yemeni government and of other governments in the region.[13]

Then the fighters realized that the gang in the White House could not see things clearly, and that their leader (that idiot they obey) was claiming that we envied their lifestyle—when the truth, which this Pharaoh would like to hide, is that we are attacking them because of their injustice toward the Muslim world, and especially Palestine and Iraq, as well as their occupation of the land of the two sanctuaries.[14] When the fighters saw this, they decided to come out of the shadows and take the fight into their territory, into their homes.

That holy Tuesday, the 23rd of Jumada al-Thani 1422, corresponding to September 11, 2001, the American-Zionist alliance was pursuing its work among our sons and parents on the blessed land of Al-Aqsa. Jewish hands piloted American planes and tanks, while our sons in Iraq were dying because of the unjust embargo imposed by America and its agents. During this time, the Muslim world was living as far as possible from the true religion, and the situation had reached an unbearable degree of frustration, despair, and distress among Muslims—apart from those who fear God. There was such injustice, arrogance, and aggression within the American-Zionist alliance that Uncle Sam's country was sinking in sin, feasting on despotism, scowling at the world, going on its merry way, convinced that it was invulnerable. Then the catastrophe struck. What was this? They leapt forth, disheveled, their feet in the dust, those who had been chased out of everywhere. "They were youths who believed in their Lord, and we advanced them in guidance."[15] Their doctrine was firm, and they held their faith close; they feared no blame save God's. They desired only what God possessed, and so refused to sleep.

And so, thanks to the enemy's aircraft, they undertook a brave and beautiful operation, unprecedented in the history of humanity, and struck down America's totems. They hit at the heart of the Department of Defense, they struck the American economy with full force, rubbed America's nose in the dirt, and dragged its arrogance through the mud. New York's Twin Towers tumbled down, dragging down with them things far higher and greater.

The myth of America the great crumbled!
The myth of democracy crumbled!
People realized that American values are misguided.
The myth of the land of the free collapsed.
The myth of American national security collapsed.
The myth of the CIA crumbled, thanks be to God.

The most important positive consequence of the attacks on New York and Washington was that they showed the truth about the fight between the crusaders and the Muslims.[16] They revealed how much the crusaders resent us, once these two attacks stripped the wolf of its sheep's clothing and showed us its horrifying face. The entire world awoke, Muslims realized how important the doctrine of loyalty to God and separation is,[17] and solidarity among Muslims grew stronger, which is a giant step toward the unification of Muslims under the banner of monotheism, in order to establish the rightly guided caliphate, please God.[18] Finally, everyone realized that America, that oppressive force, can be beaten, humiliated, brought low . . .

I advise young people to wage jihad, because they are the first to be affected by this obligation, as al-Shatbi showed in *The Concordances*.[19]

The first duty and the best of the works you can undertake for God is to aim at the Americans and the Jews everywhere on earth. I advise you to gather around sincere ulema, such as devoted, active preachers; I advise you to resort to dissimulation, especially when it comes to jihad and its military actions.

I want to tell all of you, and especially our brothers in Palestine, that your mujahedeen brothers are on the march, on the path of jihad, to strike the Jews and the Americans. The operation in Mombasa was just the first drop in a long downpour.[20] We will not forsake you. Carry on the struggle, with God's grace, and we will carry on too, if God wills it.

Before concluding, I want to cite these verses, to encourage my Muslim brothers and myself to carry on jihad along God's path:

> I lead my horse and throw myself into battle with him like an
> oar into the waves,
> God, let my death come not on a bier embroidered with
> green,
> But let my grave be in the belly of a vulture, dozing on its
> perch,
> May I die a martyr in a troop attacked in a trembling ravine,
> Like the heroes of Shayban, united in piety, as they lead the
> assault.
> When they depart this world, they leave suffering behind, and
> find what the Quran has promised.[21]

In conclusion, I call on my Muslim brothers, and on myself, to fear God, in private and in public, to pray constantly and to beg him to accept our repentance and take away our sorrows. "Our Lord! Grant us good in this world and good in the hereafter, and save us from the torment of the Fire."[22]

We ask God to free us from the Americans and their allies, and to free Sheikhs Omar Abdel Rahman and Said Ibn Zuwayr, as well as our brothers in Guantánamo.[23] We ask him to support the mujahedeen in Palestine and the other Muslim countries, and to help us overcome our enemies.

Our last prayer is in praise of God.

SECOND LETTER TO THE
MUSLIMS OF IRAQ

Praise the Lord. Praise the Lord.

Praise the Lord, who said: "O Prophet! Strive against the unbelievers and the hypocrites! Be harsh with them. Their ultimate abode is hell, a hapless journey's end."[1]

Praise and blessings upon our Prophet, Muhammad, who said: "Whoever is killed defending his property is a martyr, whoever is killed defending himself is a martyr, whoever is killed defending his religion is a martyr, and whoever is killed defending his family is a martyr."

This is my second letter to the Muslim brothers in Iraq.

O sons of Saad and Muthanna, of Khalid and Mu'anna, O descendants of Saladin,[2]

Peace be with you, and the mercy and blessings of God.

I salute you and your efforts, as well as your blessed holy war. With God's assistance, you have showered blows upon your enemies, restoring hope in the hearts of all Muslims, and especially the Palestinians. May God reward you. We thank you for your holy war; may God strengthen your steps and make your aim true.

Rejoice, because America is sinking in the quagmire of the Tigris and the Euphrates. Bush thought Iraq and its oil would be easy prey, but he is now in a difficult situation. Thank God, America is now crying out and falling to its knees before the eyes of the world. Praise God, for he punished it for having drafted the dregs of humanity and gone to beg for mercenaries from east and west.[3]

It is not surprising that you were able to do this to America, to strike such blows against it, because you are the sons of the courageous knights who gave Islam to the East, all the way to China.[4]

You should know that this war is a new crusade against the Muslim world, and that it will be decisive for the Muslim community all over the world. It can have dangerous repercussions and damaging effects on Islam and Muslims, to an extent that only God knows.

So, young Muslims from everywhere, and especially from neighboring countries of Iraq and from Yemen:

You must lead the holy war suitably, follow the truth, and beware of listening to men who obey only their desires and lie on the ground, or those who put faith in their oppressors, fear for you, and seek to turn you away from this blessed holy war.

There are those who have raised their voices in Iraq, as they did before in Palestine, Egypt, Jordan, Yemen, and elsewhere, calling for a peaceful and democratic solution, calling for collaboration with apostate regimes, or with Jewish and crusading invaders, instead of leading a holy war. It is necessary to beware of this false and misleading way, which is contrary to God's law, and which hinders holy war.

How can you support the holy war if you do not fight for God's cause? Are you going to backtrack? Those men have weakened sincere Muslims and taken as their reference point human passions, democracy, and religions ignorant of Islam;[5] by participating in parliaments, they have lost their way and led many others astray with them.

What are they thinking, those who enter the parliaments of idol worshippers, which Islam has destroyed? If the heart of religion existed no longer, what would remain for them? And they claim they are right! They are very wrong, and God knows Islam is innocent of their faults. Islam is God's religion, and parliaments are an ignorant religion, so those who obey princes and ulema (who allow what God has forbidden, like entering legislative councils, and forbid what God has allowed, like jihad) commit the sin of making these men lords in place of God—when there is strength only in him![6]

I am speaking to Muslims in general, and Iraqis in particular, when I say: beware of supporting America's crusaders and those who have taken their side, because all those who collaborate with them or belong to them, whatever their names or titles, are unbelievers and apostates.

The same judgment applies to all those who support impious political parties, like the Baath, the Kurdish democratic parties, and others like them.[7]

Everyone knows that any government formed by the United States is a treacherous puppet regime, like the governments of our region, including those of Karzai and Mahmoud Abbas, which were created in order to extinguish the flame of jihad.[8]

The "road map" is just another episode in the series of plots aimed at liquidating the intifada.[9] Jihad must continue until an Islamic government is ruling according to revealed law.

Muslims!

This is a serious matter. Those who strive, reason, have principles, courage, or money should know that their time has come. It is at such times that men think of dying, and at such times that one can tell the difference between sincere men and liars, between those who cherish their religion and cowards.

We must hope that noble, honorable Muslims will play their part.

I want to say to my Muslim brothers who are fighting in Iraq:

I share your concerns, feel as you do, and envy you your jihad. God knows that if I could, I would join you.[10] How could I stay here, knowing that God's apostle, whom we take as our example and model, said: "Had I not found it difficult for my followers, then I would not remain behind any *sariya* [military expedition] going for jihad"? He also said: "I would have loved to be martyred in God's cause and then brought back to life, and then martyred and then brought back to life, and then again martyred in his cause." This, then, is our Prophet's way (peace be upon him), and the way to follow in order to bring about the triumph of religion and establish the Muslim state.[11] Follow it; but only sincere believers will be able to.

Muslims, people of Rabia and Mudar, O Kurds![12]

Raise the banner and God will raise you up. Do not be intimidated by these armed mules, because God has weakened them.[13] Do not be impressed by their numbers, because their hearts are empty and their situation has begun to deteriorate, not only on the military front but also economically, especially since that blessed day in New York, thanks be to God.

The losses inflicted by that blow and its repercussions have reached over a trillion dollars—a thousand thousand million— and for the third consecutive year they have also had a budget deficit. This year it reached a record high, since it is estimated at over 450,000 million dollars, praise be to God.[14]

To conclude:

To my brothers fighting in Iraq, to the heroes of Baghdad—the seat of the caliphate—and its environs;[15]

To the companions of Islam, Saladin's heirs;[16]

To the free men of Baaquba, Mosul, and al-Anbar;[17]

To those who left their countries to wage jihad and die defending their religion, having left behind fathers and sons, families and homelands;

I greet all of you, and say:

You are the soldiers of God, the spears of Islam, and, today, you are on the front line in the defense of the Muslim community.

Christians have gathered beneath the banner of the cross to fight the community of Muhammad (may God bless and save him).[18] Be satisfied with your holy war. No Muslim is worthy of going before you, because you have placed your trust in God alone.

The hopes that are placed in you, after God, cannot shame today's Muslims. Follow the example of Saad (may God be pleased with him), who, on the day of the Battle of the Trench, said: "Wait awhile, the fight will follow the attack. Death matters little, if your hour is come."[19]

Death matters little, when the time is come.

God, this is one of your days of glory. Turn the hearts of young Muslims and their brows toward the jihad in your cause.

Strengthen their faith and their footsteps. Make their aim true and their hearts united.

O God, let your creatures triumph everywhere: in Palestine, Iraq, Chechnya, Kashmir, the Philippines, and Afghanistan.

Free our brothers whom the tyrants have jailed, in America, Guantánamo, occupied Palestine, and in Riyadh—everywhere, for you are all-powerful.

God, give us patience, strengthen our steps, and grant us victory over the unbelievers. "God has full power over things, but most people know it not."[20]

May God bless our Prophet Muhammad, his family, and his companions.

Praise be to God, Lord of this world and the next.

MESSAGE TO THE
AMERICAN PEOPLE

"To those against whom / War is made, permission / Is given (to fight), because / They are wronged;—and verily, / God is Most Powerful / For their aid."[1]

Peace be with those who follow the righteous path.

American people: my speech to you is about the best way of avoiding a repeat performance of Manhattan, as well as the causes and consequences of the war.[2] By way of introduction, let me say that security is an indispensable pillar of human life and that free men do not forfeit their security, contrary to Bush's claim that we hate freedom.[3] If that were true, then let him explain to us why we do not attack Sweden, for example.

Freedom haters do not possess defiant spirits like those of the nineteen[4]—may God have mercy on them. No, we fight because we are free men who do not slumber under oppression. We want to restore freedom to our nation, and just as you lay waste to our nation, so shall we lay waste to yours. Only a witless wrongdoer plays with the security of others and then fools himself into thinking he will be secure, whereas rational people, when disaster strikes, make it their priority to look for its causes.[5]

I am amazed at you. Even though three years have passed since the events of September 11, Bush is still engaged in distortion, deception, and hiding the real causes from you. And thus, the reasons are still there for a repeat of what occurred. I shall tell you why those events took place, and speak to you frankly about the moments that led me to make this decision, so that you can think about them. God knows we would never have thought of striking the towers, had we not seen such tyranny and oppression from the American-Israeli alliance against our people in Palestine and Lebanon. Only when we could take no more did we think of it.

The events that affected me personally began in 1982, when America gave the Israelis the green light to invade Lebanon and the American Sixth Fleet helped them.[6] When the bombardment began, many were killed and injured, and others were terrorized and displaced. I cannot forget those unbearable scenes of blood and severed limbs, the corpses of women and children strewn everywhere, houses destroyed along with their occupants and high-rise buildings burying their residents, rockets raining down on our land without mercy. It was as if a crocodile had seized a helpless child, who could do nothing but scream. Tell me: Does the crocodile understand any language other than that of force? The whole world watched this tragedy and did nothing. In those difficult moments many thoughts that are difficult to describe boiled up within me. They produced an intense rejection of tyranny, and a strong resolve to punish the oppressors.

And as I looked at those demolished buildings in Lebanon, it entered my mind that we should punish the oppressor in kind and destroy the towers of America, so that they could experience some of what we had experienced, and so that they would stop killing our women and children. And that day, I realized that killing innocent women and children is a deliberate American policy. State terrorism is called freedom and democracy, while resistance is terrorism and intolerance. This means that millions of people must suffer oppression and embargo until death results, as inflicted by Bush Sr. in Iraq in the greatest mass slaughter of children ever.[7] It means millions of children are subjected to mass bombardments because Bush Jr. wanted to overthrow a former ally and replace him with a new puppet to assist in the theft of Iraq's oil and other crimes.[8]

The events of September 11 unfolded against this background, as a response to these grave injustices. Can one blame a man who is only defending himself? Is defending oneself, and punishing an aggressor in kind, terrorism? If that is the case, then we had no choice.

This is the message I sought to communicate to you in word and deed, repeatedly, for years before September 11. You can read it, if you like, in my interview with Scott in *Time Magazine* in 1996, or with Peter Arnett on CNN, or with John Miller in 1998.[9] You can see it in practice, if you wish, in Kenya and Tanzania and Aden.[10] And you can read it in my interview with Abdul Bari Atwan, as well as my interviews with Robert Fisk.[11] The latter is one of your compatriots and co-religionists, and I consider him to be neutral. Did the alleged defenders of freedom at the White House and the channels controlled by them bother to speak with these people, so that they could tell the American people the reasons for our fight against you?

If you avoid these causes, you will be on the right path to enjoy the security that you had before September 11. So much for the war and its causes.

As for its results, they have been, thanks to Almighty God, extremely positive, and indeed beyond all expectations. This is owing to many factors, chief among them that we have found it easy to deal with the Bush administration because it is just like the regimes in our countries, half of which are ruled by the military and the other half by the sons of kings and presidents. We know them well: both types are characterized by pride, arrogance, greed, and misappropriation of wealth.

This resemblance has been visible since Bush first visited the region. While some of our compatriots were dazzled by America and hoped that these visits would have an effect on our countries, he was the one who was affected by the monarchies and military regimes, and became envious of their long hold on power and their ability to embezzle public wealth without supervision or accounting. So he passed despotism and contempt for freedom on to his son, who named them the Patriot Act, on the pretence of fighting terrorism.

Bush set his sons up as state governors and did not neglect to import expertise in election fraud from the Arab countries to Florida, for use in difficult times.[12]

All this made it easy for us to provoke and bait this administration. All we have to do is send two mujahedeen to the Far East to wave a banner proclaiming "Al Qaeda," and the generals run. In this way, they increase their human, economic, and political losses without achieving anything of note, apart from some benefits to their private corporations.

In addition, we have experience in using guerrilla warfare and attrition to fight tyrannical superpowers, as we, alongside the mujahedeen, bled Russia for ten years, until it went bankrupt and was forced to withdraw in defeat, thanks be to God.[13] So we are continuing this policy in bleeding America to the point of bankruptcy, God willing—and nothing is too great for God.

Saying that Al Qaeda defeated the administration in the White House, or that the administration has lost in this war, is not correct, however, because when one scrutinizes the results, one cannot say that Al Qaeda can take sole credit for achieving these spectacular gains. In fact, the White House policy of doing everything possible to start wars on new fronts to keep various corporations busy—whether in the field of arms or oil or reconstruction[14]—helped Al Qaeda achieve these tremendous results.

As some analysts and diplomats have pointed out, the White House seems to be playing on our team, and the goal is to score against the United States economy, even if our intentions differ. This is what the diplomat declared in his lecture at the Royal Institute of International Affairs: for example, Al Qaeda spent five hundred thousand dollars on 9/11, while America, in the incident and its aftermath, lost—according to the lowest estimate—in excess of five hundred billion dollars. This means that every dollar Al Qaeda spent conquered a million dollars by the grace of God Almighty, not to mention the loss of a huge number of jobs.[15] As for the budget deficit, it has reached astronomical numbers, estimated at over a trillion dollars.

Even more dangerous for America is the way the mujahedeen recently forced Bush to resort to emergency funds to continue the fight in Afghanistan and Iraq, thus proving that the plan to bleed the Americans dry is succeeding, God willing.[16]

True, this is evidence of Al Qaeda's victory, but it also shows that the Bush administration has gained, as is obvious to anyone who looks at the contracts acquired by the shady megacorporations linked to the Bush administration, like Halliburton and the rest.[17] All this shows that the real loser is you, the American people, and your economy.

For the record, we had agreed with Commander in Chief Muhammad Atta, God have mercy on him, that his mission would be accomplished within twenty minutes, before Bush and his administration had time to notice;[18] but it never occurred to us that the commander in chief of the American armed forces would abandon fifty thousand of his citizens in the Twin Towers to face great horrors alone, at the time when they needed him most.

But he seems to have preferred listening to a little girl talk about a butting goat, rather than occupy himself with the planes that were butting the skyscrapers, and so we were given three times the period required to execute the operations—may God be praised![19]

Nor is it any secret to you that American intellectuals and the most brilliant minds warned Bush before the war, telling him: "You have everything you need to make America safe and eliminate weapons of mass destruction—assuming they exist. The world is on your side if you continue the inspections. American interests will not be served by starting an unjustified war with an unknown outcome." The black gold blinded him, however, and he gave priority to private interests over the interests of America. This is how the war went ahead, so many have died, the American economy is suffering, and Bush is sinking in the swamps of Iraq. There is an apt proverb to illustrate this: "Like the doomed she-goat who used her hoof to dig up a knife from under the ground."[20]

I would like to remind you that over fifteen thousand of our people have been killed and tens of thousands injured, just as over a thousand of yours have been killed and more than ten thousand injured. Bush's hands are stained with the blood of all those killed on both sides, all for the sake of oil and the benefit of private corporations.

You need to know this: when a nation punishes a weak man because he has killed one of its citizens for money, while letting a powerful man go free when he kills thousands of citizens, also for money . . .[21] The same goes for your allies in Palestine. They terrorize women and children, they kill and capture men as they lie sleeping.

Just remember that for every action there is a reaction.

Finally, you need to think about the last wishes of the thousands who left you on the 11th as they gestured in despair. These are important testaments, which should be studied well.

What I will remember among their pleas, before the towers fell, is the one regretting having allowed the White House to attack oppressed peoples in its foreign policy. They want you to hold accountable those who were indirectly responsible for their death, and happy are those who give sound advice. Their messages remind me that "injustice hounds the unjust, and thieves never profit from stolen goods."

As the saying goes, an ounce of prevention is better than a pound of cure. Return to the truth, rather than persisting in error. Sensible people would never squander their security, wealth, and children for the sake of the liar in the White House.

In conclusion, honestly, your security is not in the hands of

Kerry, or Bush, or Al Qaeda. It is in your own hands, and any state that does not violate our security has automatically guaranteed its own.[22]

God is our guardian and helper, while you have none. Peace be with the one who follows the Way.

PART II

ABDALLAH AZZAM

INTRODUCTION

ABDALLAH AZZAM, THE IMAM OF JIHAD

THOMAS HEGGHAMMER

"Today, there is not a single land of jihad worldwide, not a mujahid fighting along God's path, that Abdallah Azzam's life, teachings, and works have not inspired."[1]

Abdallah Azzam (1941–1989), a Palestinian religious scholar, occupies a central place in the history of radical Islamism, for which he served as principal theoretician, inspirational figure, and organizer of Arab participation in the war in Afghanistan during the 1980s. Western analysts have described him as "the godfather of jihad," while radical Islamists call him "the imam of jihad" because of his central role in the development of the "global jihad movement" that was born with the Afghan war.

By the time an assassin set off the bomb that killed Azzam in Peshawar, in November 1989, he was already a legendary figure in Islamist circles, thanks to his writings, his charisma, and his uncontested status as a pioneer of Arab engagement in the Afghan jihad. Almost twenty years later, Azzam is still an icon of the Islamist movement, and among radicals his stature is matched only by Osama Bin Laden's.

It is impossible to ignore the influence of Azzam's written work. His two best-known books, *The Defense of Muslim Territories* and *Join the Caravan,* in which he preaches a worldwide Islamist military defense effort, are still considered classics of jihadist literature.

How and why did the Palestinian scholar end his days near the front of the Afghan jihad? What was new in Azzam's ideas, and to what extent can he be considered the intellectual godfather of Al Qaeda's global terrorism? In the following pages, we will examine his life, writing, and legacy more closely.

Beginnings

Abdallah Yusuf Mustafa Azzam was born in 1941 in a village called Silat al-Harithiyya, eight kilometers northwest of Jenin, in what was then Transjordan.[2] Little is known of his parents, apart from the fact that his father, Yusuf Mustafa Azzam (who died in 1990) was a grocer. The Azzams were a large family, well known in northern Palestine and southern Lebanon. The branch that lived in the Jenin region was dubbed the sheikhs, because its men grew their beards. The family was pious but not excessively so and, throughout Azzam's career, never hesitated to criticize his political activism. At the same time, he inspired several younger members of his family to join the Muslim Brotherhood.

In most of his biographies, Azzam is described as having been a child who liked to read and was exceptionally bright. He excelled in class and studied topics above his grade level. It is difficult to distinguish between hagiographical material and fact on this point, because the theme of the gifted child is extremely widespread in biographies of ulema. What seems certain is that he joined the Muslim Brotherhood in the mid-1950s after having been influenced by a local teacher who belonged to the Brotherhood: Shafiq Asad Abd al-Hadi. This elderly man, who lived in the same village, appreciated young Azzam's brilliant mind, gave him a religious education, and introduced him to the movement's main figures in Palestine. As a result, Azzam grew more interested in Islamic studies and set up a study group in his village. Then Shafiq Asad introduced him to Muhammad Abd al-Rahman Khalifa, the "general supervisor" of the Muslim Brotherhood in Transjordan, who visited Silat al-Harithiyya several times to meet with and encourage the young man. During this period, Azzam discovered the work of Hassan al-Banna and read the Brotherhood's other publications.

Azzam stayed in his village until he had finished secondary school. In the late 1950s he began attending the Al-Khaduriyya agricultural college, near Tulkarm, thirty kilometers southwest of his native village. No one knows why he chose to study agriculture, but the proximity of the college and the pressure exerted by his parents must have influenced this decision. He got good grades, although he was a year younger than his classmates. Once they had graduated, the students were sent out to teach in the local schools of the West Bank. Azzam was sent to the village of Adir, in central Jordan (near the town of Kerak, ninety kilometers south of Amman). One of his biographers notes that Azzam had wanted to find a job nearer to home, but was sent to a distant institution after an argument with the dean of his college.

After spending a year in Adir, he went back to Transjordan, where he taught in a school in Burqin, a village four kilometers east of Jenin. Later, his colleagues there remembered him as being conspicuously more religious than they were; during coffee breaks, while the others were eating sandwiches, Azzam would sit and read the Quran.

Religious Studies in Damascus (1964–1966)

At one point during his stay in Adir or Burqin, Azzam must have had second thoughts about his teaching career and decided to study religion. In 1963 he went to Syria, registered at the Islamic law school at Damascus University, and went on to obtain a diploma in sharia studies in 1966. He wrote his thesis on "the dissolution of marriage in Islamic jurisprudence and civil law"; it was a comparative study of divorce in Islamic law and in Syrian and Jordanian civil law. His thesis adviser was Abd al-Rahman al-Sabuni, a respected Syrian academic and author of several books on divorce and other subjects relating to family life and personal status in Islamic law.

While he was in Damascus, Azzam met many Syrian clerics who later became religious authorities or Islamist leaders, such as Muhammad Adib Salih, Said Hawa, Muhammad Said Ramadan al-Bouti, Mullah Ramadan Sheikh al-Shafia, and Marwan Hadid.[3] Azzam certainly took part in the political debates raging in Islamist circles at the time, especially about the attitude to adopt toward oppressive regimes, which most Islamists considered un-Islamic. A biographer recounts that when he visited Azzam, Mullah Ramadan initially refused to share the meal. When his hosts insisted, he accepted but explained that he never ate food served by his son, Muhammad Buti, because Muhammad earned a salary as a civil servant. According to Mullah Ramadan, public money was unclean because it might come from such sources as taxes on alcohol.

The death of Azzam's mentor, Shafiq Asad Abd al-Hadi, in 1964, affected Azzam deeply, strengthening his determination to keep working for the Islamic cause and to "take up the banner" in Shafiq Asad's memory. This in particular is the reason he preached and taught at the mosque in his village whenever he went back there on holiday.

In 1965, probably during the summer holidays, which he spent in the village, Azzam married a young Palestinian woman from Tulkarm, who gave him five sons and three daughters. The spouses' families had known each other since 1948, when the creation of Israel forced the young woman's family to flee their village in northern Palestine. They arrived in Silat al-Harithiyya, where the Azzams welcomed them. The Azzam family was therefore indirectly affected by the 1948 war and its consequences, but Abdallah was soon directly affected by the Israeli occupation and the Arab-Israeli conflict.

In 1966, after he had graduated with highest honors from Damascus University, he went home to the West Bank, where he taught in elementary schools, preached in mosques, and gave talks in the region surrounding his village.

Shortly after the June 1967 war and Israel's occupation of the

West Bank, Abdallah and the rest of the Azzam family moved to Jordan. Like many Palestinian refugees forced to flee during this period, they had to settle in a refugee camp: Al-Rusayfa in Al-Zarqa, a town with a majority population of immigrants, a few kilometers northwest of Amman. In the 1990s Zarqa became the center of Islamist radicalism in Jordan, fueled by economic difficulties and the arrival in 1990 and 1991 of radical Palestinians returning from Afghanistan and of migrants returning from Kuwait strongly influenced by Wahhabi doctrine. Zarqa also gave its name to the infamous Abu Musab al-Zarqawi, and today many of its inhabitants have left it to go and fight in Iraq.[4] Abdallah Azzam stayed there for a short while before heading for Amman with his wife and their eldest daughter, Fatima. In Amman, he taught at the Taj Secondary School for Girls.

Azzam's Palestinian Jihad (1967–1969)

The way in which events unfolded between the time he arrived in Amman in late 1967 and the date when he started working at the university there, in early 1970, is unclear. It was at this time that Azzam participated in guerrilla warfare against Israel, like thousands of other young Palestinians in Jordan. In his own words, he fought "for a year and a half in the Palestinian jihad." He also obtained a master's degree from Al-Azhar University in Cairo in 1969—an endeavor that required at least a year of work. Further historical research is necessary to establish the exact chronology of his life during this period.

All the hagiographies emphasize his "Palestinian jihad," but the fact that he participated in armed resistance against Israel is indisputable. It would seem that he made the decision suddenly. A biographer writes: "One night, Abdallah heard young men chanting slogans in the street, calling people to arms for Palestine. He said to himself: 'Isn't it shameful that young people should be leaving for the battlefield before me?'" This is when he decided to join the fedayeen's incursions into Jordan. Along with his wife and daughter, he left the apartment in Amman's Taj neighborhood for a shack in Zarqa. There, Azzam gathered a group of adherents, set up a base in the Irbid area, and began to launch operations across the border, supposedly "in agreement with the Islamic movement in Jordan." He became the chief of a paramilitary base dubbed Bayt al-Maqdis (another name for Jerusalem in Arabic, though less commonly used than al-Quds) in the village of Marw, not far from Irbid. The base was part of a network of camps linked to Fatah and called the sheikhs' bases (qawa'id al-shuyukh). The name referred to some Fatah founders, like Abu Jihad, who were members of the Muslim Brotherhood.

Azzam's decision to leave his salary and his respectable position for a shack in a Jordanian slum disappointed his parents, who, according to one biographer, had hoped to see him become a respected judge in Amman. His wife lost the respect of his family and her brothers, but she accepted, and later came to admire, her husband's decision. Azzam's father even ordered him to go back to teaching, which angered the newly minted jihadist. This confrontation with his father, it is said, convinced Azzam that it was unnecessary to obtain his parents' permission before going on jihad.[5]

Although he had disobeyed his father in order to carry on his "Palestinian jihad," Azzam did not give up on his academic ambitions. In autumn 1968, he registered at Al-Azhar, the prestigious university in Cairo, and obtained his master's degree in Islamic law with high honors in 1969. He then returned to Jordan to continue fighting with the fedayeen. In early 1970, he was offered a teaching position at Jordan University, and accepted. His decision to return to academia must have been the result of two factors: he was disillusioned with the secular and nationalist character of the Palestinian resistance movement, which the PLO dominated, and he wanted to satisfy his intellectual inclinations. A year later, in 1971, Azzam obtained a doctoral fellowship at Al-Azhar.

During the events of Black September 1970, when the PLO was

expelled from Jordan, Azzam remained neutral. Consequently, he avoided the sanctions that the Hashemite monarchy slapped on the Palestinian fedayeen, since he had been working at the university since the beginning of the year. At the same time, his role in the Palestinian jihad did not hinder him from obtaining his teaching position in Amman, which may indicate that his participation in the jihad was not as significant as his biographers claim.

Doctorate from Al-Azhar (1971–1973)

When Abdallah Azzam arrived in Cairo, the Islamist scene was in the process of changing completely. In 1966, Gamal Abdel Nasser had severely repressed the Muslim Brotherhood, ordering the execution of Sayyid Qutb as well as the jailing and torture of thousands of others. This served to radicalize some of the younger Brothers, who found in Qutb's last writings the ideological basis for a more militant approach to Islamism. In 1970, when the new president, Anwar Sadat, took power, he distanced himself from the Nasser legacy and from Nasser's political support base. One of the elements in his strategy was to court the Islamists, setting most of them free and relaxing restraints on their political activities.

Still, several years passed before these underground currents surfaced in the form of militant activism, but it is clear that, during the two and a half years he spent in Cairo, Azzam was immersed in the turmoil of the Islamist environment. Furthermore, his political affiliation with the Muslim Brotherhood and the fact that he was registered at Al-Azhar gave him the unique opportunity to create an enormous network of contacts in the Egyptian Islamist movement. He became a close friend of the Qutb family, and it is very likely that he met Omar Abdel Rahman, who became the spiritual leader of militant Islamists in Egypt. By contrast, he probably did not meet Ayman al-Zawahiri at this time.

While he was in Cairo, Azzam also attracted the attention of the Egyptian security forces, in part because of his relations with Egyptian Islamists and in part because the authorities were investigating him as the possible author of an anonymous telegram sent from Palestine to the Egyptian government in 1966 deploring the execution of Sayyid Qutb. They were right: Azzam had sent such a telegram, but the Egyptian authorities were unable to prove it, and he was never detained in Egypt.

When he left the country in late 1973 holding a doctorate in Islamic law, he had not only the immense religious prestige of a graduate of Al-Azhar University, but also a network of relations in what was then the capital of the Islamist movement. Azzam, while studying in Damascus, had made contacts in local Islamist circles, and he was now ready for the kind of transnational Islamist mobilization he undertook in Afghanistan in the 1980s.

Amman (1973–1980)

When he returned from Cairo, Azzam worked briefly in the information department of the Ministry of Pious Endowments, but he asked to be transferred to the university because he liked academic life, wanted to teach young people, and wanted to spread Muslim awareness in Jordanian society. He taught a course on sharia for six years. A few months after he had started, word spread around campus that a new and very eloquent professor was teaching sharia. During the same period, in 1972, the university had introduced a more flexible system that allowed students to choose annual seminars rather than following a fixed syllabus. This allowed students from all departments to take classes with Azzam. He had a conservative influence on the university, advocating less coeducation and encouraging male students to grow their beards. During the years he spent as a university professor in Jordan, he taught an entire generation of students and left his mark on the Islamists. Cassette tapes of his lectures circulated, and his growing influence earned him the sobriquet the Jordanian Sayyid Qutb.

Apart from his official university duties, Azzam gave evening classes at mosques and received visits from students at home. He traveled all over the country, preaching and lecturing. He rapidly rose through the echelons of the Jordanian Muslim Brotherhood and became one of the five members of the organization's advisory council *(majlis al-shura)* in 1975.[6]

One of his biographers writes that Azzam also went to America, in response to an initiative undertaken by the Muslim Student Association. He is said to have lectured in several states for the association's various branches.

By the late 1970s Azzam had become an influential Islamist figure in Jordan, and his classes were increasingly politicized and increasingly critical of the government. Even though relations between the Muslim Brothers and the Jordanian regime were relatively cordial, the authorities were clearly paying more attention to Islamist discourse, owing to the appearance of a strong and sometimes violent Islamist opposition in neighboring countries such as Egypt and Syria. The authorities pressured Azzam to tone down his sermons and finally threatened to jail him, but Azzam was aware that his popularity made that option difficult.

What apparently triggered his dismissal was a dispute with a newspaper, *Al-Ra'y,* which erupted in early 1980. The newspaper had published a caricature mocking religious figures: it showed a group of sheikhs holding M-16s, with the caption "American Spies." Azzam was outraged, and called the head of Al-Ra'y Foundation to demand an apology. The director refused, and Azzam insulted and threatened him. The director reported Azzam to the authorities, who dismissed him from his position. But this episode was simply a pretext for a decision the Jordanian authorities had long intended to make to silence an increasingly vehement opponent.

Azzam understood that the security services were going to prevent him from giving sermons and teaching freely in Jordan. He seems to have attempted to join the Palestinian struggle, but, having realized that this would be too difficult, he decided to leave the country and go to Saudi Arabia, which was then the favorite haven of Islamist intellectuals.

Stopping in Jidda

In mid-1980, Azzam began teaching at King Abdul Ibn Saud University in Jidda. He probably obtained the position through his connections with the Muslim Brotherhood. In the 1960s and early 1970s the country had taken in many Egyptian and Syrian Brotherhood members who were fleeing persecution at home; they had found work in Saudi Arabia, especially in the field of higher education, which was new there and lacking in intellectual resources. As a consequence, many Saudi universities, especially in the Hejaz, were strongly influenced by these individuals. One of the most visible was Muhammad Qutb, Sayyid's brother, whose family Azzam had frequented during his studies in Cairo. It is possible that Qutb, who was teaching at King Saud University, helped Azzam find a place there.

It is tempting to think that Azzam might have met the young Osama Bin Laden at this time. In 1980 Bin Laden was twenty-three and was studying business at King Saud University. He was more pious than the other members of his wealthy family and was beginning to show an interest in politics from following developments in the Islamist opposition in Syria, his mother's country.[7] He must have been interested in the lectures delivered by this brilliant new orator who was beginning to preach on campus. One source asserts that, in Jidda, Azzam and his family lived in an apartment rented by Bin Laden.[8] There is no proof, however, that the two men knew each other at this time, and neither said that they had met in Jidda. Even if Bin Laden attended Azzam's classes, or if their paths crossed in another way, it is difficult to argue that Azzam had a profound and decisive ideological influence on Bin Laden, for the simple reason that he did not stay long in Saudi Arabia.

In October 1980, shortly after the beginning of the academic year, Azzam traveled eighty kilometers from Jidda to Mecca to carry out the pilgrimage. There he was to meet Sheikh Kamal al-Sananiri, the man who opened his eyes to his great destiny: jihad in Afghanistan. Sananiri was a member of the Egyptian Muslim Brotherhood, and he had gone to Afghanistan in 1979. In 1980 he mediated among the mujahedeen factions, whose internecine squabbles undermined any attempt at effective resistance against the Soviet-backed regime. Sananiri forged an agreement that served as a basis for the creation of the Islamic Union of Afghan Mujahedeen, headed by Abdul Rasul Sayyaf.[9] The agreement was signed during the pilgrimage in 1980. We do not know the circumstances in which Azzam met Sananiri, but this was certainly a turning point in his life, for he was so influenced by what Sananiri had to say that he decided to go to Afghanistan himself.[10]

He asked the dean of his university whether it would be possible for him to teach at the new international Islamic university in Islamabad, which was funded by King Saud University. In 1981, probably at the end of the academic year in Jidda, Azzam left for Islamabad.

At the Heart of the Afghan Jihad

Just after arriving in Pakistan, Azzam began to make contact with Afghan military leaders, most probably through Sananiri's relations. It took him some time to find his place in the resistance, but from the first day he was an intermediary between the Afghan mujahedeen and Islamists in the Middle East. Indeed, this is the role that defined Azzam's whole involvement in the jihad: sometimes he followed and supported military efforts on the ground in Afghanistan; the rest of the time he wrote, preached, and used his influence to convince the rest of the Muslim world to send men and money into the country. It is important to note that he saw himself more as a writer and a thinker than as a combatant; if he considered that he was a mujahid, in the sense of someone who waged jihad, his field was more the propagation of the faith *(da'wa)* than it was armed action *(qital)*. That is why his Islamist comrades described him as the "heart" and the "brain" of the jihad in Afghanistan.

Little is known of Azzam's activities between 1981 and 1983, apart from the fact that he worked at the Islamic University in Islamabad, traveled regularly to Afghanistan, formed ties to the mujahedeen leaders, and worked to develop sympathy for the Afghan cause in the Muslim world. Starting in 1982, he scaled down his teaching at the university in Islamabad to two or three days a week, so that he could spend the rest of the time in Afghanistan, writing letters and pamphlets or receiving visitors. In late 1983, however, it was clear that Azzam was frustrated to see his efforts bear so little fruit. The number of Arab volunteers was negligible, in the range of ten or twenty men. Furthermore, Azzam felt he had not managed to convince the Muslim world that jihad in Afghanistan was an individual duty, incumbent upon every Muslim. He had the impression that many ulema in the Middle East were working toward goals opposed to his and discouraging men from going to Afghanistan.

To remedy this situation, Azzam made three important decisions. First, in early 1984 he wrote a book titled *The Defense of Muslim Territories*, in which he argued, as a religious scholar, that the Afghan jihad was an individual obligation *(fard 'ayn)* for Muslims worldwide. In this book, he elaborated on a fatwa he had delivered a year earlier, and published in *Al-Mujtama*, an Islamist periodical in Kuwait. In order to reinforce the legitimacy of his fatwa, he had colleagues at the university (who went on to attain eminent positions) write the preface to the book. This was also the time when he clashed with the supreme authority of the Muslim Brotherhood in Jordan, Muhammad Abd al-Rahman Khalifa, who refused to send fighters to Afghanistan out of preference for humanitarian and financial support. The disagreement led to a formal break, for Azzam's membership in the Jordanian Muslim Brotherhood was later suspended. Then he left his job at the Islamic University and went to Peshawar, near the Afghan border, where it was easier to coordinate the volunteers who were beginning to arrive in increasing numbers. Finally, he formalized his cooperation with the newcomer Osama Bin Laden, by establishing an organization called the Service Bureau *(maktab al-khadamat)* in Peshawar.

The Service Bureau

The main aim of the Service Bureau was to facilitate the arrival of Arab volunteers and to coordinate the distribution of recruits to the various battlefields, training camps, or support activities for the jihad in Afghanistan. Azzam was the official director, but assistants took care of daily business in various subcommittees and local branches. There were four subcommittees, responsible for training, military affairs, health services, and logistics. The Service Bureau managed a certain number of hostels *(mada'if)* in Peshawar, where foreign volunteers could stay as long as necessary while waiting to go to Afghanistan. During the second half of the 1980s, Peshawar became an ideological and political melting pot for men from many different backgrounds and countries of origin, each with his own ambitions. A good number of the ideological processes and personal relations that would mark the evolution of radical Islamism in the 1990s had their origin in what a radical Islamist veteran called the Peshawar kitchen.[11]

In 1984 Azzam and Bin Laden received permission from the Afghan mujahedeen leader Abdul Rasul Sayyaf to establish the first training camp exclusively for Arabs in Afghanistan. This was a significant step toward what later became a separate military structure for Arabs. Over the years more and more camps were set up in Afghanistan to receive the thousands of recruits that began to pour into Peshawar starting in 1986.

That year, the next step toward the creation of an autonomous military force was taken, when the Service Bureau decided to create Arab combat units. But this was a source of disagreement between Azzam and Bin Laden. While Azzam favored the usual practice of sending Arab volunteers to complete their training with mujahedeen and Islamic NGOs, Bin Laden wanted to constitute independent foreign (mainly Arab) forces. This difference did not lead to a conflict between them, but it was the first move Bin Laden made toward emerging from Azzam's shadow and becoming an independent actor in the Afghan jihad. Thus, in October 1986 Bin Laden set up the companions' den *(ma'sadat al-ansar)* near the border town of Jaji, to train exclusively Arab forces. Egyptian instructors provided most of the training, heralding the current predominance of Egyptian jihadists around Osama Bin Laden. The impact of these Arab units on the war was fairly limited, and it seems that contrary to the mythology spun by the Afghan Arabs, they did not participate in many battles against the Red Army.[12]

Despite these minor differences, Abdallah Azzam was still on good terms with Bin Laden. According to all accounts, the two men worked together, heading the Service Bureau until the end of the war. Azzam does not seem to have participated in Bin Laden's military projects, but he continued and stepped up his efforts in the political arena.

Whereas Bin Laden and many foreigners lived apart from the Afghan mujahedeen, Azzam maintained good relations with the various politicians, warlords, and local military chieftains. He traveled to Afghanistan frequently to visit the different mujahedeen factions; and when at the end of the war rivalries exploded between two of the warlords, Ahmed Shah Massoud and Gulbuddin Hekmatyar, Azzam mediated between them.[13]

Ambassadors for the Afghan Cause

Azzam's good offices were not limited to the Afghan domestic scene. He also acted as ambassador for the jihad throughout the Muslim world and worked tirelessly to spread knowledge of the situation that mujahedeen faced worldwide. His goal was clear: to guarantee the maximum possible amount of financial and humanitarian aid for the cause. He followed a tripartite strategy: canvassing of the main Islamic institutions; many international trips; and a voluminous ideological output.

Although Azzam was no longer officially a member of the Muslim Brotherhood, by virtue of his long experience and his vast network he was uniquely well placed to lobby for political and financial support from most Islamic organizations, such as the World Muslim League. He also benefited from the support of eminent Saudi ulema and from that of the government in Riyadh, which became one of the principal donors and suppliers of men to Peshawar. Financial support was provided through an institution established in 1985, the Islamic Coordination Council. This was a conglomerate of around twenty Muslim charitable organizations, headed by the Saudi and Kuwaiti Red Crescent Societies in Peshawar with help from Azzam, who became its director.[14] Azzam also set up international branches of the Service Bureau, in the United States in particular.

He traveled a good deal: his fundraising trips took him mainly to the Gulf countries, but also throughout the Middle East, to Europe, and to the United States. Between 1985 and 1989, for example, he and his second-in-command, a Palestinian sheikh named Tamim al-Adnani, visited dozens of American cities. But these visits did not preclude a strong opposition to American foreign policy; the lectures he gave in the United States, many of which were recorded on video, were very critical toward the West generally.

The third pillar of Azzam's strategy was his ideological work. He was a productive author, and his numerous books, articles, and recorded lectures on jihad in Afghanistan circulated worldwide, from India to America and from the palaces of Saudi Arabia to the Palestinian refugee camps.

As a result of these efforts, Azzam managed to gather considerable sums of money for his Service Bureau and other organizations participating in the jihad. No verified figures are available, but according to rough estimates several hundred million dollars flowed into Peshawar between 1985 and 1989.

The Assassination of Abdallah Azzam

The retreat of the Red Army from Afghanistan in February 1989 put an end to the Soviet occupation, but it did little to stabilize the country. The U.S. support for the Afghan mujahedeen ended,

Saudi support diminished, owing to the rivalry with Iran, and many countries expressed perplexity at the civil war and the emergence of what they saw as extremist factions under Gulbuddin Hekmatyar and Abdul Rasul Sayyaf. At the same time, the Afghan Arab leaders were discussing ways of dealing with the new political situation and were looking to the future. At this difficult time, the Afghan jihad lost its "heart and soul."

At around seven in the morning on Friday, November 24, 1989, Abdallah Azzam was killed when a bomb exploded as he was driving down one of Peshawar's main streets, heading toward a mosque where he was supposed to deliver the Friday sermon several hours later. His two eldest sons, Muhammad and Ibrahim, aged twenty and fifteen, were killed with him in the explosion. Some sources assert that Tamim al-Adnani's son was also in the car. Azzam was buried in Martyrs' Cemetery in Babi, near Peshawar. Abdul Rasul Sayyaf and Burhanuddin Rabbani, as well as a large group of Afghan Arabs, attended the burial.

Until today, the assassins have not been identified, but there is no lack of speculation, since at least five theories exist to explain the assassination. The first and most widespread is that a conflict had broken out between Azzam and Bin Laden over the future of the Arab combatants, and that Bin Laden ordered Azzam's assassination. According to this theory, Bin Laden wanted the Afghan Arabs to undertake military operations against Middle Eastern regimes, whereas Azzam wanted to continue the struggle in Afghanistan until a true Islamic state could be founded. The second interpretation holds that Ayman al-Zawahiri organized the assassination, on account of a power struggle between Azzam and the Egyptian jihadists. Several people have said that cold mutual suspicion reigned between Azzam and the Egyptians in Peshawar, as a result of the Egyptians' radicalism and their attempts to manipulate Osama Bin Laden. Zawahiri and Azzam supposedly had different plans for the Afghan Arabs: Zawahiri wanted to lead a jihad against the "nearby enemy" (the Arab regimes), whereas Azzam wanted the Afghan Arabs to stay in Afghanistan. According to the third theory, Azzam fell victim to rivalries among the Afghan factions, and his mediation attempts incited someone from the ranks of Massoud or Hekmatyar to liquidate him. The fourth is that Pakistani intelligence (the Directorate for Inter-Services Intelligence, or ISI) carried out the attack, and the fifth attributes responsibility to the CIA and Mossad. As might be expected, the fifth theory prevails in jihadist circles: barely a week after the assassination, *Al-Jihad* magazine in Peshawar published an article suggesting that the Americans and the Israelis had killed Azzam.

Legacy and Influence

Azzam's influence on the jihadist movement requires no further demonstration. His enormous legacy has three dimensions: first, the political dimension and Azzam's role in moving the Afghan conflict from the regional to the global scale; second, the organizational aspect, which highlights Azzam as "the father of the Afghan Arabs"; and third, the ideological dimension, with Azzam becoming the preeminent theoretician of global jihad.

Jihad in Afghanistan in the late 1980s was an arena for massive international involvement; it would be possible to argue that the military and financial resources invested were out of all proportion to Afghanistan's strategic value, and indeed greater than in any other secondary conflict during the cold war. In the context of the Islamic world, the level of mobilization and the support extended by states, organizations, and individuals for the Islamist resistance in Afghanistan had no precedent. This mobilization can be explained by regional political factors (for example, the rivalry between Iran and Saudi Arabia) and structural changes in Islamic banking and NGOs (which facilitated the transfer of funds). Still, no single individual played a more important role than Abdallah Azzam in gathering support for this cause in the Muslim world. His systematic propaganda work, fundraising activities, and creation of networks were essential to the internationalization of what would otherwise have remained a regional conflict on the margins of the Muslim world.

Another, perhaps more tangible, consequence of Azzam's activity is his contribution to shaping the "Afghan Arab" phenomenon. Azzam and the Service Bureau recruited, received, and trained thousands—perhaps tens of thousands—of foreigners with the aim of providing military support to the Afghan resistance. The result was the creation of an Islamist International made up of men whose strong feelings of brotherhood transcended national and cultural differences as well as ideological perspectives—those of the nation-state and of the struggle against specific Arab governments. Perhaps more important still is way the Service Bureau and its branches created a cadre of extremely motivated, experienced, and hardened activists, whose paramilitary prowess was superior to that of any previous Islamist group. The most remarkable product of the Afghan Arabs was Osama Bin Laden and the Al Qaeda phenomenon. Azzam, who is said to have opposed Bin Laden's strategy of constituting purely Arab fighting units starting in 1986, can be held responsible only indirectly for the transformation of some Afghan Arab factions into terrorist organizations. Still, he will always be considered the "father" of the Afghan Arabs—a category of radical Islamists whose influence could be felt in many regions of the world starting in the 1980s.

At any rate, Abdallah Azzam's most lasting legacy is incontestably his contribution to radical Islamist thought and doctrine. A religious cleric by training and a theoretician by vocation, he was a far more prolific author than Bin Laden or Zawahiri. Azzam left an immense oeuvre of over a hundred books, articles, and recorded conferences, of which only a tiny part has been translated into Western languages.

It is said that Azzam was successful in rejuvenating the concept of jihad among the Arab masses. But he was not the first modern Islamist to focus attention on jihad as a means of political change. Nor was he the first to declare that jihad is an individual duty, incumbent upon all Muslims, and the highest form of devotion. Egyptian Islamists, and most notably Abd al-Salam Faraj in *The Absent Imperative*, published in 1981, had already expressed these ideas.[15] Why, then, was Azzam seen as the pioneer who revived jihad in the twentieth century, and why was he more widely read than Faraj? The answer to this question is to be found in his political justification of jihad and his strategic vision for its implementation. On many points, Azzam's thought differs from that of the radical ideologues.

Primarily, Azzam shifted the target from combat against the enemy within to combat against the external enemy. He redefined the main casus belli of jihad: occupation of Muslim territories by foreign aggressors. This marked a change in relation to the Egyptian radicals, who asserted that jihad was essentially a fight against the tyranny of Islamic governments. Azzam, of course, may well have been favorable to the establishment of an Islamic state, by force if necessary, but he considered that self-defense against a foreign aggressor was more urgent and important than overthrowing domestic tyrants.

Second, Azzam developed a more territorial form of Islamism. He redefined the main point of contention in jihad as Muslim territories, not the political system prevailing there. Hence, in Islamism as formulated by Azzam, land *(al-ard)* is more important than the state *(al-dawla)*. This marked another break in relation to the perspective of the Egyptian jihadists. Azzam's territorial discourse played an important role in Islamizing many separatist struggles in the 1990s: Bosnia, Chechnya, and Mindanao, to cite only a few. Azzam's influence was particularly strong in his native land, Palestine, where it may be said that his writing helped redefine the conflict with Israel. As many actors saw it, Palestinians were no longer engaged in a nationalist struggle to found a state; rather, they were leading an uncompromising struggle to reconquer Muslim land. "The Palestinian problem will be solved only through jihad," wrote Azzam; "jihad, a rifle, and that is all. No negotiations, no conferences, no dialogue."

Third, Azzam's opinion of the strategy to be followed in jihad represented a change in that he preferred the military approach to the revolutionary approach. He rejected the idea of a vanguard *(tali'a)* and proposed instead that of a "solid base" *(qaeda sulba)*. He mocked the idea, which was widespread among Egyptian radicals at the time, that a small clandestine group could establish an Islamic state by carrying out a coup d'état. What the Islamist movement needed, he argued, was a territorial base where young Muslims could receive an "education in jihad" *(tarbiyya jihadiyya)* and build up the military force necessary for a reconquest of Muslim territories. Azzam asserted that the Islamist movement needed a vanguard of combatants, but he believed that this vanguard had to start from a solid base, and not from within an oppressive state. In several of his texts, the expression "solid base" refers to a geographically defined territory. In one of his last works, he used the expression to refer to the groups of people who would lead the fight, and it is likely that this slight semantic modification later incited some Afghan Arabs to baptize their organization Al Qaeda.

Fourth, Azzam minimized the importance of the nation-state and embraced pan-Islamism as the political platform for the Islamist movement. In theory as in practice, Azzam promoted a form of Islamic internationalism that represented a marked change in relation to the rather nationalist orientation espoused by other radical Islamist groups before the 1980s. Azzam's obsession with Afghanistan was due to his great love not for the Afghan nation, but for the Muslim community: the *umma*. Azzam wanted Afghanistan to be the solid base from which to launch the reconquest of other Muslim territories. As he wrote: "Palestine, Bukhara, Lebanon, Chad, Eritrea, Somalia, the Philippines, Burma, South Yemen, Tashkent, and Andalusia are still left."[16] It is not surprising that Azzam, as a Palestinian in exile, having studied and worked in different countries, should have adopted a pan-Islamist vision. That being said, he was not exempt from nationalist emotions or from love for Palestine. He often said: "If my body is in Kabul like a specter, my heart, soul, and spirit are in Jerusalem."[17]

Finally, Azzam contributed a great deal to developing a cult of martyrdom among radical Sunni Islamists. In several texts he praised martyrdom as the ultimate form of devotion to God, and the peak of jihad. A central theme in his work is thus "the divine favors granted to martyrs" *(karamat al-shuhada)*. The benefits of being martyred during jihad were widely discussed in traditional Islamic theology, but Sunni Islamist writers before Azzam had not emphasized the idea. For example, the notion of martyrdom barely appears in Faraj's book *The Absent Imperative*. Since Azzam, martyrdom has become a central concept in radical Islamist literature, and suicide operations—its logical consequence—have been one of the most powerful and widespread tactics employed Islamist terrorist groups since the mid-1990s.

Still, it seems important to note that on many points Azzam's ideas were far more moderate than those of Bin Laden and Zawahiri in the late 1990s. Although Azzam turned attention from the enemy within to the external enemy, he was never in favor of carrying out strikes on the territory of the faraway enemy. He may have argued enthusiastically for jihad, but he seems to have envisaged a strategy closer to guerrilla warfare than to terrorism. And despite his pan-Islamist, internationalist perspective, he never called for a "global insurrection" against the enemies of Islam.

Whatever the case may be, Azzam's ideas and perspectives were new and different from the dominant paradigm in jihadist circles in the early 1980s, and especially from social-revolutionary jihad. Azzam took the first step toward a more global vision of jihad, opening the way for Osama Bin Laden and Al Qaeda's total global war against "the alliance of Jews and crusaders." In that sense, Azzam was really the first theoretician of global jihad.

What would have happened to the Islamist movement and the Afghan Arabs if Azzam had lived until the 1990s? Years later, an eminent Afghan Arab asserted, "Azzam would have been more dangerous than Osama Bin Laden, because he had more credibility as the founder of the jihadist movement in Afghanistan."[18] This is possible, because Azzam himself saw the Afghan jihad as the beginning of the fight. In 1989 he said: "I feel as if I'm nine years old: seven and a half years of Afghan jihad, and a year and a half of Palestinian jihad. The rest of my life doesn't count."

THE DEFENSE OF MUSLIM TERRITORIES CONSTITUTES THE FIRST INDIVIDUAL DUTY

(EXCERPTS)

Introduction

It is to God that all praise is due—we beg for his help and implore him to protect us against our own evil and against our bad deeds; he whom God guides will not stray, but he whom God leads astray will not find the way.[1] I bear witness that there is no god but God and that Muhammad is his servant and messenger. O God, things are simple only through you, even sadness.

When I first wrote this fatwa, it was longer; I showed it to the great and respected sheikh Abd al-Aziz Bin Baz, then read it to him, and he appreciated it, saying: "This is a good fatwa."[2] He approved it but suggested that I abridge it before he wrote the introduction. I did so, but the sheikh's time was short because of the pilgrimage, and I was not able to show it to him again.[3]

Then, at Bin Laden Mosque in Jidda and at the great mosque of Riyadh, the sheikh, God preserve him, decreed that today waging jihad in person is an individual duty.[4] Afterward, I showed this fatwa as is (without the six additional questions it deals with) to Sheikh Abdallah Alwan, Said Hawa, Muhammad Najib al-Muti'i, Husayn Hamid Hassan, and Omar Sayf.[5] I read it to them, they approved, and most of them signed it.[6] Sheikh Muhammad Ibn Salih Ibn Uthaymin, too, signed it after I had read it to him. Sheikhs Abd al-Razzaq Afifi and Hassan Ayub did so as well, as did Dr. Ahmad al-Assal.[7]

Then I raised the question during a conference in Mina, during the pilgrimage season, at the center for religious orientation, where more than a hundred ulema from all over the Muslim world were gathered.[8] I said to them: "The Ancients and the Moderns, all the jurists and hadith scholars, at all times during the Muslim era, have agreed that 'if a portion of Muslim territory is invaded, jihad becomes an individual duty for all Muslim men and women. Children can go to fight without their parents' permission, and a wife can go without that of her husband.' I declared before Sayyaf, the leader of the mujahedeen, and after three years of experience in the Afghan jihad, that this jihad needs men.[9] So, esteemed ulema, those among you who have objections should pose them now." No one objected. On the contrary, Dr. Sheikh Idris told me: "Brother, there is no disagreement on this subject."[10]

In consequence, I am publishing this fatwa. May God make it beneficial in this world and the next, and useful to all Muslims.

Dr. Abdallah Azzam

. . .

It is to God that all praise flows, it is him we beg for help, and it is him we implore to protect us against our own evil and against our bad deeds; he whom God guides will not stray, but he whom God leads astray will not find the way. I bear witness that there is no god but God and that Muhammad is his servant and messenger. May God bless him, his family, and all his companions.

God chose this religion as a blessing for living creatures, and sent the best of messengers to be the seal of the prophets. Then he caused this religion to triumph by the spear and the sword, once the Prophet had explained it by proof and eloquence, before Judgment Day. The Prophet said, in an authentic hadith reported by Ahmad and Tabarani: "I was sent before Judgment Day, so that God alone would be worshiped, with no associates. He placed my livelihood in the shadow of my spear and promised humiliation to those who oppose me" (*Precise Anthology of Authentic Hadith*, 1818, by al-Albani).[11]

Through God's wisdom, the good in this world rests on the law of defense: "And did not God check one set of people by means of another, the earth would indeed be full of mischief: but God is full of bounty to all the worlds" (Quran 2:251).[12]

This means that God gave humanity this law and enjoined it to follow this rule (that of defense)—or in other words, the fight between truth and falsehood—in the interest of humankind, for the supremacy of truth and the development of the good, and even so that religions and places of worship might be erased by this law: "Did not God check one set of people by means of another, there would surely have been pulled down monasteries, churches, synagogues, and mosques, in which the name of God is commemorated in abundant measure. God will certainly aid those who aid His (cause); for verily, God is full of Strength, Exalted in Might (able to enforce His Will)" (22:40).[13]

This law (of defense) or jihad takes up many pages in the book of God, because truth cannot do without a force to protect it. How many truths have been lost because those who should have upheld them abandoned them? And how many errors have won the day because they had partisans and men ready to sacrifice themselves for their sake?

Jihad rests on two pillars: patience, which reveals the heart's fortitude, and generosity, which consists in spending money and giving one's soul (this is the height of generosity). The authentic hadith narrated by Ahmad says as much: "Faith is patience and generosity" (al-Albani, *The Chain of Authentic Hadith*, 554).

Ibn Taymiyya said: "Since the wealth of human beings in their life on earth and their religion depends on courage and generosity, God has shown (may he be exalted!) that he who turns away from jihad of the self will be replaced by someone else.[14] 'Unless you go forth, He will punish you with a grievous penalty, and put others in your place; but Him you would not harm in the least. For God hath power over all things'" (*Collection of Fatwas*, 28, 157).[15]

This is why he has singled out the worst flaws[16]—in other words, meanness and cowardice—which lead to the ruin of the soul and the downfall of society, in this authentic hadith: "The worst flaw in a man is sordid avarice and flagrant cowardice" (authentic hadith narrated by Abu Dawud).[17]

Much time has passed since our pious ancestors, by following this rule, came to rule the world and became the masters of humanity, as God said: "And We appointed, from among them, leaders, giving guidance under Our command, so long as they persevered with patience and continued to have faith in Our Signs" (Quran 32:24).

As the Prophet said in his authentic hadith: "The welfare of this community was born of abstinence and certainty, and it will end in avarice and hope" (narrated by Ahmad and Tabarani in *The Median*, and by Bayhaqi in the *Small Anthology of Authentic Hadith*, 3739).[18]

Then came other generations of Muslims, who neglected God's laws and forgot God, and God forgot them in turn; they lost his rulings and went astray: "But after them there followed a posterity who missed prayers and followed after lusts; soon, then, will they face Destruction" (19:59).

They found their actions admirable, but the authentic hadith says: "God hates those who strut arrogantly in the marketplace; at night they are cadavers, by day donkeys, knowledgeable in this life and ignorant in the hereafter" (*Small Anthology of Authentic Hadith*, 1874).

One of the most important obligations and the main duties forgotten is jihad, which has disappeared from the lives of Muslims. This is how they came to resemble detritus borne by the flood, as the Prophet said: "Other nations stand ready to surround you on all sides, like guests around a single pot."

They asked him: "O messenger of God, is this because there are few of us?"

"No," he replied, "but because you are like detritus borne by the flood; you love this world too much and despise death, you allow weakness to creep into your hearts and cause it to disappear from the hearts of your enemies." According to another version:

They said: "What is weakness, O messenger of God?"

"Your love of life," he replied, "and your hatred of war" (*The Chain of Authentic Hadith*, 958, narrated by Ahmad, following a sound chain of narrators, and by Abu Dawud.[19] There is a variation: "Hatred of death." This is an authentic hadith.

There are two sorts of jihad against unbelievers:

Offensive jihad [*jihad al-talab*], which means attacking unbelievers in their countries. When unbelievers are not mobilized to fight Muslims, jihad is a collective duty, and the least one can do is to guard the borders of the Muslim world in order to intimidate God's enemies. For this purpose, one can send out an army at least once a year.[20] The imam may also send a unit to the land of war once or twice a year, and the population must help him; if this does not happen, it is a sin (*Commentary* by Ibn Abdin, 168, 3).[21] Jurists have compared it to the *jizya*.[22] Theologians have said: "Jihad is forced preaching, and it is necessary to accomplish it as much as possible, so that only Muslims or people who accept conciliation remain" (Shirwani, *Commentary*, and Ibn al-Qasim, *Tuhfat al-Muhtaj alal-Minhaj*, 213, 9).[23]

Defensive jihad [*jihad al-daf*] consists of expelling unbelievers from our territory. This is an individual duty, indeed the most important of all individual duties, in the following cases:[24]

1. when unbelievers enter one of the Muslim territories;
2. when two armies meet and exchange blows;
3. when the imam mobilizes individuals or a group: then they must gather to fight;
4. when unbelievers imprison Muslims.

. . .

Combat in Afghanistan and Palestine

As we have seen, it is clear that if a stretch of Muslim territory is attacked, jihad is an individual duty for those who inhabit that territory and those who are neighbors. If there are too few of them, or if they are incapable or reticent, then this duty is incumbent upon those who are nearby, and so on until it spreads throughout the world.

In such a situation, a husband's permission is not required for his wife to fight; nor is the father's permission necessary for the son, or the creditor's for his debtor. As a consequence,

1. all Muslims are sinners as long as any country that was once Muslim is still in non-Muslim hands;
2. sin increases according to power, possibilities, and capabilities: so the ulema, leaders, and preachers who are eminent members of their societies are then considered greater sinners than the masses and the people;
3. the sin that our generation has committed in neglecting contemporary issues like Afghanistan, Palestine, the Philippines, Kashmir, Lebanon, Chad, and Eritrea is graver than the sin committed by former generations who allowed former Muslim territories to fall.[25] This is what we were saying: now we must concentrate all our efforts on Afghanistan and Palestine, for these are central questions—the enemies who occupy them are fearsome, and they have expansionist plans for the entire region—because their solution holds the key to many issues in all the Muslim countries, and our defense is the key to the defense of all these regions.

Let's Begin with Afghanistan

Every Arab who wants to wage jihad in Palestine may start there, but those who cannot should go to Afghanistan. As for other Muslims, I think they should begin their jihad in Afghanistan. Not because Afghanistan is more important than Palestine: Palestine is the sacred cause of Islam, the heart of the Muslim world, and a blessed land; but there are several reasons for starting with Afghanistan.

1. The battle in Afghanistan is still raging; it is at its peak. The mountains of the Hindu Kush are the theater of battles without precedent in the history of the Muslim world.[26]

2. The banner flying over Afghanistan is clearly Muslim. ("There is no god but God, and Muhammad is his Prophet.") The goal is clear as well. ("The word of God is exalted to the heights.")[27] Article 2 of the charter of the Islamic Union of Afghan Mujahedeen stipulates: "Our goal derives from his word."[28] "None can command except God"; and so absolute sovereignty belongs to the Lord of the worlds.[29]

3. The Islamists preceded others onto the battlefield in Afghanistan, and those who lead the jihad are the sons of the Islamist movement, the ulema and those who have learned the Quran by heart. Things are different in Palestine, where all sorts of people have taken over leadership: some are sincere Muslims, but others are communists, while others still are simple Muslims. The banner they raised was that of the secular state.[30]

4. In Afghanistan, the cause is led by the mujahedeen, who refuse assistance from unbelieving states, whereas the Palestinian cause has been supported by the Soviet Union, and Russia abandoned them in the worst possible way, leaving them to their destiny in the face of a global conspiracy.[31] This matter has become a plaything in the hands of the superpowers who gambled with the land, people, and honor of Palestine, even into the territory of the Arab states, in order to end their military power and to annihilate all their capabilities.[32]

5. Afghanistan's borders are open to the mujahedeen. There are over three hundred kilometers of open borders, not to mention that surrounding the country are tribal regions that the authorities have not subjugated and

that form a shield for the mujahedeen.[33] In Palestine, the situation is totally different. Its borders are closed and its hands are tied. On all sides, the authorities are on the lookout for whoever might attempt to infiltrate it to fight the Jews.[34]

Join the Caravan

(excerpts)

Preface to the First Edition

Glory to God, Lord of the worlds, and peace and praise upon the noblest of messengers.[1]

Here is a treatise I wrote for those who burn with desire to carry out jihad and who have a taste for martyrdom along the path of God. It is made up of two parts:

1. The justifications for jihad
2. Islam, come to our aid! And a few concluding remarks.

We pray God that it will be useful, improve us, and improve others through us, for God is he who hears. He is near and replies. I dictated it in response to the many letters sent to me asking for advice about coming to Afghanistan.

> Come to the garden of Eden, where you first dwelt,
> We camped there
> But fell into enemy hands—
> Do you think we shall return in safety?[2]

THE HUMBLE SERVANT OF GOD ABDALLAH AZZAM,
17th of Sha'ban 1407 (April 15, 1987)

The Justifications for Jihad

Praise God! We praise him, ask him for assistance, pray that he will forgive us our evil ways and protect us against our bad deeds.

Whoever considers the situation in which Muslims find themselves today will see that the most important trial they have under-

gone has been abandoning jihad (out of love for this world and disgust at death).³ This is how tyrants have come to rule them on all sides
and all over the world, because unbelievers fear only battle:⁴ "Then
fight in God's cause—you are held responsible only for yourself."⁵

We call on Muslims and encourage them to come fight for many
reasons, the main ones being:

So that unbelief does not win out;

Because real men are few and far between;

For fear of hellfire;

To fulfill the obligation and respond to God's call;⁶

To follow the pious ancestors' example;

To establish a solid base for the expansion of Islam;

To defend the oppressed;⁷

Out of predilection for martyrdom.⁸

. . .

SO THAT UNBELIEF DOES NOT WIN OUT

It is said in the noble verse: "And fight them on until there is
no more tumult or oppression, and there prevail justice and faith
in God altogether and everywhere; but if they cease, verily God
doth see all that they do."⁹ If the fight were to cease, unbelief would
triumph and sedition (which means worshipping idols alongside
God) would win the day.¹⁰

BECAUSE REAL MEN ARE FEW AND FAR BETWEEN

The crisis besetting the Muslim world is due to the lack of responsible men who are capable of bearing the burden of integrity. As
the *Sahih* says: "Men are like a hundred camels, among which not
one is fit to ride."¹¹ This means that the ideal of austerity in this
world and of longing for the next is reserved for only a few steeds.

A good steed signifies a camel that can endure long journeys and bear heavy burdens, is beautiful to look at, and so on.[12] In other words, out of a hundred camels, a person might not find the one he needs. It is said that Omar Ibn al-Khattab told a few of his companions: "Make a wish!"[13] Each of them did so, and then they told him to do the same. "I would like to see this house full of men like Abu Ubayda," he replied.[14]

Men of knowledge are few and far between, and men of action are rare. Those who go on jihad are fewer still, and those who continue on that path are too few to mention.

I have often watched young Arabs reciting the Quran in the land of honor and glory—I mean Afghanistan:[15]

> Honor rides the steeds of glory
> And glory comes through night journeys and night watches

I watched the faces of these young men to see which of them could recite properly, so that I could ask him to lead the lessons, but I did not find a single one.[16] So I told myself: "Our people have been unjust with us," which is exactly what the Prophet said when seven of his partisans were killed before his eyes at the Battle of Uhud.[17]

Our educated brothers and the experienced preachers never helped us, and they even advised those who wanted to join us to stay at home, although they could not say a word because of the injustice of tyrants and the despotism of dictators. Some of them issue fatwas in ignorance, and say: "The Afghans need money, not men." I am on the ground in this jihad, and I can tell you that the Afghans desperately need money, but they need men too, and preachers most of all. This is the eighth year I have spent among the mujahedeen.[18]

If you do not believe me, let us travel through Afghanistan together, and you will see an entire battlefront where no one knows how to read the Quran. Follow me to another, and you will realize that no one knows how to pray over the dead, which forces them to transport their martyrs—according to the Hanafi school of law, martyrs must be buried after a prayer—over long distances in order to find someone capable of performing the burial rites.[19]

As for the laws of jihad, such as those pertaining to the distribution of spoils and the treatment of prisoners, they are ignored on many fronts, which makes it imperative to take them to ulema who can give their opinion according to Muslim law. You will come face to face with the urgent need for preachers, imams, Quran readers, and ulema when you see the deep marks left by young Arabs whose education is rudimentary—sometimes it does not go beyond grade school. I could tell you, for example, about our brothers Abdallah Anas, Abu Dujana, Abu Asim, Tahir, and many others, not to mention the illiterate Arab Abu Shu'ayb and the virtuous impressions he left throughout the province of Baghlan—you would be astounded[20] . . .

Thus, we told the judge, Mazlum, a member of the high command of Ahmed Shah Massoud—the most brilliant leader in Afghanistan: "Tell us about Abu Asim, the Quran reader who was martyred among you at Andarb [a region in the north of Afghanistan]."[21] He replied: "We never saw anyone arouse such respect, consideration, and admiration. None of us dared to speak in his presence, let alone joke or laugh." What would you say, my brothers, upon learning that Abu Asim, who was barely twenty-three years old, had only a secondary school diploma but knew the Quran by heart?

This is why the time has come for true men. This is not the time for long speeches.

. . .

FOR FEAR OF HELLFIRE

God Almighty, the Majestic, says: "Unless you march forth, He will punish you with a severe punishment, and will replace you with another people, and you will not harm Him at all. And God has power over all things."[22]

Ibn al-Arabi said: "Severe punishment is being conquered in

this life by the enemy, and in the hereafter by hellfire" (*Commentary* by al-Qurtubi, 42, 8).

In his commentary, Qurtubi added: "It has been said that what is meant by this verse is that going out on jihad is compulsory in times of need, if the unbelievers arrive, and when they are the aggressors."

God says: "Those whose souls the Angels take (in death) while they are wronging themselves—they (the Angels) say (to them), 'In what state were you?' They reply, 'We were weak and oppressed in the land.' (The Angels) say, 'Was not God's Earth spacious enough for you to emigrate therein?' Then, the abode of those people shall be Hell—how evil a destination! Except for such weak and oppressed men, women and children who were neither able to come up with a stratagem (to emigrate) nor shown any way (to do so)—those God will surely pardon, and God is Most Pardoning, Oft-Forgiving."[23]

Al-Bukhari has narrated, through his sound chain of narration, that Ikrimah said:[24] "Ibn Abbas informed me that people from among the Muslims were with the polytheists, swelling their numbers, during the time of the Prophet. Arrows that were shot would come and hit some of them, killing them, and then God revealed (the verses meaning), 'Those whose souls the angels take while they are wronging themselves.'"

Thus, the believers in Mecca who were clinging to their religion but had not emigrated went out in shame and fear of the unbelievers, so that the ranks of the disbelievers were increased on the day of the Battle of Badr.[25] Then some of these Muslims were killed, and according to al-Bukhari's narration, they merited hell. If that is so, what of the millions of Muslims who are being martyred and forced to live like animals? They cannot repel attacks on their honor, lives, and property—they cannot even grow their beards, because this marks them as Islamists. Nor, in fact, can they decide how their wives should dress, or have them wear the long garments required by revealed law, because it is a crime for which we are blamed on all sides.[26] Nor can a Muslim teach the Quran to three young Muslims in the mosque because it is an illegal gathering according to the laws of the ignorant.[27] Even in the countries that are called Islamic, his wife cannot cover her hair; nor can this Muslim prevent security officers from leading his daughter in the dark of night wherever they wish.[28] Can he refuse an order issued by the tyrant, to whom he is sacrificed as a cheap victim?

Are these millions of people not living in subjugation, crushed and weakened; and when the angels call them, will they not be taken by surprise? What will be their reply when the angels ask them: "What state were you in?"

"We were weak and oppressed in the land."[29]

Weakness is not an excuse before God; it is a crime for which one risks going to hell. God has excused only the elderly, small children, and women, who cannot free themselves, do not know the way to the land of honor, and are unable to emigrate to the land of Islam or to arrive at the base for jihad.[30]

. . .

Jihad, and emigration in order to wage jihad, are fundamental aspects of this religion, because a religion that does not have jihad cannot establish itself anywhere, and its trunk cannot hold up its topmost branches. The truth of jihad, which is an integral part of this religion and weighs so heavy in the scales of the Lord of the worlds, is not an accident peculiar to the period in which the Quran was revealed; it is a necessity accompanying the caravan that this religion guides.[31]

In his work *In the Shade of the Quran*, Sayyid Qutb says of this verse: "If jihad were a transient phenomenon in the life of Muslims, all these sections of the Quranic text would not be flooded with this type of verse! Likewise, it would not have taken up so many chapters in God's book—and in such a manner! Nor would it have occupied so much of the *sunna* of the Prophet."[32]

If jihad were a temporary phenomenon, the Prophet would not have addressed the following words to every Muslim, until Judgment Day: "Whoever dies without having fought (in a jihad), or having prepared his soul for this battle, dies on a branch of hypocrisy" (narrated by Muslim, after Abu Hurayra).[33]

God knows how princes hate this. He knows that the ruler's men will combat it, because God's way is not theirs, not only then, but now and tomorrow and in every land and in every time . . .

TO RESPOND TO GOD'S CALL

God says: "March forth, whether light or heavy, and fight with your wealth and your lives in the Path of God; that is better for you, if only you knew."[34]

In his commentary, Qurtubi quoted ten different reports for the interpretation of "light" and "heavy:"

1. Narrated from Ibn Abbas: young and old.
2. Narrated from Ibn Abbas and Qatada: active and inactive.
3. "Light," rich. "Heavy," poor, according to Mujahid.
4. "Light," youthful; and "heavy," old, according to Hassan [al-Basri].
5. Busy and unoccupied, according Zayd Ibn Ali and Al-Hakam Ibn Utayba.
6. "Heavy" is the one with family, and "light" is the one without, according to Zayd Ibn Aslam.
7. "Heavy" is the one with work which he does not want to abandon, and "light" is the one without any work, according to Ibn Zayd.
8. "Light," infantry; and "heavy," cavalry," according to al-Awza'i.
9. "Light" are those who rush to war in the vanguard.
10. "Light," brave; and "heavy," cowardly, according to al-Naqqash.[35]

We interpret this verse as meaning that the order extends to everyone: that is, "Go forth," whether mobilization is light or heavy. It is narrated that Ibn Um Maktum came to the Prophet, and asked him, "Do I have to do battle?"[36]

The Prophet said, "Yes," and God revealed the verse meaning, "There is no blame on the blind."[37]

These reports are a simple parable, and no sensible person doubts that the situation in Afghanistan and Palestine—and even in most of the Muslim world—is summed up in this verse. Exegetes, specialists in hadith, jurists, and experts in principles of jurisprudence have reached a consensus: when enemies enter Muslim territory, or territory that was formerly Muslim, its inhabitants must confront them.[38] If they do not, or are incapable, reluctant, or insufficient in number, the obligation extends to those around them, and so on, until it encompasses the whole world.[39] Nobody can abandon it, just as one cannot abandon prayer and fasting, and at that time the son may go out without the permission of his father, the debtor without that of his creditor, the wife without that of her husband, and the slave without that of his master. The individual obligation to wage jihad remains in effect until the lands are purified from the pollution of the unbelievers. That being said, a woman going out on a journey must be accompanied by a close male relative.[40]

In my limited reading, I have not found a single book of jurisprudence, exegesis, or hadith that affirms the contrary. None of the pious ancestors ever said that in this situation jihad was a collective obligation; nor did they say that permission was necessary. The sin will not be erased as long as a Muslim land (or one that was once Muslim) remains in the hands of the unbelievers, and only those who fight will be absolved.

A Muslim who is not performing jihad today is just like one who breaks the fast in Ramadan without permission, or a rich person who withholds legal alms.[41] Indeed, failing to carry out jihad is more serious still.

As Ibn Taymiyya said: "As for the occupying enemy who corrupts religion and life, nothing is more urgent after faith than repelling him."[42]

. . .

TO FOLLOW THE PIOUS ANCESTORS' EXAMPLE

Jihad was life itself for the pious ancestors; the Prophet was the master of jihad combatants, and a leader for unexperienced young men. When combat raged, they sought the protection of the messenger of God, who led them up to the enemy. He participated in twenty-seven expeditions and fought in nine of these: Badr, Uhud, al-Muraysi, al-Khandaq, Qurayza, Khaybar, the conquest of Mecca, Hunayn, and Taef.[43] According to that which is said: "Mecca was taken by force, and he sent forty attachments, fighting the Banu Nadir himself" (*The Seeker's Goal,* 8, 16).[44] This means that the messenger of God used to go out on an expedition or send out a detachment at least once every two months . . .

TO ESTABLISH A SOLID BASE FOR THE EXPANSION OF ISLAM

Establishing a Muslim society on an area of land is as necessary for Muslims as water and air, and this territory will exist only through an organized Islamic movement that wages jihad, in actions and words, and makes of combat its goal and its defense. The Islamic movement will be able to establish an Islamic society only through a general popular jihad.[45] Its movement will be a beating heart and a shining mind, similar to a small detonator that triggers a large explosion, by freeing the Muslim community's contained energy and releasing the sources of good that it contains deep down. The Prophet's companions were only a handful of men, compared to the troops that overturned Chosroes' throne and tarnished Caesar's glory.[46]

Even the tribes that had apostatized from Islam under the caliphate of Abu Bakr were sent by Omar, after they had repented, to fight against the Persians. Tulayha Ibn Khuwaylid al-Asadi, who had previously claimed to be a prophet, was one of the heroes of the Battle of Qadisiyya; indeed, Saad sent him to spy on the Persians, and he demonstrated great courage on this mission.[47]

As for the few officers who thought they could establish a Muslim society, they were the victims of an illusion and a trap that runs the risk of repeating the tragedy experienced by the Islamic movement under Gamal Abdel Nasser.[48]

The popular jihadist movement, which has a long way to go, given the bitter suffering endured and the magnitude of the sacrifices and losses sustained, can purify souls and elevate them above reality . . . Interest is turning away from mundane conflicts over money and short-term needs . . . Hatred dissipates, souls are polished, and the caravan is climbing from the narrow valley toward the highest peak, far from the stench of the marshes and the law of the jungle . . .

Islamic society needs to be born, but birth takes place in pain and suffering[49] . . .

OUT OF PREDILECTION FOR MARTYRDOM

In the authentic hadith narrated by Ahmad al-Tirmidhi, on the authority of Miqdim Ibn Ma'd, who heard it from Muhammad:[50] "The martyr is granted seven special favors by God: He is forgiven his sins with the first drop of his blood, he sees his place in Paradise, he is clothed in the raiment of faith, he is wedded with seventy-two wives from among the beautiful maidens of paradise, he is saved from the punishment of the grave, he is protected from the Great Terror (of the Day of Judgment), on his head is placed a crown of dignity, one jewel of which is better than the world and all it contains, and he is granted intercession for seventy people of his household" *(Complete Anthology)*.

Al-Bukhari reported from Abu Hurayra that the Prophet said: "In paradise God has prepared one hundred levels for the mujahedeen; the difference between every pair of these is like the difference between heaven and earth, so if you ask God, ask for Paradise" (*The Conquest*, 9, 6) . . .

Islam, Come to Our Aid!

O Muslims, peace be with you, and God's mercy and blessings.

No one is ignorant of the enormous sacrifices the Afghan Muslim people has made: more than nine years have passed since the communist coup d'état of Nur Taraqi in April 1978, and since then Afghan Muslims have borne the greatest suffering to defend their religion, their honor, and their children.[51] Indeed, there is not a home left in this country where a woman does not mourn her husband, and the children their father.

These people have an excuse before God: they have taken him as their witness to the piles of skulls and amputated limbs, the withered souls and flowing blood.[52] They no longer have arrows to shoot; their quivers are empty. During this long period the Afghans hoped their Muslims brothers would come forth in their thousands, that their brothers in Islam would march to their aid, but until today the Muslims have not answered the call, as if they could not hear the mothers crying for their sons, the virgins screaming, the orphans sighing, and the elderly groaning. Many fine people felt it was enough to send their leftovers by way of assistance.

The situation is more serious than that, however. Islam and Muslims in Afghanistan live in anguish and must face a grave peril.

This blessed jihad has been led by a handful of young men raised according to Islam, and a group of ulema devoted to God. But this first generation, for the most part, fell on the path to martyrdom, and the second generation that has come forth has neither instruction nor guidance, for it did not receive the benefits of a proper education. These people urgently need someone who will live among them, linking them to God and to the revealed law.

Given our humble experience and limited reading, in the current situation we consider that jihad in Afghanistan is an individual duty, to which Muslims must contribute personally and financially. The jurists of the four schools have stated this, as have all commentators, hadith specialists, and theologians . . .

Conclusion

1. When enemies enter Muslim territory, jihad becomes an individual duty, according to all the jurists, exegetes, and hadith experts.

2. When jihad becomes an individual duty, there is no difference between it and prayer or fasting, according to the three imams. The Hanbalis, however, give priority to prayer.

In *Bulghat al-Salik li-Aqrab al-Masalik fi Madhhab al-Imam Malik* (The Voyager's Sustenance on the Nearest Path Leading to Imam Malik's School), one can read the following: "Annual jihad along the path of God, causing his word to prevail, is a collective duty: if some accomplish it, the others no longer need to. It becomes an individual obligation, like prayer and fasting, if the imam declares it is so, or if a region is subjected to attack by the enemy."[53] In the *Majma' al-Anhar* (Confluence of the Rivers), a Hanafi work, it is said: "If the collective obligation is fulfilled by all men, then it becomes an individual obligation, like prayer." In his *Commentary*, the Hanafi Ibn Abdin writes: "When the enemy attacks a Muslim border, it is an individual obligation, like prayer and fasting, that no one can abandon" (238–2).

3. Since jihad is an individual duty, no permission is required from one's parents, just as such permission is unnecessary for those performing the dawn prayer or fasting during the month of Ramadan.

4. There is no difference between those who abandon jihad and those who fail to fast during Ramadan.

5. Donating money does not exempt anyone from accomplishing jihad and risking his life, no matter how much money is given. The duty of jihad remains, just as it is not permissible to pay a poor man to pray or fast in one's stead.

6. Jihad is a lifelong duty, like prayer and fasting. Just as it is not permissible to fast one year and abstain the next, or to pray one day but not the next, so is it forbidden to accomplish jihad one year and desist for several years running, if one is still capable of continuing.

7. Jihad, which entails donating one's money and risking one's life, is an individual duty in every place conquered by the unbelievers, and remains so until every piece of land that was once Muslim has been liberated.

8. The word "jihad" refers exclusively to armed combat, as Ibn Rushd said.[54] The four imams agreed upon this.

9. The meaning of the expression "along the path of God" is jihad, as Ibn Hajar wrote in his *Conquest* (22–6).[55]

10. The sentence "We returned from the lesser jihad (battle) to the greater (jihad of the soul)," which some cite as if it were a hadith, is a forgery, and baseless. It is simply something Ibrahim Ibn Abi Abla, one of the successors, once said, and it is in contradiction with texts and reality alike.[56]

11. Jihad is the peak of Islam, and one reaches it in stages: emigration [*hijra*], preparation, guarding the borders,[57] and combat. Emigration is absolutely necessary for jihad, for it is said in the authentic hadith narrated by Imam Ahmad on the authority of Junada (and this is a hadith that can be traced back to the Prophet), that "emigration will not cease as long as there is jihad" (*Al-Sahih al-Jami* [The Complete Anthology], 1987).[58]

As for guarding the borders of Islam in order to defend Muslims, this is essential to combat, for soldiers cannot go out to fight every day. A man can stand guard for long periods and participate in only one or two battles during his lifetime.

12. Today, committing one's wealth and personal safety to jihad is an individual duty for all Muslims, and the Muslim community as a whole will remain in sin as long as the last piece of Muslim territory has not been freed from the unbelievers. Only the mujahedeen may be absolved from this sin.

13. There were different sorts of jihad in the time of God's messenger. The Battle of Badr was delegated, whereas the Battles of the Trench and of Tabuk were individual obligations for each Muslim, and so the entire community was mobilized.[59] In the case of the trench, this was because the pagans had invaded Medina, the land of Islam. As for Khaybar, it was a collective duty, and the messenger of God allowed only those who had been present at Hudaybiyya to participate.[60]

14. Jihad in the time of the companions and the successors

was mainly a collective duty, because new conquests had taken place.[61]

15. Today, risking one's life in jihad is an individual duty.

16. God has not allowed anyone to abandon jihad, except for the sick, the infirm, and the blind, as well as children who have not reached puberty, women who cannot experience emigration and jihad, and the elderly. Even those who have a minor illness, such as the lame and the blind, can go to training camps to assist the mujahedeen, teach them the Quran, speak to them, and encourage them. They must do this; it is better that they come, as Abdallah Ibn Umm Maktum did at Uhud and Qadisiyya.

No one else has any excuse before God: not employees, artisans, merchants, or important businessmen. They cannot refuse to participate personally in jihad; nor can they content themselves with donating funds.

17. Jihad is a collective act of devotion, and each community must have a commander.[62] Obeying the commander is imperative in jihad, and therefore people must grow accustomed to obeying the commander at all times. "You must listen and obey, whether this is difficult or not, when it pleases you and when it does not" (hadith narrated by Muslim, on the authority of Abu Hurayra).

Note for Those Who Come to Perform Jihad

1. Jihad for ordinary people is different from jihad for preachers. The latter are generally few in number and make up the community's elite. They cannot undertake a long jihad by themselves, or clash with states; the community must participate with them. All men have faults; no people are pure angels.

2. Afghans are like other human beings, with their ignorance and defects, and so we must not expect to find perfection in them. The difference between the Afghans and the others, however, is that the Afghans have refused to stand by and watch as their religion is dishonored, and they have paid the price for this resolve

with bloodbaths and piles of corpses. In contrast, others immediately submitted to colonization and evil.[63]

3. The Afghan people are ignorant, educated in the Hanafi school alone. It has no rival in Afghanistan, which is why many Afghans believe that whatever is not mentioned in Hanafi jurisprudence does not exist in Islam. The absence of other schools in their country has bred in them a fierce attachment to Hanafism; whoever seeks to accomplish jihad with the Afghans, therefore, must respect the teachings and rulings of that school.[64]

4. The Afghans are a valiant people, virile and proud, without ruse or flattery in their nature. If they love a person, they give their blood and soul. If they detest someone, nothing stands in the way of that hatred. By abandoning some ways of praying, at the beginning of your stay among them, you will be able to affect them, guide them, and eventually educate them, in order to reform their religion and their way of life. This is authorized in the religious opinions of Ahmad Ibn Hanbal, Malik, and Ibn Taymiyya.[65]

5. You must know that the path of jihad is long and difficult. Many find it difficult to persevere and preserve their enthusiasm. The overflowing emotions aroused by jihad must go hand in hand with the ability to withstand hardship and to adapt to suffering and grief. How many young men arrived full of zeal and lost it little by little, until one day they came to question the very need for jihad.

6. God has committed himself to helping the mujahedeen. He embraces all those who go along the path of God, assists them, fortifies their resolve, and makes their hearts and their steps firm. "Three people deserve God's help: the mujahid on the path of God, the slave who wishes to buy his manumission, and the married man who seeks to remain chaste" (hadith narrated by Ahmad, al-Tirmidhi, and Nasa'i, authenticated by Hakim, and certified by Dhahabi).[66]

7. He who wants to come to Afghanistan must call the following numbers in Peshawar: 42708, 43203, and 42397. Once there, he

must call one of these numbers and tell the person who answers where he is. Someone will come and get him.[67]

The mailing address is: Peshawar University, P.O. Box 977, Peshawar, Pakistan.

Praise God. In praising you, O Lord, I bear witness that there is no god but you. I beg your pardon and I repent.

Morals and Jurisprudence of Jihad

(EXCERPTS)

Etymology of the Word "Jihad"

The word *jihad* comes from the verb *jahada*.[1] The verbal noun is *juhd* or *jahd*, which means energy or possibility. Some say that *juhd* means energy or potential, while *jahd* means pain or grief.[2] The word *jahd* is also used to mean extremity ("They swear their strongest oaths by God"), meaning to the furthest point of their strongest oath.[3]

Therefore, *jahd, juhd,* and *jihad* mean to give all one's energy to obtain something that is appreciated or to repel something that is detested (see *Lisan al-Arab* and *Al-Bahr al-Muhit*).[4]

Meaning and Usage of the Word "Jihad"

The four great jurists agree that jihad is fighting and assisting combat.[5] These are the definitions given by the four legal schools:

1. The Hanafis: Ibn al-Humam, in his work *The Almighty's Victory* (5, 187), defines it as "calling unbelievers to true religion, and combating them if they do not accept."[6] In *The Marvels*, Kasani defines it as follows: "Expending all efforts and all energy to combat along the path of God, in person, by words, and so on."[7]
2. The Malikis: "Muslims' battle against unbelievers with whom no pact has been concluded to cause God's word to prevail."
3. The Shāf'īs: according to Ibn al-Qasim's *al-Bajuri*, "Jihad

is combat along the path of God."[8] Ibn Hajar, in *Victory,* said: "Legally, it means making every effort to fight the unbelievers."

4. The Hanbalis: ("fighting the unbelievers") see *The First Requests* (2, 497): "Jihad is fighting and doing everything in one's power to cause God's message to triumph." See *The Pillar of Jurisprudence* (p. 661) and *The Spirit's Aim* (1, 203).

In sum, the word "jihad" means fighting, and the expression "along the path of God" refers to jihad.

Ibn Rushd, in his *Prolegomena* (1, 369), said: "Regarding jihad of the sword: fighting pagans for religious purposes; whoever exerts himself in order to know God wages jihad along his path, but jihad along the path of God simply means combating infidels by the sword until they become Muslim, or until they submit and pay the head tax."

Ibn Hajar, in *The Conquest* (6, 29), wrote: "What comes to mind when one hears the expression 'God's path' is jihad."

Morals and Jurisprudence of Combat

In Islam, fighting is legitimate when its aim is to spread God's word, save humanity from unbelief, and lead humanity from the darkness of this world to its light and the light of the next life. This is why, in our holy religion, combat was established to transcend political, economic, and social obstacles to preaching the Muslim faith.[9] It may even be said that the function of jihad is to bring down the barriers preventing this religion from spreading across the face of the earth. When people accept this religion, there is no need to unsheathe a single sword, spill a drop of blood, demolish institutions, or waste money, because this religion came to reform, build, and gather together, not to destroy.

Killing and fighting are duties that have been imposed on Muslims because they must bear the banner of God's oneness, and because they have received the order to propagate it on every hill and every plain.[10] If we are unable to reach people with this message without fighting the current political systems and regimes, we must fight them because they are a hindrance on the path that leads to people. If political authorities, wealthy men, and tribal groups stand in our way, we are forced to confront them with weapons until they submit to this religion, and there is a clear path between us and the people we have been commanded to save.

"And fight them until there is no more tumult or oppression, and there prevail justice and faith in God altogether and everywhere; but if they cease, verily God does see all that they do."[11] The function of fighting is to eliminate tumult and sedition (*fitna*), and to eliminate the group that wants men to worship it instead of worshipping God. If this clique submits peacefully, there will be no need to unsheathe swords or kill people.

This is why Islam encourages its adherents to save people, and even tyrants, from hellfire: the hell of ignorance in the world here below, and hell in the world beyond. This is why the Prophet told Ali, on the day of Khaybar:[12] "By God, if you obtain the conversion of a single man, this will be better for you than the most perfect grace." This is an accepted hadith.

This is why Islam asserts great principles and sets out clear limits that constitute the general rules of jihad. The most important of these is that the aim in fighting is to propagate the Muslim faith. As a consequence, those who do not oppose this aim must not be fought. This is why:

1. People must be called to religion before they are fought; it is forbidden to combat them without warning them first.[13]
2. It is forbidden to kill those who do not fight[14] . . . It is forbidden to combat those who are unarmed, who cause no harm, and from whom sedition is not feared, like children,

women, the helpless, those who pay tribute, monks, and hermits.

3. It is forbidden to waste money, cut down trees, or burn houses, unless this is necessary to remove the barriers that impede the summons to Islam.

4. It is forbidden to inflict punishment after combat and to mutilate corpses.

5. It is forbidden to continue fighting after the enemy has conceded defeat and promised or signed a truce. It is forbidden to violate one's word once a pact has been concluded, "(But the treaties are) not dissolved with those Pagans with whom you have entered into alliance and who have not subsequently failed you in aught, nor aided anyone against you. So fulfil your engagements with them to the end of their term: for God loves the righteous."[15] Every traitor will wear a banner on Judgment Day: this is an authentic hadith. Now for a detailed explanation of these general principles . . .

On the Execution of Monks

Monks can be killed, depending on whether or not they live among people. If they do, they may be killed; if they live isolated in order to devote themselves to God, they may not be killed.

In the hadith of Ibn Abbas, it is said: "When the Prophet sent soldiers out, he would tell them: 'Fight in the name of God Almighty, along the path of God, against those who are unbelieving. Do not be traitors; do not pillage, do not punish, and do not kill children or hermits.'" This is narrated by Abu Dawud, but Ibrahim Ibn Ismail is in the chain of authentification, and he is not entirely reliable. Still, Ahmad considered him to be reliable.

Sarakhsi's *Exposition* (10, 27), Abu Yusuf, Muhammad, and the narrators of the *Book of Expeditions* all say: "You must not kill them."[16]

Abu Yusuf, however, said: "I asked Abu Hanifa what should be done with hermits and monks, and he told me they could be killed. He even added: 'They are the masters of unbelief.'"[17] If one synthesizes Abu Hanifa's two opinions, one will conclude that monks living in society must be killed, but those living apart must not.

On the Execution of the Elderly, the Sick, the Blind, and the Weak among the Unbelievers

Jurists disagree on this point and have two main opinions. Some, like the Hanafis and Malik, classify the elderly along with women and children and base their opinion on the hadith narrated by Abu Dawud on the authority of Anas Ibn Malik, who heard it directly from the Prophet: "Do not kill decrepit old men, or small children"[18] . . . Jurists add that the reason is the same as for children: they are of no use to the unbelievers and cause no disturbance to the Muslims . . . Others, like the Shāf'īs, permit killing them, on the basis of a hadith included in the two Sahihs, and according to which Abu Amir al-Ash'ari killed Durayd Ibn al-Simma, who was over a hundred years old[19] . . .

Our conclusion—but God knows better than anyone[20]—is as follows: those who can be useful to the unbelievers or to others must be killed, whether they are old people, priests, or invalids. But the elderly who are senile, isolated monks, and the invalid who are suffering cannot be useful to the unbelievers and cause no harm to the Muslims. Therefore, it is better to leave them be . . .

On the Execution of Communist Women in Afghanistan

As for communist women in Afghanistan, they must be killed, whether they participate in combat, give their opinion, or do not participate, whether they are isolated or not, and whether they are single or in a group, because their doctrine is inimical to Islam and harmful to Islam and Muslims. The Prophet of God said of two women from the Banu Abd al-Muttalib, who had spoken ill of him, of his family, and of Islam, along with a group of men: "Kill them, even if you find them hanging from the curtains of the Kaaba"[21] . . .

The Prevalent Opinion on the Treatment of Prisoners

Of course, the prevalent opinion is that held by the vast majority: that the imam chooses, according to the Muslims' best interest, between execution, slavery, pardon, ransom of a Muslim, or liberation in exchange for money. This point of view requires proof, before the imam chooses what is best for the community.

In Ibn Qudama's *Al-Mughni fi Sharh Mukhtasar al-Khiraqi* (10, 407), it is said: "Among the prisoners, if there are strong men who can harm the Muslims, it is better to kill them. If there are weak men who are very wealthy, it is better to exchange them for a ransom. If one finds men who have a high opinion of the Muslims, one can incite them to convert, or to help Muslims free or ransom their prisoners, and so it is better to invite them to convert. If there are people who can serve without harming, it is better to enslave them, like women and children. The imam is the best qualified to judge what is in the Muslims' interest, and so the decision should be left to him" . . .

Afghan Communist Prisoners

Many communists, when the mujahedeen take them prisoner and they feel they are going to be executed, make the Muslim declaration of faith.[22] The mujahedeen execute them regardless, which some people have condemned, considering that such converts are preserved from sin once they have pronounced the profession of faith.

These people quote the hadith of Osama: "How could you kill him, after he had said, 'There is no god but God'?"[23] In reality, however, the situation in Afghanistan is different, because the mujahedeen are accustomed to taking prisoners whom they bring before the party tribunal. They carry out an investigation, because these people know each other, and when they are certain that the prisoner is a communist, since the people of his village know him, they kill him, even if he has professed Islam, prayed, or even restored the laws of Islam.

True, revealed law has ruled that, if an unbelieving prisoner converts to Islam, he cannot be killed because his sins are forgiven. He then becomes a slave, and the same treatment is applied to him as to children: he can be enslaved but not executed, because the sentence "There is no god but God" differentiates between unbelief and Islam.

In Afghanistan the situation is different, because Babrak Karmal and Najib, the head of the Afghan communist party, who have done everything in their power to eradicate Islam in that country, say, "I am a Muslim" and pray in front of the television cameras[24] . . .

Origin of the Word "Martyr"

Opinions differ on the origin of the word "martyr."[25] Azhari wrote: "This is because God and his Prophet bear witness in his favor for paradise."[26]

Nadr Ibn Shumayl said: "'Martyr' refers to a living person; martyrs are designated in this way because they remain alive with their Lord."[27]

It has been said: because the angels of mercy help the martyr and take his soul.

It has been said: because he bears witness before other nations.

It has been said: because there has been testimony to his faith and to an auspicious fate.

It has been said: because there is a witness to his death, because he will be born again and his blood will gush forth.

It has been said: because his soul sees paradise, while others will see it only on Judgment Day (Nawawi, *The Entirety,* 1, 772).[28]

Definition of Martyrdom

1. The Shāfʿī definition, provided in *The Entirety,* a gloss on *The Refined:* "The martyr is he whose body is not washed and over whom no funeral prayers are pronounced: he is

the one who died fighting the unbelievers—whether he was killed by an unbeliever; accidentally, by a Muslim's weapon; by his own weapon; by falling from his mount; by a blow from a horse's hoof; trampled by the steeds of Muslims or others; by an arrow from the bow of a Muslim or an unbeliever; whether he was found dead after war was declared, without the cause of his death being known; whether there is a trace of blood on him or not; whether he died on the battlefield or later, before the end of the war; whether or not he ate, drank, and made his will. All this is established among us, as Shāf'ī decreed."

2. The Hanafi definition: in Ibn Abdin's *Commentary* (2, 247), "the martyr is any pure adult Muslim who was killed unjustly, without the blood-price being paid, and who was not borne wounded from the battlefield."

Conditions Necessary for Martyrdom

1. That combat took place along God's path ("He who fights for God's word to prevail is on the path of God": this is an accepted hadith). This text has the force of law: Whoever was killed while he had the intention of supporting Islam is a martyr; otherwise, he is not.
2. Having shown endurance and courage.
3. Attacking and not fleeing.
4. Not having stolen spoils of war before they were distributed . . .

Funerary Rites for Martyrs

The four imams [founders of the four law schools] agree that the martyr's body must not be washed [before burial] . . .

Prayers for Martyrs

The ulema have different opinions regarding funerary prayers for martyrs: they fall into two categories. The first, majority opinion is that no funerary prayer is necessary. This is the opinion of Malik, Shāfʿī, all the Hanbalis, Ishaq, and Ahmad's sources.[29] The second, to which the Hanafis, Thawri, and some of Ahmad's sources adhere, is that funerary prayers must be pronounced[30] . . .

This is why no funerary prayers are said for martyrs, because they are alive; because martyrdom is an elevation, and funerary prayers constitute intercession—whereas the martyr's faults have been pardoned and the sword erases sin . . .

Indeed, martyrs are those who intercede for sixty members of their family. Finally, since the martyr was not purified, how could funerary prayers be pronounced for him?

Can Someone Be Called a Martyr?

When it is said that someone is a martyr, this means that in this world he is treated as such. In other words, his body will not be washed before burial and no one will say funerary prayers over his corpse. This does not mean, however, that we are testifying that he will go to paradise, or to hell, because all hearts are in God's hands and he is the one who knows the mysteries of heaven and earth. All decisions are his. The first Muslim historians adopted this usage, referring to the martyrs of Uhud, Hunayn, Yarmuk, and Qadisiyya: he was martyred at Yamama, he died a martyr at Qadisiyya, and so forth.[31]

Those Who Fall Victim to Rebels and Highway Bandits

The Hanafis and Hanbalis consider that those who fall victim to rebels and bandits are martyrs, and must be treated as such. This goes against the Shāfʿī opinion.

The Hanafis provide the following as proof: Imam Ahmad reported, according to a reliable chain of guarantors, from Ibrahim Ibn Abdallah Ibn Farrukh, who had it from his father: "I attended Uthman's burial in his clothes, without funerary garb" (*Divine Victory*, 7, 951).[32] As for the Shāfʿī: Malik, according to Nafi, according to Ibn Omar, said that Omar was washed and wrapped in a shroud before the funerary prayers were pronounced.[33] Shāfiʿī himself wrote: "The Muslim leaders washed Omar's body and performed the prayer for the dead. He was therefore a martyr, but reached martyrdom without warfare." In the same work, he wrote: "If someone is devoured by a wild beast or killed by rebels or brigands, without its being known who killed him, his body is washed and prayers for the dead are pronounced."

To the Young Muslims of
the United States

(EXCERPTS)

Peace be with you, and God's mercy and blessings.[1]

I pray that the Almighty will guide you in the midst of this turbulent ocean of temptation, preserve you from hidden and visible sedition, reveal the Truth and cause us to follow it, and show us Falsehood and cause us to avoid it.[2] I pray that he will inspire us with wisdom, establish love of the faith in our hearts, cause us to despise unbelief, immorality, and rebellion, and make well-guided men of us.

I pray that he will give each one of us a beatific life and a martyr's death, before resurrection with the prophets (may God bless them), that in this world he will gather us together in his care, and that in the next he will hold us in his merciful embrace.[3]

Dear brothers, my heart rejoices and my soul overflows at the sight of your zealous piety in this arid desert, in the darkness of ignorance and paganism. May God make you thirsty for the good word and impatient to meet the messengers of this religion, who will bring shining light to the four corners of the world.[4]

What comforts me and eases my pain is your taste for jihad, the interest you take in news of it, the concern you show for its progress and the lives of its heroic leaders. I also know what a great difference there is between the reality in which you live and the land of warfare to which you aspire; but sincere intention and declared resolve—with God's help—can lead you to high places. The longest journey begins with a single step: "And those who strive in Our (cause),—We will certainly guide them to our Paths: For verily God is with those who do right."[5] Martyrdom will be granted to those who seek it sincerely, even on their deathbeds, because sincerity follows preparation: "If they had intended to come out, they would certainly have made some preparation."[6]

I liked so many things in the United States.

The congress of the Muslim Arab Youth Association is among the greatest gatherings worldwide of educated Muslims, although its organizers are students of modest means whose resources and possibilities are limited and whose experience of Islamic action is recent.[7] Still, its remarkable organization, security, and coordination did not escape those Muslims whom God favored with the opportunity of cooperating with this association.

Its centers are cool oases in exile and luxuriant gardens in the caverns of ignorance; they are lifeboats in the raging ocean of perdition.

God gave these centers the noble task of saving young people who run the risk of drowning in the stinking swamp of promiscuity. With God's permission, they preserve these youth from the mud of sin, which has become this society's daily bread. This society, which having escaped from its Lord, does nothing but flee from itself;[8] having destroyed every moral boundary and every human value, it continues on its way without paying heed to anything.[9]

In the branches I visited, what caused me to rejoice was the members' fervent zeal for jihad as well as their . . . love for Afghanistan and for the events that have caused the land of Palestine to tremble.[10]

I also appreciated the ingenious means used by the brothers there to collect money in support of jihad: for example, T-shirts with the slogan "Help Free Afghanistan" were made in Melbourne and Orlando, Florida, and were sold from a van that toured U.S.

cities to raise awareness of the Afghan cause, then distributed these T-shirts to HCI centers.[11] I liked the prayer beads they made, and the cakes baked each week and sold after Friday prayers in Tucson, with the proceeds going toward jihad.

I was delighted by the interest shown by the community in New York (Al-Faruq Mosque) and Brooklyn for jihad in general, and the Afghan jihad in particular.[12] I was happy to see their overflowing enthusiasm, their sincere impulses, their resolve and determination: one can read these in the faces of young and old alike.

I also appreciated the fact that they opened an office to serve the Afghan jihad, hired a lawyer, and received permission from the authorities; then they sent fighters to Afghanistan, paying for their tickets and obtaining visas for them from the embassy in New York.[13] In this manner, we received seven groups of volunteers without spending a penny (may God reward and support them).

I opened an account at the Independence Savings Bank in Brooklyn; the number is 644417610.[14] Whoever would like to send a check or make a deposit to this personal account should do so at the following address: Service Bureau, 552 Atlantic Avenue, Brooklyn, N.Y. 11217, telephone (718) 797–0207. On the back of the check, write: Abdallah Y. Azzam.

In conclusion, I would like to thank the brothers who organized these visits, accompanied me on the trip, and helped me endure its difficulties, especially Hisham Yusuf, Muhammad Tawba, Muhammad Balata, Abd al-Razzaq al-Aradi, Abdallah al-Shaybani, Muhammad Uwaynat, Abdallah the American, and others—I hope you will ask those whose names I have been unable to mention to forgive me.[15]

I advise you to worship God, to be sincere, to recite a passage from the Quran every day, to read invocations to God morning and night, taken from the *Ma'thurat* [Famous Words] or the Prophetic Invocations or the hadith;[16] to hold your tongue; to respect our food prescriptions piously; to avoid foreign women; to love Muslims; to read Tahawi's *Book of Doctrine,* the *Commentary of* the Two Jalal al-Dins, *In the Shade of the Quran,* Muhammad al-Ghazali's *Jurisprudence of the Prophet's Life,* Sayyid Sabiq's *Jurisprudence of Sunna,* and the books of Mawdudi and Ibn Qayyim—especially *The Sufficient Response to Those Who Seek a Remedy.*[17]

Praise to you, O Lord. Praising you, I testify that there is no god but you, and I repent.

THE SOLID BASE

(EXCERPTS)

Praise be to God, and prayers and blessings upon the last of the prophets.[1]

Every principle must be supported by a vanguard, which clears a path for itself toward society, at the price of vast efforts and heavy sacrifices.[2] There is no creed [aqida], whether earthly or heavenly, that can dispense with such a vanguard, which spends all it has to cause this dogma to triumph.[3] The vanguard has a long and difficult path to travel before it can implant this dogma in real life, if God allows it to appear and grow stronger; the vanguard represents the solid base of the society we hope to create.[4]

Every dogma, even if it comes from the Lord of the worlds, will be stillborn if it does not find a vanguard that sacrifices itself and expends every effort in order to defend it.

The slogan of those who bear this dogma must be: "Say: 'Call your "god-partners," / Scheme (your worst) against me, / And give me no respite! / For my Protector is God, / Who revealed the Book . . . And He will choose / And befriend the righteous.'"[5]

I had not realized exactly how important the duration of the Meccan education was before I participated personally in the Afghan jihad, as I am now doing for the seventh consecutive year (thanks be to God).[6] After having examined the question in all its depth, I discovered that a long education in doctrine is the basis and the pillar of Islamic society, without which there can be no godly society. Otherwise, society would be merely a fragile structure; it would crumble with the slightest gust of wind, or at the first storm.

I have deduced a fundamental rule for the creation of Islamic society: such a society cannot be founded without a movement that has been forged in the fire of trials, and unless its members have developed in the heat of conflict. This movement is the thunderbolt that causes the community's energy to burst forth, and triggers a long jihad in which its members take the role of leaders, pioneers, imams, and spiritual guides. During this long struggle, men's resources shine through, their energy is deployed, and their positions become clear; their leaders step forward to show the way and seize the reins. These leaders will be strengthened after long suffering, God making use of his power behind them and making of them the instruments of his religion's victory. Therefore, taking up arms before having undergone the long education of the group of believers would be dangerous, because armed men quickly become gangs that might endanger people's security and poison their lives.[7]

Here are the main points in the education of the small group of believers, and its pioneering vanguard:[8]

1. It must develop amid trials and calamities.
2. Its educators must share the sweat and blood of this painful march; they must be the incubator within which its young grow, and no growth is possible without a long period of care and education.[9]
3. The vanguard must rise above the vanities of this world and distinguish itself through its asceticism and frugality.
4. It must also be convinced of its creed and brimming with hopes of victory.
5. It must persevere and convince itself of the need to continue the struggle, no matter how long.
6. Provisions for the road are essential: these are constant prayer and patience.[10]
7. It must practice loyalty and separation.[11]
8. It must comprehend the magnitude of international conspiracies against Islam.

There are essential reasons for such a long education.

1. Without a profound education, which provides the safety valve for the long march, the enormous sacrifices and disproportionate costs it exacts cause boredom and despair in time.
2. Because along this path there are constant temptations and compromises, but the closer one gets to victory, the more the proposals and attempts at disruption proliferate. The leadership must therefore be made up of solid members.
3. Because if God strengthens the leadership in this world, it will hold treasures in its hands: it will be the guardian of the Muslim people's money, honor, and life. If it is not secure, woe to the community it leads . . .

The Importance of the Solid Base in the Afghan Jihad

Now we have understood the importance of this base, which has educated Muslims in Islam since the earliest times.[12] Having looked all around us, we have observed that the whole world is criticizing this jihad. We have witnessed the international conspiracies that seek to pluck its fruits and extinguish its fire. We have also noticed the sordid struggle taking place on a global scale to reduce the jihad and prevent its authentic leadership from continuing its guidance of the Muslim people.

We have looked all around and found that only the sons of pious discourse and those of the solid base stood against the whole world, saying: "No. We are here." When God's enemies bared their fangs, when their friends ceased to support them and were content with the role of spectators, the remarkable leaders of jihad rose up: Sayyaf, Hekmatyar, Rabbani, and Khalis said, "God is enough for us, and he is the best support."[13] These four men rebelled and, raising the veil of the ghastly conspiracy, cried out: "Our Lord is stronger than any earthly power; 'Nor is God to be frustrated / By anything whatever / In the heavens / Or on earth: for he / Is All-Knowing, All-Powerful.'"[14]

We have observed that throughout the experiences of the Muslim peoples, it is the servants of the West or America's allies, the secularists of the old Afghanistan, in Algeria, Tunisia, and Egypt, who have ultimately enjoyed the fruits of jihad.[15]

Today, America is attempting to seize the fruits of this marvelous jihad and to prevent legislation on the basis of God's book.[16] The solid base is facing international pressure and global encouragement; but [its members] have refused to bow their heads before the storm, and have decided to carry on their exhausting march along a road of blood, sweat, and tears.

As for the Muslim world, its duty is to support the solid base firmly, with financial and personal contributions. "The Unbelievers are / Protectors, one of another: / Unless you do this, / (Protect each other), / There would be / tumult and oppression / On earth, and great mischief."[17] Finally, it is necessary to continue the jihad, no matter how long it takes, to the last man, or until we see the Islamic state.

May you be praised, Lord; in praising you, I testify that there is no god but you. I beg your forgiveness and I repent to you.

PART III

AYMAN AL-ZAWAHIRI

INTRODUCTION

AYMAN AL-ZAWAHIRI, VETERAN OF JIHAD

STÉPHANE LACROIX

The doctor [Ayman al-Zawahiri] passed through many phases in his life: first, there was his youth, marked by enthusiasm for the writings of Sayyid Qutb; then his encounter with other young people like him, to organize their passage to action; then the divisions, trials, and debates that roiled the jihadist movement in prison after Sadat's assassination; then Jihad's departure for Afghanistan; then the sedition that broke out within the organization, followed by its physical and intellectual dislocation; then the difficult task of rebuilding under terrible conditions; then the reunion with Sheikh Osama Bin Laden in Afghanistan, under the rule of the Taliban; and finally the conflict with America. All these phases and situations were full of experiences, events, and contributions, the result being that today the doctor holds the place of the sage within the Islamist jihadist movement. How precious his experience and wisdom are for our young people, and for History!

ABU QATADA AL-FALASTINI, *Hakim al-Haraka al-Islamiyya: Ayman al-Zawahiri* (The Sage of the Islamist Movement: Ayman Zawahiri)

Of all the figures of the international jihadist movement, it is Ayman al-Zawahiri, an Egyptian, who best illustrates the story of contemporary radical Sunni Islamism.[1] An activist from the start, he joined the Egyptian jihadist movement, which was then working to overthrow the regime and establish an Islamic state, in 1966, when he was only fifteen. For thirty years, in Egypt, Afghanistan, and Sudan, among others, he pursued this sole objective and indeed in the 1980s was one of the principal opponents of the regime of Egyptian president Hosni Mubarak. In the late 1990s, in circumstances that will be explained later, he made a spectacular strategic shift that spurred him to give priority to the struggle against the United States, and more generally against the Christian West, whose interference in the Middle East was denounced as a war on Islam. Zawahiri's importance then derived from the fact that shortly afterward he and Osama Bin Laden founded Qaedat al-Jihad as a joint venture. He became chief ideologue and brain of this organization; in particular, he is considered to be the true thinker behind the September 11 attacks on the United States.

Zawahiri's Childhood and Political Awakening

Ayman al-Zawahiri was born in Cairo in 1951 in the chichi neighborhood of Maadi, where the new Egyptian middle class rubbed shoulders with the cosmopolitan crowd of Western expatriates.[2] The scion of two prestigious families, Ayman had all it took to ensure a brilliant future: on his father's side, his great-uncle had been the great imam of Al-Azhar University, the bastion of Sunni Islam, where his grandfather and great-grandfather had also served. At another level, his father, Rabi al-Zawahiri, a renowned professor of pharmacology at Ayn Shams University, had made his name in medicine, as had many of Ayman's uncles and cousins. On his mother's (Omayma Azzam's) side there were even bigger names: as in the case of the Zawahiris, many members of the family had graduated from Al-Azhar, starting with Omayma's father, Sheikh Abd al-Wahhab Azzam, who had gone on to head the Cairo University Faculty of Literature, before leaving for Saudi Arabia, where he founded King Saud University in Riyadh. Other relatives on his mother's side were well-known politicians: Abdul Rahman Azzam, for instance, was secretary-general of the Arab League when it was founded in 1948. Furthermore, both families traced their origins to the Arabian Peninsula; Omayma's family even claimed descent from the Prophet Muhammad.[3]

Rabi and Omayma, however, were very different from the high society to which they belonged by virtue of their background. They lived in a relatively modest fashion and seemed more pious and socially conservative than many members of their generation. This sharp contrast between a traditional, fairly austere family environment and a very Westernized social environment, is certainly key to understanding young Ayman's subsequent political involvement. As a child, he had a sweet, sensitive, and—from the start—extremely pious temperament. At school he stood out because of his great intelligence and a certain precociousness. This latter quality may also be observed in his political activity: in 1966, when he was fifteen, he created his first clandestine cell, along with some school friends. Its objective was to overthrow the regime and to institute the reign of Islam.

As it happened, 1966 was a key date in the history of Egyptian Islamism. It was then that the Islamist thinker Sayyid Qutb was condemned to death and hanged. The event marked the end of a phase and—especially—the beginning of another, more violent and radical one. Qutb had joined the Muslim Brotherhood (founded in 1928 by Hassan al-Banna with the aim of creating an Islamic state in Egypt) after returning from a trip to the United States, where he studied in the late 1940s. During his time there, he had been shocked to discover the "moral decadence" in which he felt the West lived. After the coup d'état of 1952, which the Muslim Brotherhood supported, Qutb became an adviser to the new president, Gamal Abdel Nasser. The honeymoon between the Free Officers and the Muslim Brothers was short-lived, however: after Brotherhood members were accused of having attempted to assassinate Nasser, in mid-1954 the movement was outlawed and thousands of members were arrested. Sayyid Qutb was among them; he was sentenced to life imprisonment, but his sentence was commuted to fifteen years. More important, he was subjected to horrific torture, which continues to mark Islamists' memories today. This inhuman treatment, according to many observers, is responsible for the intellectual radicalization he underwent in his cell, where he penned *Signposts,* a book some have described as the Egyptian Islamist movement's *What Is to Be Done?* In it, Qutb argues that humanity is essentially divided into two camps: that of Islam, and that of *jahiliyya*—the classical term designating the period of "ignorance" that preceded the rise of Islam. Everywhere, according to Qutb, *jahiliyya* has taken the place of Islam, even at the heart of societies that consider themselves Muslim. The counterpoint of the concept of *jahiliyya* is that of *hakimiyya* (divine sovereignty): in Qutb's work, the latter makes it imperative to render power unto God, by overthrowing the impious leaders that govern and establishing in their stead Islamic regimes regulated by divine law. In taking these positions, Qutb set himself apart from the line followed by the Muslim Brothers, who had officially adhered to a legalistic, nonviolent approach since their very inception.[4]

The stories of Sayyid Qutb's life and martyrdom were on everyone's lips in Islamist circles at the time; they most certainly played an essential role in raising Zawahiri's political awareness. In the same manner, Qutb's work—especially *Signposts,* as well as his famous commentary on the Quran, *In the Shade of the Quran*—provided the foundation for Zawahiri's political ideology. Indeed, Zawahiri devoted a whole passage of his book *Knights under the Prophet's Banner* to the influence Qutb had on the Egyptian jihadist movement in general, and on him in particular.

Sadat's Assassination and the Ordeal of Prison

The Arab armies' defeat by Israel in the 1967 war engendered a terrible trauma in Egyptian society. Secular left-wing ideologies, discredited and delegitimized, were gaining no new recruits, while the Islamist movements—the only ones to put forth an alternative—

were growing increasingly popular. Starting in 1970, Sadat implemented a policy of de-Nasserization and looked to the Islamist movements for support; he therefore freed most of the militants his predecessor had jailed, and tacitly encouraged their activities. This policy was also beneficial to the most radical Islamists, such as those in Zawahiri's cell, of whom there were forty in 1974. At the same time, cells of this type were multiplying. In the late 1970s four of them fused to form Jihad under the leadership of Abd al-Salam Faraj, the author of an influential pamphlet, *The Absent Imperative,* which made of armed struggle against an "impious" government the "sixth pillar of Islam." In 1980 Faraj concluded an agreement with the Islamic Group (Al-Gama'a al-Islamiyya), led by Karam Zuhdi, with a view to combining their forces. The Islamic Group, originally made up of student organizations, had become the foremost radical Islamist group in Egypt in the course of the 1970s. It was very prominent in Upper Egypt, and it was a mass movement, in contrast to the elitist jihadist groups mentioned previously—especially Zawahiri's—which saw themselves as a revolutionary vanguard. This union of radical Islamist organizations in Egypt took place under the aegis of Sheikh Omar Abdel Rahman, a graduate of Al-Azhar and an influential religious personality. The coalition was behind the assassination of President Sadat on October 6, 1981, after he had signed his death warrant, as many saw it, by concluding a peace treaty with Israel in 1978.

The enormous wave of arrests that followed the assassination, however, culminated in the imprisonment of most Egyptian Islamist leaders. Among them was Ayman al-Zawahiri. The following three years were truly a turning point in his life. Zawahiri had been a sincere revolutionary before experiencing prison—indeed, since his adolescence—but the strategy he wanted to follow then was that of a coup d'état carried out by a small elite, which would lead to the regime's overthrow without entailing losses of anyone other than the "pharaoh," and which would somehow bypass society. To that end, Zawahiri had endeavored to recruit within army ranks—since he felt the military was most capable of carrying out such a mission—notably through a childhood friend, Isam al-Qamari, who had become an officer. This much is clear: the bloody operations carried out by Jihad and the Islamic Group in the 1990s were not even contemplated at this early stage.

The experience of prison, for Zawahiri, was therefore both traumatic and foundational: traumatic because he was beaten, tortured, and humiliated, even more than his comrades. The reason—although Zawahiri had only a tenuous connection with Sadat's assassination—was that he had already come to occupy a fairly central position in the radical Islamist movement in Egypt, which led the authorities to believe that he knew more than he was saying. The supreme humiliation for him, according to Islamist lawyer Montasser al-Zayyat, was that he betrayed his friend and mentor Isam al-Qamari under torture.[5] On the basis of the information Zawahiri revealed, Qamari was arrested and thrown into prison. He managed to escape, but he was killed soon after in a gun battle with the police. Recurring allusions and stories of torture in Ayman al-Zawahiri's writing show how important this ordeal was. In 1992 he even devoted an entire book to the question, titled *The Black Book: Torturing Muslims under President Hosni Mubarak.*[6] Basing his account on Amnesty International reports and articles from the Arabic-language press, Zawahiri catalogued all the cases of torture documented in Egyptian prisons through the 1980s, emphasizing that although Islamists were not the only victims, they paid the highest price. Regarding his own case, he noted in the introduction: "We will not include our own testimony here, although what we saw with our own eyes, and even felt in our own flesh, may be worse than what we have mentioned. Still, we have preferred to let foreigners and journalists speak, for they cannot be described as extremists working to shatter social peace and threaten national unity."

The ordeal was also foundational because during these years

Zawahiri relived Sayyid Qutb's martyrdom. More than ever, he identified with his spiritual father, whose work he felt he had to carry on. It is also in prison that Zawahiri truly emerged as the leader of the Egyptian radical Islamist movement: during his trial, following Sadat's assassination, from the huge cage where the prisoners were held, he is the one who spoke in the group's name, addressing the foreign journalists gathered there in English:[7] "Now, we want to speak to the whole world. Who are we? Who are we? Why [did] they bring us here, and what [do] we want to say? About the first question: We are Muslims. We are Muslims who believe in their religion, both in ideology and practice, and hence we tried our best to establish an Islamic state and an Islamic society." All the prisoners responded in chorus: "There is no god but God." Zawahiri continued: "We are not sorry, we are not sorry for what we have done for our religion, and we have sacrificed, and we stand ready to make more sacrifices." He added: "We are here—the real Islamic front and the real Islamic opposition against Zionism, communism, and imperialism . . . And now, as an answer to the second question: Why did they bring us here? They bring us here for two reasons. First, they are trying to abolish the outstanding Islamic movement . . . and secondly, to complete the conspiracy of evacuating the area in preparation for the Zionist infiltration." The prisoners shouted: "We will not sacrifice the blood of Muslims for Americans and Jews." As they showed the marks of torture on their bodies, Zawahiri continued: "We suffered the severest inhuman treatment. They kicked us, they beat us, they whipped us with electric cables, they shocked us with electricity! They shocked us with electricity! And they used the wild dogs! And they used the wild dogs! And they hung us over the edges of the doors with our hands tied at the back! [He bent over to demonstrate.] They arrested the wives, the mothers, the fathers, the sisters, and the sons!" He went on to recite the names of prisoners who, he said, had died under torture, and concluded with what already sounded like a warning to the West: "So where is democracy? Where is freedom? Where is human rights? Where is justice? Where is justice? We will never forget! We will never forget!"

The Afghan Jihad and the Meeting with Bin Laden

A few months after he was freed in 1984, Ayman Zawahiri left Egypt for Saudi Arabia, where he worked in a clinic on the coast in Jidda, before traveling on to Peshawar and then to Afghanistan. There were two reasons for this journey: one was pragmatic, for Zawahiri knew he was now under close surveillance in Egypt, and that all the clandestine networks he had spent years constructing had been destroyed; the second was ideological, for, as Zayyat notes, Afghanistan was the best place for these activists to settle, because the country offered what they were looking for—fighting and jihad.[8] Zawahiri, a physician, had already made two humanitarian trips to Peshawar, Pakistan, and to Afghanistan, in 1980 and 1981. At the time, he was freshly graduated from medical school and was practicing as a surgeon at a clinic run by the Muslim Brotherhood in the Cairo neighborhood of Sayyida Zaynab. He spent over six months in the country, and was dazzled by the jihad taking place there. In 1985, then, he landed in familiar territory; apparently, he was already thinking of establishing a secure base from which to organize Islamic Jihad.[9] Starting in 1987, the structure was indeed formed anew, around Egyptian militants on the run, whose numbers were increasing steadily.

When he arrived in Peshawar, however, Ayman al-Zawahiri did not bother paying allegiance to Abdallah Azzam—then widely seen as the father and the theoretician of jihad against the Soviets—but directed his attention instead toward a young Saudi, who was quite discreet but highly respected: Osama Bin Laden. Zawahiri quickly managed to place members of his organization in the key posts around Bin Laden. The first aim was to ensure that Islamic Jihad would receive the lion's share of financial aid from the Saudi billionaire, against contenders like the Islamic Group, which was also present in Peshawar. More generally, however, the goal was to pull Bin Laden away from his mentor, Abdallah Azzam. The young Saudi thus became the object of fierce competition between Zawahiri and Azzam, the conflict growing so intense that Zawahiri, with the sole aim of weakening Azzam's position, propagated the rumor that Azzam was a spy for the Americans.[10]

In 1988 Bin Laden, surrounded by a few faithful supporters, laid the foundations of a new organization called Al Qaeda: "the base." It was supposed to be very structured, with ideological contours that were still vague: its aim, as its charter stated, was "to bear the word of God and make His religion triumph."[11] Still, the fact that among its founding members and its close entourage were many members of Egypt's Islamic Jihad group—notably Zawahiri—and the assertion made in its founding statement that "this future project is in the interest of the Egyptian brothers" suggest that the struggle against the Muslim world's "apostate" regimes—especially the Egyptian and Saudi governments—was one of the movement's priorities.[12] Yet Azzam, who was concerned with maintaining the unity of the Muslim community against its external enemies, had always been against turning jihad against the Arab regimes. Furthermore, the creation of Al Qaeda was a clear challenge to Azzam's authority, for it was set up as a structure competing with his Service Bureau. For both these reasons, the creation of Al Qaeda marked the break between Azzam and Bin Laden, the latter now falling under Zawahiri's influence. On November 24, 1989, Azzam was killed in a car bomb explosion. Although there was never any evidence that Zawahiri and Bin Laden were implicated, some observers singled them out as having been behind the attack.[13]

The Struggle Against the Egyptian Regime

This honeymoon between Bin Laden and Zawahiri was short-lived, however, and their interests rapidly diverged. After Saddam Hussein invaded Kuwait on August 2, 1990, the Saudi regime refused the assistance offered by the young Saudi mujahid and his "Arab legion" in protecting the borders of the kingdom.[14] Instead, the Saudis preferred to accept protection from a U.S.-led international coalition. Long after the end of the Gulf War proper, though, U.S. forces were maintaining bases in Saudi Arabia, a situation Bin Laden interpreted as "occupation of the land of the two holy sanctuaries." He was now opposed not only to the power of the Saud dynasty, but also—and indeed especially—to the United States, whose unconditional support for Israel he vehemently condemned. In other words, in his hierarchy of priorities, the nearby enemy gave way to the faraway one. At this time, however, Zawahiri did not hold the same opinion at all. Not that he liked the United States any more than Bin Laden did; but he considered that establishing an Islamic regime in Egypt was the first priority, and that it was only in this way that Muslims would one day be able to conquer Palestine anew. As he wrote in 1995 in *Al-Mujahidun,* "the road to Jerusalem passes through Cairo."[15]

Internecine warfare among former Afghan mujahedeen commanders bred chaos in Afghanistan after the war against the Soviets ended. This impelled Bin Laden, Zawahiri, and their Egyptian comrades to begin looking for a new base. Sudan—where a coup d'état in 1989 had brought to power a military regime led by Omar al-Bashir and directed behind the scenes by an Islamist, Hassan al-Turabi—seemed like a good alternative. At the same time, the Sudanese authorities were desperately seeking funds to develop the country, and Bin Laden committed himself to providing financing. In 1992 Bin Laden, followed by Zawahiri and the members of their organizations, left Kabul for Khartoum.

During the period that followed, Zawahiri devoted himself almost exclusively to reorganizing Islamic Jihad. He hoped that, thanks to geographical proximity, Sudan would become the dreamed-of rear base from which to destabilize the regime in Cairo. The first problem he encountered was that of funding, for his Saudi ally's generous donations were insufficient to restore Islamic Jihad to its former strength. At this time, therefore, with the aim of raising funds and establishing cells in various countries, he traveled tirelessly to the Balkans, Austria, Dagestan, Yemen, Iraq, Iran, the Philippines, and even Argentina. Still looking for money, he even went to the United States in 1993, under cover of the Kuwaiti Red Crescent Society, for which he had already worked at the time of the Afghan jihad.[16]

Finally, starting in 1993, a new series of operations was unleashed on Egyptian territory, in large part to maintain competition with the Islamic Group, which was engaged in an all-out war with the regime in Cairo. In August an attempt to assassinate then minister of the interior Hassan al-Alfi failed, and in November a bomb that was supposed to kill Prime Minister Atef Sidqi killed a little girl instead. Islamic Jihad emerged from this period profoundly weakened once again: on the one hand, because the schoolgirl's death finally turned public opinion against Zawahiri and his group, and on the other because a wave of arrests unprecedented since Sadat's death deprived him of many of his partisans in Egypt. In 1995, in a bid to stop the hemorrhage and reinvigorate the movement, Zawahiri and the Islamic Group decided to carry out a spectacular operation: the assassination of President Hosni Mubarak while he was visiting Addis Ababa. Once again, however, the operation was a failure, which was followed by fierce repression of Egyptian Islamists. In response, Zawahiri and his colleagues organized an attack against the Egyptian embassy in Islamabad, which was a success—if one can call it that—claiming sixteen dead and many wounded. This first nontargeted violent operation carried out by Zawahiri's group gave birth to an internal debate that forced Zawahiri to explain his position, in an article titled "Suicide Operations: The Reasons for the Attack on the Egyptian Embassy in Islamabad in 1995" and published in *Al-Mujahidun.*

The 1995 attack also brought renewed pressure from the U.S. administration and the Egyptian regime on the Sudanese government, which was increasingly unhappy with the presence of a veritable "state within the state" at the heart of its territory. Bin Laden, Zawahiri, and their supporters were ultimately forced to leave Sudan the following year. Bin Laden went immediately to Afghanistan, a large part of which was under the control of the Taliban by this time, after several years of civil warfare among the warlords who had emerged from the jihad of the 1980s. As for Zawahiri, he made short trips to various countries in Europe (the Netherlands, Switzerland, Bosnia-Herzegovina), Asia, and the Middle East. These also seem to have been part of his quest for new bases for the movement and an ongoing search for funds. His last expedition to Dagestan was a complete fiasco: he was arrested there as an illegal alien. He was quickly freed, but only because the Russian authorities proved incompetent and unable to identify him. After these voyages, he understood that the best sanctuary for him and his supporters was Afghanistan, and he joined Bin Laden in Jalalabad. There, Bin Laden had already begun to set up training camps. The duo was thus reunited, and this time—in contrast to 1989, when a loose structure had been created—their proximity was no longer merely organizational; it took on an ideological dimension as well.

From the Nearby Enemy to the Distant Enemy

In Ayman al-Zawahiri's political and intellectual trajectory, 1998 marked a fundamental break. On February 26, in the name of Islamic Jihad, he signed a joint declaration with Bin Laden and representatives of different radical Islamist movements, announcing the creation of the World Islamic Front for Jihad against Jews and Crusaders and containing the famous fatwa that made the murder of Americans and their allies an individual duty for Muslims. This was more than the renewal of his alliance with Bin Laden: in this declaration, Zawahiri was renouncing the priority he had always given to the "nearby enemy"—the Egyptian regime—and subscribing to Bin Laden's worldview, in which the fight against the "distant enemy"—the Americans and their allies—was always more important. Two types of reasons might serve to explain this change.

First, Zawahiri was finding it increasingly difficult to obtain funding. In addition, the various waves of arrests carried out by the Egyptian authorities had severely weakened his movement. Only ideological alignment with Bin Laden's positions held out the promise for Zawahiri of garnering a greater share of the resources at the Saudi billionaire's disposal.

It is also necessary, however, to take into account the challenge posed in July 1997, when the historic leaders of the Islamic Group, from their cells in Egyptian jails, called for an initiative to halt violence *(mubadarat waqf al-unf)* on Egyptian territory. Using an argument very close to the one Zawahiri adopted the following year, these leaders recognized that the strategy of direct confrontation with the regime had failed, and they laid plans to abandon the struggle against the nearby enemy, in order to concentrate on the fight against Israel, and beyond it the United States. Although the two analyses were similar, however, the conclusions to which they led were diametrically opposed: whereas Zawahiri opted for global jihad, the leaders of the Islamic Group advocated a return to preaching *(da'wa)* and Islamization of society from the ground up. Whereas Zawahiri kept the Egyptian regime in his crosshairs, merely reversing his priorities, the leaders of the Islamic Group considered that violence against the regime really had to end, for any weakening of the government and any threat to civil order ultimately benefited only Israel. This initiative, which heavyweights within the Egyptian Islamist movement backed, and which even seemed seductive beyond the circle of the Islamic Group, thus forced Zawahiri, who feared he would find himself isolated, to respond promptly.[17] His response took the form of the World Islamic Front for Jihad against Jews and Crusaders, of which many consider him to have been the principal architect.

Zawahiri's move, however, provoked upheavals within Islamic Jihad, many of whose members opposed the alliance with Bin Laden and the strategic reorientation it implied. These members reproached their leader for having acted in the group's name without consulting them.[18] An emergency meeting was called in Afghanistan: Zawahiri, who found himself in the minority, threatened to abandon the leadership of the organization. The meeting ended with the withdrawal of several important figures, among them Ayman's brother, Muhammad al-Zawahiri. It was only in the summer of 1999, however, that Zawahiri, exasperated by the opposition he was still facing, especially from those who supported the group's adherence to the nonviolence initiative, threw in the towel and abandoned his office as emir. He finally, a few months later, resumed command of Islamic Jihad, which was drained by this time. In the end, the movement was officially dissolved in June 2001 and fused with Al Qaeda (led by Bin Laden) as a joint venture named Qaedat al-Jihad.

The creation of the World Islamic Front for Jihad against Jews and Crusaders led to renewed interest in Islamic Jihad on the part of the CIA, and consequently to the arrest of several of the Islamic Jihad leaders living in exile. Zawahiri presented the attacks on the U.S. embassies in Nairobi and Dar es Salaam, carried out during the summer of 1998, as a response to the successful American clampdown. From that point on, the situation escalated: the U.S. administration responded by bombing training camps linked to Bin Laden's network in Afghanistan, and—by mistake—a pharmaceuticals factory in Khartoum. In the fall of 2000 the USS *Cole* was attacked in the port of Aden. Finally, on September 11, 2001, in the most spectacular operation ever carried out by Qaedat al-Jihad, four American airplanes were hijacked and three of them were flown into the World Trade Center and the Pentagon, killing over three thousand people.

Zawahiri after September 11

The Western media had ignored Zawahiri for the most part until 9/11, but after he appeared seated next to Bin Laden and a Kuwaiti, Sulaiman Abu Ghaith, on a videotape broadcast by Al-Jazeera on October 7, 2001, and shown on American and European television channels, attention in the West focused on him. Little by little, analysts realized that even if Bin Laden was the charismatic figure and the symbol of Qaedat al-Jihad, Zawahiri was its unofficial spokesman, chief polemicist, and principal ideologue.

Spokesman

The first function Zawahiri gradually took on after 9/11 was that of the group's unofficial spokesman. After a year's absence, during which some observers began to believe he had been killed and was buried in a collapsed tunnel of the Tora Bora complex, Zawahiri suddenly became visible in the media once again. In October 2002, he reappeared on another recording, warning the Americans of what was still only a possible military operation in Iraq and reproaching the allies of the United States for supporting Washington's policies. Thereafter, he was a regular, self-invited guest on Al-Jazeera's screens: in May 2003 he denounced the invasion of Iraq, which he described as the preamble to an attack on all the countries in the region. Consequently, he encouraged his partisans to attack the interests of the United States and some of its allies, wherever those interests might be found. In August 2003 he denounced the treatment of prisoners at Guantánamo and called for revenge. In September he attacked the president of Pakistan, Pervez Musharraf, a faithful ally of the United States, and called on the Pakistani people to overthrow him. In December, on the second anniversary of the battle of Tora Bora in Afghanistan, he intervened to demonstrate that the invasions of Afghanistan and Iraq had been resounding defeats for the United States, and that the jihadist movement was stronger than ever.

During the following period he was even more present in the media than Bin Laden, whose declarations became less frequent. In February 2004 Zawahiri took on President Bush on the one hand and the French law forbidding the display of visible religious signs (notably Islamic headscarves) in state schools on the other: the latter, to him, was "another example of the crusaders' evil intentions," demonstrating that France, although it had opposed the war in

Iraq, was still deeply hostile to Islam and Muslims. In March 2004 Zawahiri renewed his attacks on Pervez Musharraf, and in June 2004 he warned the Arab countries that the reforms imposed by the United States were designed only to ensure American control of the Middle East and its resources. In September 2004 Zawahiri reviewed the situation in Afghanistan and Iraq three years after the attacks on New York and Washington and concluded that the United States was bogged down in both countries. In October 2004 he insisted that the Palestinian cause lay at the heart of Al Qaeda's struggle; as in every other case, he called for strikes against America and its allies. Finally, in late November 2004 he criticized Egypt, Saudi Arabia, and the United States and reasserted that the international jihadist movement was determined to pursue the fight.

From 2005 onward, he kept up the same rhythm: Zawahiri seems to have felt the need to react to every current event, clarifying his position and, beyond it, Al Qaeda's. This was the case in October 2005, for example, after a devastating earthquake hit Pakistan: Zawahiri enjoined his coreligionists to show solidarity in denouncing Western NGOs. During Israel's war on Hezbollah in the summer of 2006, he called on the "oppressed" *(mustad'afun)* to rally around his movement. Around the symbolic date of September 11 every year, he also made it a point to provide a detailed review of the balance of power between Al Qaeda and its adversaries, intended to mobilize the organization's supporters even more. Finally, shortly after the attacks on London on July 7, 2005, Zawahiri appeared in the prelude to the will of Muhammad Siddique Khan, a British terrorist of Pakistani origin, vaunting the virtues of the "knights of monotheism," who had "taken . . . the battle into enemy territory."

Zawahiri's omnipresence in the media allowed Al Qaeda to fulfill the function it sought as a spokesman, but it also contributed to diluting its message. Though Zawahiri's early interventions, in 2002 and 2003, had been front-page news worldwide, his last appearances were barely mentioned, meriting a brief note at best. His only true audience, from that point on, was the crowd of jihadist sympathizers on the Internet, at the very time when the increasing use of English and sometimes French subtitles was intended to give his speeches a far broader reach. In striving to make himself widely heard, Zawahiri became, in a sense, inaudible.

The Polemicist

By speaking out repeatedly, Zawahiri also sought to portray himself as the jihadist movement's "chief polemicist." From the time he had first been involved in the Islamist movement, his preferred target had been "reformist" Islamist groups, which abided by the law and presented themselves as hostile to any form of political violence. In his eyes, such groups were crucial, especially since they constituted the prime force, on the ground, for mobilization in the name of Islam.

The archetype of such groups was the Muslim Brotherhood. Starting in the early 1970s, it openly distanced itself from the ideological legacy of Sayyid Qutb and opted for the same strategy of reconciliation with the regime that it had followed before Nasser took power. In the early 1990s Zawahiri devoted an entire work to the Brotherhood, titled *Bitter Harvest*, in which he drew up a tally for the sixty years that had passed since the movement was founded. He accused its leaders of having transgressed Islam's fundamental principles by forsaking "jihad against tyranny (*al-taghut*)" and agreeing to play the "democratic" political game, implicitly meaning that they recognized the regime on one hand and popular sovereignty on the other. By contrast, Zawahiri, like Qutb, believed authority was God's alone and could derive only from the strict implementation of Islamic law. In other writings, he made even more virulent attacks on the Muslim Brothers, accusing them of having taken the government's side in the struggle that pitted radical Islamist movements in Egypt against the regime of Hosni Mubarak in the 1990s.[19]

When Brotherhood members and affiliates stepped up their political participation in various Arab countries, they triggered renewed criticism. In January 2006 Zawahiri once again attacked the Egyptian Muslim Brothers for participating in legislative elections, and accused them of treason because it "[served] U.S. interests." In May 2007, he lambasted Hamas, which had agreed to cooperate with Fatah on a national unity government created after the Mecca accords, thereby consolidating "the loss of the sharia and of most of Palestine."

The conflict between Zawahiri and those who supported the "initiative to halt violence" also unfolded in this context. It had already held an important place in his work *Knights under the Prophet's Banner,* which he wrote after September 11 and excerpts of which are presented here. After a period of calm, the same conflict broke out once more, with renewed virulence, during 2006. On August 5 Zawahiri insinuated, rejoicing openly, that several of the Islamic Group's historical leaders had just joined Al Qaeda, chief among them Sheikh Omar Abdel Rahman, the emblematic figure of radical Islamism in Egypt and the presumed author of the fatwa ordering the assassination of Sadat. Abdel Rahman had been in jail in the United States since 1993, when he was found guilty of involvement in the first attack on the World Trade Center. Among these leaders also was Muhammad al-Islambuli, the brother of Sadat's assassin, as well as Abd al-Akhar Hammad and Mustafa al-Muqri, both eminent members of the group, exiled in Germany and Britain, respectively. Zawahiri's announcement was made in tandem with an interview of Al-Sahab, Al Qaeda's "production company," with Muhammad al-Hakayima, who presented himself as one of the group's historical leaders. Hakayima, who said he was speaking in the name of "those who are loyal to their pledge within the Islamic Group" *(al-thabitun alal-ahd bil-jama'a al-islamiya),* confirmed the "good news." Within the next few days, however, several of those mentioned in the announcement (especially Hammad and Muqri) had denied any affiliation with Al Qaeda.[20] At the same time, spokesmen for the Islamic Group—

which had taken the initiative in calling for a cessation of violence—accused Zawahiri of being dishonest and manipulative.[21] The members also declared that they did not know Hakayima and suggested that he was at best a low-ranking cadre whom Zawahiri had chosen to use in order to carry off a "media scoop" *(farqa'a i'lamiyya)*. In the following weeks the debate grew more venomous: Hakayima sought to prove he was involved in the Islamic Group, and wrote a "history of jihadist movements in Egypt,"[22] which was supposed to demonstrate his intimate knowledge of these circles; the Islamic Group, for its part, asserted that he was in Iran, enjoying the assistance and protection of the authorities there—a particularly damaging accusation.[23] The war of words also revolved around Sheikh Omar Abdel Rahman's position, each side claiming that he supported it, although the sheikh, in a high-security U.S. jail, could neither confirm nor deny the allegations.[24] Since then, the quarrel has played out on the Internet, notably between the Web site created by Hakayima to represent the members of the Islamic Group who remained "loyal to their commitments" and the official Web site of the group in Egypt.[25]

To the uninformed observer the intensity of the debate may appear surprising: What could Zawahiri, and Al Qaeda in general, want from a few jailed or exiled former leaders of a depleted group? The fact is that Al-Jihad and the Islamic Group have long waged a fierce battle for leadership of radical Islamism in Egypt. Their competition grew more intense when the initiative to halt violence was announced in 1997: the Islamic Group took the lead in this "ultimate act of treason." By announcing these defections, Zawahiri hoped to win the upper hand in a long-standing rivalry. Even more than his attacks on the Muslim Brothers, the conflict that pitted him against those members of the Islamic Group who had remained in Egypt was therefore indicative of Zawahiri's imaginary political landscape. His politics remained locally rooted, even though he had joined the global jihad advocated by Bin Laden, and for Zawahiri time seems to have frozen in 1981.

The Ideologue Who Ensured Al Qaeda Orthodoxy

At the same time, Zawahiri imposed himself as the movement's chief ideologue, by writing two books in which he theorized about the struggle being waged by Qaedat al-Jihad—or simply Al Qaeda—against the "faraway enemy." He also sought to produce the elements of religious legitimation necessary to pursuit of the struggle. These works were widely read in jihadist circles. The first was titled *Knights under the Prophet's Banner,* and long excerpts from it were published in daily installments in late 2001 in *Al-Sharq al-Awsat,* a pan-Arab daily financed with Saudi capital.

In this text, which is presented as the probable testament of a man who did not know whether he would survive the U.S. strikes on Afghanistan, Zawahiri reflects at length on his life and the history of the jihadist movement, his aim being to justify the change in strategy that had led to the September 11 attacks. He takes stock of the successive failures that he and more generally the movement as a whole has faced, to conclude that on one hand a change in rhetoric and indeed in strategy (from the nearby to the distant enemy) is necessary, and on the other only a spectacular act can mobilize anew those he calls—in a perfectly Marxist vein—the masses.[26] The importance of the text therefore derives largely from the fact that he recapitulates in it the intellectual changes that had led to the September 11 attacks.

A year after *Knights under the Prophet's Banner* was published, another of Zawahiri's works, titled *Loyalty and Separation,* came out. The difference between the two texts was significant: *Knights* resembled a journalistic pamphlet, with a few passages drawn from sacred texts interspersed, and *Loyalty* was a more ambitious attempt to produce a work of religious literature in its own right.[27] It contains incessant references to the Quran, the sunna, and works of exegesis; this entire textual apparatus is placed in the service of a single idea—that the dogma of loyalty and separation is central to the faith and, according to Zawahiri, imposes the necessity of supporting Muslims in all circumstances, and of breaking completely with unbelievers at every level. This approach implies a political separation, attained through refusal to ally with a state governed by a non-Muslim regime (or a regime that fails to apply God's law as defined by Zawahiri), as well as individual separation, meaning a refusal to frequent or befriend unbelievers. In sum, the principle of jihad, and nothing else, must regulate relations with "non-Muslims," in Qutb's definition of the term.

Although the notions of *wala* (loyalty) and *bara* (separation) have always been part of dogma (even if interpretations of what they meant changed over time), the formula *al-wala wal-bara* was manufactured fairly recently. It seems that it was given theoretical form for the first time in 1818 by Sulayman Ibn Abdallah, the grandson of Muhammad Ibn Abd al-Wahab and the representative of the most intransigent strain of Wahhabism, at the time when Diriyah, the capital of the first Saudi state, was being besieged by the "infidel" Egyptian troops of Muhammad Ali Pasha, whom the Ottoman sultan had sent to eliminate the "Wahhabi heresy."[28] Sulayman Ibn Abdallah, who was the city's most respected religious scholar at the time, felt called upon to react and to find a means of galvanizing the troops of the young state: this was the function of *al-wala wal-bara*. More recently, under the influence of several ideologues, chief among them a Palestinian named Asim Barqawi (also known as Abu Muhammad al-Maqdisi, the author of *Millat Ibrahim* (Abraham's People, a very influential work),[29] the dogma acquired great importance in the ideology of the contemporary Salafist jihadist movement. Some observers even consider that this principle is to contemporary jihadist movements fighting the distant enemy what the principle of *hakimiyya* was to the jihadist movements at war against the nearby enemy in the 1970s.[30] It is precisely this move, from the central place of *hakimiyya* to that of *al-wala wal-bara*, that Zawahiri, the jihadist veteran, carried out. His work on the topic, of which we present large excerpts here, consecrates this epistemological break, which was so crucial to his intellectual evolution.

For Zawahiri, nevertheless, the principle defining friends and enemies according to *al-wala wal-bara was* first and foremost a political one. Christians and Jews—perceived as being collectively at war against Islam—were to be fought, as were the regimes of the Muslim world, but Muslims who failed to adhere to Sunni orthodoxy, by contrast, were not targeted specifically. As he explained regarding Iraq, "It is clear that whoever is fighting the Americans must be particularly careful to reduce the number of his enemies and increase that of his friends; how could he do otherwise when he is confronting the world's Number 1 power? . . . In Iraq, there are many non-Muslim communities, like Christians, Jews, or 'devil worshippers,' and Al Qaeda never attacked them in any way.[31] Al Qaeda in Iraq focused on fighting the crusading occupiers, and we target only those who help the Americans, in word or in deed."[32] During the war in Lebanon in the summer of 2006 Zawahiri even spoke out in the following terms, most likely addressing Hezbollah, and perhaps an even wider audience: "As for you, the oppressed who are victims of injustice worldwide, victims of the iniquity and tyranny of Western civilization, led by America, join the Muslims to resist this oppression, the likes of which humanity has never seen before. Unite with us, because we are united with you against this injustice and oppression . . . Resist with us, until those who have been stripped of their rights have recovered them, until the symbol of tyranny in human history has collapsed."[33] As Zawahiri himself emphasized, this position also corresponded to Bin Laden's: anti-Shiism was not part of Zawahiri's stock in trade, as the texts presented here show.

In the Wahhabi tradition from which it emerged, however, the dogma of *al-wala wal-bara* tended to take on a far more exclusive, and ultimately more religious, sense than Zawahiri gave it. It designated primarily all those who do not adhere to Sunni orthodoxy, and especially the Shiites. Since the nineteenth century, ulema from the Arabian Peninsula have produced very rich literature on this theme—literature from which Abu Musab al-Zarqawi took his cue, starting in 2004, to justify the idea of an all-out war against

Iraq's Shiites. The increase in anti-Shiite violence that resulted from his interpretation initially evoked a muted reaction from Al Qaeda's leaders, and especially Zawahiri.[34] In a letter intercepted by U.S. forces in October 2005 (its authenticity is still contested, although its content is unsurprising given Zawahiri's other declarations, mentioned earlier), Zawahiri openly questioned Zarqawi's strategy of conflict with the Shiites:[35] "Is this inevitable? Can it be deferred until the jihadist movement's strength increases? And even if some operations can be qualified as self-defense, are they all necessary? Or have there been unjustified operations? Is it wise to open a new front, in addition to those with the Americans and the government? Or is the conflict with the Shiites, rather, lightening the burden for the Americans, by directing the mujahedeen's attention toward the Shiites, while the Americans continue to control the situation from afar? Even if attacks on Shiite leaders were necessary in order to foil their plans, why have there been attacks on ordinary Shiites? … Can the mujahedeen kill all the Shiites in Iraq? Has any Islamic state in history attempted this? And why kill ordinary Shiites, when their ignorance ensures that they will be forgiven? What will we lose if we do not attack the Shiites?"[36]

Despite these reservations, Zarqawi—who had officially joined Al Qaeda and pledged allegiance to Bin Laden in October 2004, nevertheless pursued the path of militant anti-Shiism. As for Zawahiri, his initial reticence notwithstanding, he was compelled to accept a fait accompli and to honor the man who had brought Al Qaeda some of its most outstanding triumphs in 2005 and 2006. Zawahiri, the self-declared guarantor of the movement's doctrinal orthodoxy, was thereby obliged to give in to Zarqawi, who held a central place on the battlefield (as Zawahiri did not).

In 2004 Zawahiri still appeared to be one of the most important cogs in the Al Qaeda "system." Three years later, in 2007, he has never seemed less influential. He is barely audible in the media and is lost in inter-Egyptian quarrels whose stakes are incomprehensible to the "masses." Furthermore, Zawahiri's authority as an ideologue is being challenged by those who practice daily jihad, as Zarqawi did. Besides the circumstantial reasons already mentioned, there is a more largely structural cause: because of repression and the proliferation of increasingly decentralized jihads, Al Qaeda is no longer the hierarchical vertical organization it was at the beginning of the twenty-first century. As a result, its leaders and ideologues are partially isolated today: prisoners in an ivory tower from which their voices are heard more and more faintly. All their importance, therefore, now lies not in their personalities but in their oeuvre, and especially in canonical works like *Bitter Harvest* or *Loyalty and Separation,* which (regardless of local reinterpretations) still constitute the heart of the jihadist ideological corpus.

BITTER HARVEST:
SIXTY YEARS OF THE MUSLIM BROTHERHOOD

(EXCERPTS)

Now, as we conclude our survey of the examples drawn from a mountain of the Brotherhood's words and deeds, we must pause for a few conclusions.[1]

First: the questions we cited in the first chapter of this book (governing in spite of God's revelation, democracy, loyalty, and separation) are not secondary matters on which legal disagreements are acceptable. They constitute bases of the faith, and are even related to the most fundamental basis of all: monotheism.[2]

Governing in spite of God's revelation:[3] either we govern according to God's revelation, making our actions agree with our words ("There is no god but God"), or we govern in spite of God's revelation, which means associating other gods with God, because sovereignty is God's alone.[4] He said: "The command is for none but God," and he said: "Nor does he share his command with any person whatsoever."[5]

Democracy: either legislation comes from God alone, and one refers to him in case of conflict, in accordance with our words ("There is no god but God"), or one gives the right to legislate to others, like the people and their delegates, referring to them in case of conflict. This is tantamount to worshipping gods, peers, and associates alongside God, whereas he said: "What! Have they partners (in godhead) who have established for them some religion without God's permission?"[6]

Loyalty: we cannot reconcile loyalty with God's unbelieving enemies, affection for them, or praise for them and their impious doctrines, like consultation, positive law, and democracy.[7] None of this can be reconciled with faith. He said: "You see many of them turning in friendship to the Unbelievers. Evil indeed are (the works) which their souls have sent forward before them (with the result), that God's wrath is on them, and in torment will they abide. If only they had believed in God, in the Messenger, and in what has been revealed to him, never would they have taken them for friends and protectors, but most of them are rebellious wrongdoers."[8]

Second: the Muslim Brothers, from a religious perspective—apart from the teacher Sayyid Qutb and a few others who do not represent the Brotherhood's official position—have avoided taking a clear stand on anathema against tyrants.[9] They even closed the debate on this subject by adopting the principle "Preachers and not judges" declared by the second guide, Hassan al-Hudaybi.[10]

Third: not only did the organization fail to condemn rulers who do not govern according to revealed law; it went so far as to recognize, in words and in deeds, these rulers' legitimacy, and allowed this judgment to spread in its ranks.[11] The Brotherhood recognized the legitimacy of secular parliamentary institutions (parliament and its democratic elections), which was of invaluable use to the tyrants, since it enabled them to accuse the jihadist groups of illegitimacy—according to infidel laws, of course.[12]

Fourth: the organization concluded agreements with most of the regimes under whose authority the Brotherhood's branches live. It has sometimes participated in government. The organization's agreements with such impious governments often took the form of pacts: the government left the Brotherhood some leeway to develop, and in return the organization recognized the regime's legitimacy and provided assistance in countering a strong opposition. For example:

- King Farouk used the organization to strike against the Wafd Party and counter its influence on the masses.[13] Shortly before he was assassinated, Hassan al-Banna also offered the king his assistance in combating communism, because Banna had understood the point of this game.[14]
- Gamal Abdel Nasser used the organization to increase the revolution's popular appeal. He excluded it from the law banning political parties until he had become a popular leader; then he turned on the Brotherhood.[15]
- Anwar Sadat openly used the organization in combating the communist and Nasserist movements.[16]
- Hosni Mubarak used the organization to counter the extremist tendency (jihadist organizations). Ma'mun al-Hudaybi did not hesitate to express this, saying: "The organization's existence is in the government's interest.[17] It often has recourse to us in order to contain the extremist religious current" (*Al-Sharq al-Awsat*, May 11, 1987). We provide examples of this in the second part of the book.

Fifth: When the organization failed to reach agreement with certain regimes, it sought substitutes among hostile governments. This shows how much the Brotherhood needs a strong ally, even if that ally is infidel, in order to survive, because this is the way it was formed. Here are a few examples.

To begin with, their agreement with the Saudi regime, which was opposed to Nasser, when their relations with Nasser deteriorated. King Faisal was happy about this, because it revived the Islamic flame against the Arab nationalist movement led by Nasser that threatened the thrones and chiefdoms of the Gulf in the 1960s.[18]

Another example is their agreement with the Iraqi Baath re-

gime when their relations with the Syrian Baath deteriorated, before and after the Hama events of 1982.[19] Many members of the
Syrian Brotherhood, among them Adnan Saad al-Din and Said
Hawa, sought refuge in Iraq, and it is there that the Brotherhood
allied with the remainder of the Syrian opposition: Baathists,
Nasserists, and nationalists.[20] Finally, Rifaat al-Assad, who had formerly butchered the Brotherhood, joined this alliance too, with the
aim of overthrowing Hafez al-Assad's regime and establishing a
secular, democratic state.[21] This says a lot about their decadence.

Sixth: In the early 1980s, the Brothers were implicated in partisan conflicts in Egypt, during which they changed their tune
several times. One day they were allied with a party, and the next
they were fighting and insulting it, as they did with the Wafd and
Nuqrashi.[22] All this contradicts the Brotherhood's characteristics as
established by Hassan al-Banna: "To abandon the dominance of
the notables and grandees, to abandon parties and organizations."
See "Letter to the Fifth Congress," in *Correspondence* (n.p.: Shihab
Press, p. 159).[23] The Brotherhood was thus compromised in partisan conflicts, which even led to a schism, with certain of its members forming the Youth Association of Our Master Muhammad
(praise and blessings upon him).[24]

Seventh: the organization, and all its branches, were satisfied to
trust democracy, the people's power, and elections as a means of
change and access to power. Hassan al-Banna even declared: "The
things we criticize in the constitution may be changed by means
prescribed in the constitution," meaning in a democratic way.[25]
This is true of the Brotherhood in Kuwait, Jordan, Yemen, Sudan,
Algeria, and Tunisia, as well as in Egypt.[26]

Eighth: The organization agreed to reject violence—which is
what tyrants call jihad along God's path—and forsook those who
adopted it, even though they might be its supporters.[27]

Ninth: Today, all the Brotherhood leaders have adopted these
ideas (constitutional legitimacy, democracy, support for the regime, and rejection of violence). No contrary idea reaches the

leadership level, meaning that the former permeate the entire hierarchy.

Tenth: Hassan al-Banna was already guilty of all the infractions to religious prescriptions that the organization has committed: flattering rulers and praising them unduly, giving them legitimacy, recognizing constitutional legitimacy, respecting the constitution and democratic practice, participating in democratic elections (as Hassan al-Banna did twice), demonstrating political opportunism by participating in partisan conflicts, and rejecting violence. Hassan al-Banna had already committed all these sins.[28] We might add, addressing those who claim that the Brotherhood today has moved away from Banna's methods and policy, that it is inaccurate to say so. The data cited in this book show without a doubt that Banna was the first to adopt such deviations. God's messenger said: "He who issues a bad law bears the fault, as do those who obey this law" (narrated by Muslim). Is this how one goes about reviving religion? Is this how the renewer of the fourteenth century A.H. would behave?[29] In his book *Our Contemporary Reality* Muhammad Qutb sought to exonerate Hassan al-Banna of the Brotherhood's mistakes, but he was not fair, because when he criticized democracy and the Brotherhood's adherence to democratic rules, describing its members as old men exhausted by a long march, he did not mention the fact that Hassan al-Banna preceded these old men in participating in elections and other sins. See Muhammad Qutb, *Our Contemporary Reality* (Al Medina Press, 1407 A.H.), pp. 427–460.[30] God, may He be exalted, said: "O you who believe! Stand out firmly for justice, as witnesses to God, even as against yourselves, or your parents, or your kin."[31]

Eleventh: The Brotherhood's biased methods have not encountered much internal opposition, except from a few individuals, like Sayyid Qutb (God rest his soul) and his sister Amina Qutb. As for the Brothers who seceded because they disagreed with the method followed or the guides' behavior, they were no better inspired than the Brotherhood from which they emerged, and they fell into mistakes that were similar and others that were far worse: this is the case of the Youth Association of Our Master Muhammad, Muhammad al-Ghazali's schismatic group, and that of Shukri Mustafa, al-Takfir wal-Hijra.[32]

Twelfth: those who read this book will see clearly that within the organization this apple has had a worm in it since the 1940s. There are several reasons for this: the lack of method, and even the bad methods followed, which consist in a policy justifying deviation. There is also the failure to command good and prohibit evil, under the pretext that one must obey rulers blindly and trust them absolutely.[33] Another reason is the members' general, chronic intellectual poverty in the sharia sciences, especially those related to monotheism and dogma.[34] Often, we have observed that the members who do study these sciences end up leaving the organization.

The organization suffered a great loss during this period: that of commanding good and forbidding evil within its ranks. This trial was brought about by the material comfort the Brotherhood came to enjoy, thanks to its relations with the Gulf countries, after many of its members fled Nasserist repression, to the extent that the organization took over the leadership of many preaching and charity associations in the Gulf and Saudi Arabia and now has control of regional and international banks and societies.[35] Joining the Brotherhood has become for young people a means of making a living; how, in the midst of such temptation, could it be possible to hear the voice commanding good and forbidding evil? God said: "We test you through evil and through good by way of trial. To us must you return."[36]

Thirteenth: The Brotherhood presents some of its acts to young people as great feats of courage, like combat in Palestine in 1948, or on the banks of the Suez Canal in 1951.[37] This is in order to make people believe that the Brotherhood has participated in jihad, and that its current pagan political practices are just a provisional tactic to bring about its victory. We have to counterbalance these acts, which the Brotherhood uses to glorify itself and to delude young people, with the following remarks.

A. The organization was not the only group participating in combat in Palestine and near the canal. Other groups and individuals participated as well.[38]

B. Since combat in Palestine and the Canal Zone was compatible with the state's policies, and even encouraged by the state, members of the Brotherhood in Palestine fought under Egyptian army command. The Egyptian army, in turn, was led by a Briton, Glubb Pasha, who was commander of the Jordanian forces and the Arab armies. As for the canal, the supreme guide Hassan al-Hudaybi firmly opposed the Brotherhood's participation in the fight against the British, as we showed in this book. When we say that combat was compatible with state policy, this means that the organization undertook nothing—not even jihad—without the government's agreement or in opposition to the government's will, let alone any act it might have directed against the government.[39]

C. Confirming the assertion just made is that the Jews have been in Palestine since 1948 and the Brothers never bothered them in forty years, for the government did not allow it.

D. Combat and other pious acts, and even acts in support of religion, are not in themselves a sign of piety and a mark of justice. Just as pious people can carry out these acts, so can debauched people. The word of God's messenger shows this: "God helps this religion through the debauched" (an accepted hadith). So we should not consider that the Brothers' participation in combat in Palestine alone shows the organization's rectitude, without also considering its method, practices, and other acts. In this book, we have supplied proof of how corrupt the Brotherhood's method is in the most important questions currently facing Muslims. Still, we assert that those who were killed in Palestine or in the Canal Zone so that God's word would triumph will be rewarded, if it should please God. The Brotherhood's corruption will not affect these people, because acts are judged according to intentions and each man is rewarded according to what he wished for.

E. We consider that the fight against apostate regimes in Muslim countries must come before other fights, because they are apostates and the fight against apostates must take precedence over the fight against unbelievers; this is also true because they are closer to Muslims. God said: "Fight the unbelievers who gird you about."[40] Their nature as apostates and their proximity to Muslims make them more dangerous for Muslims, as experience shows. We consider that Israel would not have taken Palestine and would not have stayed there so long had it not been for the treachery and complicity of apostate governments. Do not allow yourselves to be deluded by the Arab-Israeli wars: these were all operettas, full of betrayals. This is why we consider the fight against apostate governments to be more urgent, as God commanded: "Then let those beware who withstand the Messenger's order, lest some trial befall them, or a grievous penalty be inflicted on them."[41] The Brothers returned from Palestine only to be thrown into jail.

What does the group Al-Jihad expect of the Muslim Brothers and of all those who committed such deviations?

A. We want the Brotherhood to repent publicly of all its errors, for whatever is secret remains secret, just as whatever is public is public. God said: "Except those who repent and make amends and openly declare (the Truth): To them I turn; for I am Oft-returning, Most Merciful."[42] In order for repentance to be effective, one must make amends publicly.

B. This will be achieved by denouncing the apostasy of the tyrants who rule in spite of revealed law, and the positive laws that the crusading colonizers spread in our countries and that the apostate Muslims maintain.[43]

C. They must announce that they disavow these tyrants and their impious laws. God said: "There is for you an excellent example (to follow) in Abraham and those with him, when they said to their people: 'We are clear of you and of whatever you worship besides God . . . unless you believe in God and Him alone.'"[44]

D. The Brotherhood must announce that it rejects constitutions, positive law, democracy, and parliamentary elections. It must abandon all the practices linked to these things.

E. The Brothers must believe in the duty of jihad against these tyrants, or they must call on their members to wage it. They must consider jihad an individual duty that is incumbent upon every Muslim governed by these tyrants.

F. The Brothers must know that what we are calling for is not a secondary matter nor a manner of taste, but one of the pillars of monotheism, and one of the two pillars of the Muslim confession of faith ("There is no god but God"), which means that if one does not consider tyrants to be unbelievers, one's faith is incomplete. God said: "Whoever rejects evil and believes in God has grasped the most trustworthy hand-hold, that never breaks. And God hears and knows all things."[45]

G. The Brothers must act according to the laws we cited in the first chapter of this book, concerning the need to know before acting and the need to refer to the sharia in case of conflict, not to the actions of previous guides, as they have done to justify running as candidates for parliament, on the pretext that Banna did so.[46] These laws also concern the duty to govern according to God and his prophet, and to reply to everything that contradicts the sharia in word or opinion, whatever the rank of the person expressing these words or opinions.

H. The Brotherhood must reinstate commanding good and forbidding evil within its ranks, because this is a fortress against persistent deviation. The good of this community rests on this practice. God said: "You are the best of peoples, evolved for mankind, enjoining what is right, forbidding what is wrong, and believing in God."[47] To neglect this duty arouses God's displeasure and condemnation. God said: "Curses were pronounced on those among the Children of Israel who rejected Faith, by the tongue of David and of Jesus the son of Mary: because they disobeyed and persisted in excesses / Nor did they (usually) forbid one another the iniquities which they committed."[48]

God said: "And if they strive . . . they do so for their own souls: for God is free of all needs from all creation."[49] He also said: "O men! It is you that have need of God. But God is the One Free of all wants, worthy of all praise. / If He so pleased, He could blot you out and bring in a New Creation. / Nor is that . . . difficult for God."[50]

God therefore has no need of us, the Brotherhood, or his other creatures. Praise him: he causes his religion to triumph through whomever he wills. Thus, when the Quraysh refused to hear the message of the Prophet of God, God replaced them with the Prophet's partisans, so that they could care for this religion. God said: "These were the men to whom We gave the Book, and authority, and prophethood: if these (their descendants) reject them, Behold! We shall entrust their charge to a new people who reject them not."[51]

In this way, if someone refuses to wage the jihad that God commanded, God will replace him with someone else; but God will send punishment in this world and the next to those who refuse to fight. For God said: "O you who believe! What is the matter with you that, when you are asked to go forth in the cause of God, you cling heavily to the earth? Do you prefer the life of this world to the Hereafter? But little is the comfort of this life, as compared with the Hereafter. / Unless you go forth, He will punish you with a grievous penalty, and put others in your place; but Him you would not harm in the least. For God has power over all things. / If you help not (your leader), (it is no matter): for God did indeed help him, when the Unbelievers drove him out: he had no more than one companion; they two were in the cave, and he said to his companion, 'Have no fear, for God is with us': then God sent down His peace upon him, and strengthened him with forces which you saw not, and humbled to the depths the word of the Unbelievers. But the word of God is exalted to the heights: for God is Exalted in might, Wise."[52]

In conclusion, we ask God to strengthen us and all Muslims in Truth. We ask him to show us the Truth and cause us to prosper by serving it, to show us Error and cause us to prosper by avoiding it.

Our last word is this: May God, Lord of the worlds, be praised, and may he grant his messenger blessings and salvation.

Advice to the Community to Reject the Fatwa of Sheikh Bin Baz Authorizing Parliamentary Representation

(excerpts)

Published under the supervision of Ayman al-Zawahiri

. . . Dear brothers, we will speak today of the error committed by one of our ulema, Sheikh Abd al-Aziz Bin Baz, who authorized entering the National Council (parliament).[1] In order to trick the community and lead it astray, the Muslim Brotherhood promulgated the sheikh's fatwa (if it is indeed his), and published it in *The Banner of Islam*[2] . . .

The Legal Means of Eliminating the Corruption That Affects Our Lands

God said: "As to the thief, male or female, cut off his or her hands: a punishment by way of example, from God, for their [*sic*] crime: and God is Exalted in power." And he said: "In the Law of Equality there is (saving of) Life to you."[3] Preserving the state of the world and eliminating corruption, dear Muslim brother, depends on carrying out God's rulings, pronounced to reform his creatures.[4] "Should He not know, He that created? and He is the One that understands the finest mysteries (and) is well-acquainted (with them)."[5] When the impure unbelievers came to dominate Muslim countries at the end of the nineteenth century, the revealed law of

Islam was put aside in governing our countries, and they brought in impious positive law instead.[6] When they left, the colonizers handed the reins to a group of Muslims who had reached power through these laws, which do not give truth and error their real importance: they allow such illicit behavior, as fornication, usury, wine, and gambling but forbid that which is licit, like jihad along God's path, commanding good, and forbidding evil.[7] These positive laws protect the corruption spreading through the land and are a threat to all those who do not want to obey them and who call for reform.

Evil, my brothers, lies in the group that defends positive law, the rulers and their assistants; these rulers are unbelieving apostates whom it is necessary to fight until the unbelief and the corruption that hover over our countries are eliminated.[8]

The fact that they are apostates is proved by God's word: "And if any fail to judge by (the light of) what God has revealed, they are (no better than) wrong-doers."[9] What they are doing is the very same thing that caused the revelation: they are abandoning government according to revealed law and creating a new authority imposed on all men, just as the Jews abandoned stoning according to the Torah and created another legislation (al-Suyuti, *Mastery of Sciences Relative to the Qur'an*, 1:28, 30).[10]

As Ibn Hajar wrote, and Qadi Ismail referred to this: "Ismail the judge said, regarding the rulings of the Quran, after having reported this conflict: 'The verses' apparent meaning shows that whoever imitates them and creates a ruling that contradicts God's command and makes of it a practiced religion must receive the judgment promised in the verses, whether or not he puts it in practice'" (*Conquest*, 13, 20).[11]

I would add: "and makes of it a practiced religion" refers to a prevailing order, because religion—according to one of its meanings—designates the way one follows, whether true or false. God has called unbelievers' straying from the path a religion too, saying: "To you be your Way, and to me mine."[12]

The Essence of Democracy

Democracy is a new religion.[13] In Islam, legislation comes from God; in a democracy, this capacity is given to the people. Therefore, this is a new religion, based on making the people into gods and giving them God's rights and attributes.[14] This is tantamount to associating idols with God and falling into unbelief, since God said: "The command is for none but God. He has commanded that you worship none but Him."[15]

Sovereignty in Islam is God's alone; in a democracy, it belongs to the people. That is why Abul-Ala al-Mawdudi said of Western-style democracy that it gives godlike powers to the people (*Islam and Modern Civilization*, p. 33).[16] In democracy, the people legislate through the majority of deputies in parliament.

These deputies are men and women, Christians, communists, and secularists. Their legislation becomes a law imposed on all people, according to which taxes are levied and death sentences are passed. Take the example of the Egyptian constitution: article 3 proclaims that "sovereignty is for the people alone who will practise and protect this sovereignty and safeguard national unity in the manner specified by the Constitution," and article 86 declares: "The People's Assembly shall exercise the legislative power, approve the general policy of the State, the general plan of economic and social development, and the general budget of the State. It shall exercise control over the work of the executive authority in the manner prescribed by the constitution."[17] In this manner, they made the people equal to and similar to God. God said: "Have they partners (in godhead), who have established for them some religion without the permission of God?"[18]

According to one definition, religion is a system of life for men, whether true or false. God said: "To you be your Way, and to me mine."[19] He therefore called the infidels' unbelief a religion; in consequence, the human beings who legislate for the people in a democracy are idols, associated with God and worshipped in his place. They are the lords God mentions: "That we erect not, from among ourselves, lords and patrons other than God."[20] Is there a worse form of unbelief?

Adi Ibn Hatim, a Christian convert to Islam, said:

> I went to see the messenger of God when he was reciting the sura of Repentance, and had reached this verse: "They take their priests and their anchorites to be their lords in derogation of God."[21]
>
> I told him: "O messenger of God, we did not take them to be our lords."
>
> He replied: "You did. Do they not allow you that which is forbidden, and make it licit for you? Do they not forbid what is allowed, and make it illicit for you?"
>
> I said: "Yes."
>
> He replied: "This is the same as worshipping them" (hadith considered valid, narrated by Ahmad and al-Tirmidhi).[22]

In his exegesis of this verse, al-Alusi said: "Most exegetes say that 'lords' here is not the same as 'gods,' but it means that they obey their orders and respect their prohibitions" (quoted in *In the Shade of the Qur'an,* vol. 3).[23]

Let us briefly cite what Sayyid Qutb said about God's words, "that we erect not, from among ourselves, Lords and patrons other than God":[24]

> This entire universe lives and prospers only through the existence of one God, Who organized it: "If there were, in the heavens and the earth, other gods besides God, there would have been confusion in both."[25] The most manifest of God's characteristics relative to humanity is worship from His creatures, legislation in their existence, and balance among them. Therefore, if someone claims to possess

these things, he claims for himself the most manifest of the divine qualities and establishes himself as a god for men instead of God. There is no corruption like that which spreads when gods multiply on the earth, when men worship men, when one of God's creatures claims the right to be obeyed as such, and claims to the right to legislate, and establish values and rules as such. All of this is tantamount to claiming divinity, even if the creature does not claim, as Pharaoh did: "I am your Lord, Most High."[26]

This is tantamount to associating other gods with God; it is unbelief, corruption on earth—and what corruption! God said: "Say: 'O People of the Book![27] come to common terms as between us and you: That we worship none but God. That we associate no partners with Him; that we erect not, from among ourselves, Lords and patrons other than God.' If then they turn back, say: 'Bear witness that we (at least) are Muslims (bowing to God's will).'"[28] This is a call to worship God alone, without associating anything or anyone else, whether humans or stones.[29] It is a call to refrain from taking each other as lords in God's place, or as prophets or messengers, for all of these are God's servants.[30] God chose them only as vehicles for his message, not to share in his divinity.

"If then they turn back, say: 'Bear witness that we (at least) are Muslims.'" Here is an opposition between Muslims and those who take each other as lords instead of God; it shows clearly that Muslims are those who worship only God: "that we erect not, from among ourselves, Lords and patrons other than God." This is their main characteristic, by contrast with other confessions and communities, and their way of life sets them apart from the rest of humanity: either this characteristic is real and they are true Muslims, or it is not and, no matter what they say, they are not Muslims.

In all earthly systems, men take each other as lords instead of God . . .

This takes place in the most advanced democracies and in dictatorships alike. The first of God's characteristics is the right to be worshipped by men, the right to establish rules, doctrines, laws, regulations, values, and arbitration . . . This is a right in all earthly systems to which people aspire in one way or another: matters are decided by a group of men in all cases, and this group subjects others to its legislation, values, decisions, and conceptions. It is made up of earthly lords, whom some obey instead of obeying God, and to which some allow the claim of godliness. They worship this group instead of God, even if they do not prostrate themselves or kneel before it; prayer is a form of worship that can be directed only toward God. In this sense, for God, Islam is the religion . . . This is the message conveyed by all the prophets sent by God: God sent them to lead people from worshipping creatures to worshipping God, from the injustice of creatures to the justice of religion.[31] Whoever refuses this is not a Muslim [*or*, is not subject to God's testimony] according to God's testimony, whatever the commentators may say and whatever those who seek to lead people astray would like to have us believe . . . For God, religion is Islam (*In the Shade of the Qur'an*, 1:406–408).

As you can see, my dear Muslim brother, democracy is based on the principle of the power of creatures over other creatures, and rejects the principle of God's absolute power over all creatures; it is also based on the idea that men's desires, whatever they may be, replace God absolutely, and on the refusal to obey God's law.[32]

In Islam, when there is a disagreement or a difference of opinion, one refers to God, his Prophet, and the commands of sharia: "If you differ in anything among yourselves, refer it to God and

His Messenger, if you do believe in God and the Last Day." He also said: "Whatever it be wherein you differ, the decision thereof is with God."[33] But in a democracy, one has recourse to human beings (the people) in case of disagreement: Can one go further in unbelief? God commands that decisions be referred to him, and democracy commands that decisions be referred to the people; can one go further in unbelief?

In addition, they call their countries republics to show that legitimacy is derived from the masses and not from God's commands. Thus, in the Egyptian constitution (article 1): "The Arab Republic of Egypt is a democratic, socialist state."

In some countries, the people are even consulted and their opinion is solicited with regard to implementation of the sharia: Do the people agree or not?[34] This shows clearly that in a democracy, when disagreements arise, the people, rather than God and his Prophet, resolve them. This means that the ruler and the people give themselves the right to judge what God has revealed . . .

Even if their constitutions affirm that the state is a democracy and the state religion is Islam, this does not lessen unbelief.[35] It is as if someone were to say: "I testify that there is no god but God, and Muhammad is his Prophet, and Musaylima is his Prophet."[36] Would anyone doubt that this is heresy? Therefore, someone who claims to be a Muslim and cites a democratic or socialist thinker becomes an unbeliever and an apostate; God said: "And most of them believe not in God without associating (others as partners) with Him."[37]

Islam has no need of all these impious principles. God said: "This day have I perfected your religion for you."[38] So whoever thinks Islam is not perfect and may need the unbelievers' systems is himself an unbeliever and goes against the verse we have just cited. God said: "None but Unbelievers reject our signs."[39] Islam is elevated, and has no need of elevation; it does not accept mingling with anything else. God said: "Say: O you that reject Faith! . . . To you be your Way, and to me mine."[40] This is a total break and an utter disavowal. God said: "Verily it is We Who have revealed the Book to you in Truth: so serve God, offering Him sincere devotion. / Is it not to God that sincere devotion is due?"[41] Sincere, here, means exempt from mixing of any sort.

This is what impious democracy is like, my brother; and the members of the People's Assembly are lords who seek to take God's place; those who elect them and take them for lords in God's place make them tyrants and worship them instead of God.

And if a member of that assembly were to tell us that he serves in it not to legislate but to advise, we would reply:[42] What about the oath of unbelief you took when you entered? What about the fact that you recognize democracy as a regime? and the fact that the majority opinion applies to all? Remember, if he refused the majority opinion, he would not have been allowed to be a candidate, let alone to stay in the assembly. (See Law for the Protection of the Interior, 33, 1978, articles 1, 6, and 10; and Law of the People's Assembly, 38, 1982.[43])

The articles to which we have referred, my brother, show that, among the conditions for entering the People's Assembly and forming political parties, is that one must assert that the regime is democratic and socialist, and one must recognize the peace agreement with Israel (Camp David), among other things. Whoever refuses these conditions does not have the right to run for the People's Assembly or to form a political party and will even be accused of corruption.

You will readily understand, dear brother, that it is impossible for anyone who rejects idolatrous democracy to enter this assembly. No one enters it who has not recognized democracy and committed to it. This is how we must understand the words of the former guide of the Muslim Brotherhood, Omar Talmasani: "We conform to positive law, even if we do not respect it and call for its abolition" (Omar Talmasani, *Memories, Not Memoirs,* p. 212)[44] . . .

If you consider, my dear brother, that positive law is impious, as well you should, you must also know that democracy is more impious still, because the capacity to legislate in positive law is in the hands of legal specialists, whereas in a democracy, the capacity to legislate is entirely in the hands of the people . . .

Conditions for a Legal Opinion

You must know that legal opinions are "the knowledge of duty in reality." Therefore, someone who does not know the real circumstances to which a question relates, or does not know which legal judgment applies in a given case, can only err in his legal opinion.[45]

Ibn Qayyim said: "The mufti or the judge cannot give a legal opinion or judge according to law if he does not possess two sorts of understanding: 1) an understanding of reality and jurisprudence, and deduction of what really happened through signs, traces, and indications; 2) an understanding of duty, meaning that one must understand God's command as delivered in his book or through the mouth of his Prophet on a given subject, since one of the two applies to the other" (*I'lam al-Muwaqqi'in*, 1, 87–88).

Abdallah Ibn Batta added, in his chapter on divorce, according to Imam Ahmad, that he had said: "A man must not give a legal opinion if he does not possess five qualities: 1) intention, for if he is deprived of this, neither he nor his words will be enlightened; 2) knowledge, wisdom, dignity, and tranquillity; 3) strength, and confidence in what he knows; 4) efficiency, or else people will make a mouthful of him; 5) knowledge of men" . . .

What we think of Sheikh Bin Baz's legal opinion is that it is erroneous, because—with all due respect—he does not grasp the truth of the situation; he does not understand that elections are simply part of democracy, that the People's Assembly is nothing more than an assembly of lords who legislate for people and flout what God has revealed, and that this is idolatry. We think that the sheikh does not know that a member of the People's Assembly swears that oath when he is admitted to serve: "I swear by God to remain loyal to the good of the nation and the republican regime, to preserve the people's interests and to respect the constitution and the law."

Does Sheikh Bin Baz know that the constitution, which the member of parliament must swear to respect, stipulates that "sovereignty is for the people alone" (article 3), that "the People's Assembly shall exercise legislative power" (article 86), and that "the principal source of legislation is Islamic jurisprudence" (article 2)? It clearly says jurisprudence, and not the commands of revealed law; and it clearly says the principal source, and not the only source.[46] This means that the constitution, which a member of parliament commits to upholding, accepts un-Islamic sources of legislation. This in turn means that the constitution encourages the creation of other gods, who legislate with God: this stands in clear contradiction to the profession of faith, according to which there is no god but God.

Does Sheikh Bin Baz know that the laws that members of parliament swear to respect fornication between consenting adults, usury, consumption of alcohol, gambling, and apostasy, which in the name of freedom of belief it does not punish (article 46)? We think Sheikh Bin Baz does not know these things.

This is why his legal opinion is not based on precise knowledge of reality. It is erroneous, and this constitutes the error of a religious scholar.

Harmful Consequences of a Religious Scholar's Error

Omar Ibn al-Khattab said: "Three things can harm Islam: a religious scholar's error; a hypocrite's contestation of the Quran; and a lying imam's ruling" (narrated by Darimi, whose chain of transmitters is accurate, according to al-Albani, *Mishkat al-Masabih*, 1, 89)[47] . . .

Advice to Sheikh Bin Baz

God's messenger said: "Religion is sincere counsel" (narrated by Muslim).[48] We would therefore advise the sheikh to investigate the situation to which his legal opinion relates.

We also advise him to promulgate another fatwa, abrogating his previous one, because God's messenger said: "If someone promulgates a legal opinion without knowledge, the sin falls upon the person who requested it" (narrated by Abu Dawud, and considered authentic by al-Albani, *Mishkat al-Masabih*, 1, 81). Omar Ibn al-Khattab told Abu Musa al-Ash'ari in *The Book of Judgment*:[49] "If you have passed judgment today and thought about your ruling while inspired, nothing prevents you from revising it to the better, for the truth is valid for all eternity, and to return to it is better than to persist in error" (cited in Ibn Qayyim, *I'lam al-Muwaqqi'in*, 1, 86). What use was it if the sheikh spent his life preaching monotheism, rejecting idolatry, and dismissing pretexts for paganism, if he is now authorizing participation in idolatrous democracy, whether through participation in the People's Assembly or through elections?

This legal opinion emitted by Sheikh Bin Baz leads to the suspension of jihad against tyrants who rule without bothering with revealed law. By making it licit to follow the democratic path, the sheikh opened the door for Muslims to forsake this jihad, which is an individual duty; he is even combating it. That is why his legal opinion is deplorable from a religious perspective, now and in the future. We therefore request that God will inspire him to revise his legal opinion, and we ask God to give the sheikh and all of us a favorable conclusion. God's messenger said: "The (results of) deeds done depend upon the last actions" (accepted hadith) . . .

KNIGHTS UNDER
THE PROPHET'S BANNER

(EXCERPTS)

It is now time to explore the future of the jihad movement in Egypt in particular and the world in general.[1]

Emerging Phenomena

Any neutral observer can discern a number of phenomena in our Muslim world and in Egypt.

The Universality of Our Battle

The Western forces that are hostile to Islam have clearly identified their enemy. They refer to it as Islamic fundamentalism. They are joined in this by their old enemy, Russia. They have adopted a number of tools to fight Islam, including the United Nations; the servile rulers of the Muslim peoples; multinational corporations; international communications and data exchange systems; international news agencies and satellite media channels; international relief agencies and nongovernmental organizations, which are used as a cover for espionage, conspiracies, proselytizing, and arms smuggling.[2]

In the face of this alliance, a fundamentalist coalition is taking shape.[3] It is made up of the jihad movements in the various lands of Islam as well as the two countries that have been liberated in the name of jihad (Afghanistan and Chechnya).[4] If this coalition is still in its early stages, it is growing at a rapid pace. There is no longer any need to prove its scope: its actions speak for themselves, while the fear it has engendered allows it to dominate thinking in the West, cause it to worry, and keep it in a state of high alert.

It is a growing force that is rallying under the banner of jihad, against the scope of the new world order. This force is free of servitude to the dominant Western imperialism and promises destruction and ruin to the new crusades against the lands of Islam. This force thirsts for revenge against the heads of the global gang of infidels, the United States, Russia, and Israel. This force is anxious to seek retribution for the blood of martyrs, the grief of mothers, the deprivation of orphans, the suffering of detainees, and the wounds of tortured people throughout the lands of Islam, from Eastern Turkistan to Andalusia.[5]

Today we are witnessing a new phenomenon that continues to gain ground: young Muslim fighters who have abandoned family and country, neglected wealth, left their studies and jobs to join the battlefields of jihad.[6] With the emergence of this new kind of Islamists, who have been long awaited, a new awareness is developing among the sons of Islam, who are eager to ensure their victory: namely, that no solution is possible without jihad.

The spread of this awareness has been assisted by the failure of all other methods that sought to evade the burden of jihad. The Algerian experience has provided a harsh lesson in this regard. It proved to Muslims that the West is not only unbelieving but also hypocritical and lying. The principles it brags about are exclusive to it: the Muslim peoples can enjoy these principles only in the way that a slave gathers the crumbs left over after his master's meal.

The Islamic Salvation Front (FIS) in Algeria overlooked the tenets of the creed, the facts of history and politics, the balance of power, and the laws of control. It wanted to use the ballot boxes in a bid to reach the presidential palaces and ministries, but at the gates tanks were waiting, loaded with French ammunition, their barrels pointing at those who had forgotten the rules of the battle between justice and falsehood.[7]

The shots fired by officers of the "French party" brought them crashing down from their soaring illusions to the hard earth of reality.[8] The Islamic Salvation Front men thought that the gates of power had been opened to them, but they were astonished to see themselves pushed through the gates of detention camps and prisons and into the cells of the new world order.

What led us to the conclusion that "jihad is the only solution" was the brutality and injustice of the new Jewish crusade, which treats the Muslim community with utter contempt. As a result, the Muslims in general and the Arabs in particular have lost everything and are threatened by all powerful parties. We have become like orphans at a banquet for the villains.[9]

Some may say I am contradicting myself: I am talking about a widespread jihad awakening when just now I said despair was spreading among leaders of the movement. The answer is simple. All movements go through a cycle of erosion and renewal, but it is the ultimate result that will lead the jihad movement to disappear or to survive.

Necessary Duties

The Islamic movement in general, and the jihad movements in particular, must train themselves and their members to persevere, have patience, remain steadfast, and adhere to firm principles. The leadership must set an example for the members to follow. This is the key to victory. "O you who believe. Endure, outdo all others in endurance, be ready, and observe your duty to God, in order that you may succeed."[10] If signs of slackening and retreat start to show among the leadership, the movement must find ways to replace it and not permit it to deviate from jihad.

Loyalty to the leadership and acknowledgment of its primacy and merit are confirmed duties and fundamental values. But if loyalty to the leadership reaches the point of sanctification, and if the acknowledgment of its primacy and merit leads to claims that it is infallible, the movement will suffer from methodological blindness. Any leadership flaw could lead to a historic catastrophe, not only for the movement but perhaps also for the community as a whole.[11]

Hence the importance of the issue of leadership in Islamic action in general and jihad in particular, and the community's need for an educated, militant, and rational leadership that can guide it toward its goal through storms and hurricanes, with awareness and wisdom, without losing its way, striking out blindly, or reversing its course.

Mobilizing the Fundamentalist Movement

Mobilizing the community to participate in the struggle, and taking good care not to engage in an elitist struggle against authority:[12] the jihad movement must come closer to the masses, defend their honor, fend off injustice, guide them, and lead them to victory. It must sacrifice itself first and convey its message in a way that makes the truth accessible to all those who seek it. It must simplify access to the origin and facts of religion and free them of complex terminology and intricate expression.

The jihad movement must dedicate itself to working with the masses, preaching in the community, providing services to the Muslim people, and sharing their concerns through all available avenues for charity and educational work.[13] We must not leave a single area unoccupied. We must win the people's confidence, respect, and affection. The people will not love us unless they feel that we love them, care about them, and are ready to defend them. In short, the jihad movement must enter the battle in midst of the community and lead it to the battlefield. It must guard against isolating itself from its community in an elitist battle against the authorities.

We cannot blame the community for not responding or not doing enough without blaming ourselves for the times when we failed to seize the opportunity to communicate clearly or to show compassion and sacrifice.

The jihad movement must enable the Muslim community to

participate with it in the jihad, and believers will participate only if the mujahedeen's slogans are comprehensible.

The one slogan that the community has understood well, and to which it has responded for the past fifty years, is the call to jihad against Israel. In addition, for a decade the community has been galvanized against the U.S. presence and has responded favorably to calls to jihad against the Americans.[14] A single look at the history of the mujahedeen in Afghanistan, Palestine, and Chechnya will show that the jihad movement took a central leadership position in the community when it adopted the slogan of liberating the nation from its external enemies and when it portrayed national liberation as a battle of Islam against unbelief and unbelievers.[15]

Strangely, secularists, who caused so much harm to the community, particularly during the Arab-Israeli conflict, and who began the long march of treachery by recognizing Israel with the armistice agreement of 1949, as we explained earlier, are the ones who talk the most about the Palestinian cause.[16] Stranger still, however, is the fact that the Muslims who have sacrificed the most for Jerusalem, whose creed and conviction prevent them from abandoning any part of Palestine or recognizing Israel, as we explained earlier, and who are the most capable of leading the jihad against Israel, are the least active in championing the Palestinian cause and causing its slogans to be heard among the masses.[17]

The opportunity for the jihad movement to lead the community in jihad to liberate Palestine is greater than ever, for all the secular factions that bellowed so loudly about Palestine, competing with the Islamic movement to lead the community in this cause, are now exposed before the community, having recognized Israel's existence, undertaken negotiations, and complied with international resolutions to liberate what is left of Palestine, or what Israel is willing to relinquish.[18] The only difference lies in how many crumbs Israel will leave the Muslims and the Arabs.

The undeniable truth is that Palestine is not only the cause that has been igniting the feelings of Muslims from Morocco to Indonesia for the past fifty years, but also a rallying point for all the Arabs, believers or unbelievers, good or bad.[19]

Small Groups Can Spread Fear among the Americans

Through this jihad the positions of the rulers and their supporters among the ulema, intellectuals, judges, and security agencies will be exposed. The Islamic movement will thus prove these groups' betrayal to the Muslim masses and demonstrate that the reason for their betrayal is their idolatry, for they have allied themselves with the enemies of God; they fought the mujahedeen because of their Islam and jihad, in the service of the Jewish and Christian enemies of the nation. They have sinned against monotheism by supporting idol worshippers against Muslims, precisely because of their Islamic faith.

It is always possible to track an American or a Jew, to kill him with a bullet or a knife, a simple explosive device, or a blow with an iron rod.[20] Setting fire to their property with a Molotov cocktail is not difficult. With the means available, small groups can spread terror among Americans and Jews.

The Islamic movement in general and the jihad movement in particular must lead the battle to raise the community's awareness by doing the following:

- exposing the rulers who are fighting Islam;
- emphasizing the importance in the Muslim faith of Muslims' remaining loyal to Muslims, and not to unbelievers;
- making every Muslim responsible for defending Islam, its sanctuaries, nation, and homeland;
- cautioning against palace ulema and reminding the community that the ulema of jihad and the imams of sacrifice have a right to be defended and supported;[21]
- exposing the extent of aggression against our religion and its holy places, and the plundering of our wealth;
- finally, by pursuing the goal of establishing an Islamic state in the heart of the Muslim world: the jihad movement must

follow a plan aimed at establishing an Islamic state it can defend on a territory in the Muslim world; from there, it will lead the struggle to restore the rightly guided caliphate after the Prophet's model.[22]

Toward a Fundamentalist Base in the Heart of the Muslim World

Just as armies achieve victory only when the infantry occupies territory, the Islamic movement of jihad will not triumph against the world coalition unless it possesses an Islamic base in the heart of the Muslim world. All the means and plans that we have reviewed for mobilizing the nation will be for naught, unless they lead to the establishment of a caliphate in the Muslim world.[23]

Nur al-Din Ibn Zanki, and Salah al-Din al-Ayyubi [Saladin] after him, fought dozens of battles before Nur al-Din managed to rid Damascus of the hypocrites and unify Syria under his command.[24] He sent Salah al-Din to Egypt, where he waged one battle after another until he brought Egypt under his control. When Egypt and Syria were unified after the death of Nur al-Din, the mujahid Sultan Salah al-Din managed to win the Battle of Hattin and free Jerusalem. Only then did the wheel of history turn against the Crusaders.[25]

If successful operations against the enemies of Islam and the severe damage inflicted on them do not form part of a plan aiming to establish an Islamic state at the heart of the Muslim world, they will be, no matter what their magnitude, nothing more than harassment, which can be contained and overcome after some time and despite a few losses.

Clearly, the establishment of an Islamic state at the heart of the Muslim world is not an easy goal, but the hope of the Muslim community lies in the restoration of the caliphate.

If the goal of the jihad movement in the Islamic world in general and Egypt in particular is to bring about real change by establishing an Islamic state, it must neither precipitate confrontation nor delay victory.

The militant movement must prepare its plans and pool its resources, then gather its supporters in order to fight the battle at the time and in the place it chooses.

At this point, however, an extremely important and serious question arises: What if the members of the movement are identified or its plans are revealed? What if its members are jailed, its existence threatened, and a campaign of arrests and harassment targets its members, funds, resources, and leaders?[26]

Could it hide from the storm and withdraw from the field with the fewest possible losses? Or should we consider that patience would be vain and lead to defeat and that one must take the field at any cost?

Perhaps the answer lies in a middle ground between these two scenarios, meaning that the movement will have to usher some of its leaders and members to safety and leave others to face jail and oppression.[27]

In my opinion, the answer is that the movement must remove whatever it can to a place of safety, without hesitating, showing reluctance, or succumbing to illusions. The greatest risk for someone under siege would be to escape. Nothing is harder than to leave one's family, job, position, and normal life for the unknown, uncertainties, and a life of instability.

But as soon as the doors of the cell close behind the prisoner, he wishes that he had spent his entire life wandering without shelter, rather than face the humiliation of captivity.

Yet if the entire movement, or part of it, is encircled and its collapse is a matter of days or hours, the movement, or at least one of its branches, must set off a confrontation with the regime, so that none of its members is captured or killed in vain.

How must this confrontation take place?

Here, we must repeat what we have already explained about the composition of the new anti-Muslim world order and its relationship with the regimes in our countries. As we emphasized earlier, we must mobilize the community for the battle of Islam against unbelief. We warned earlier against the risk of seeing the Muslim vanguard killed in silence in a battle waged by this elite against the authorities.

Striking at the Americans and the Jews

If the forces of injustice drag us into a battle at a time we have not chosen, we must respond in an arena of our choosing: we must strike at the Americans and the Jews in our countries. This has three advantages:

- first, we deal a blow to the master, which is protecting its lackey;
- second, we have the community on our side, since we are aiming at a target that it favors, and that sympathizes with those who attack the community;
- third, we show the Muslim people that when this regime oppresses us, it does so to defend its American and Jewish masters. We thereby force it to uncover its ugly face, the face of the hired policeman who is faithfully serving the occupiers and the enemies of the Muslim nation.[28]

If our goal is comprehensive change and if our path, as the Quran and our history teach us, is a long road of jihad and sacrifice, we must not lose hope in the face of repeated strikes and recurring catastrophes. We must never lay down our arms, regardless of the casualties or sacrifices.

We must remember that countries do not fall all of a sudden. They must be fought to the ground.

Taking the Battle to the Enemy

Our Islamic movement and its jihadi vanguard, as well as the entire community, must bring the major criminals—the United States, Russia, and Israel—into the battle, rather than allowing them to guide the battle between the jihadist movement and our governments from afar and in safety.[29] They must pay the price—and dearly.

The masters of Washington and Tel Aviv use regimes to protect their interests and to fight the Muslims on their behalf. If shrapnel from the battle reaches their homes and wounds them, however, they will fight with their agents. In that case, they will face a dilemma, in which both terms are equally bitter: either wage the battle against Muslims directly, which will turn the struggle into clear-cut jihad against the unbelievers, or reconsider their plans, after acknowledging the failure of the violent and unjust confrontation against the Muslims.[30]

This is why we must move the battle to the enemy's territory, to burn the hands of those who have set fire to our countries.[31]

The struggle for the establishment of the Muslim state cannot be waged as a regional struggle. It is clear from the foregoing that the Judeo-crusader alliance, led by the United States, will not allow any Muslim force to attain power in any Muslim country. If such a thing ever occurs, it will mobilize all its power to strike it down and remove it from power. It will open a global battlefront and punish all those who support the Muslim power, if not declare war against them itself. Therefore, given this new reality, we must prepare ourselves for a battle that is not confined to a single region but that extends to apostates at home and the Judeo-crusaders abroad.

The struggle against the external enemy cannot be postponed: it is clear from the foregoing that the Judeo-crusading alliance will not allow us a moment's respite, as long as we have not defeated the domestic enemy, then declared war against it. The Americans, the Jews, and their allies are now present with their forces, as we have demonstrated.[32]

Unity against the common enemy: the jihad movement must realize that half the road to victory is attained through union, unity, rising above minor matters, self-sacrifice, and putting the interests of Islam above personal conflicts.[33]

The importance of unity for the jihad movement is clearer now than ever before. It must build a union as soon as possible if it sincerely intends to win.

It is necessary to rally around the struggling countries and support them. The first of all duties is that of backing and supporting Afghanistan and Chechnya and defending them with words, deeds, and advice, for they are the true assets of Islam at this time.[34] As we have seen, the Judeo-Christian crusade was formed to crush them. But we must not be content with safeguarding them. We must do everything in our power to move the fight to the heart of the Islamic world, which represents the true battlefield for the defense of Islam.[35]

Besides, these two fortresses may not be of much use to us, owing to many circumstances, especially the tremendous pressure to which they are being subjected and their apparent weakness. That is why we must solve this problem ourselves, rather than expose them to pressure and strikes. This may be one of the great problems of the jihad movement, but as difficult as it may be, God willing, it will be solved. "And whosoever keeps his duty to God, God will appoint a way out for him."[36]

The Choice of Targets and the Importance of Martyrdom Operations
Changing the method of provocation and attack: the Islamic jihad movement must escalate its strikes and means of resisting its enemies, to keep up with the extraordinary increase in their number, the quality of their weapons, their destructive capacity, and their disregard for all taboos, even for the rules of engagement. In this regard, we must

1. be sure to inflict maximum casualties on the enemy, kill the greatest number of people, for this is the language understood by the West, no matter how much time and effort such operations take;
2. concentrate on martyrdom operations as the most suc-

cessful way of inflicting damage on the opponent and the least costly to the mujahedeen in terms of casualties;[37]

3. choose our targets and weapons to reach the vulnerable spots of the enemy and thus dissuade it from its brutal ways, arrogance, and violations of every sacred custom and restore it to its normal place;

4. reemphasize that at this stage focusing on the domestic enemy alone would be pointless.

Our battle is that of every Muslim: we must reiterate that this battle, which we must wage to defend our faith, community, sanctuaries, honor, values, wealth, and resources, is that of every Muslim, young or old. It is a battle that touches every one of us in our work, our families, our children, and our dignity.

In order for the masses to move, they need the following:

1. a leadership that they can trust, follow, and understand;
2. a clear enemy to strike at;
3. for the shackles of fear and the bonds of powerlessness to be broken.

These conditions show the disastrous consequences of the so-called initiative to end violence and similar calls aimed at discrediting the leadership and dragging the community back into weakness and fear.

To demonstrate this point, let us ask ourselves: What will we tell future generations about our achievements?

Will we tell them that we took up arms against our enemies then dropped them and asked them to accept our surrender?

From the perspective of jihad, what value will future generations gain?

We must communicate our message to the masses and break the media embargo imposed on the jihad movement.[38] This is an independent battle that we must wage side by side with the military battle.

Liberating the Muslim community, attacking the enemies of Islam, and waging a jihad against them require a Muslim authority, established on Muslim territory, that raises the banner of jihad and rallies Muslims around it. If we do not achieve this goal, our actions will be nothing more than small-scale harassment and will not bear fruit—the restoration of the caliphate and the departure of the invaders from the land of Islam.

This goal must remain the basic objective of the Islamic movement, regardless of the time needed to attain it and the sacrifices we must make.

Loyalty and Separation

CHANGING AN ARTICLE OF FAITH AND
LOSING SIGHT OF REALITY

(EXCERPTS)

In the name of God, Most Gracious, Most Merciful.[1]

The last decades of the community's history have been a time of fierce conflict pitting the forces of unbelief, injustice, and arrogance against the *umma* and its jihad vanguard. The conflict reached its peak with the two blessed raids on New York and Washington, then Bush's declaration of his new crusade against Islam, which he later called the war on terror.[2]

In light of the events of this war, two things become apparent: First, the urgent need to understand the importance of loyalty and separation, for this fundamental tenet of Islamic doctrine has been neglected and forgotten; and second, the extent of the treachery of the enemies of Islam, and of their servants and lackeys, toward the community in aggregate when they seek to undermine this solid foundation, by causing enemies to appear as protectors and good people to appear bad.

These enemies are leading—along with their military crusade—an operation to confuse minds and pervert dogma.[3] They are trying to put the fragments of the regimes in our countries back together, despite their corruption, depravity, and servility toward the international forces of Judeo-crusader brutality.

This crusade, which seeks to erase the lines between Truth and

Falsehood, and to mix enemies and allies, also aims—in its feverish bid to counter the growth of the Islamic jihadi wave—to conceal the reality of the recklessness, dependence, submission to others than God, government by laws other than his, not to mention the perversion of the call to Truth, jihad, and honor that the vanguard of the community, along with its partisans and the masses around them, has raised.

The stronger that the call to jihad, truth, and honor grows, the stronger also grows the call to falsehood, passivity, and disgrace: indeed, the advocates of falsehood were not even ashamed to adopt the ideas of the extremist *murji'a* of old, although they clamor that they are defending the religious legacy of the pious ancestors and the virtuous first centuries of Islam.[4] They did not hesitate to borrow the ideas of corrupt secularists, although they claim to guard and defend revealed law. In their minds, there is no harm in being a civil servant, a soldier, a security agent, a journalist, a judge, and a partisan of secularism, preaching recognition of Israel and submission to its superior force, while also claiming to be a pious Muslim who fears God, fasts, prays, goes on pilgrimage, and donates legal alms.[5]

Thus, we saw the noblest of dynasties placing itself in the service of American interests while claiming to defend monotheism;[6] we saw impious imams imposing secular constitutions, judging on the basis of positive law, and rushing to normalize relations with Israel, while supervising Quran memorization competitions among students at universities where women are not allowed to wear the veil; we saw the most brutal oppressors of the Muslims undertaking the lesser and greater pilgrimages; we saw Afghan brigands in the pay of the Americans, who sent them out in front of the U.S. troops to confront the mujahedeen, seeing good omens in the martyrs' uniforms and the dust that covers their tombs.[7] As the Sheikh al-Islam, Ibn Taymiyya, said of the Mongols: "Until people realize how important this region was to them and see them pillaging its wealth, honoring a man and then stripping him of his clothes, insulting his women, subjecting him to various torments such as only the most brutal and depraved can inflict, for he who claims to interpret religion punishes only those who rebel against it, but they honor the religion of those they punish, then assert he is more observant than they: What interpretations can such people make?" (*The Major Fatwas*, question 813, 4:332ff.).[8]

This is not surprising in the least: it is characteristic of falsehood, which roils and confounds everything in its wake, so that depravity may linger, floating above us like this occupation that has sullied our nation's pure soil, especially in the most sacred lands: the two sanctuaries, and Jerusalem.

Any rational observer will realize that this is the result of their proselytism: the persistence of a corrupt and corrupting government that does not follow revealed law, the nation's subjection to the forces of the new Judeo-Christian crusade—these are their aims, every time they speak or write a single word.

The Quran unmasked this group's predecessors, laid bare their true nature, showed that they were spreading sedition in the Muslim ranks, that they were the most willing to accept it, and that they rushed to join the unbelievers in order to preserve their personal interests and their material benefits. "If they had intended to come out, they would certainly have made some preparation therefor; but God was averse to their being sent forth; so He made them lag behind, and they were told, 'Sit among those who sit (inactive).' / If they had come out with you, they would not have added to your (strength) but only (made for) disorder, hurrying to and fro in your midst and sowing sedition among you, and there would have been some among you who would have listened to them."[9] He also said: "And behold! The Hypocrites and those in whose hearts is a disease (even) say: '(God) and His Messenger promised us nothing but delusion!' / Behold! A party among them said: 'You men of Yathrib! you cannot stand (the attack)! therefore go back!' And a band of them ask for leave of the Prophet, saying, 'Truly our houses are bare and exposed,' though they were not exposed; they intended nothing but to run away."[10]

This is why we consider that the gravest sedition in our time that threatens monotheism and the faith is to abandon the alliance of Muslims and hostility toward the unbelievers.[11] We wrote these pages as a warning to our blessed community, in its uprising and its victorious jihad, if it please God, against the Judeo-American crusade being waged against the Muslim nation.

We have divided our thesis into two chapters and a conclusion. The first chapter is devoted to the basis of loyalty and separation in Islam; the second examines examples of deviation from this doctrine; and the conclusion presents the main ideas we would like to emphasize.

Whatever is good in this book is due to God; the rest is our responsibility, and Satan's. "My success (in my task) can only come from God. In Him I trust, and unto Him I look."[12] Our last prayer is in praise of God, Lord of the worlds; we ask him to grant peace and blessings to Muhammad, his family, and his companions.

AYMAN AL-ZAWAHIRI, Shawwal 1423 / December 2002

The Basis of Loyalty and Separation in Islam

On the Prohibition against Collaborating with Unbelievers

God said: "Let not the believers take for friends or helpers Unbelievers rather than believers: if any do that, in nothing will there be help from God, except by way of precaution, that you may Guard yourselves from them. But God cautions you (To remember) Himself; for the final goal is to God."[13] Al-Tabari said:[14] "This means: O believers, do not take unbelievers as helpers or assistants, do not help them in their religion, do not help them against Muslims, do not show them what is intimate; whoever does that has nothing to do with God, meaning that he will have disavowed God and God will have disavowed him, because of his apostasy and his return to paganism" (*Commentary*, 3:227).

God said: "To the Hypocrites give the glad tidings that there is for them (but) a grievous penalty; / Yes, to those who take for friends unbelievers rather than believers: is it honour they seek among them? No, all honour is with God."

God said: "O you who believe! Take not for friends unbelievers rather than believers."[15] Al-Tabari noted: "He asked them (may he be exalted): 'Do you wish to offer God an open proof against yourselves?'[16] Do not ally with the infidels and do not help them instead of helping the people of your community and your religion, because that would make you similar to the hypocrites to whom hellfire is promised" (*Commentary*, 5:337).

God said:

> O you who believe! take not the Jews and the Christians for your friends and protectors: They are but friends and protectors to each other. And he among you that turns to them (for friendship) is of them. Verily God guides not a people unjust. / Those in whose hearts is a disease—you see how eagerly they run about amongst them, saying: "We do fear lest a change of fortune bring us disaster." Ah! perhaps God will give (you) victory, or a decision according to His will. Then will they repent of the thoughts which they secretly harboured in their hearts. / And those who believe will say: "Are these the men who swore their strongest oaths by God, that they were with you?" All that they do will be in vain, and they will fall into (nothing but) ruin. / O you who believe! if any from among you turn back from his Faith, soon will God produce a people whom He will love as they will love Him, lowly with the believers, mighty against the rejecters, fighting in the way of God, and never afraid of the reproaches of such as find fault. That is the grace of God, which He will bestow on whom He pleases. And God encompasses all, and He knows all things. / Your (real) friends are (no less than) God, His Messenger, and the (fellowship of) believers, those who establish regular prayers and regular charity, and they bow down humbly

(in worship). / As to those who turn (for friendship) to God, His Messenger, and the (fellowship of) believers, it is the fellowship of God that must certainly triumph. / O you who believe! take not for friends and protectors those who take your religion for a mockery or sport, whether among those who received the Scripture before you, or among those who reject Faith; but fear God, if you have faith. / When you proclaim your call to prayer they take it (but) as mockery and sport; that is because they are a people without understanding."[17]

Al-Tabari said: "His words (may he be exalted), 'And he among you that turns to them (for friendship) is of them,' mean that whoever allies with Jews and Christians rather than with Muslims is like the Jews and Christians, and *whoever allies with them and supports them against the believers is of their religion and belongs to their community.* Whoever makes an alliance becomes like the ally and shares his religion, like the one with whom he is satisfied; if he is satisfied with him and his religion, the same judgment applies to both of them" (*Fath al-Bari* [Commentary], 6:277).[18]

In his commentary on the hadith of Omar, Ibn Hajar al-Asqalani said: "When God punishes people, he punishes also those who are with them, and then they are brought back to life according to their works (narrated by al-Bukhari). One deduces the legitimacy of shunning unbelievers and iniquitous people, since to reside with them jeopardizes one's soul; and this is so if one does not help them or approve of their actions, but if one helps them or shows satisfaction with them, then one is like them" (*The Conquest,* 31:61).[19]

This is why God imposed on them an eternal sojourn in hell, saying: "You see many of them turning in friendship to the Unbelievers. Evil indeed are (the works) which their souls have sent forward before them (with the result), that God's wrath is on them, and in torment will they abide. / If only they had believed in God, in the Messenger, and in what has been revealed to him, never would they have taken them for friends and protectors, but most of them are rebellious wrong-doers."[20]

God said: "O you who believe! take not for protectors your fathers and your brothers if they love infidelity above Faith: if any of you do so, they do wrong. / Say: If it be that your fathers, your sons, your brothers, your mates, or your kindred; the wealth that you have gained; the commerce in which you fear a decline: or the dwellings in which you delight—are dearer to you than God, or His Messenger, or the striving in His cause; then wait until God brings about His decision: and God guides not the rebellious."[21] Ibn Kathir said: "Bayhaqi narrated an account by Abdallah Ibn Shawdhab, saying:[22] 'On the day of the Battle of Badr, Abu Ubayda Ibn al-Jarrah's father began to praise the idols to him, and so Abu Ubayda moved away; but when the father insisted, his son took aim and killed him. Then God revealed this verse.'"

The Prophet is reported to have said: "By him who holds my soul in his hand, none of you believe if you do not love me more than your father, your children, and all others" (Ibn Kathir, *Commentary*, 2:343–344) . . .

On the Prohibition against Befriending Them

God said: "O you who believe! Take not into your intimacy those outside your ranks."[23]

In this verse, God prohibited believers from taking unbelievers, Jews, and heretics as advisers or from trusting them with money. It is said that you must not speak to anyone whose creed or religion is different from yours. The poet said:

> Ask not about someone but about his kin,
> For anyone follows the example of those close to him.[24]

In Abu Dawud's *Sunan*, there is a hadith of the Prophet narrated by Abu Hurayra: "Men are of their friends' religion, so beware of those you would take as friends." Ibn Masud is said to have warned: "Examine men according to what their brothers do."[25]

. . .

On the Prohibition against Placing Unbelievers in
Important Positions

Ibn Taymiyya said:

> Imam Ahmad narrated, according to an accurate chain of transmitters, following Abu Musa al-Ash'ari: "I told Omar that I had a Christian secretary." "What is wrong with you?" he replied, "God damn you. Did you not hear God's words: 'O you who believe! take not the Jews and the Christians for your friends and protectors: They are but friends and protectors to each other. And he among you that turns to them (for friendship) is of them. Verily God guides not a people unjust. / Those in whose hearts is a disease—you see how eagerly they run about amongst them, saying: "We do fear lest a change of fortune bring us disaster." Ah! perhaps God will give (you) victory, or a decision according to His will. Then will they repent of the thoughts which they secretly harboured in their hearts.' Why did you not take a Muslim?" "Commander of the faithful," I replied, "I keep what he writes, and he keeps his religion." "Do not do them this honor, for God dishonored them; do not exalt them, for God debased them; do not draw close to them, for God distanced them." (*Iqtida al-Sirat al-Mustaqim* [Following the Straight Path], 1:50).[26]

Al-Qurtubi narrates:

> According to Omar: "Do not take people of the book as governors, for they are corrupt. Seek assistance in your af-

fairs from those of your subjects who fear God." Some told Omar: "There is a Christian from Hira here, who writes better than anyone and whose calligraphy is the most beautiful.[27] Would you not take him as your secretary?" He replied: "My only confidants are believers." Therefore, one must not take protected peoples as one's secretaries, not for other tasks related to commerce, and one must not trust them.[28] Times have changed, for today people of the book are employed as secretaries and intimates; this is how they rule over stupid governors and ignorant emirs (al-Qurtubi, *Commentary*, 4:179).

Ibn Taymiyya said: "Do not rely on protected peoples to head provinces, nor as secretaries, because corruption will be the result."

Ahmad [Ibn Hanbal] was asked about Abu Talib's account: "And to collect the land tax?"[29] He replied: "One must not rely on them for anything." "If someone gives them an office [*Diwan*] in the Muslim administration, does he break his oath?" "Whoever has harmed Muslims or is corrupt must not be employed. In any case, anyone else is better, because Abu Bakr vowed never to employ an apostate, even if he were to return to Islam, for fear that he might corrupt their religion" ("Scientific Selections," *Great Fatwas*, chapter on jihad, 4:607ff).[30]

On the Prohibition against Respecting the Unbelievers'
Laws, Accepting and Approving of the Errors Committed by
Unbelievers and Apostates, and Praising Them

The Sheikh al-Islam said:[31]

Chapter on alliance and hostility. The believers belong to the fellowship of God, and are allied among themselves; the unbelievers are the enemies of God and of the believers. God commanded Muslims to ally with one another, and explained that this was an *article of faith*. He forbade alliance with the unbelievers and explained that this was a *betrayal of the believers.* He showed that those who pay allegiance to the unbelievers are hypocrites.

And he said: "Those who turn back as apostates after Guidance was clearly shown to them, the Evil One has instigated them and busied them up with false hopes. / This, because they said to those who hate what God has revealed, 'We will obey you in part of (this) matter'; but God knows their (inner) secrets."[32] He explained that paying allegiance to the unbelievers was the cause of their apostasy.

This is why, in [the sura entitled] "The Table Spread," he recalled the imams of the apostates immediately after having forbidden any alliance with the unbelievers, saying (may he be exalted): "And he amongst you that turns to them (for friendship) is of them,"[33] and saying: "O Messenger, let not those grieve you, who race each other into unbelief: (whether it be) among those who say 'We believe' with their lips but whose hearts have no faith; or it be among the Jews, men who will listen to any lie, will listen even to others who have never so much as come to you. They change the words from their (right) times and places: they say, "If you are given this, take it, but if not, beware!" If anyone's trial is intended by God, you have no authority in the least for him against God. For such—it is not God's will to purify their hearts. For them there is disgrace in this world, and in the Hereafter a heavy punishment."[34] He spoke of the hypocrites and the conciliatory unbelievers, and He explained that they obey others, who did not come to the Prophet; this refers to the hypocrites and the conciliatory unbelievers obeying declared unbelievers, who, for their part, are not conciliatory.

As there are those among the believers who listen to the hypocrites—as he said: "There would have been some among you who would have listened to them"—some consider that this means spying.[35] But in fact it means that some obey and follow them, as in the expression "God heeds those who praise him," which means that God answers those who honor him. When someone is said to heed or listen to someone else, that means he obeys and follows that person.

Therefore, those in the community who ally with the unbelievers, whether with idol worshippers or people of the book in any way at all—for example, by repeating their lies or imitating their words or deeds—will be blamed and punished in the appropriate way.

God (may he be exalted!) loves to separate Good from Evil, Truth from Falsehood, and he knows that they are hypocrites, or show hypocrisy, even if they are Muslims; for the fact of being Muslim in appearance does not prevent one from being a hypocrite in his heart.

All the hypocrites, indeed, are Muslims in appearance, and the Quran has described them precisely at the time of the Messenger of God and at the time of revelation, when the signs of prophecy were becoming clear and the light of his message was shining forth; they can be only more numerous at a more distant time, especially since the cause of hypocrisy is unbelief, in other words opposition to that which the prophets brought (*Compendium of Fatwas*, 28:190–202).

On the Prohibition against Helping Them against the Muslims

God said:

O you who believe! take not the Jews and the Christians for your friends and protectors: They are but friends and protectors to each other. And he among you that turns to them (for friendship) is of them. Verily God guides not a people unjust. / Those in whose hearts is a disease—you see how eagerly they run about amongst them, saying: "We do fear lest a change of fortune bring us disaster." Ah! perhaps God will give (you) victory, or a decision according to His will. Then will they repent of the thoughts which they secretly harboured in their hearts. / And those who believe will say: "Are these the men who swore their strongest oaths by God, that they were with you?" All that they do will be in vain, and they will fall into (nothing but) ruin.[36]

Of the circumstances in which this verse was revealed, al-Tabari said: "What seems most correct, in our opinion, is that God (may his name be exalted) forbade all believers to take Jews and Christians as assistants and allies instead of taking those who believe in God and his prophet, and he informs us that whoever takes them as *assistants, allies, or friends instead of God, his Prophet, and the believers, is one of them, among the opponents of God, his Prophet, and the believers;* and that God and his Prophet are innocent of this" (*Commentary*, 6:267).[37]

Ibn Taymiyya said, with regard to the Mongols: "Each time a commander of the army goes toward them, his judgment becomes similar to theirs, which constitutes apostasy. If the ancestors called those who abstained from paying legal alms apostates, even though they prayed and fasted, without fighting the Muslims, then what must we say of those who have become enemies of God and his Prophet by fighting the Muslims?" (*Great Fatwas*, 4:332ff.).

Ibn Hazm said: "We know that whoever leaves the land of Islam to go into the land of war flees God (may he be exalted), the imam of the Muslims, and his community, as shown in the Prophet's hadith: 'He is innocent of any Muslim who lives among the idolaters.' He disowns only the unbelievers. God said: 'The Believers, men and women, are protectors one of another.'"[38]

Abu Muhammad [Ibn Hazm] also said:

This means that whoever enters the land of war of his own free will and fights the Muslims pursuing him is an apostate and will receive the same judgment as any apostate: execution when he is captured, the distribution of his wealth, the annulment of his marriage, and so forth, because the Prophet did not allow any Muslim to leave Islam.[39]

As for those Muslims who live in India, China, or Sind,[40] among the Turks, the blacks, or the Byzantines, if they cannot leave because they are burdened by a family or have insufficient funds, because of physical weakness or because the roads are closed, they are pardoned; but if they combat the Muslims and assist the unbelievers, serving them or working for them as secretaries, then they are unbelievers too.

If a hostile unbeliever conquers Muslim land, allowing the Muslims to practice their religion but governing alone and professing a religion other than Islam, then those who assist him and reside with him are unbelievers, even if they claim to be Muslims, for the reasons we have given (*Al-Kitab al-Muhalla bil-Athar* [The Book Ornamented with Traditions], 11:199–200) . . .

What would Tabari, Ibn Hazm, and Ibn Taymiyya say if they saw the forces of the Americans and their allies striking Muslims in Iraq from their bases in the Gulf?[41] What would they say if they could see American fighter jets taking off from Pakistan to kill Muslims in Afghanistan?[42] What would they say if they saw American and Western ships and planes, armed and supplied by the Gulf states, Yemen, and Egypt on their way to Iraq to impose the embargo there, occupy the Arabian Peninsula, and defend Israel's security?[43] What would they say if they could see American weapons (those of the friends of our governments) demolishing homes around their Muslim residents in Palestine, and what would they say at the sight of American planes bombing mujahedeen in Yemen, with the full complicity of the Yemeni government?[44]

On the Order to Wage Jihad against Them, to Refrain from Loving Them, and to Shun Them

The Lord commanded us not only to refrain from allying with unbelievers, but also to wage jihad against the original unbelievers, the apostates, and the hypocrites.

JIHAD AGAINST THE UNBELIEVERS, AND ITS OBLIGATORY CHARACTER WHEN THEY SEIZE MUSLIM LANDS

Ibn Taymiyya said: "If enemies enter Muslim territory, it is absolutely necessary to push them farther and farther back, because *Muslim lands are like a single country.* It is necessary to mobilize, without asking one's father or one's creditor for permission: Ahmad [Ibn Hanbal] is clear on this subject." He added: "As for defensive combat, *it is the most forceful form of defense against those who attack our honor and religion.*[45] *It is therefore a duty, according to all the jurists. Nothing, after faith, is more necessary than to repel hostile enemies who corrupt religion and life. This is not conditional but depends on possibility.* This is what the ulema, our masters and others, have decreed. But it is important to distinguish between repelling unbelieving aggressors, and confronting them in their own land" (*Great Fatwas,* 4:607ff.).[46]

Consider, then, these powerful words, written by a mujahid scholar, the Sheikh al-Islam Ibn Taymiyya, as he reflected on the ulema's consensus regarding jihad against unbelievers who conquer Muslim countries. Consider, too, his assertion that nothing, apart from faith, is more important than repelling them: all the community's ulema have agreed on this. Now compare these opinions with those of the palace ulema, the preachers of resignation who do everything they can to turn Muslims away from jihad, so that the invading unbelievers can conquer our lands securely and so that they can reach their goal easily, calmly, and serenely.

JIHAD AGAINST THE APOSTATES GOVERNING MUSLIM LANDS

One of the most important forms of personal jihad today is the one waged against apostate governments that flout revealed law and ally with the Jews and the Christians.[47] This is a command on which all the ulema agree, and for which there is abundant proof, but we will cite only some of the evidence here.

God said: "But no, by the Lord, they can have no (real) Faith, until they make you judge in all disputes between them, and find in their souls no resistance against Your decisions, but accept them with the fullest conviction."[48]

Shāfiʿī said, in his chapter on the obedience owed to the Prophet:[49]

> God (may he be exalted) said: "Obey God, and obey the Messenger," and he said: "We sent not an apostle, but to be obeyed, in accordance with the will of God," and he said: "He who obeys the Messenger, obeys God," and he also said: "But no, by the Lord, they can have no (real) Faith, until they make you judge in all disputes between them, and find in their souls no resistance against Your decisions, but accept them with the fullest conviction."[50]
>
> He (praise him) therefore affirmed in these verses that it is a duty to obey the Prophet, and He explained that obeying the Prophet is the same as obeying God, which implies that disobeying him is the same as disobeying God, for God said: "Then let those beware who withstand the Messenger's order, lest some trial befall them, or a grievous penalty be inflicted on them."[51] He therefore threatened those who showed insubordination toward the Prophet, those who disobeyed his orders and who refrained from transmitting what he had brought or who doubted and were outside faith. God said: "But no, by the Lord, they can have no (real) Faith, until they make you judge in all disputes between them, and find in their souls no resistance against Your decisions, but accept them with the fullest conviction" . . .
>
> It is clear from these verses that *whoever does not obey one of God's or the Prophet's commands is outside Islam,*

*whether this is because he doubted, or because he rejects and
refuses to follow it.*[52]

This proves what the Prophet's companions used to say:
he who refuses to pay legal alms is an apostate, and it is
therefore permitted to execute him and seize his children.
Because God said that he who does not pronounce the formula saluting the Prophet, his judgment, and his decisions,
is not a man of faith (*Ahkam al-Qur'an* [Legal Interpretations of the Quran], 3:180–181).

God said: "Do they then seek after a judgment of (the days of)
ignorance? But who, for a people whose faith is assured, can give
better judgement than God?"[53] Ibn Kathir said: "He who does that
is *an unbeliever, and must be fought until he returns to the laws of
God and his Prophet, for only God can judge in matters minor and
major*" (Ibn Kathir, *Commentary,* 2:68).[54]

JIHAD AGAINST HYPOCRITES WHO SOW DOUBT
God commanded his Prophet to wage jihad on hypocrites with severity and rigor, by setting an example and carrying out the requisite punishments.

God said: "O Prophet! Strive hard against the Unbelievers and
the Hypocrites, and be firm against them."[55] Al-Qurtubi said: "There
is only one subject at hand here: the emphasis placed on God's
religion. He therefore commanded [the Prophet] to fight hypocrites with the sword and the good word, by calling them
to God, with severity and by setting an example." Hassan said:
"This means, fight them by carrying out the requisite punishments" (*Commentary,* 18:201).[56]

*Unacceptable Excuses of Those Who Ally Themselves with
the Unbelievers*
The Lord accepted no excuses from the hypocrites in their attempt
to ally with the unbelievers and support them for fear of accidents
of fate and history, since at times the unbelievers vanquished the

Muslims in battle, and the hypocrites thought they would find support among them. But God said:

> O you who believe! take not the Jews and the Christians for your friends and protectors: They are but friends and protectors to each other. And he among you that turns to them (for friendship) is of them. Verily God guides not a people unjust. / Those in whose hearts is a disease—you see how eagerly they run about amongst them, saying: "We do fear lest a change of fortune bring us disaster." Ah! perhaps God will give (you) victory, or a decision according to His will. Then will they repent of the thoughts which they secretly harboured in their hearts. / And those who believe will say: "Are these the men who swore their strongest oaths by God, that they were with you?" All that they do will be in vain, and they will fall into (nothing but) ruin.[57]

Ibn Kathir said: "'Those in whose hearts is a disease' means those who harbor doubt, suspicion, or hypocrisy; 'how eagerly they run about amongst them' means that they rush to pay allegiance to them and love them, in public and in secret, saying: 'We do fear lest a change of fortune bring us disaster. They explain their affection and allegiance by their fear that victory of the unbelievers over the Muslims should require support among the Jews and the Christians" (Ibn Kathir, *Commentary*, 2:71).

On the Duty of Allying with the Muslims and Supporting Them
Now that we have explained what God has forbidden us in regard to allying with the unbelievers, we will sum up what he has commanded us in regard to supporting the Muslims.
God said:

> Those who believed, and adopted exile, and fought for the Faith, with their property and their persons, in the cause

of God, as well as those who gave (them) asylum and aid, these are (all) friends and protectors, one of another. As to those who believed but came not into exile, you owe no duty of protection to them until they come into exile; but if they seek your aid in religion, it is your duty to help them, except against a people with whom you have a treaty of mutual alliance. And (remember) God sees all that you do. / The Unbelievers are protectors, one of another: Unless you do this, (protect each other), there would be tumult and oppression on earth, and great mischief. / Those who believe, and adopt exile, and fight for the Faith, in the cause of God as well as those who give (them) asylum and aid, these are (all) in very truth the Believers: for them is the forgiveness of sins and a provision most generous. / And those who accept Faith subsequently, and adopt exile, and fight for the Faith in your company, they are of you. But kindred by blood have prior rights against each other in the Book of Allah. Verily God is well-acquainted with all things.[58]

Al-Qurtubi said: "His words (may he be exalted) 'those who give them asylum and aid' mean: if they leave the believers who did not quit the land of war, support you by mobilizing or paying money to save you, then help them, it is a duty for you; do not abandon them, unless they help unbelievers with whom you have concluded a pact. In that case, do not support them, and do not break the pact until its conclusion."

Ibn al-Arabi:[59] "Unless they are poor prisoners; in that case, mutual support is appropriate, and it is a duty to support them, so that no eye of ours sheds a tear without our undertaking an expedition to save them, if our numbers allow it, or without our spending all our wealth to deliver them, to the last *dirham,* as Malik and all the ulema said.[60] We belong to God, and to him we shall return" (al-Qurtubi, *Commentary,* 8:57).

Ibn Kathir said:

He mentioned different sorts of believers and divided them into categories: the emigrants, who left their homeland and their belongings, to assist God and his Prophet and help establish his religion, for which they spent their money and gave of themselves; the helpers, the people of Medina at the time, who welcomed their brothers the emigrants and . . . helped God and his Prophet by fighting with them; they allied with each other, meaning that each of them has rights over the others . . . which is why God's messenger considered the emigrants and the helpers alike as brothers.

God said: "As to those who believed but came not into exile, you owe no duty of protection to them," and these belong to the third category of believers: those who believed and did not emigrate but stayed in the desert. They will not have a share in the spoils, not even a fifth, unless they take part in combat.

God said: "If they seek your aid," and these are the Bedouins who did not emigrate—to combat in the name of religion against an enemy—and . . . [your] duty is to help them, for they are your brothers in religion unless they supported the unbelievers with whom you have a pact, meaning a truce. Do not violate your pact and do not break your oath to those with whom you have allied; all this is narrated by Ibn Abbas.

God said: "The Believers, men and women, are protectors one of another: they enjoin what is just, and forbid what is evil: they observe regular prayers, practise regular charity, and obey God and His Messenger. On them will God pour His mercy: for God is Exalted in power, Wise." After having mentioned the hypocrites' reprehensible characteristics, he described the believers' praiseworthy qualities, saying: "The Believers, men and women, are protectors one of another," meaning that they support and help one another, as in the authentic hadith: "Believers are to believers like the fingers of a single hand." It is also said: "Believers in their mutual affection and compassion are like a single body: if a limb complains, the rest of the body responds with fever and wakefulness" (Ibn Kathir, *Commentary*, 2:329–330, 370).

Summary

. . .

1. *Rulers have impeded revealed law on alliance with Jews and Christians.* Among the groups that have deviated the most from the doctrine of loyalty and separation in our time, although they pretend to be part of the Muslim community, are the rulers of our countries, who flout revealed law.

The threat they pose to the nation has become so great that it is the gravest menace to our creed: they use force to prevent the community from obeying its religion, because they have strayed far from the path of Islam but continue to dominate Muslims completely, through control of their minds and their wealth.[61] At the same time, this group is so present that not a single Muslim country escapes the harm it does.

The rulers have strayed doubly, because they have not only failed to govern according to revealed law, but also pledged allegiance to Islam's enemies abroad and submitted to them, especially to the Jews and the Christians.

If we consider their allegiance to the Jews and the Christians, we will observe that they have transformed the Muslim countries, and especially the Arab world, into a supply base and rallying point for Jewish and Christian forces. Looking at the situation in the Arabian Peninsula, the Gulf emirates, Egypt, and Jordan, one sees that these countries have become bases or camps for the administrative and technical support of crusader forces in the heart of the

Arab world—not to mention that these governments have obliged their armies to serve the goals of the new Judeo-Christian crusade against the Muslim community.

This phenomenon, whereby rulers of Muslim countries violate revealed law, has its roots in past episodes of contemporary history. The enemies of Islam, especially the Americans, the Jews, the French, and the British, through conspiracies, secret relations, direct support, bribery, secret salaries and bank accounts, corruption, and enlistment, have been able to place the destiny of Muslims in these rulers' hands. This is not the place to write about the history of these events, but we are referring to the fact that in the post–World War II period forces hostile to Islam have been able to contain these governments and place them at the heart of the world order, represented by the allies that won the war and that went on to make up the core of the United Nations.[62]

Briefly, the United Nations are, from the Muslim point of view, an impious international institution. We should not be members, and we should not rely on its arbitration, because its ability to judge is based on the refusal of revealed law and docile submission to the will of the world's top five criminals, who dominate the leadership body known as the Security Council.

We are also referring to the fact that the enemies of Islam forced these governments to accept the legal existence of the Zionist entity in Palestine through many official agreements and practical policies, from the 1949 armistice to the 1993 Oslo accords. Finally, the Beirut summit of 2002 confirmed that the Arab states have reached a consensus on unconditional acceptance of Israel's presence.[63]

Remember that the armistice and the recognition of Israel's takeover of Palestine imply forsaking an imperative and well-known religious obligation. The armistice contains a renunciation of individual jihad, which Muslims must wage to expel the unbelievers who have invaded the Muslim countries, as we demonstrated earlier, and contains a renunciation of the duty to support Muslims in Palestine, another well-known individual religious obligation. God said: "And why should you not fight in the cause of God and of those who, being weak, are ill-treated (and oppressed)? Men, women, and children, whose cry is: 'Our Lord! Rescue us from this town, whose people are oppressors; and raise for us . . . one who will protect; and raise for us . . . one who will help!'"[64] Al-Qurtubi said: "The words 'Why should you not fight in the cause of God' are an exhortation to jihad, which implies delivering the unfortunate from the unbelieving pagans who have inflicted suffering upon them and are leading them out of religion. Therefore he (may he be exalted) made jihad a duty, so that his word would prevail, his religion would be revealed, and the weak believers would be saved, even if that results in human deaths" (al-Qurtubi, *Commentary*, 5:279).

Nor is this a matter of simply delaying the accomplishment of a religious duty: most of the Arab states also participated in the Sharm al-Sheikh conspiracy of 1996 with Israel, America, Russia, and most of the Western states. Everyone agreed and promised to defend Israel against the mujahedeen's attacks.[65]

In this context of submission to the will of the greatest criminals, the forces hostile to Islam, led by the new crusaders, managed to enslave the governments of our countries to serve their own military and economic objectives.

Things reached such a pass that we arrived at our current situation of complete allegiance to the new crusaders. Palestine is being torn apart and destroyed. Every day, its sons' throats are slit, while its Arab neighbors look on in silent complicity. Iraq is being battered by attacks aimed at killing its Muslim inhabitants, dividing up its territory, and pillaging its oil, while its Arab neighbors rush to help the new crusaders. Afghanistan has become a toy that the crusaders toss back and forth, while its neighbors sign agreements allowing the Americans to dominate the country and its people.[66]

These rulers violate revealed law; their corruption is infamous, as are their depravity and the crimes they have committed against the Muslim masses and elites, not to mention the alliances they have concluded with the Jews and the Christians.

Because they fear that the Muslim nation and the jihadist youth will rise up against them, especially as American-Zionist aggression escalates in Palestine, Iraq, Chechnya, and Kashmir, these rulers resorted to other groups to lull the nation and maintain its weakness, demoralize it, and control it. The most fearsome of these groups is the one that has dressed itself in the garb of Islamic preachers, to get to the heart of our religion, just as deadly germs bypass or destroy the immune system, before spreading through the body's cells. This is what we will sum up below.

2. *The rulers' supporters.* These are the official ulema, journalists, the media, writers, thinkers, and civil servants, who in return for their wages support falsehood and disguise it, while concealing the truth and opposing its backers.

This group causes the greatest commotion in supporting treacherous regimes and the crusaders who attack Muslim lands, or *dhimmis,* as they claim. But unfortunately, they avoid addressing a question of capital importance: who is paying the *jizya* to whom?

This group, made up of different sorts of people, confuses various perverted articles of faith, which all the imams of Islam, both ancient and modern, the followers of tradition, and the community of believers, reject.[67] Thus, this group has confused the following:

a. The doctrine of deferred judgment characteristic of the *murji'a* in its most scandalous form, applied without a trace of shame to confer a measure of legitimacy on the most blatant corruption and dependence shown by the apostate regimes and their violation of revealed law.

b. The adoption of the Kharijite point of view on anathema, accusations of depravity, and the authorization to spill the blood of the mujahedeen fighting for Islam and to discredit them.[68]

Thus, the mufti of the Egyptian republic, a civil servant who takes wages to carry out the job for which he was hired (which is to provide legal window dressing for the secularist regime that tyrannizes Muslims and pays allegiance to the Jews in an even more flagrant way than did the *murji'a* of old), was the one who authorized a secular military tribunal to execute five mujahedeen who were heroes of Islam in Egypt: Muhammad Abd al-Salam Faraj, Abd al-Hamid Abd al-Salam, Khalid al-Islambulli, Husayn Abbas, and Atta Tayil—the men who killed Anwar Sadat. Why? Because Sadat had signed four peace agreements with Israel, whereby he recognized its existence as a state and its position on Palestine, committed himself to refrain from attacking it or providing any support to a state that might attack it, and even agreed to demilitarize Sinai in order to ensure Israel's security, not to mention the secret agreements.

The best-known of these accords is the peace treaty of 1979, which put an end to hostilities between Egypt and Israel forever, prevents Egypt from helping any state that Israel has attacked, and normalizes all political, economic, and intellectual relations with Israel. After it was signed, Al-Azhar issued a fatwa blessing the agreement and actually declaring that it was in accordance with revealed law![69]

Another kind of mufti is calling for obedience to the government and considers the mujahedeen to be spreading sedition, after having authorized recourse to the Americans, and believes that we can trust their enormous armies, which block the horizon, their gigantic fleets, which clutter up the sea, and the hundreds of thousands of soldiers who have invaded our territory.[70] One doesn't know quite whom to believe. Collective fatwas have been issued authorizing recourse to American forces to confront the Baathist Iraqi regime if necessary; they have conferred religious legitimacy on the vast armies of unbelievers that have invaded the holiest Muslim land. These forces, which are still present almost twelve years after the withdrawal and defeat of the Iraqi army, have killed half a million children without the civil servants' uttering a word about it.

The aim was not to ask for help from forces of unbelievers against Saddam's Baathist forces, but rather to take control of oil wells in the Arabian Peninsula. There was no need to go looking for the Americans: the armies of the Arab and Muslim countries were quite capable of defending and liberating Kuwait.[71]

These governments, however, are irresolute; they are the result of the British plans that drew their borders and hoisted the rulers onto their thrones, before the Americans inherited the British influence. They are laying down the law at present to all the rulers of the Arabian Peninsula and the rest of the Arab world. The masters came in to defend their belongings, and the sheikhs and kings have nothing to do with the security or defense of the Arabian Peninsula.

Iraq admitted defeat, an air embargo was imposed on half its territory, the Kurds in the north declared their independence from Baghdad, inspection teams were imposed on it, and the state agreed to pay damages:[72] despite all this, the crusader presence in the Arabian Peninsula continues to grow. The crusaders are even preparing another attack on Iraq, an attack that is expected to kill hundreds of thousands of Muslims—in order to seize Iraq's oil wealth.

Then, as they told Congress, they will turn to Saudi Arabia and divide it among themselves, before looking to Egypt, which they describe as "very valuable."[73]

This is not a matter of assistance but of occupation, spoils of war, pillage, domination, and crusader hegemony over the Muslims in their most sacred territory, the Arabian Peninsula. These rulers are a thin layer of whitewash on the wall of the U.S. presence. The ulema follow, signing fatwas that have been dictated to them from above authorizing this domination, this pillaging, the crusaders' hegemony, and even the murder of Iraqi Muslims. Afterwards, the grand mufti of Saudi Arabia will authorize an armistice with Israel, because Yasir Arafat, who concluded it, will be responsible for the Muslims there . . .

Conclusion

In conclusion, we wish to reassert the following crucial points.

1. Allying with believers and confronting the unbelievers are essential pillars of the Muslim faith, without which this faith remains incomplete. God said: "O you who believe! take not the Jews and the Christians for your friends and protectors: They are but friends and protectors to each other. And he amongst you that turns to them (for friendship) is of them. Verily God guides not a people unjust."[74] And hostility toward the unbelievers implies denouncing the tyrant's wickedness, because God said: "Whoever rejects evil and believes in God has grasped the most trustworthy handhold, that never breaks. And God hears and knows all things."[75] He also said: "Have you not turned your vision to those who declare that they believe in the revelations that have come to you and to those before you? Their (real) wish is to resort together for judgment (in their disputes) to the Evil One, though they were ordered to reject him. But Satan's wish is to lead them astray far away (from the right)."[76] Therefore, we must sever connections with the tyrants and their partisans, and rebuff them.

2. To neglect this essential pillar is to open up a breach through which the enemies of Islam can pass to destroy the Muslim nation, deceive it, put it to sleep, and lead it into disaster and calamity. God said: "If they had come out with you, they would not have added to your (strength) but only (made for) disorder, hurrying to and fro in your midst and sowing sedition among you, and there would have been some among you who would have listened to them. But God knows well those who do wrong."[77]

3. Neglecting this essential pillar leads to breaking up the Muslim creed and changing it. God said: "O you who believe! If you obey the Unbelievers, they will drive you back on your heels, and you will turn back (from Faith) to your own loss."[78]

4. More than ever, we need to distinguish between the servants of Islam, who defend it, its enemies, who attack it, and those who waver and work only for their own interests, weakening the community's resistance and distracting it from its true battlefield. God said: "When you look at them, their exteriors please you; and when they speak, you listen to their words. They are as (worthless as hollow) pieces of timber propped up, (unable to stand on their own). They think that every cry is against them. They are the enemies; so beware of them. The curse of God be on them! How are they deluded (away from the Truth)."[79] He also said: "(They are) distracted in mind even in the midst of it, being (sincerely) for neither one group nor for another whom God leaves straying, never will you find for him the way."[80]

5. How can we accept calls to abandon the battlefield to the nation's enemies? How can we remain silent as they try to deprive the Muslims of their right to self-defense against their enemies, when this is a right guaranteed to all human beings? How can we stay silent as they try to demoralize us, when the community has prodigious support in the abilities of sincere fighters? How can we allow these calls to spread among us when criminals attack us? They respect nothing: neither modesty nor morals nor family nor any covenant. Any Muslim who cares about the victory of Islam must reject calls to stop jihad or slow it down, or to remove responsibility for jihad from the shoulders of the community, despite all the abilities we have mentioned, at a time when our enemies are continually attacking our sanctuaries, our wealth, and all that we hold most sacred. God said: "In a Believer they respect not the ties either of kinship or of covenant! It is they who have transgressed all bounds."[81] According to a hadith narrated by Ibn Omar: "I heard the messenger of God (praise and blessings upon him) say: 'If you start selling on credit, then seizing the tails of cattle and contenting yourselves with agriculture, then you will abandon jihad and God will abase you until you return to your religion' (from Ahmad and Abu Dawud)."[82]

6. Not only do we reject all calls to cease jihad, we call on the nation and all those who constitute it to join the caravan of jihad, to follow its path and strike at the enemy. God said: "O you who believe! Shall I lead you to a bargain that will save you from a grievous Penalty? / That you believe in God and His Messenger, and that you strive (your utmost) in the Cause of Allah, with your property and your persons: That will be best for you, if you but knew! / He will forgive you your sins, and admit you to Gardens beneath which Rivers flow, and to beautiful mansions in Gardens of Eternity: that is indeed the Supreme Achievement. / And another (favour will He bestow,) which you do love, help from God and a speedy victory. So give the Glad Tidings to the Believers."[83]

7. We extend a hand to all Muslims who care about the victory of Islam so that they may participate in our working plan (to save the community from its painful straits), based on hostility toward tyrants and infidels, allegiance to the believers, and jihad along God's path. In this working plan, each Muslim who cares about the triumph of Islam will try to outdo his fellows in showing generosity and giving liberally to free Muslim land, restore Islam's dominion over its territory, and spread its call throughout the world.

8. We want to warn our community against passivity and disregard for the colossal dangers that face us. The Judeo-crusading military apparatus occupies holy Jerusalem, lurks ninety kilometers from the sanctuary in Mecca, and surrounds the Muslim world with a chain of military bases and navies. The aggressors use a network of submissive governments to wage their campaigns.

We do not live on another planet, and we do not want to behave as if we were a thousand years away from danger: every morning, we awake to the sight of Jewish tanks destroying houses in Gaza and Jenin and laying siege to our homes.[84]

The campaign against Iraq will not be the last, and the assassination of Abu Ali al-Harithi in Yemen by American missiles bears the traces of Israel's technique of liquidating the mujahedeen in Palestine, which is now developing in the Arab world. Tomorrow any one of us could be targeted by an American missile. The finger will be pointed at every sincere preacher and every decent writer.

We have wasted enough time and must act quickly.

Young Muslims need not wait for anyone's permission, because jihad against the Americans, the Jews, and their allies, hypocrites and apostates, is now an individual duty, as we have demonstrated. *Every group of young people must support the community and prepare to defend it against any attack.*[85] We must scorch the earth beneath the feet of the invaders, or they will never leave.

In conclusion, we call on the community, and especially young fighters, to have endurance and remain steadfast. You must have endurance to bear the responsibilities of religion, and especially the highest of its obligations: jihad along God's path. God said: "O you who believe! Persevere in patience and constancy; vie in such perseverance; strengthen each other; and fear God, that you may prosper."[86] For he also said: "God has decreed: 'It is I and My apostles who must prevail': For God is One full of strength, able to enforce His Will."[87] Muslim narrated a hadith from Uqba Ibn Amir: "I heard the messenger of God (praise and blessings upon him) say: 'Part of my community will continue to fight for God, overcoming its enemies, without suffering from those who oppose it, until Judgment Day.'"

Our last word is one of praise for God, Lord of the worlds. We ask him to grant peace and blessings to Muhammad, his family, and his companions.

AYMAN AL-ZAWAHIRI Shawwal 1423 / December 2002

PART IV

ABU MUSAB AL-ZARQAWI

INTRODUCTION

ABU MUSAB AL-ZARQAWI, JIHAD IN "MESOPOTAMIA"

JEAN-PIERRE MILELLI

After the guerrilla war in Afghanistan waged in the 1990s came to an end, and following the 2001 attacks, the terror campaign led by Abu Musab al-Zarqawi in Iraq from 2003 to 2006 allowed jihadist fighters to remain at the forefront of international events by defying U.S. power, and thus to give the entire world the impression that a lasting, if not eternal, jihad had been unleashed.

On the international level, this will probably be Zarqawi's legacy. On the Iraqi domestic scene, however, it will be that Zarqawi—a Jordanian by birth—ignited and fueled a civil war with religious overtones between Shiites and Sunnis. As a result, it is difficult to know whether his assassination at the hands of the U.S. army, on June 7, 2006, renewed the violence of jihadist operations or whether these operations are destined to disappear in the general conflagration between Iraqi Shiites and Sunnis.

The conditions in which Zarqawi was assassinated did not shed further light on his past, but his death gives reason to wonder whether he will enter jihadist martyrology as so many others did before him or whether he will also be a source of inspiration, reviving the jihadist flame in a different arena.

This, at least, is how Zawahiri intended to use the figure of Zarqawi, adorned with the halo of martyrdom. In an elegy posted on the Internet a few days after Zarqawi's death, Zawahiri unambiguously cited verses that Ahmad Shawqi, a neoclassical Egyptian poet, had dedicated to Omar al-Mukhtar, the leader of the Libyan resistance, hanged by the Italian colonial authorities to serve as an example in 1931:

> They planted your corpse in the sand like a banner
> That rouses the valley, noon and night.
> Woe to them who raised a bleeding emblem
> That will instill violent resentment in tomorrow's generations.

It is nevertheless plausible that Zawahiri and Bin Laden did not experience Zarqawi's death as an irreparable loss, for he had demonstrated such independence from them as to challenge their sovereign authority. It's possible to suppose that he died conveniently at the point where he could be pronounced a martyr before he had achieved the success he anticipated, which would have made him an outright rival.

Zawahiri's opportunistic attitude was clear as early as July 2006, during Israel's thirty-three-day attack on Lebanon: in a speech, citing Zarqawi, he denounced Israel and the United States but gave no credit to Hezbollah. The short reference, which alluded to the Prophet Muhammad's night journey, situated what Hezbollah would soon call its divine victory firmly within the perspective of global jihad: "The imam and martyr—or so we hope—Abu Musab al-Zarqawi said: 'In Iraq, we are fighting a stone's throw from the path the Prophet traveled during his night journey. And if we are fighting in Iraq, it is with our eyes fixed on Jerusalem, which we will recover only by following the Quran and raising the sword.'"

Outside the circles of jihadists and sympathizers, in any case, Zarqawi was an example of further radicalization in this ideological orientation, because of his cold determination to wreak havoc on an Arab country that had already suffered cruelly under dictatorship and war. This probably estranged a good part of Muslim public opinion worldwide.

His first appearance in a propaganda film, posted on the Internet a few months before his death on April 26, 2006, also suggests that he may have resorted to this means of communication—which Bin Laden in particular had used before him—to assert himself within the context of rivalry with Iraqi fighters or the historical leaders of the jihadist movement. It was almost as if he intended to follow in his masters' footsteps and produce a propaganda clip that conformed to stylistic requirements: it featured the logo of the Consultative Council of Mujahedeen, which grouped several organizations around the one he headed (Al Qaeda in Mesopotamia); Zarqawi made a speech of about twenty minutes in classical Arabic, standing in front of a wall mounted with a machine gun; there were images of a meeting headed by Zarqawi during which a map of operations in Iraq was consulted; and finally the clip showed a missile being fired in the desert, after which Zarqawi, facing the camera, generously emptied several rounds from a heavy machine gun.

Unlike Bin Laden and Zawahiri, who were cut off from the battlefield and could only attempt to intervene on various questions of international importance, Zarqawi was mainly concerned with efficiency. He did not seek to stand out in any way, but rather echoed the theme of the war's underlying causes. He promised even "more bitter and devious" developments, addressed George Bush, whom he accused of lying to the American people about the way the war was going, criticized the formation of an Iraqi parliament, and concluded by calling on Iraqis to join the guerrilla war.

Zarqawi was a stout man with fleshy cheeks and a dull gaze. Dressed in black and carrying his machine-gun cartridges slung across his chest, he appeared athletic and sure of himself—something like a Muslim Rambo. The film, indeed, was the best possible recruitment agent for young Muslims longing for adventure and convinced that this was a just cause.

The question of his relations with the Iraqis was one of those raised in a document that U.S. intelligence published in October 2005, presenting it as a letter intercepted on its way from Zawahiri to Zarqawi. If it is proved to be authentic, this document will give an idea of relations, no matter how loose, between Zawahiri and Zarqawi, and of what Zawahiri thought of Zarqawi's policy in Iraq. Zawahiri's opinion can be detected through the rhetorical precautions proffered by Al Qaeda's ideologue, and may be summed up as follows: although they agreed on the strategy to be pursued, Zawahiri considered Zarqawi's tactics to be risky and dangerous. The most he could do, however, was to try to convince Zarqawi to change his policy; Zawahiri's authority was merely intellectual.

The letter, about fifteen pages long, enumerated in detail points of politics, doctrine, tactics, and strategy, embellished with historical examples and verses of classical poetry. Its goal was to convince Zarqawi to adopt a more measured attitude in his anti-Shiite policy, to restrain his enthusiasm for beheading foreign hostages and showing footage of the executions on the Internet, to preserve the unity of the mujahedeen, and thus to pave the way for an Islamist government in Iraq once the Americans had been defeated.[1]

At any rate, the last months of Zarqawi's life show no tendency toward moderation, which may be what his only "self-portrait as a mujahid" may have sought to demonstrate. The difficult relationship with Zawahiri, and Zarqawi's desire for independence, do not seem to have been exceptions in Zarqawi's life, of which the main phases will be outlined below.

Zarqa

Abu Musab al-Zarqawi was the pseudonym of Ahmad Fadil Nazzal al-Khalayla.[2] Abu Musab chose his name in homage to Musab Ibn Omayr, one of the Prophet's companions, who was martyred at the Battle of Uhud in 625.[3] As for the second part of his name, meaning "from Zarqa," it is significant because, starting in the 1990s, this city fostered the propagation of jihadist ideas in Jordan.

Zarqa's ethnic composition is fairly unique in the Middle Eastern context: Circassians settled on the banks of the Zarqa (the "Azure River," the Arabic name for the Biblical Jabbok) in the late nineteenth century.[4] They were joined by settled Bedouin tribes (among them the Bani Hasan, Abu Musab's tribe) and finally by Palestinian refugees, who poured in after the Arab-Israeli wars of 1948 and 1967 and today make up 80 percent of the population.

In "O my people, hearken to the one who invites you,"[5] a text subtitled "Letter to the Bani Hasan," Abu Musab marshaled numerous Quranic verses, hadith, lines of classical poetry, and citations from Ibn Taymiyya to criticize the Jordanian monarchy for supporting U.S. military policy in the region. In particular, he openly attacked King Abdullah for having allied himself with Jews and Christians. "He fights God's allies and banishes them, then throws the sons of this blessed religion in jail. With Apache helicopters, he bombs Muslims in Maan, while in Jenin the same helicopters are killing our brothers and mothers in Palestine[6]—all this to defend Israel's security and extinguish any movement that might disturb the sleep of those pigs and monkeys. Jordan is Israel's release valve and its defensive wall." On May 29, 2004, however, representatives of the Bani Hasan publicly dissociated themselves from Zarqawi's actions.[7]

Palestinian militants brought Zarqa to the world's attention on September 6, 1970, when PFLP[8] fighters diverted three airliners (TWA and SwissAir carriers, then three days later a BOAC flight) to its airport. Once the passengers had disembarked, the fedayeen dynamited the three planes on September 12 and renamed the airport Revolution Airport. This challenge to King Hussein's authority triggered the crisis that had been brewing between the Palestinian organizations and the Hashemite monarchy. Mass repression of the Palestinian organizations followed, and the period went down in history as Black September. According to the Palestinian Red Crescent Society, three thousand people were killed and ten thousand wounded in Amman and Zarqa.

In the 1960s, Islamists like Abdallah Azzam had settled in Zarqa: Azzam's organization, the Jordanian Muslim Brotherhood, took King Hussein's side during Black September. Previously, in order to guide fedayeen incursions into Israel from Jordanian territory, Azzam had headed a training camp in the "sheikhs' camps," a zone where a stricter and more pious atmosphere reigned than in the other, Marxist or nationalist camps. When he returned to Jordan in 1973, Azzam taught at the university in Amman, where he had considerable influence, spreading radical Islamist ideas among the students there.

Apart from Abdallah Azzam, who found in Afghanistan the jihad battlefront he had dreamed of in Jordan, another renowned figure in radical Islamist circles was a Salafist Syrian sheikh of Albanian origin, Nasir al-Din al-Albani, who was invited by the Muslim Brotherhood to lecture in Jordan. One of his disciples at the time was Sheikh Yusuf al-Barqawi, a relative of Asim al-Barqawi.

Because of the influence exerted by these charismatic individuals, the enduring Arab-Israeli conflict, and fragile socioeconomic circumstances, Zarqa became a focus of radical Islamist activity in Jordan in the 1990s, and especially after Jordanian emigrants began returning from Kuwait after the first Gulf war. Among these returnees was Abu Qatada, the Afghan Arab who later became a fixture of Londonistan; Abu Anas al-Shami, who went on to become the mufti of Zarqawi's organization in Iraq; and Zarqawi's spiritual master, Asim al-Barqawi, also known as Abu Muhammad al-Maqdisi.[9]

Zarqawi

Zarqawi, who received no secondary or religious education, was a jihadist from the rank and file, whose lightning-swift ascent from amid the motley ranks in the radical Islamist milieu was unexpected; his apparent mediocrity seems to have misled several observers until the three-year period when he became the main Islamist opponent to U.S. policy in the Middle East.[10]

Born on October 20, 1966, into a modest family of three sons and seven daughters, Zarqawi left primary school to work intermittently at odd jobs. Influenced by an imam at his neighborhood Salafist mosque, he decided to leave for Pakistan in 1989. In Hayatabad, near Peshawar, he stayed in the dormitories run by the Service Bureau, which Osama Bin Laden headed at the time. In the spring of 1989, after the fall of Khost, in eastern Afghanistan, he went to the front. More important, however, during the same period Zarqawi met al-Maqdisi, who introduced him to the head of a jihadist newspaper in Peshawar, *Al-Bunyan al-Marsus*, where he worked as a journalist.[11]

During the civil war that followed the Soviets' retreat from Afghanistan, Zarqawi took up arms again alongside Gulbuddin Hekmatyar's faction. He also frequented Al-Sada, an Afghan Arab camp in the zone controlled by Abdul Rasul Sayyaf's party.

Back in Jordan in 1993, Zarqawi made contact once again with al-Maqdisi, who had returned home as well, and founded a group named Bay'at al-Imam (Allegiance to the Imam). Zarqawi was arrested in 1994 and sentenced to fifteen years for carrying arms and false documents, then jailed in Suwaqa. During this period in prison, he wrote *Ifadat Asir* (Deposition of a Prisoner of War), addressing a Jordanian judge, criticizing positive law, and refusing any un-Islamic form of justice. "In your courts, you run your cases according to positive law; but know, judges, that if you die in your current state, we will meet again in the court of an all-powerful Sovereign, and you will find all your actions inscribed in a register there. If they are to your credit, praise God; but if not, you will have no one to blame but yourselves."

On March 29, 1999, Zarqawi was freed during an amnesty declared by Abdullah II when he acceded to the throne. He left again for Pakistan a few months later. In an article published on his Web site, Abu Muhammad al-Maqdisi related the reasons Zarqawi had given to explain his return to Afghanistan: "He answered those who reproached him for leaving his country that he loved jihad, and did not have the patience to learn, teach, or preach. This is how he recruited a group of brothers who left with him for Afghanistan, where they were able to benefit from the situation in that country and in its military camps." In Pakistan, Abu Musab apparently became close to Bin Laden, but was careful not to submit to his authority.

Thus, in early 2000 he was running a training camp near Herat, in western Afghanistan, not far from the Iranian border, while Bin Laden was in the east of the country. The camp was called Al-Tawhid wal-Jihad (Monotheism and Jihad), a name that bore al-Maqdisi's imprimatur (it was also the name of his Web site). In July 2001, Kurdish Islamists were hosted at the camp, and in September of the same year a small delegation of jihadists from the camp moved to Iraqi Kurdistan,[12] where they set up an organization called Jund al-Islam (Soldiers of Islam). Zarqawi sought refuge in this region after the American invasion of Afghanistan, after crossing Iran, where he was detained for a time by the security services.

In late 2001, Ansar al-Islam (Partisans of Islam) was created. The organization brought together several Islamist groups (Jund al-Islam among them) and had several training camps in Kurdistan, where it fought the Patriotic Union of Kurdistan and launched a suicide attack on its headquarters on February 2, 2004, that killed over a hundred people.

In the meantime, Zarqawi had organized several operations in Jordan: an attack on several tourist sites, including an American hotel in Amman, intended to mark the millennium, but which was foiled during the preparation stage; the assassination of U.S. diplomat Laurence Foley, on October 28, 2002; and a chemical-weapons attack on Amman, which was thwarted by the Jordanian police. To prepare for these attacks, Zarqawi and his accomplices had traveled to Iraq and Syria.

Furthermore, Ansar al-Islam was mentioned in one way or another in connection with most of the investigations into terrorist attacks in Europe: the Madrid train bombings that left 192 dead and 1,400 wounded on March 11, 2004, but also attacks in Germany and Italy, where support cells were dismantled in April 2002 and March 2003, respectively.

On February 5, 2003, U.S. Secretary of State Colin Powell addressed the U.N. Security Council, declaring: "Iraq today harbors a deadly terrorist network headed by Abu Musab Al-Zarqawi, an associate and collaborator of Osama bin Laden and his Al Qaida lieutenants." Whatever reservations one might have about the motives behind this statement, it was the first time the extent of Zarqawi's network had received public acknowledgment. The U.S. invasion of Iraq opened the way for its expansion. In the early stages of the U.S. offensive, on March 23, 2003, Ansar al-Islam suffered heavy losses due to American bombardments coordinated with a ground offensive by Kurdish secularists: the attack allegedly killed 180 Islamist fighters and led to the capture of 150. This did not prevent a new organization from taking over in June 2003: Ansar al-Sunna (Partisans of the Sunna), which joined several others under the aegis of Al-Tawhid wal-Jihad, led by Zarqawi.

The terrorist operations carried out by Zarqawi's organization reached their peak after the U.S.-British coalition's intervention in Iraq: footage of the kidnapping and execution of foreign hostages was shown on the Internet. In his "Recommendations to Jihad Fighters," Zarqawi reminisced about the assassination of Nicholas Berg,[13] whom he was said to have personally beheaded: "Emissaries tried to save that infidel mule, offering us all the money we wanted (and we needed it badly to keep the wheel of jihad turning), but we preferred to avenge our brothers and take revenge for our community . . . In order to strengthen their wills and cause Muslims east and west to rejoice, we decided that this infidel would not be bought back, even if they offered us his weight in gold. We swore we would not release this prisoner for money, whatever we thought, so that the enemies of God would know that there is no truce for them in our hearts, nor pity for them."[14]

An equally notable, and far more brutal, aspect of Zarqawi's policy was the murder of Iraqi Shiites, either because they showed willingness to work with the new government's police and health services (as in Hilla on February 28, 2005, when a hundred civilians were killed in a marketplace near a recruitment center), or during religious gatherings (for example, the Ashura commemorations of March 2004 and February 2005), not to mention the assassination of religious dignitaries like Ayatollah Baqir al-Hakim on August 29, 2003.

Al-Maqdisi

This is why, in a text written in 2004 and entitled "Zarqawi: Support and Advice" (and subtitled "Hopes and Fears"), Abu Muhammad al-Maqdisi criticized his former protégé, whom he now seemed to consider little more than a desperado. Al-Maqdisi—who was in jail at the time, and therefore subject to pressure from the Jordanian security services—criticized Zarqawi's policy in Iraq, although his points concerned tactics rather than principles. He condemned the haphazard, unproductive (not to say harmful) attacks that had killed Muslims ("The error that spares the blood of a thousand unbelievers is not as grave as the one that kills even a single Muslim"); the decision to attack Shiites in their places of worship, rather than fighting the occupiers ("Whatever their history, their hostility toward Sunnis, or the harm they have done, people of modest means must not be lumped together with military leaders"); the policy of targeting Christians and churches ("Do not attack civilians, even if they are unbelievers or Christians, and do not strike their churches or places of worship"); the suicide attacks ("which, according to the principles of our ulema, we call jihad operations") as an end in themselves rather than a means; the reduction of jihad to a series of punitive measures; and finally, the failure to entrust more responsibility to Iraqi jihad fighters.[15]

Furthermore, this text reveals the reasons for Zarqawi's second departure for Afghanistan, mentioned earlier, and explains his attitude toward Bin Laden, alluded to in a sentence about his mufti, Abu Anas al-Shami: "I rejoiced and found new hope when I learned that Abu Anas al-Shami had joined Abu Musab, although this man did not share all our opinions; I saw there proof of a flexibility that Zarqawi had lacked previously, and which had prevented him from finding a place in Al Qaeda and submitting to the authority of Sheikh Osama Bin Laden (God preserve him)."[16]

Al-Shami

Abu Anas al-Shami, also known as Omar Yusuf Jumaa, was born in 1968 in Kuwait to a Jordanian family of Palestinian origin. In the city of Salmiyya, he met al-Maqdisi, then went to study in Saudi Arabia at the Islamic University in Medina from 1988 to 1991. There, he was influenced by the ideas of Safar al-Hawali, Salman al-Awda, and Nasir al-Omar. In the summer of 1990 he went to Afghanistan and spent three months in Al-Faruq training camp. In 1991 he graduated with a degree in theology, married a young woman of Palestinian origin,[17] and settled in Jordan, in the town of Suwaylih, where he served as imam in a mosque. He spent a short time in Bosnia-Herzegovina and was jailed briefly on his return to Jordan for having made a public statement at the Bukhari Center, where he worked, in the north Amman neighborhood of Marka, to the effect that the Jordanian regime had made the country into barracks for U.S. soldiers and that the coming war was not against Iraq but against Islam. Finally, in September 2003, claiming that he was going to Saudi Arabia to perform the lesser pilgrimage, he went to Iraq, where he joined Zarqawi's organization and became its mufti and the author of its statements.

These statements, letters, and narratives, published on the Internet, also provide information. In a text titled "The Document," Abu Anas indirectly admits that his organization was responsible for assassinating Ayatollah Baqir al-Hakim, a Shiite cleric and political leader, and head of the Supreme Council for the Revolution in Iraq, probably the country's largest opposition group. Mentioning one of his Iraqi comrades who had died in battle, Thamir al-Ramadi, he adds: "He is one of Iraq's glorious heroes: he organized the operation against Muhammad Baqir al-Hakim and many suicide operations, also taking charge of preparation, surveillance, and equipment, in collaboration with the martyr Hamza Abu Muhammad (God rest their souls), called Nidal Muhammad Arabiyyat, from one of the noblest tribes of the town of Salt in Jordan."[18]

Another piece of information this text provides concerns Zarqawi's attitude during the first U.S. attack on Falluja, in April 2004. Although he wanted to take part in the fighting, his comrades apparently asked him not to do so, and their sending word to him through an emissary who had to cross a river every time he conveyed a message seems to indicate that Zarqawi was some way away from the combat zone. This may also be why the second attack on Falluja, which took place in autumn of 2004, may have allowed U.S. forces to discover arms stockpiles and torture chambers in the city but did not lead to Zarqawi's capture.

On September 17, 2004, Abu Anas al-Shami and around thirty other combatants were killed by U.S. troops near Abu Ghraib, in the course of an operation against the now infamous prison.[19] On October 19, through a spokesman and on the Internet, Abu Musab al-Zarqawi publicly declared his allegiance to Bin Laden and stated that this was the result of eight months of contacts between his organization and Al Qaeda. Zarqawi's group was now renamed Qaedat al-Jihad in Mesopotamia.[20]

On January 22 of that year, at which point jihad operations against U.S. and British forces in Iraq had already been under way for six months, secularist Kurdish fighters arrested Hasan Guhl, a Pakistani veteran of the Afghan war, in Kalar, Kurdistan. They found on him a CD-ROM recording of a twelve-page text of which extracts were published on February 9 by Dexter Filkins, the *New York Times* correspondent in Baghdad.[21] Given the shady circumstances of the text's publication, some observers suspected that the document was a fake. It was written in impeccable classical Arabic, however, and exposed a strategy that was subsequently followed in large part, indications that may lead us to suppose that the text was in fact the work of Abu Anas al-Shami.

Since the allegiance to Bin Laden has been confirmed, it is useful to reexamine the strategy exposed in the letter from Zarqawi, in an attempt to understand the goals he had set himself and what Bin Laden's blessing might have meant. The offer of allegiance was formulated in the following manner: "We will be your readied soldiers, working under your banner, complying with your orders, and indeed swearing fealty to you publicly and in the news media, vexing the infidels and gladdening those who preach the oneness of God. On that day, the believers will rejoice in God's victory. If things appear otherwise to you, we are brothers, and the disagreement will not spoil [our] friendship."[22]

The main characteristic of the letter was its crude exposition of the project to attack Iraq's Shiites, constantly referred to as heretics or cunning enemies (*rafida; uduww makir*), particularly those who enlisted in the police and the army. "This is why I say again that the only solution is for us to strike the heretics, whether they are men of religion, soldiers, or others, until they submit to the Sunnis. You might object that it is too soon, and unfair to throw the nation into a battle for which it is unprepared; that this will cause losses and spill blood; but this is precisely what we want."[23]

The second characteristic of Zarqawi's strategy was to precipitate operations before a new government could be formed: "It would be ideal if we could do as we wish, upset the applecart and cause their plan to fail. If not, God forbid, the government will extend its control over the country and we will have to pack our bags and break camp to head for another land in which we can resume carrying the banner, unless God prefers to have us die as martyrs."

Zarqawi's media strategy was also clearly formulated: "Perhaps we will announce this soon, even if we do so gradually, so that everyone will know about it. The waiting period is over, and we intend to give the media something to think about, in such a way as to reveal the truth, inspire vocations, and rally men's wills. Then, the pen and the sword will work together in this jihad."

By publishing the document found on the emissary, the Americans also got the message through to Bin Laden, if he had not already received it. The U.S. administration may have shown a slightly naive belief in the "ruse of history," which was meant to bring democracy in the troops' knapsacks, but Zarqawi believed in the "ruse of God," as he said in another of his texts: "Praise God, who will cause Islam to triumph and paganism to crumble, who will dispose of all things and draw the unbelievers in through his ruse, who will share out the days of victory but will give final victory to the believers alone."[24]

Letter to Bin Laden and Zawahiri

(excerpts)

In the name of God, the Merciful, the Compassionate,

From . . . to the proudest of leaders and men in the age of the servants. To the dwellers on the mountaintops, the hawks of glory, the lions of [the] mountains, to the two honorable brothers[1] . . .

Peace and the mercy and blessings of God be upon you.

Even if our bodies are far apart, the distance between our hearts is small.

Our solace is in this saying of the Imam Malik. I hope that both of you are well. I ask God Almighty that this letter finds you in good health and savoring the winds of victory and triumph . . . Amen.[2]

I send you an account that is appropriate to the situation, lifting the veil to reveal good and evil in what is taking place in Iraq.

As you know, God graced the Muslim nation with jihad in the land of Mesopotamia.[3] You know that this is a battlefield unlike any other. It offers both benefits and drawbacks not found elsewhere.

Among the greatest benefits is that this is jihad in the Arab heartland, a stone's throw from the lands of the two sanctuaries and Al-Aqsa [Mosque]. We know from God's religion that the true, decisive battle between unbelief and Islam is in this land, that is, in [Greater] Syria and its surroundings. Therefore, we must spare no effort in establishing a foothold in this land. Perhaps God may help us thereafter. The current situation, dear and courageous sheikhs, requires that we examine this matter carefully, on the basis of our religion and the reality in which we live . . .

Here is the current situation as I, with my limited vision, see it. I ask God to forgive my omissions and weaknesses. First, having sought help from God, I say that the Americans, as you know, entered Iraq on a contractual basis and to create the State of Greater Israel from the Nile to the Euphrates and that this Zionized American administration believes that accelerating the creation of the State of [Greater] Israel will accelerate the coming of the Messiah.[4] It came to Iraq with all its allies, with pride and arrogance, defying God and his Prophet.[5] It thought that the matter would be easy, despite a few minor obstacles. But it found a completely different reality. From the first, the operations of the mujahedeen brothers began, which complicated matters. Then, the pace of operations quickened in the Sunni Triangle, if it can be called thus.[6] This forced the Americans to conclude a deal with the rejectionists [the Shiites], the dregs of humanity, whereby the Shiites would get two-thirds of the booty for having stood by the crusaders against the mujahedeen.[7]

First, the composition [of Iraq]: In general, Iraq is a political mosaic, an ethnic mixture made up of confessional and sectarian differences that only a strong central authority and a despotic ruler have been able to lead, from Ziyad Ibn Abihi to Saddam.[8] Difficult choices lie ahead, for it is a land of great hardship and difficulties for anyone. As for the details:

The Kurds

Whether they belong to Barzani's faction or to Talabani's, they applauded the Americans and gave them their hearts, then opened their land to the Jews, becoming their rear guard and a Trojan horse for their plans.[9] They [the Jews] infiltrate through their lands, hide beneath their banners, and use them as a bridge by which to reach financial control and economic hegemony. They use them as a base for espionage, which is what all their territory has become.

The voice of Islam has fallen silent among them and the light of religion has gone out in their lands.[10] Iraqi propaganda has intoxicated them, and the good people among them, few as they are, are weak and cowardly.[11]

Heretics

[They are] an insurmountable obstacle, a lurking snake, a crafty and malicious scorpion, a spying enemy, and a mortal venom. Here, we are entering a battle on two levels. One is open, against a furious enemy and patent unbelief; the other is more difficult and fierce, against a cunning enemy who wears the garb of a friend, pretends to agree, and calls for solidarity, but harbors evil and takes tortuous paths.[12] He is the heir to the esoteric gangs that traversed the history of Islam and left indelible scars on its face. The attentive observer and careful witness will realize that Shiism is a looming danger and a true challenge. "They are the enemies; so beware of them. The curse of God be on them! How are they deluded (away from the Truth)."[13] History's message, confirmed by the current situation, demonstrates most clearly that Shiism is a religion that has nothing in common with Islam except in the way that Jews have something in common with Christians as people of the book. From patent polytheism, tomb worship, and circumambulating shrines to calling the companions of the Prophet infidels and insulting the mothers of the believers and the best of the Muslim nation, they arrive at distorting the Quran as a logical means of defaming those who know it, in addition to claiming that the imams are infallible, that believing in them is a tenet of faith, that revelation came down to them, and other forms of unbelief and heresy that fill their favorite books and reference works—which they continue to churn out incessantly.[14] The dreamers who think that a Shiite can forget this historical legacy and the old hatred of the *nawasib*, as they say, are deluded:[15] this is like asking a Christian to renounce the idea of the crucifixion, which no rational person would do. These are a people who gathered in their unbelief and masked their heresy with political cunning and a feverish effort to seize on the crisis of governance and overturn the balance of power in the state: with the assistance of their allies, the Americans, they are trying to redraw this state and determine its size by means of their political banners and organizations.

Throughout history and over the centuries, these people have been a treacherous and disloyal sect. The true face of their creed is war against the people of sunna and the community. When the accursed Baath regime collapsed, the heretics took as their slogan: "Revenge on Tikrit and Anbar." This shows their hidden hatred for the Sunnis.[16] Their religious and political leaders, however, have been able to keep their community in order, so as to avoid having a battle break out between them and the Sunnis and turn into a sectarian war, because they know they would never succeed in this way.[17] If a sectarian war were to break out, a large part of the Muslim community worldwide would support the Iraqi Sunnis.[18] Because their religion is one of dissimulation [taqiyya], they maliciously and cunningly adopted a different method, and began by taking control of the state institutions and security, military, and economic strategic points. As you know, security and the economy are the main components of any country; therefore, they infiltrated the most strategic sectors of the state. Take the example of the Badr Brigade, the military wing of the Supreme Council of the Islamic Revolution, which exchanged its heretical garb for police and military uniforms in order to embed its cadres in these institutions and, under the pretext of preserving the nation and its citizens, has begun to settle scores with the Sunnis.[19] The American army has begun to pull out of some cities and deemphasize its presence. The Iraqi army has begun to take its place, and this is a real problem for us: fighting the Americans is easy, because the enemy is clear and exposed. He does not know the land or the situation of the mujahedeen because his intelligence is weak, especially since we know full well that the crusader forces will pull out very soon:[20] this is clear to anyone observing the enemy's haste in putting together an army and a police force that have started to carry out the missions assigned to them. But the other enemy, made up of heretics and the Sunnis on their payroll, is ultimately the real danger that we face, because these are compatriots: they know our hiding places and are far more cunning that their crusader masters. As I said, they began by attempting to dominate the security forces and liquidated many Sunnis in the ranks of the Baath Party whom they saw as their enemies. In an systematic, careful way, they assassinated jihad fighters, scientists and thinkers, physicians and engineers, and many others.[21] This is why I think—but only God knows for sure—that before the year is out, the American army will put forth a plan to hand over power to the secret army of heretics and its military brigades.[22]

They are creeping in like snakes to seize the army and police apparatus, which is the striking force and iron fist in our Third World, while dominating the economy like their Jewish masters. Every day, their hopes are growing that they will establish a heretical state stretching from Iran through Iraq, Syria, and Lebanon to the cardboard kingdom of the Gulf.[23] The Badr Brigade entered the game brandishing the slogan of revenge against Tikrit and Anbar, but then it took up the slogans of the army and police to oppress the Sunnis and kill the Muslims in the name of law and order. All this was embellished with syrupy words, full of falsehood, for their gnostic religion adorns itself with lies and veils itself in hypocrisy, exploiting the naïveté and good-heartedness of many Sunnis. How long will it take for our community to learn history's lessons and listen to the testimony of centuries past? The Shiite Safavid dynasty was an insurmountable obstacle in the path of Islam—indeed, a dagger that stabbed the Muslims in the back.[24] As one of the Orientalists said: "Had the Safavids not existed, we in Europe would be reading the Quran just as the Algerian Berbers do." Yes, the vast armies of the Ottoman state stopped at the gates of Vienna, and the city walls almost crumbled before them. Islam would have spread in the shadow of the swords of honor and holy war; but these armies were forced to retreat because the Safavids had occupied Baghdad, demolished its mosques, killed its people, raped its women, and plundered its wealth, thereby forcing the Ottomans to turn back in order to defend Islam and the Muslims. For two centuries, fierce fighting raged, provoking the collapse and dwindling of the Islamic empire. During this time, the community slumbered, awakening only to the drums of the invading Westerners.

The Quran tells us about the hypocrites' conspiracies, the machinations of this fifth column, and the cunning of our compatriots, whose tongues speak honeyed words in our name but whose hearts are those of demons. Evil resides in them: they are the secret cause of our distress; they are the worm in the apple. "They are the enemies; so beware of them." Ibn Taymiyya—after describing the anathema they pronounced against the Muslims—was right to say: "This is why they help the unbelievers against the Muslims. They were the main reason for the arrival of Genghis Khan, the king of the unbelievers, in the lands of Islam, Hulagu's arrival in Iraq, the taking of Aleppo, the pillage of Salihiyya, and other things.[25] This is why they plundered the Muslim armies when they marched to Egypt the first time. This is why they attacked Muslims on the highways and helped the Mongols and the Franks against them. This is why they felt such deep sadness at the triumph of Islam, because they are allied themselves with the Jews, Christians, and polytheists against the Muslims. This is typical of the hypocrites . . . Their hearts are full of bitterness and gall against the Muslims, young and old, good and bad. Their greatest act of faith is to curse the Muslims, from first to last. They are the people most anxious to divide the Muslim community; they insult the best Muslim leaders—like the Rightly Guided Caliphs and the ulema—and accuse them of apostasy, being convinced that anyone who does not believe in the infallible imam (a figment of their imagination) does not believe in God or his Prophet, praise and blessings upon him.

"The heretics love the Mongols and their dynasty because they have found with them privileges they did not enjoy with the Muslim states . . . They are the greatest collaborators with the Mongols in conquering the Muslim countries, killing Muslims, and raping their women. The story of Ibn al-Alqami and others like him, as well as that of Aleppo, is well known.[26] When Muslims defeat Christians and polytheists, it breaks the heretics' hearts, but when the polytheists and Christians defeat the Muslims, this is cause for celebration and joy among the Shiites" (*Book of Fatwas*, chapter 28, pp. 478–527).[27]

Praise God: it is as if this author had seen the invisible and glimpsed the future, then spoken as if he were describing his experience.

Our teachers, then, clearly showed us the way and revealed the truth about these people. Imam al-Bukhari said: "Unhappy is he who has prayed behind Shiites, Jews, or Christians. Do not greet them, do not wish them a happy celebration, do not take them in marriage, do not take them as witnesses, and do not eat the animals they slaughter" (*The Acts of God's Creatures*, p. 125).

Imam Ahmad [Ibn Hanbal] was asked about those who insulted Abu Bakr, Omar, and Aisha.[28] He replied: "I do not see them as Muslims." Imam Malik said: "He who curses the companions of the Prophet is not part of Islam" (al-Khallal, *Kitab al-Sunna*, number 779).[29]

Faryabi said:[30] "I see the Shiites as atheists" (*Al-Lalika'i*, chapter 8, p. 1545).

As for Ibn Hazm, he brought evidence that the Jews and Christians had distorted the Bible and the Gospels; their only reply was that the Shiites claimed that the Quran had been distorted too. He said: "As for the Shiites' alterations, the Shiites are not Muslims.[31] They are disciples of the Jews and Christians in lying and unbelief" (*The Difference between Sects*, part 2, p. 78).

Ibn Taymiyya said: "It is thus clear that they are worse than those who have gone astray, and worthier of being fought than the Kharijites.[32] This is why people generally say that the Shiites are heterodox. This is what popular belief expresses when people say that the opposite of Sunni is Shiite: they are more clearly hostile to the Prophet's example and the laws of the Muslims than are the others who have gone astray" (*Sa'ir Ahl al-Ahwa*, chapter 28, p. 482). He also said: "If the Prophet's tradition and the consensus of the ulema agree on one thing, it is that if an attacker is Muslim and intends to kill, then he can be overcome only by killing him, even if he wanted to seize only half a dinar[33] . . . What, then, must be said of those who have left the laws of Islam and fight God and his Prophet?" (chapter 4, p. 251).

Still, the Muslims should know that we did not take the first step down this path. We were not the first to unsheathe our swords. These people have experience killing the preachers of Islam and the jihad fighters: they stab them in the back, while the world looks on in silence and complicity—even, sadly, those who are considered as outstanding figures of Sunni Islam. These people are a thorn in the side of the jihad fighters and a dagger in their backs. Everyone knows that most of the jihad fighters who fell during the war were killed by these people, who twist the daggers of hatred and malice night and day in open wounds.

The Sunnis

They are more lost than sheep among the wolves. They have no guide and wander in the desert of gullibility and neglect, divided and fragmented, without a leader capable of bringing them together and preserving the best of them. They are also of various kinds.

The People

These masses are the silent majority, an absent presence. "The distracted mob, ready to follow the first to croak, deprived of the enlightenment knowledge brings and of any solid support."[34] Even if they hate the Americans and hope that they will disappear, so that the dark clouds above can dissipate, they do nothing but wait for a sunny day and a bright future, an easy life, luxury and opulence. In the meantime, however, they are easy prey for the lying media and ferocious politicians . . . Still, they are the people of Iraq.

Sheikhs and Ulema

Most of them are errant mystics.[35] Their religion is limited to commemorating anniversaries, chanting and dancing to the songs of camel drivers, and concluding it all with a greasy banquet. They are the real opium of the people:[36] they are misleading guides for a nation fumbling through the dark night. As for the spirit of jihad, the jurisprudence of martyrdom, and the refusal of allegiance to unbelievers, they know nothing of it, just as the wolf knew nothing of Joseph's blood.[37] Despite the horrors and dire straits we are in, not one of them says a word about jihad or calls for sacrifice. They are powerless, and good for nothing.

The Brotherhood

As you know, they trade in the blood of martyrs and draw unwarranted glory from the piled-up skulls of the faithful.[38] They dismounted, threw down their arms, and declared—the liars—"No jihad!" All they do is extend their political control and seize their slice of the posts reserved for Sunnis from the pie of future government, meanwhile taking care to preserve their domination over jihadi groups through financial support.[39] This is for two reasons: first, in order to spread propaganda abroad, so that they can get money and support, as they did during the events in Syria;[40] and second, to control the situation and scatter these groups once the show is over and they can distribute the prizes. They are determined to create an Islamic shura (council) that will speak on behalf of the Sunnis, because they are used to playing a double game. They follow the twists and turns of politics, and their religion changes mercurially; it has no foundation or solid base. God preserve us from them.

The Mujahedeen

They are the best of the Sunnis, the cream of this country. On the whole, they are Sunnis and Salafists. Naturally, Salafism splintered when tested, and thus experienced a delay. These fighters are defined by the following:

A. Most of them are inexperienced, especially in organized collective action, because they are the product of a repressive regime that conscripted the entire country, spread terror and dread, and destroyed trust among the people. For this reason, most groups work in isolation, with no political prospects or foresight, or even any preparation for the time when they will inherit this earth. True, the idea has begun to ripen, and people began to whisper, then to speak out loud, about the need to rally and unite under the banner. Still, things are only beginning, and, praise God, we are trying to make them ripen more quickly.

B. Here, jihad is unfortunately reduced to planting mines and firing rockets or mortars from a distance. The Iraqi brothers still prefer to stay safe and go home to their wives at night, where they have nothing to fear. Some groups have even boasted that they have sustained no losses. But we often told them that safety and victory do not go together, that the tree of triumph and power can grow only if it is watered with blood and persistence, that the global Muslim community can live only on the odor of martyrdom and the perfume of blood spilled in God's name.[41] We have told them that people will awake from their stupor only if martyrdom and martyrs become their topic of conversation, day and night, something that requires patience and conviction; but our faith in God is great.

The Foreign Mujahedeen

Their numbers continue to be negligible as compared with the vast magnitude of the battle.[42] Still, we know that there are many brave men, and the army of jihad is already on the move . . . The only thing preventing us from declaring a general mobilization is that this country has no mountains in which to seek refuge and no forests in which to hide.[43] Our backs are exposed and our movements are known. There are eyes everywhere. "The enemy is before us and the sea behind."[44] Many Iraqis have shown us hospitality and see us as brothers, but when it comes to making their homes a base for launching operations, this is rarer than gold. This is why some brothers are occasionally a burden: we train new recruits while wearing this ball and chain, so to speak—even though, thanks be to God, through sustained effort and a resolute search we have been able to find safe places. These are growing more numerous with time and have become gathering points for the brothers who are waging the war and training the people of the country, so that a real war will break out, God willing.[45]

The Current Situation and the Future

There is no doubt that the Americans' losses are very heavy, because they are deployed over a vast area, among a population that can easily procure weapons. This makes them easy targets, which cause the believers' mouths to water. But America did not come here only to leave again, and it will not leave no matter how numerous its wounds are and how much of its blood is spilled. It is eager for the near future, when it hopes to disappear into its bases, safe and sound, turning Iraq over to the bastard government with an army and police force that will replay for the people the story of Saddam and his agents.[46] There is no doubt that the margin for maneuver has begun to shrink and that the noose around the mujahedeen's throats is growing tighter. With the deployment of soldiers and police, the future grows darker.

What Is Our Situation?

We have little support, friends have abandoned us, and we are in difficult straits, but God has graced us with strikes against the enemy. For all the martyrdom operations, except those in the north, we were the instigators, praise be to God. I have launched twenty-five operations up to this point, thanks be to God, including several among the heretics and their leaders, the Americans and their soldiers, [and] the police, soldiers, and the forces of the coalition. God willing, others will follow. We could not publicize them, because we wanted to establish ourselves and were waiting to have the appropriate means to bear the consequences of such declarations, so that we could show our strength and avoid suffering a setback (God preserve us). Thank God, we have made great strides as the moment of truth approaches. We feel our forces spreading and taking advantage of the security vacuum, freeing up strategic points that will serve as the germ of further operations and a rebirth, God willing.

The Work Plan

After study and reflection, we can classify our enemy into four groups.

The Americans

As you know, they are the most cowardly of men.[47] They are an easy prey, thank God. We ask God to enable us to kill and capture them, in order to sow panic among those behind them, and to trade them for our sheikhs and brothers in jail.[48]

The Kurds

These are a calamity, but they are a thorn it is not yet time to extract. They are last on our list, although we are making efforts to attract some of their leaders, God willing.

Soldiers, Police, and Collaborators

These are the eyes, ears, and arms of the occupier. We are determined to strike them hard in the coming months, before the situation has stabilized and they are able to consolidate their grip.[49]

The Heretics

In our opinion, they are the key to change, because attacking their religious, political, and military aspects will reveal their rage against the Sunnis. They will bare their fangs and show the secret hatred simmering in their hearts. If we manage to drag them into a religious war, we will be able to awaken the slumbering Sunnis, who will sense the imminent danger and the cruel death that these

Sabeans have in store for them.[50] Despite their weakness and dispersion, the Sunnis are the sharpest blades: they are bolder and more courageous than these devious and cowardly heretics, who show arrogance only toward the weak and attack only the powerless. For the most part, the Sunnis know how dangerous these people are: they are wary of them and fear the consequences if they take power. Were it not for the spiteful Sufi sheikhs and the Brothers, people would speak differently. What we can hope for is that these words will alarm those who have dozed off, and awaken the sleepers. We hope to disarm these people and reduce their ability to harm us before the decisive battle, in the anticipation that this battle will enrage the people against the Americans, who have brought ruin and caused this catastrophe. Still, we fear that the population will savor the pleasures it has been deprived of for so long, give in to an easy life, and become attached to it. Then it will choose safety and turn away from the clashing of swords and the neighing of horses.

Modus Operandi

As I have told you, the situation demands that we act courageously and decisively in an attempt to remedy it; otherwise we will find no solutions that allow us to serve religion. The solution we propose, but God knows best, is to drag the heretics into the fray, because this is the only way to prolong our battle against the unbelievers.[51] It is essential to engage with them for several reasons:

1. The heretics are the ones who secretly declared war against the Muslims. Therefore, they are the Sunnis' nearby, deadly enemy, even though the Americans are the archenemy.[52] The danger from the heretics, however, is greater, and the harm they can cause the community is greater, because there is virtual unanimity regarding the Americans, who attacked us.

2. They pledged allegiance to the Americans, backed them, and stood in their ranks against the mujahedeen. They will do everything in their power to cause the jihad and the mujahedeen to fail.

3. Fighting the heretics is the best means of taking the nation

into the battle. Here, we will review in some detail what we have said before: that the heretics have put on the uniforms of the Iraqi army and police, under the watchword of defending the nation and its citizens. On this pretext, they have begun to liquidate the Sunnis, while alleging that they are the destroyers, the remnants of the Baath, and terrorists spreading evil. Thanks to the propaganda of the Governing Council and the Americans, they have come between the Sunni masses and the mujahedeen.[53] Take the example of the so-called Sunni Triangle, where the army and the police have begun to deploy and are growing stronger every day. They are led by local Sunni collaborators, so that the army and police are linked to the population by blood and honor. This area, however, is the base from which we started and to which we return. When the Americans pull out, which they have already begun to do, and when they are replaced by collaborators who enjoy indestructible ties to the population, what will happen to us? We find ourselves forced to make a choice.

A. Either we fight them, even though this will create a division between us and the population.[54] We will be fighting their cousins and their sons, and under what pretext after the Americans, who hold the reins of power, pull out and Iraqis take power? Once democracy is established, there will be no excuse;

B. Or we pack up and go in search of another land. This is the sad story that has repeated itself on jihad's other battlefields, because our enemy grows stronger every day and his information grows more precise. By the Lord of the Kaaba, I swear we will be suffocated and wear down the roads. People practice the same religion as their rulers. "If their hearts are with you, their swords are with the Umayyads," meaning with power and victory (may God forfend).[55]

This is why I say again that the only solution is for us to strike the heretics, whether they are men of religion, soldiers, or others, until they submit to the Sunnis. You might object that it is too soon, and unfair to throw the nation into a battle for which it is unprepared; that this will cause losses and spill blood; but that is precisely what we want. There is no longer any place for right or wrong in our current situation. The heretics have destroyed all equilibrium, and God's religion is more precious than lives and souls. Since when has the majority stood on the side of right? Therefore, we must sacrifice for this religion, no matter how much blood is spilled. We will hasten on their way to paradise those who have been good; as for those who have not, we will be delivered from them. By God, this religion is more precious than anything: it is more important than people, wealth, and children. The best example is what happened to the makers of the pit.[56] Nawawi said the story proved that if the whole world fought to the death to prove the oneness of God, it would be good. People live, protect themselves, and preserve their honor only through sacrifice for this religion. By God, my brothers, we will do battle against the heretics and pass dark nights that we can no longer postpone, because the threat they pose is imminent . . . Know that they are the most cowardly of men, and that killing their leaders will only weaken and frighten them further.

When one of their leaders dies, the community will die with him. The situation is not the same among the Sunnis, because, if a leader dies or is killed, another arises, and the death of the first is a challenge that gives weak Sunnis heart. If you knew how afraid the Sunni population is, you would be distressed. How many mosques have been converted into *husayniyyas,*[57] how many houses have been brought down around their occupants' ears, how many brothers have been killed and mutilated, and how many sisters have been raped by these depraved unbelievers? If we could inflict painful, repeated blows upon them, in order to drag them into battle, we would be able to deal the deck anew. Then, the Governing Council and even the Americans will have no value or influence; the Americans will come back to battle with the heretics, which is what we want. Then, whether they like it or not, many Sunni regions will stand with the mujahedeen, and the mujahedeen will have assured themselves of a territory from which to strike the Shiites in the heart of their regions. In this way, strategic depth will be created, as well as a path for communication between the brothers abroad and the fighters within.

1. We are doing everything in our power and racing against the clock to form brigades of mujahedeen that can retreat to safe places, reconnoiter the territory, and pursue the enemy—Americans, police, and soldiers—on every road. We are busy training and recruiting. As for the heretics, God willing, they will receive their due from martyrdom operations and car bombs.

2. For some time now, we have been endeavoring to observe the situation and sort through those working in it. We are searching for sincere men, using a sound method to cooperate with them—coordinate with a view to associating and uniting with them—after having put them to the test. We hope that we have made great strides, and perhaps we will announce this soon, even if we do so gradually, so that everyone will know about it. The waiting period is over, and we intend to give the media something to think about, in such a way as to reveal the truth, inspire vocations, and rally men's wills. Then, the pen and the sword will work together in this jihad.

3. Alongside this action, we wish to erase doubt and explain legal prescriptions through tapes, tracts, lessons, and lectures. This will develop collective awareness, affirm the doctrine of the oneness of God, prepare the infrastructure, and clear people's conscience.

Time to Act

We hope to accelerate the pace of work and to form experienced brigades, while awaiting the moment when we begin to act and take control of the country—first at night, and then in broad daylight, with the blessing of God almighty. Approximately four months remain before the government is constituted, and, as you can see, we are racing to meet the deadline.[58] It would be ideal if we could do as we wish, upset the applecart and cause their plan to fail. If not, God forbid, the government will extend its control over the country and we will have to pack our bags and break camp to head for another land in which we can resume carrying the banner, unless God prefers to have us die as martyrs.

What about You?

You, dear brothers, are our leaders and guides, the representatives of jihad and battle. We do not see ourselves as worthy of competing with you or of striving to achieve glory for ourselves. Our only hope is to serve as a spearhead, a vanguard, a bridge the nation will cross toward the promised victory and the future to which we aspire. We have explained our way of seeing things, and our intentions. If you make your plan and agree to the idea of fighting heretical sects, we will be your soldiers, standing ready.[59] We will rally to your banner, obey you, and even pledge our allegiance to you, publicly and in the media, to irritate the unbelievers and please Muslims, for believers will see this as a sign from God.[60] But if you gauge things differently, we will still be brothers, and no quarrel will come between us. We will support each other and stand by each other in jihad. Awaiting your response, God keep you—you are the keys of all good and the only resource of Islam and the Muslims, amen, amen.

Peace be with you, and the mercy and blessings of God.

ANNOTATION

INDEX

Notes

Introduction: Osama Bin Laden

1. He belongs to the same generation as Ayman al-Zawahiri, born in 1951. In the Arab and Muslim world, which consists largely of the gerontocracy, both men are therefore among the youngest actors on the political scene.

2. Jonathan Randal, *Osama: The Making of a Terrorist* (New York, Knopf, 2004).

3. Ibid.

4. Peter L. Bergen, *Holy War, Inc.: Inside the Secret World of Osama bin Laden* (New York: Free Press, 2001).

5. In retrospect, the crises that broke out after September 11 may be seen as outstanding debts from the two wars of the 1980s, Iran-Iraq and Afghanistan. The link existed, at least, for Bin Laden and Saddam Hussein, both of whom were disappointed veterans and sword bearers for the West in the last phase of the cold war.

6. Regarding the Islamists' social base, made up of middle-class elements and young, disenfranchised urban dwellers, and the way the Arab regimes managed to dissociate these components from each other, see Gilles Kepel, *Jihad: The Trail of Political Islam*, trans. Anthony F. Roberts (Cambridge, Mass.: Harvard University Press, 2002).

7. The late Abu Musab al-Zarqawi started out as a serious challenger: an evanescent, ubiquitous star, he was even more of a "bad guy," and in any case he benefited from added value due to his presence on Iraqi territory.

8. Georges Lavau, *A quoi sert le parti communiste français?* (Paris: Fayard, 1981), pp. 342–343.

9. Ibid., p. 346.

10. Hadith narrated by al-Tirmidhi.

11. Of course, one can detect the obvious influence of Egyptian jihadist literature from the 1970s, and the concept of jihad as a neglected duty. In general, see radical twentieth-century thinkers, who often tended to deconstruct Islam, breaking it down into primary "elements" that believers should put together again: for example, the Pakistani ideologue Abul-Ala al-Mawdudi, *Four Basic Quranic*

Terms, presented in Gilles Kepel, *Muslim Extremism in Egypt: The Prophet and Pharaoh*, 2nd ed. (Berkeley: University of California Press, 2003).

12. In Bin Laden's *Tactical Recommendations*.

13. Bergen, *Holy War, Inc.*

14. Sigmund Freud, "Group Psychology and the Analysis of the Ego," trans. James Strachey (New York: Liveright, 1951).

15. Cited in Randal, *Osama*.

The Companions' Den

1. The texts presented here are "authenticated," having been published in a book titled *Ma'sadat al-Ansar al-'Arab bi Afghanistan* (The Arab Companions' Den in Afghanistan), written by an Egyptian author, Isam Diraz, and published in Cairo in 1991. Diraz, an Egyptian filmmaker, went to Afghanistan in the 1980s to film the Afghan front and visited the Afghan Arab training camps. The two first paragraphs record the testimony of an Afghan Arab, Abu Muhammad al-Suri— "the Syrian"; with respect to the Service Office, see "Abdallah Azzam, the Imam of Jihad."

2. Al-Urduni means "the Jordanian." On the jihadists' noms de guerre, see the first note in the introduction to the section on Zarqawi.

3. This was the first jihadist boarding house *(madhafa)* in Peshawar, dubbed the partisans' house *(bayt al-ansar)*. Soon, there were dozens of boarding houses in this town on the Afghan border.

4. Bin Laden is now speaking.

5. The emir of the Union of Mujahedeen in Afghanistan was Abdul Rasul Sayyaf. See notes to Azzam, "The Defense of Muslim Territories."

6. In Arabic, the term used *(nafila)* designates a religious action that is not a duty, like an additional prayer after the five ritual ones. As mentioned earlier, however, Abdallah Azzam—and his disciples, Bin Laden among them—had declared that "jihad" in Afghanistan was an individual duty *(fard 'ayn)*.

7. The village of Jaji is located in the eastern province of Paktīā, not far from the border with Pakistan.

8. Other sources emphasize the presence of many Egyptian instructors in the "den's" early phase, most of them former army or police officers, like the renowned Egyptian fighter Abu Ubayda al-Banshiri. See note below. Most of the inhabitants of Mecca initially rejected the Prophet's message, and it was in Medina, where he sought refuge in 622, that he found many partisans. Here, the parallel with early Islamic history is clear, as Bin Laden implies, since the first converts— not to Islam but to "jihad"—were also from Medina. Such narratives aim to give a mythical dimension to the mujahedeen's activities in Afghanistan. It is possible that Bin Laden broadened the affiliation to Medina, including within it other ar-

eas of the Hejaz or the environs of Medina. This would explain why Bin Laden—who hails from Jidda, and not Medina—presents himself as one of the Medinans.

9. The difficulties encountered in mobilizing Arab combatants illustrate the phenomenon of "jihad tourism," which many young Arabs engaged in: they would go to Peshawar during the summer holidays and then return to school, convinced that they had participated in the jihad.

10. In Arabic, *Ma'sadat al-Ansar.* The word *ma'sada* means den, or region populated by lions. Many mujahedeen drew on the symbolism associated with lions, as did the members and groups of the Al Qaeda network at a later date. It should also be noted that the name Osama means lion. As for the term *ansar,* it designates the inhabitants of Medina who welcomed the Prophet upon his arrival from Mecca and converted to Islam. Although the term was widespread among the Islamist movements, given the idea of "Muslim vanguard" that it implies, the decision to use it in these circumstances was perhaps also motivated by the fact that, as Bin Laden explained earlier, most of the group's members were from Medina (or the Hejaz).

11. It was precisely this type of collective social experience in the training camps set up in Afghanistan that produced the strong internal cohesion of the "Afghan Arab networks," whether among the generation of the 1980s or among that of the Al Qaeda period, 1996–2001.

12. The Prophet's mosque in Medina.

13. Jalalabad lies in eastern Afghanistan, halfway between Kabul and Peshawar. In spring 1987, the Jalalabad region was the scene of a series of violent battles between the Red Army and the mujahedeen. The events of Jalalabad have an important place in the Afghan Arabs' mythology, because the first purely Arab combat units, trained in the "den," participated in these battles.

14. *Al-Ansar* designates the companions of the Prophet Muhammad. See notes to Azzam, "Join the Caravan."

15. Kaab Bin Malik is said to have declaimed these verses on the day when the trench around Medina was dug, in 627. They must have been quoted from memory, since the citation is inaccurate. The verses can be found in the classical dictionary *Lisan al-'Arab* (The Arabs' Tongue), where it is cited to illustrate the entry "h-b-y." See Ibn Manzur, *Lisan al-'Arab* (Beirut: Dar Bayrut, n.d.), 14:6.

16. Gulbuddin Hekmatyar, born in 1947, is an Afghan warlord, the founder of the Hezb-i Islami in Afghanistan; he has been important figure on the Afghan political scene since the early 1970s. On Sheikh Sayyaf, see notes to Azzam, "The Defense of Muslim Territories."

17. The Spetnatz, Russian special forces.

18. City in Saudi Arabia, southeast of Mecca.

19. Abu Ubayda al-Misri ("the Egyptian") or al-Banshiri (from Panshir), was Al Qaeda's "military commander in chief." This former police officer, an Egyptian,

called "the man from Panshir" because of his military feats in Afghanistan, died in spring 1996, when the ferry he was on sank off the coast of Kenya. He was probably preparing the attacks that were carried out on August 7, 1998, in Nairobi and Dar es Salaam.

20. See Abdallah Azzam, "Morals and Jurisprudence of Jihad."

21. According to some estimates, 50,000 Arabs participated in combat operations, out of 175,000 to 250,000 Afghans every year. See Mark Urban, *War in Afghanistan* (London: Macmillan, 1988), p. 244. Nevertheless, all estimates of the number of Afghan Arabs who participated in the Afghan jihad remain uncertain.

22. The tribal areas on the Afghan-Pakistani border are the site of an enormous open-air market for all sorts of weaponry. The Red Army had pulled out of Afghanistan on February 15, 1989. The forces confronting the "den's" mujahedeen were therefore those loyal to Afghanistan's communist president, Muhammad Najibullah.

Declaration of Jihad against the Americans

1. On August 23, 1996, a fax was sent from the mountains of the Hindu Kush, in Afghanistan, to several Arab newspapers. It was signed as follows: "A message from Osama Bin Laden to his Muslim brothers worldwide, and in the Arabian Peninsula in particular, dated Friday, April 9, 1417 / August 23, 1996. From the mountains of the Hindu Kush, Khorāsān, Afghanistan." It also bore the title "Expel the Jews and Christians from the Arabian Peninsula," or "Expel the Pagans from the Arabian Peninsula." The title is taken from an unauthenticated hadith the Prophet is said to have uttered shortly before he died. Various translations are circulating online: see, for example, http://www.pbs.org/newshour/terrorism/international/fatwa_1996.html.

2. On April 18, 1996, over two hundred civilians were killed in an Israeli bombardment—part of Operation Grapes of Wrath—of a United Nations refugee camp in Qana, southern Lebanon, triggering international outrage. Bin Laden issued his declarations a few months later.

3. It is interesting to note that Bin Laden makes no distinction here between massacres of Muslims and the political repression of Islamist movements. Tajik independence, secured after the Soviet Union collapsed in 1991, led to a civil war between "neo-Communists" and a coalition of Islamists (linked to the Islamic Revival Party) and democrats, which claimed tens of thousands of victims. A peace agreement among the different factions was concluded in 1997, but its implementation was slow and tentative. In August 1996 battles were still raging. There is a Muslim minority in Burma, concentrated especially in the region of Arakan, on the border with Bangladesh. Since the early 1990s, Islam served as a scapegoat for

Burman nationalism, and multiple repression campaigns and pogroms took place. ARNO (the Arakan Rohingya National Organization), calling for Arakan's independence, was active in the region starting in 1988. Rumors of ties between ARNO and the Al Qaeda movement were propagated, but an expert on the matter, Michel Gilquin, considers that they are unfounded (http://religioscope.com/info/notes/2002_033_myanmar_islam.htm). In Kashmir, different movements are active, with ties of varying closeness with Al Qaeda (especially Jaysh-i-Muhammad and Lashkar-i-Tayyiba)—see Abdallah Azzam, "The Defense of Muslim Territories." Assam is a federal state of the Indian Union, located on the border with Bangladesh, where a large Muslim minority lives. The main separatist movement active there is the United Assam Liberation Front, founded in 1979. Originally Marxist in orientation, it seems—according to certain sources—that it drew closer to the Al Qaeda movement in the 1990s. On the Philippines, see notes to Azzam, "The Defense of Muslim Territories." Pattani is a Thai province where the population is mainly Malay Muslim. A separatist movement developed there in the 1960s, led especially by the Pattani United Liberation Organization. Like many of the region's movements, in time it adopted Islamist rhetoric. Ogaden is a region with a Muslim majority in Ethiopia, near Somalia, where separatist movements are active. They demand either complete independence or integration with Somalia. In the 1990s, a Somali Islamist movement, al-Ittihad al-Islami, some of whose members are suspected of having ties to Al Qaeda, placed such demands at the heart of its political program. It carried out several attacks in Addis Ababa in 1996 and 1997, to which the Ethiopian government responded with repression. As for Somalia, Al-Ittihad al-Islami, the main Somali Islamist organization, clashed with several local warlords who made bids for power during the 1990s and was drawn into combat against the Ethiopian army in Ogaden. It emerged from these conflicts depleted, and thereafter virtually ceased to exist. On Eritrea, see notes to Azzam, "The Defense of Muslim Territories." In 1991 the Republic of Chechnya, whose population is Muslim—in Russia, where the vast majority is Orthodox Christian—seceded. In 1994 Boris Yeltsin, then president of Russia, sent out a military expedition to reintegrate it into the federation. After extremely violent battles, the Russian army was forced to admit defeat and left Chechnya. A small number of Afghan Arabs participated in the battles. And finally, the Dayton Accords, signed in 1995, put an official end to the war in Bosnia, dividing the Republic of Bosnia-Herzegovina in two: the Croatian-Muslim federation and the Serbian republic of Bosnia. Still, everyone remembers the horrors of the war, especially the atrocities perpetrated against Muslims in Srebrenica. It is to this history, which was very recent at the time, that Bin Laden is referring.

4. *Dar al-Islam*, in Arabic, may be rendered as "abode of Islam," continuing the metaphor of home and hearth, or "Muslim territories," according to the medieval Muslim geographical view. The reference is to the non-Muslim, American or

allied troops stationed in Saudi Arabia, at King Fahd's invitation, on August 7, 1990, five days after Saddam Hussein invaded Kuwait.

5. On Ibn Taymiyya, see Abdallah Azzam, "Join the Caravan." Abd al-Aziz Ibn Abd al-Salam was a religious scholar from Damascus belonging to the Shāfi'ī school of jurisprudence, who died in 1262. He wrote *Qawa'id al-Ahkam* (The Rules of Judgment), among other works. Like Ibn Taymiyya, Ibn Abd al-Salam did not hesitate to criticize the regime of his time, which was then led by al-Salih Isma'il Ibn al-Adil: Ibn Abd al-Salam reproached this ruler for having handed over the fortress of Safad to the Crusaders. As in the case of Ibn Taymiyya, his outspokenness landed him in prison. Here, Bin Laden is celebrating the example of the intellectual who "speaks the truth to power," by comparing him implicitly to the "palace ulema" who kowtow to the ruling regimes.

6. This phrase alludes to the Quran 24:21: "And were it not for the grace / And mercy of God on you, / Not one of you would ever / Have been pure: but God / Doth purify whom He pleases."

7. Bin Laden is accusing the Americans of having killed Azzam. This is the version of events that is most widespread in Islamist circles. See "Abdallah Azzam, the Imam of Jihad." Ahmad Yassin was born in Gaza in 1936. He graduated from Al-Azhar University in Cairo and worked as a preacher in various Gaza mosques before establishing the Islamic Resistance Movement (Hamas) in December 1987. He was arrested and jailed by the Israeli forces in 1989 and released in a 1997 prisoner swap with Jordan. He resumed leadership of Hamas, but Israeli forces killed him in March 2004, as part of the targeted assassination campaign carried out by Ariel Sharon's government. At the time when Bin Laden issued this declaration, in August 1996, therefore, Sheikh Yassin was still a prisoner in Israel. The nocturnal voyage *(al-isra' wal-mi'raj)*, according to Muslim tradition, took Muhammad from "the nearest mosque" (Mecca) to "the farthest" (literally, *al-Masjid al-Aqsa*, taken to designate the Dome of the Rock in Jerusalem): Quran 17:1. As Oleg Grabar points out, it is important to note that the Quran mentions neither Jerusalem nor an ascent. Still, starting in the seventh century, the reference to a faraway (or distant, or the farthest, or the Last Oratory, depending on the translation) mosque was understood to mean a sanctuary in Jerusalem. See Oleg Grabar, *The Dome of the Rock* (Cambridge, Mass.: Harvard University Press, 2006).

8. Omar Abdel Rahman, known in the media as the blind Egyptian cleric, graduated from Al-Azhar University and played an important role in the plot to assassinate Egyptian president Anwar Sadat, by serving as mufti to the group of assassins. In the trial that followed, he was judged but acquitted—officially, owing to lack of evidence. He left Egypt for Sudan in 1989, then traveled to the United States, where he obtained residency in July 1990. He then launched his career as a radical preacher in New York. In August 1993 he was arrested by the FBI and ac-

cused of involvement in the attack on the World Trade Center, carried out in February of that year. In 1995 he received a life sentence.

9. Salman al-Awda and Safar al-Hawali spearheaded Islamist opposition to the Saudi monarchy. In particular because they criticized the American presence in the country during the early 1990s, they were arrested in 1994 and released only in 1999, three years after this declaration was issued.

10. Bin Laden is equating his departure from Afghanistan, a decision he took freely because civil war was raging among former mujahedeen commanders, with his forced departure from Sudan, which took place under pressure from the international community, and the United States in particular.

11. In Arabic, *qa'eda amina,* an expression that echoes the notion of "solid base" *(qa'eda sulba)* developed by Azzam. See notes to Azzam, "Join the Caravan." Khorāsān is the classical name of the vast region comprising eastern Iran and most of Afghanistan. Bin Laden, like most ideologues of the Islamist movement, consciously uses dated place-names when referring to certain Muslim territories. His aim is to withdraw these areas symbolically from Western influence. The same symbolic struggle occurs over dates (which he often gives according to the Hijri calendar). In Afghan Arab circles during the 1980s, a debate took place over whether to call Afghanistan by its name as a nation-state or by the older term of Khorāsān. Azzam, in particular, wrote an article on the matter, titled "Afghanistan or Khorāsān?" and published in *Al-Jihad,* issue 40, 1988.

12. Bin Laden sought to preserve the myth of Afghanistan's having fallen to the mujahedeen, although this factor was certainly not decisive in the outcome of the conflict.

13. "Path of the Prophet" is, once again, a term used to designate Palestine. The "land of the two sanctuaries" refers to Saudi Arabia.

14. Bin Laden is citing Ibn Taymiyya's best-known statement, and the most frequently repeated in jihadist literature since Abd al-Salam Faraj. In particular, see Abdallah Azzam, "Join the Caravan," and Ayman al-Zawahiri, "Loyalty and Separation."

15. Here, Bin Laden's ecumenical approach takes on its greatest significance and reaches its greatest breadth. He is not denying the dogmatic divisions that fragment the Muslim community nor the deep convictions that separate "true" Muslims from "false" believers, but these divisions subordinated, and therefore must be postponed, so that another more important division—between Muslims and Western aggressors—can be dealt with.

16. William Cohen was secretary of defense under president Bill Clinton. On November 13, 1995, five Americans and two Indians were killed when a booby-trapped car parked in front of National Guard headquarters in Riyadh exploded. Three unknown groups claimed responsibility for the act. Four radical Sunni Islamists from Saudi Arabia were ultimately sentenced and put to death. Although

they do not seem to have been acting on Bin Laden's behalf, several of them had spent time in Afghanistan in the 1980s and early 1990s and had established links with members of his organization. On June 26, 1996, a booby-trapped truck blew up on a U.S. military base in Khobar, killing nineteen Americans. The Saudi and American authorities officially accused the Saudi Hezbollah, backed by Iran. It seems increasingly likely, however, that the attacks were carried out by jihadist militants close to Osama Bin Laden's network.

17. In 1983, 241 Marines under United Nations mandate, making up part of a multinational peacekeeping force, were killed in Beirut in a suicide bombing that used a truck loaded with explosives. Hezbollah, the radical Shiite movement, claimed responsibility for the attack. Soon afterward, U.S. troops were shipped back home.

18. Bin Laden is alluding to the terrorist attacks on two hotels, the Gold Mohur and the Mövenpick, in Aden, carried out on December 29, 1992, to kill American soldiers who were traveling through Yemen on their way to Somalia. The attacks failed to kill a single American soldier (two tourists died and seven were wounded), because the jihadists attacked the wrong hotels. Still, the attacks went down in jihadist mythology as a true success, because U.S. forces left Yemen only a few days later.

19. Bin Laden is comparing the courage shown by the young jihadists to the cowardice of the American soldiers, using an expression taken from a hadith that Islamist literature cites frequently: "God will make your enemies cease to fear you, and he will place weakness in your hearts . . . 'What does this mean, Prophet of God?' Love of life and aversion to death." See notes to Azzam, "Join the Caravan."

20. In Arabic that pre-Islamic time is known as *al-jahiliyya*.

Interview with CNN

1. Osama Bin Laden was interviewed in Afghanistan by Peter Arnett and Peter Bergen; the interview was broadcast on May 12, 1997. For a transcript of the interview (© CNN), see http://www.informationclearinghouse.info/article7204.htm. For a description of the circumstances in which the interview took place, see Peter Bergen, *Holy War, Inc.: Inside the Secret World of Osama bin Laden* (New York: Free Press, 2001).

2. The editors are unaware of any attempts by the Saudi authorities to assassinate Bin Laden. The only known attempts were carried out by other Islamists: in early 1994, Sudanese Islamists, with whom he had ideological differences, apparently tried to assassinate him twice in Sudan, unsuccessfully.

3. The cult of death and martyrdom is central to jihadist culture. This, in the militants' eyes, is the source of their strength, since, by contrast with their enemies, they are not afraid of dying. See notes to Bin Laden, "Declaration of Jihad."

4. The link between action and media is consubstantial: actions must be "seen" and "heard in the media." This is part of action as Al Qaeda defines it: it must be inscribed on a media surface.

5. The mid-1990s were a time of renewed tensions and violence in the Near East, after the calm that followed the Oslo accords. A few weeks before this interview was broadcast, in March 1997, construction work began on the Jewish colony of Har Homa in East Jerusalem, triggering a serious crisis. The 1990s, which are seen today as a "posthistorical" period, or even a "sabbatical," in George W. Bush's words, were to the contrary years of intense frustration in the Middle East, owing to the persistent American presence in Saudi Arabia and the embargo on Iraq. The link established between the Clinton administration and the region's suffering during that period is a reminder that hatred for America was not linked solely to President Bush's mandate.

6. This is a leitmotif in Bin Laden's discourse: taking action, in a sort of pedagogy by example, is necessary because it is the only way to be heard by the U.S. government. Bin Laden seems to be announcing attacks on Saudi Arabia (following those of 1995 and 1996). The following jihadist terrorist attack on that country, however, took place only in May 2003, when a large-scale suicide bombing killed thirty-four people, most of them Westerners, in several residential compounds for foreigners in Riyadh.

7. Here, Bin Laden seems to be emphasizing that the U.S. Army is a volunteer force, not based on conscription, but made up of professionals who chose to belong to it; this was an aggravating circumstance. Still, this was far removed from the argument that developed the following year, which made every U.S. citizen, anywhere in the world, a legitimate target. Bin Laden is also referring here to the fact that in 1994 the Saudi government jailed several Islamist opposition figures, who had denounced "America's occupation of the country and the corruption of the royal family," among other things. Among them were Sheikhs Salman al-Awda and Safar al-Hawali, to whom Bin Laden had already referred in his jihad declaration of 1996 (see notes to Bin Laden, "Declaration of Jihad"). Paradoxically, after they were freed in 1999, the two sheikhs curried favor with the regime and condemned the outburst of jihadist violence that began with the 9/11 attacks.

8. On Muhammad's night journey, see notes to Bin Laden, "Interview with Al-Jazeera."

World Islamic Front Statement Urging Jihad

1. Quran 9:5. Sura 9, the sura of separation *(bara)* or of repentance *(tawba)* contains some of the most belligerent passages in the Quran, and for that reason it is abundantly cited by jihadist ideologues. The fifth verse of this sura, of which

only the first part is cited here, is the famous "verse of the sword" *(ayat al-sayf)*. For Islamists, this verse cancels out any others calling for a conciliatory attitude toward non-Muslims.

2. This hadith is cited in Ahmad Ibn Hanbal's *Masnad*. Various translations of this fatwa are available online. See for example http://www.fas.org/irp/world/para/docs/980223-fatwa.htm. "Crusaders," in the jihadist lexicon, is a term used to designate Western states, seen as being in a state of warfare against Islam and the "Muslim nation." The use of this term makes it possible for Bin Laden to establish a direct link between the medieval Crusades and the current political and military intervention of some Western countries in the Middle East. The term also makes it possible to insert Israeli state policy in the same lineage, since Israel is seen as a crusader state.

3. In Arabic, the Arabian Peninsula is Jazirat al-Arab, or the island of the Arabs. This alludes both to the peninsula's relatively hostile but protective geography and to its history of resistance to foreign invasions. Technically, the Arabian Peninsula includes all the countries of that geographical region: Saudi Arabia, Yemen, and the Gulf countries, from Oman to Kuwait. Still, Bin Laden, and more generally the Saudi opposition, designate Saudi Arabia as "the land of the two holy sanctuaries." This also recalls a hadith the Prophet is said to have pronounced on his deathbed, expressing his last wishes, and which Bin Laden cites frequently: "Umar Ibn al-Khattab heard the Messenger of God (peace be upon him) say: 'I will expel the Jews and Christians from the Arabian Peninsula and will not leave any but Muslims'" (*Sahih Muslim*, 4366).

4. Bin Laden's defense of the Iraqi people—of whom a majority are Shiites—is typical of the manner in which he concealed aspects of reality that were not consistent with his worldview (like the Shiites) in order to mobilize a symbol that would find an audience throughout the Arab world (Baghdad and more generally Iraq, as the emblem of the Abbasid caliphate and the golden age of Islam). One of the many reproaches Bin Laden directed against the Saudi regime at the time was its having allowed the United States and Great Britain to launch raids from bases in Saudi Arabia on the U.N.-enforced no-fly zones on Iraqi territory.

5. This estimate of the number of victims claimed by the embargo is consistent with statistics issued by various Western nongovernmental organizations, owing especially to a drastic increase in infant mortality.

6. Arab nationalist literature of the Baathist school presented Iraq as a "pivotal state," and therefore as a contender with Syria for a position at the center of a unified Arab nation. Bin Laden, therefore, is recycling Arab nationalist rhetoric to buttress his argument. The author deliberately sets up an opposition between a list of large states with considerable populations and "paper statelets" that he failed to identify but which are clearly the small oil emirates of the Gulf. Here, Bin Laden is using a cliché of Arab nationalism, which condemns the nation's "frag-

mentation" *(inqisam)* by Western imperialism. One finds the same expression in Zarqawi's statements.

7. Muwaffaq Ibn Qudama al-Maqdisi, a jurist of the Hanbali school of law, is mainly known as the author of *Al-Mughni fi Sharh Mukhtasar al-Khiraqi.* Born near Jerusalem, he left his birthplace with his family when he was still a child, probably because of the harassment the Franks were inflicting on the Muslims. He settled in Damascus, where he received an education from Hanbali teachers, and went on to pursue his studies in Baghdad. *Al-Mughni* is a Hanbali legal work. Al-Maqdisi is also known for the polemical tracts he penned against the philosophers. Like several scholars of the time, especially those belonging to the Hanbali school, he participated in a military expedition led by Saladin in 1187, which led to the reconquest of Jerusalem, then occupied by the Crusaders. Bin Laden often refers to ulema who also took up arms at crucial or critical moments in Muslim history: Ibn Hanbal, Ibn Qudama, and Ibn Taymiyya were at the same time theologians, jurists, and committed individuals, who frequently risked their lives in the political and military events of their time. Ala' al-Din Abu Bakr Ibn Mas'ud al-Kasani (1144–1189), called the king of ulema, was one of the greatest scholars of the Hanafi school of jurisprudence. His principal work was the *Bada'i' al-Sana'i' fi Tartib al-Shara'i'*, of which the first edition was published only in 1909, when it gave rise to great excitement among contemporary jurists. See W. Heffening, "al-Kasani, 'ala' al-din abu bakr b. mas'ud, called malik al-'ulama," *Encyclopaedia of Islam*, ed. P. Bearman, Th. Bianquis, C. E. Bosworth, E. van Donzel, and W. P. Heinrichs (Amsterdam: Brill, 2007); Brill Online, American University in Cairo, March 9, 2007, http://www.brillonline.nl/subscriber/entry?entry= islam_SIM-3961. Sheikh Muhammad al-Qurtubi, a Maliki scholar who lived in Andalusia in the thirteenth century, was born in Córdoba. He is known throughout the Muslim world for his works in religious studies and philology; he traveled through Asia and died in Upper Egypt in 1272. His commentary on the Quran, today a reference work, makes remarkably few references to the apocryphal or external sources (gnosis and pre-Islamic and Biblical legends) that some other commentators use abundantly. This purified aspect of his work seems to have appealed to Bin Laden."Sheikh al-Islam" is an honorific designating the famous Hanbali scholar Taqiy al-Din Ibn Taymiyya (1263–1328). See notes to Azzam, "Join the Caravan."

8. Jihad, which is usually attached to a specific territory, is thereby deterritorialized and extended worldwide by the signatories to the fatwa, something that marks a clear break with classical legal tradition. This was already the case in 1989, when Ruhollah Khomeini issued a fatwa making the murder of Salman Rushdie (the author of *The Satanic Verses*) a duty incumbent on all Muslims everywhere. Here, "the Americans" are presented not as apostates *(ahl al-ridda)*, as Rushdie was for the blasphemous tone of his novel, but as universal enemies; the

punishment they deserve thus has universal value and can be applied anywhere in the world.

9. Quran 9:36, 2:193. The term *fitna,* as it is used here, designates any discord within the Muslim community. Originally, the term referred to a trial, a temptation, or a test of faith. In that regard, *fitna* also designates the trials suffered after death. Historically, the term refers to the wars of succession that beset the early Muslim community, pitting the partisans of Ali Ibn Abi Talib, the Prophet's cousin and son-in-law, against those of the caliphs of Quraysh (first Omar and Uthman, and later the family of Mu'awiya). The word is highly polemical and is used in accordance with one's position in the debate: thus, the repression of the Hanbalis by the Abbasid regime in the ninth century was carried out in the name of fighting *fitna,* taken to mean secession in a form fatal to the community's integrity. As for the Hanbalis, they referred to this episode as a *mihna,* or calamity, imposed by despots upon the just. These word games are repeated today: jihadist Islamist movements are often accused of provoking *fitna;* meanwhile, they claim to prefer jihad to unbelief, the risk of chaos, or submission. On the dialectic of jihad and *fitna,* see Gilles Kepel, *Jihad: The Trail of Political Islam,* trans. Anthony F. Roberts (Cambridge, Mass.: Harvard University Press, 2002); and Kepel, *The War for Muslim Minds: Islam and the West,* trans. Pascale Ghazaleh (Cambridge, Mass.: Harvard University Press, 2004).

10. Quran 4:75.

11. Classical jihad doctrine permitted seizing the possessions of a defeated non-Muslim enemy, including women and children, who, once in Muslim hands, were to be converted to Islam or enslaved.

12. Bin Laden is posing here more as counselor to the prince than as leader of the Muslim community. This bears little relation to certain declarations in which he denied any legitimacy to the regimes in power in Muslim countries. This "legalistic" pose competes, in his discourse, with a more revolutionary vision.

13. Quran 8:24.

14. Quran 9:38–39.

15. Quran 3:139. This litany of Quranic verses, cited in the conclusion, is typical of classical fatwas, and allows the authors to insert their opinion with a recognized scholastic genealogy. The goal is to make of this eminently political text "a fatwa like any other."

16. Hamzah was a Pakistani Islamist.

17. Khalil was a well-known radical Islamist from Pakistan.

18. The fact that representatives of small organizations, like Khan, relatively marginal in the countries where they carried out their struggles, signed this document deserves to be emphasized. The main function of this list of names and organizations is to create the impression of widespread support for this *fatwa* throughout the Muslim world.

19. Taha subsequently withdrew from the World Islamic Front, was arrested in Syria and handed over to the Egyptian authorities, who executed him. He signed this document on his personal initiative: his organization, whose spiritual guide, Omar Abdel Rahman, is serving a life sentence in the United States, disavowed him. Most of its leadership concluded a "truce" with the Egyptian government after a dozen foreign tourists were massacred in Luxor in the fall of 1997, cutting the group off from some of its supporters.

Interview with Al-Jazeera

1. The interview was recorded in December 1998. The question posed by the journalist, Jamal Ismail, was "Who is Osama Bin Laden?" In his answer, Bin Laden spoke in the traditional manner, giving the names of his male ancestors, but referred to himself in the third person singular before reverting to the first person. A different translation of the full transcript is available at http://www.robert-fisk.com/usama_interview_aljazeera.htm.

2. At the time, many of the expatriates from other Arab countries, who had come to work in Riyadh, lived in this neighborhood. It had the reputation of being far more liberal than the rest of the city, for its residents' behavior was more consistent with the norms prevailing in the rest of the Middle East than with the Wahhabi code applied in the Najd region. For the more radical ulema of the time, Malazz was a veritable enclave of unbelief in Muslim territory. One could imagine that by leaving Malazz for Medina, Bin Laden was undertaking his own "migration"—recalling the Prophet Muhammad's flight from Mecca, which was still pagan, to Medina in 622. The reference may be read here as partaking of the symbolic construction of Bin Laden's persona as the "savior of Islam."

3. Available biographies do not mention Bin Laden spending time in Mecca and Medina, the two holy cities. The sojourns he mentions may have been brief periods when the family, or Osama alone, accompanied the father on inspection tours of construction sites. The fact that Bin Laden asserts that he lived in these cities would then contribute to the image of Bin Laden as somehow destined to save Islam. On his desire to give the impression that he was originally from Medina, see notes to Bin Laden, "The Companions' Den."

4. The title "Sheikh" is used to address wise, elderly men or those with knowledge of religious matters. Although Bin Laden's father was illiterate, and was respected mainly for his social and professional position, Bin Laden plays on the ambiguity to claim a genealogy that might serve to legitimize his religious aspirations. Hadramawt is a region of in southern Yemen, traditionally a source of emigration. Its inhabitants are known around the Indian Ocean for their zeal at work and their frugal lifestyle.

5. The expansion project, begun in 1955, increased the mosque's total surface

from thirty thousand square meters to two hundred thousand. God appears here as having favored Bin Laden's father twice: this project enriched him dramatically, while making him appear to have been "chosen" for the task. The Kaaba, the cubic edifice (each side measuring around fifteen meters) at the center of the *haram* (sanctuary) at Mecca, is the point toward which all Muslims pray *(qibla)*. According to Muslim tradition, it was founded by Ibrahim (Abraham), with the help of his son Isma'il (Ishmael): Quran 2:125. The black stone, a chunk of basalt around thirty centimeters in diameter, is lodged in one of its angles. Throughout its history, the Kaaba has been destroyed, rebuilt, and restored several times.

6. This expansion project began in 1951, increasing the surface of the mosque at Medina (the Prophet's burial place) from six thousand to sixteen thousand square meters. Bin Laden's father was therefore responsible for renovating the two holiest sites of Islam.

7. The Dome of the Rock, also known (inaccurately) as the mosque of Omar, was commissioned in 691–692 by the Umayyad caliph Abd al-Malik Ibn Marwan and stands on the site of a small mosque built by the caliph Omar on the occasion of Jerusalem's conquest by the Muslims.

8. Excessive profit *(riba)* is forbidden in the Quran (2:276–281). The expression used here evokes this prohibition.

9. This is a direct allusion to the title "servant of the two sanctuaries" that the king of Saudi Arabia took in 1986. The title was used for the first time by Saladin, to reduce the legitimacy of the Abbasid caliph in Baghdad. The same type of rivalry for legitimacy is therefore at work here: Bin Laden is challenging the Saud family's ability to serve (and defend) the holy sites of Islam.

10. The three mosques in question are the great mosque of Mecca, the Prophet's mosque in Medina, and the Dome of the Rock in Jerusalem. It might be possible to see this statement as an allusion to the nocturnal voyage *(isra')* that the Prophet Muhammad accomplished, according to Muslim tradition, between the "closest mosque" (Mecca) and the "farthest mosque" (the literal meaning of Al-Aqsa): Quran 17:1. This interpretation would support the suggestion that Bin Laden was attempting to found the myth of his father, and his family, as somehow chosen by God.

11. Muhammad Bin Laden, born in Yemen, emigrated to Saudi Arabia and established a public works company there in 1931. It later became the Saudi Binladen Group. This may be an unconscious allusion to the symbolic monopoly that King Abdul Aziz, the kingdom's founder, enjoyed over the country's history, and which Osama, the son of another founder, would like to take from Abdul Aziz's sons.

12. Osama's father died in a plane crash in 1967, while he was inspecting work on Route 15, which goes through Asir Province. Bin Laden built important infrastructure during the war in Afghanistan, and later on in Sudan. Osama is tracing

his experience as a construction expert back to his childhood, although all he did was accompany his father on trips to various construction sites. See "The Companions' Den." His way of referring to the university could be read as a critique of the Saudi royal family's tendency to appropriate the country's institutions symbolically, or as an attack on King Abdul Aziz.

13. In debates over the universal application of the concept of human rights, some Muslim thinkers have argued that the Quran defends the "rights of living creatures" and therefore contains its own definition of human rights. Here, Bin Laden is suggesting that his struggle has both universal and purely Islamic value. Although those whom Bin Laden sees as the "enemies" of the Muslim world are diverse, they appear here reduced to Americans alone, who are presented as the backbone of the system Bin Laden seeks to destroy.

14. Beyond the right Muslims have to defend themselves and their holy sites, Bin Laden is invoking the universal right to resist occupation and oppression. This oscillation between the religious, national, and universal registers is frequently found in his discourse.

15. *Qibla* is the direction Muslims face in prayer. Around 624, the Prophet directed prayers toward the Kaaba in Mecca; during the sixteen previous months, Muslims had turned toward Jerusalem. Bin Laden is using "Judeo-crusader alliance" to designate the troops of the U.S.-led coalition that arrived in Saudi Arabia in the summer of 1990, at the request of the Saudi authorities, who sought to defend the country against what they believed was an imminent Iraqi invasion. In choosing to refer to "the land of the two sanctuaries," Bin Laden appears reluctant to use the name Saudi Arabia, perhaps because it would imply recognizing the legitimacy of the Saud family. He therefore chooses to designate the country by referring to the sanctuaries of Mecca and Medina.

16. A subtle shift in the register of legitimation takes place here: from the national ("Free our land") to the eschatological ("God's word will be law").

17. In Arabic, there are several terms with connotations that correspond to "virility" or "manhood." *Muruwwa* designates the characteristics of an accomplished Arab man according to classical literary tradition (hospitality, generosity, honor). *Fuhula* has more specifically sexual implications. Here, Bin Laden is using *rujula*, signifying virility in its traditional social and moral dimensions: defense of one's family and possessions, courage, and so on.

18. Here, too, one finds a multifaceted legitimation of the right to self-defense: as men (the biological connotations echo his earlier remarks regarding the rights common to all living creatures) and as Muslims (the second point made by Bin Laden).

19. Bin Laden is referring to the presence of women soldiers among the Western troops sent to Saudi Arabia in the aftermath of Iraq's invasion of Kuwait. The most conservative elements in Saudi society were deeply shocked to see these

women at the wheel of military vehicles in Saudi towns, where women are most often confined to private space and certain do not enjoy the right to drive. Preachers in the nascent Islamist opposition took up the theme of women soldiers, making it one of the symbols of "the U.S. occupation of the land of the two holy sites." The anger these preachers felt was amplified by the reaction of more liberal Saudis, who seized the opportunity to demand that the social restrictions imposed by the Wahhabi religious establishment be lifted. One of the most spectacular protests in this context was staged on November 6, 1990, when seventy women took to the streets in their cars, demanding the right to drive. Saad, al-Muthanna, Abu Bakr, and Omar, were companions of the Prophet. The first, al-Muthanna Ibn Haritha al-Shaybani, was a great military commander during the early conquests and was named commander in chief of the Muslim armies in Iraq. The following two were the first caliphs of Islam, ruling from 632 to 634 and 634 to 644 respectively.

20. Bin Laden does not hesitate to draw on examples from the *jahiliyya,* or pre-Islamic period. The use of such examples concerning pagan Arabs, cited for their values and nobility, has been common among Arab nationalist movements since the Nahda, the Arab cultural renaissance of the nineteenth century. By contrast, Islamists refuse such usage categorically. Bin Laden is one of the few to take examples from either register indiscriminately. "Mules": in Arabic, *uluj,* a pejorative term designating non-Muslims, used by Saddam Hussein and his minister of information, Muhammad Said al-Sahhaf, in 2003 to designate Americans. Another sense, more common in North Africa, refers to Christian renegades who served Muslims as mercenaries. The term thus refers to their hybrid character, divided between two allegiances.

21. When troops from the U.S.-led coalition arrived on Saudi territory in the summer of 1990, it was with the understanding that they would not remain after the end of the war. It was only in 2003, however, after the second U.S. invasion of Iraq, that American military bases were officially transferred out of Saudi Arabia. Still, in the eyes of many Saudis, the transfer did not signify an end to the U.S. presence but meant only that this presence became more discreet than it had been.

22. The target of this comment is King Fahd Ibn Abdul Aziz, who ruled Saudi Arabia from 1982 until his death in 2005.

23. Bin Laden seems to be granting women a role in the jihad against Western forces. This position is common among jihadist ideologues, who consider that women can contribute to jihad, particularly by raising their children according to the principles of the struggle. Jihadist magazines targeting a female readership have even appeared: for example, in Saudi Arabia, the first issue of a magazine called *Al-Khansaa* appeared in August 2004. The magazine is named after an Arab poet of the pre-Islamic period, known for her elegiac compositions mourning the

death in battle of her two brothers. According to certain traditions, she met the Prophet Muhammad in 629 and converted to Islam.

24. See notes to Azzam, "Join the Caravan." The hadith cited here is central to the arguments of the jihadist movement, whose partisans seek to make jihad a canonical duty, like basic ritual prescriptions *(ibadat)*. Consequently, jihad becomes an individual obligation *(fard ʿayn)* for all Muslims everywhere, whereas the classical tradition presents it rather as a collective duty, which may be delegated to certain individuals, except in cases of direct attack, when defensive jihad is permitted.

25. According to Muslim tradition, Abraham and Ishmael built the Kaaba.

26. In this paragraph, another shift in the register of legitimation occurs, from the universal to the specifically Islamic.

Tactical Recommendations

1. Medina was the capital of the caliphate under Omar Ibn al-Khattab, 634–644. On al-Muthanna al-Shaybani, see Bin Laden, "Interview with Al-Jazeera." This text was probably published in or after December 2002, given the reference to the Mombasa attacks, which took place on November 28 of that year.

2. Note the deliberate use of anachronism: the modern term "superpower" applied to the seventh century.

3. Al-Thaqafi was a hero of the Arab conquests, who died in battle in 634. Bin Laden is citing *Al-Kamil fil-Tarikh* (The Historical Encyclopedia), by the Iraqi historian Ibn al-Athir (1160–1234), 2:322–323 (Beirut: Dar al-Kutub al-Ilmiyya, n.d.), 2:282.

4. The U.S. Army in Afghanistan began operations in Tora Bora on November 30, 2001, seeking to arrest Osama Bin Laden. Some American military officials leaked criticism of the strategy followed during combat to the media (see the *Washington Post*, April 17, 2002).

5. Once again, Bin Laden is basing his rhetoric on assumed responsibility for the victory against the Soviet Union, while ignoring the decisive role played by the United States.

6. The best-known of the Arab combatants in Chechnya were Saudis: the first, Samir Salih Abdallah al-Suwaylim, also known as Commander Khattab, was killed by the Russians on March 19, 2002, and replaced by the second, Abul-Walid al-Ghamidi, as head of the foreign combatants. The Ghamid tribe, to which Abul-Walid belonged, is very well represented among Saudi jihadists: four of the 9/11 hijackers were members.

7. Bin Laden is referring to the two wars in Chechnya. The first, launched in 1994 by Boris Yeltsin's government, aiming to retake control of the separatist republic, which had declared its independence in 1991, ended in the retreat of the

exhausted Russian army. Vladimir Putin began the second in 1999: his unstated goal was to restore the honor of Russia after the rebels had humiliated it three years earlier. Initially, the international community criticized this campaign in fairly virulent terms, but after 9/11 President Putin obtained, if not the support (as Bin Laden claims), then at least the indifference of the United States, given that he claimed to be fighting terrorism. During ten years of instability and conflict, thousands of jihadist combatants from all over the Muslim world, and especially from the Arab world, poured into Chechnya. Bin Laden is alluding to them here.

8. In 1982, as the civil war was raging in Lebanon, Israel launched Operation Peace in Galilee, invading Lebanon and laying siege to Beirut. The following year in a suicide mission, a booby-trapped truck blew up in Beirut, killing 241 U.S. Marines sent to Lebanon by the United Nations as part of a multinational peace-keeping force. The U.S. troops were called home shortly thereafter. In one of Bin Laden's last known recorded messages (October 29, 2004), he asserted that the 1982 events in Lebanon were the initial cause of his decision to carry out an attack against America (see Bin Laden, "A Message to the American People"). It is inter-esting to note that the attack on the Marines was carried out by Hezbollah, a Shi-ite group with no known links to Bin Laden or the members of his network. That Bin Laden seeks to recycle it for his own benefit here is testimony not only to the ecumenical nature of his rhetoric, but also to his desire to take away the public le-gitimacy that the Shiite group's spectacular actions have granted it.

9. Once again, the Afghan Arabs' role in Somalia seems to have been mar-ginal.

10. In December 1992, a multinational force made up mainly of U.S. troops landed in Somalia in the framework of Operation Restore Hope. Their goal was to restore peace and stability to a country torn apart by a brutal civil war. Bin Laden is referring to the events of October 1993, when Muhammad Farah Aydid's troops, probably assisted by Bin Laden's men, were able to inflict heavy losses on the American contingent: eighteen men were killed, and the media showed im-ages of corpses in U.S. military uniforms being dragged through the streets of Mogadishu. Shortly afterward, the United States, apparently traumatized, pulled its troops out of Somalia.

11. Three months later, in October 1996, U.S. troops supervising the no-fly zones in Iraq were ordered to leave Khobar. They gathered at the Kharj military base in the desert around sixty kilometers south of Riyadh. Bin Laden is referring to these events.

12. This is a reference to the creation of the World Islamic Front on February 23, 1998, and to the press conference that Bin Laden and Zawahiri organized in Kandahar in May 1998. Less than six months later, on August 7, 1998, the U.S. em-bassies in Nairobi (Kenya) and Dar es Salaam (Tanzania) were attacked simulta-neously. The attacks left two hundred dead.

13. On October 12, 2000, the USS *Cole* was attacked in Aden, a port in Yemen. Nineteen sailors were killed. According to Bin Laden's interpretation, the aim was both to punish America and to show that the Yemeni government was collaborating with U.S. forces. These goals are repeated with regard to attacks on other countries in the region: media coverage of attacks on U.S. bases publicly reveals the extent of the foreign presence in a host country.

14. Pharaoh represents unjust power in the Quran, as illustrated by Moses' sojourn in Egypt.

15. Quran 18:13. The verse designates the seven sleepers, a version similar to the Christian tale.

16. For the instigator of the 9/11 attacks, then, their value was related as much to the media as it was to strategy or operations. Here too, according to Bin Laden, attacks serve the purpose of revealing the truth about relations between the United States and the Muslim world, by forcing America to abandon its media reticence.

17. See Ayman al-Zawahiri, "Loyalty and Separation."

18. The Islamists' ultimate goal is to restore a single political structure for all Muslims worldwide. The model they look to is not the Abbasid caliphate but rather the "rightly guided" caliphate of the first four successors to the Prophet (traditionally called *al-khulafaʾ al-rashidun*). On the question of the caliphate in Salafist-jihadist discourse, see Ayman al-Zawahiri, "Knights under the Prophet's Banner."

19. Abu Ishaq al-Shatbi was a Maliki scholar, born in Granada, who died in 1388. He was the author of *Al-Muwafaqat fi Usul al-Fiqh* and famous for having been one of the first ulema to insist on the importance of determining the aims *(maqasid)* of divine laws, to guide in their interpretation. Six centuries later, reformist Muslim thought, as formulated in Egypt by Muhammad Abduh, for example, was inspired by this idea. It is interesting to see Bin Laden cite al-Shatbi, who is considered a precursor of Islamic modernism. Here too, one finds an illustration of his ecumenical rhetoric, which allows him to borrow from any legal tradition that might buttress his argument.

20. On December 8, 2002, Sulayman Abu Ghaith claimed responsibility, in the name of Al Qaeda, for the attempt to bring down an Israeli airplane and an attack on an Israeli hotel in Kenya, both carried out on November 28.

21. Excerpt from a poem by al-Tirrimah al-Taʾi, a poet from Syria who died in 743.

22. Quran 2:201.

23. Said Ibn Zuwayr was head of the department of information technology at the University of Imam Muhammad Ibn Saud in Riyadh. He was an active participant in Islamist agitation in the early 1990s and was imprisoned, like Salman al-Awda and Safar al-Hawali, during the mass arrests of 1994 and 1995. While the lat-

ter two were freed in 1999, however, Zuwayr was arrested once again after making statements to Al-Jazeera, the satellite news channel. He was still in jail in the spring of 2005.

Second Letter to the Muslims of Iraq

1. Quran 9:73. This is the transcript of a declaration recorded by Bin Laden and broadcast on October 18, 2003. It was addressed to Iraqis; another message, addressed to Americans, was broadcast at the same time. In this text, Bin Laden follows the classical rules established in Islamic legal discourse in the seventh century: an introduction praising God and the Prophet; references to poetry and Quranic verses; and a conclusion featuring an invocation.

2. Khalid and Mu'anna are the names of two of the Prophet's companions who participated in the conquest of Iraq. Saad Ibn Abi Waqqas is famous for having played an important role in the great battles against the Sassanians, especially in that of Qadisiyya (north of modern-day Iraq), which sealed the fate of the empire, and in the capture of Ctesiphon, its capital. Bin Laden named one of his sons Saad, which may indicate particular admiration for this historical figure. Khalid Ibn al-Walid was the best-known general of the Muslim armies in Iraq, which he commanded until al-Muthanna took over his leadership position. As for al-Muthanna, he was famous for his victories over the Persian armies in Iraq (the southernmost province of Iraq, on the border with Saudi Arabia, also bears this name). Al-Mu'anna was al-Muthanna's brother. Salah al-Din (1138–1193), known in the West as Saladin, is famous for his victories over the Crusaders, from whom he captured Jerusalem. This great military commander was a Kurd by birth. See Malcolm Cameron Lyons, *Saladin, the Politics of Holy War* (Oxford: Oxford University Press, 1982). The eagle, Saladin's symbol, is featured on several Arab flags. For Muslims, and for Arabs in particular, he is still a symbol of resistance against Western invasion.

3. A reference to the U.S.-led coalition.

4. In Arab-Islamic tradition, China symbolizes the Far East. A hadith exhorts Muslims to "seek knowledge, even in China." "Knights" is the translation of the Arabic word generally used to designate Muslim fighters, as, for example, in Zawahiri, *Knights under the Prophet's Banner.*

5. In Arabic, *din jahiliyya*. Religion here designates simply a system of belief.

6. Since Sayyid Qutb, this has been the principal distinction, for radical Islamist thinkers, between Islamic and pagan societies: in the first, sovereignty belongs to God alone, whereas in the latter, it belongs to the people through their representatives, who are free to contest God's law if they so choose. The Salafist-jihadist movement to which Bin Laden belongs considers parliaments to be a reprehensible innovation, contrary to the religious principles of the "pious ancestors"

(al-salaf al-salih): see Abdallah Azzam, "The Defense of Muslim Territories." For these militants, accepting the democratic system is tantamount to recognizing the legitimacy of a jurisdiction other than God's, which is a characteristic of unbelief. See Ayman al-Zawahiri, "Advice to the Community."

7. According to jihadist militants, such parties are doubly harmful: their emphasis on Kurdish specificity fragments the unity of the Muslim community, and their democratic quality (although this is really no more than an token) challenges God's sovereignty. Islamists consider the Baath to epitomize irreligious political parties: from its inception as an Arab nationalist organization, it contested the primacy of Islam, being secularist and strongly supported by Christian minorities, and even its name (signifying "resurrection" in Arabic) seemed to challenge religion by seeking to replace the cult of God with that of the nation.

8. Hamid Karzai became head of the Afghan government after U.S. forces overthrew the Taliban, and Mahmoud Abbas served as prime minister of the Palestinian Authority from March to September 2003, then again after winning the elections in January 2005. Bin Laden and his supporters saw them as traitors put in place by the Americans to serve American interests in the Middle East.

9. Bin Laden is referring here to the second intifada, which began in September 2000, and was also called the Al-Aqsa Intifada, after the mosque in Jerusalem, for it broke out in response to provocations by Ariel Sharon on the mosque esplanade on September 28, 2000, and violence by Israeli security forces. The term "Al-Aqsa Intifada" made it possible to link Fatah's strictly nationalist discourse with the more religious discourse of Palestinian Islamist groups. The "road map," presented in September 2003, was the first peace plan, after the failure of the Oslo process, to receive any support from the international community.

10. Bin Laden might be recognizing that he was not entirely free to move about. Furthermore, these words indicate that to him the jihad in Iraq was a priority, especially in relation to the struggle taking place in the Arabian Peninsula since May 2003.

11. Although the establishment of an Islamic state is secondary in Bin Laden's rhetoric, it nevertheless appears from time to time. Still, the definition of such a state has always been very vague: Bin Laden and other ideologues of his ilk simply link it with the implementation of sharia.

12. The people of Rabia and Mudar were two ancient tribes of Arabia that disappeared long ago. The tribe of Anaza, which has a very strong presence in northern Saudi Arabia, is said to be descended from Rabia, and the Quraysh, who dominated Mecca in the time of the Prophet, were supposedly descended from Mudar.

13. In Arabic, "mules" is *uluj*. See also Bin Laden, "Interview with Al-Jazeera."

14. Bin Laden has systematically mentioned the economic dimension of the war he is waging against the United States. In December 2004 he called on his

supporters in Saudi Arabia to attack petroleum-related infrastructure, in the hope of triggering a sharp increase in oil prices and a crisis for the American economy.

15. Baghdad was the capital of the caliphate under the Abbasid dynasty, from 750 to 1258, apart from a fifty-year period when the capital was transferred to Samarra. The symbolic weight of Baghdad is great in Islamic culture.

16. The Arabic phrase *ansar al-Islam* was also the name of an Islamist group in northern Iraq made up mainly of Kurds (the ethnic group to which Saladin belonged). At the beginning of the U.S. invasion, on March 23, 2003, this group suffered heavy losses inflicted by American air bombardments and a ground offensive led by secularist Kurdish combatants. The attack reportedly killed 180 men and resulted in the capture of 150 prisoners. In June 2003 a new group took over: Ansar al-Sunna (Companions of the Sunna). See the introduction to the section by Zarqawi.

17. Three Iraqi cities with a majority Sunni population.

18. The term employed here to designate Christians is *al-rum*, the epithet used in the Quran to designate the Byzantines (see Quran 30:2).

19. Attributed to Saad Ibn Abi Waqqas. In the Battle of the Trench, the idol worshippers of Mecca attacked the early Muslims in Medina, but the Muslims dug a trench around the city and withstood the siege. See Azzam, "Join the Caravan."

20. Quran 12:21.

Message to the American People

1. Quran 22:39. For this message from Bin Laden, see also http://english.aljazeera.net/English/archive/archive?ArchiveId=7403 for the unedited transcript, which appeared in subtitles on the videotape sent to Al-Jazeera on October 30, 2004, two days before the U.S. presidential elections. It was staged very differently from Bin Laden's other videotaped appearances: here, he was dressed like a Gulf notable, in an *abaya*, a coat worn over the *thawb*, the robe traditionally worn by Saudi men. He was seated behind a desk, and there was no sign of the Kalashnikov that had become a virtual trademark of Al Qaeda videos. He spoke calmly, in a didactic tone. He came across as a politician—with all the respectability that implies—and clearly sought to move away from the bloodthirsty guerrilla image that still characterizes him for many observers.

2. He is speaking of a repetition of the events of 9/11.

3. After 9/11, and after every attack carried out by Al Qaeda, the Bush administration tirelessly resorted to this rhetoric. As early as September 16, 2001, Bush told a press conference at the Pentagon: "They can't stand freedom; they hate what America stands for." On May 5, 2004, he told Al Arabiya television: "They declared war on us. And the United States will pursue them. And so long as I'm

the president, we will be determined, steadfast, and strong as we pursue those people who kill innocent lives because they hate freedom."

4. The nineteen hijackers who seized U.S. carriers with the aim of crashing them into the World Trade Center, the Pentagon, and possibly Congress (which is more likely than the White House to have been the target of the fourth plane).

5. Throughout this section, Bin Laden uses arguments to which international public opinion might be sensitive (liberty and oppression, for instance). This is another example of the strategic oscillation from one register of legitimacy to another that marks his discourse.

6. Israeli forces invaded Lebanon on June 6, 1982, and bombarded West Beirut, where left-wing Lebanese and Palestinian combatants had gathered, continuously from June 13 to August 18.

7. According to U.N. officials, five hundred thousand children under the age of five died in Iraq owing to the embargo between 1991 and 2000 (Reuters, July 21, 2000).

8. Throughout the 1980s, Saddam was one of the West's greatest allies in the Middle East. The United States and the West generally saw Iraq as a bulwark against the Iranian threat, and the West supported Iraq's eight-year war against Iran, which claimed millions of victims.

9. He refers to an interview with Scott MacLeod in Khartoum, published on May 6, 1996; one of May 10, 1997 with Peter Arnett on CNN; and an interview with Miller of ABC News, May 28, 1998.

10. The sites of three attacks: on Nairobi and Dar es Salaam on August 7, 1998 (killing 201 Kenyans, 11 Tanzanians, and 12 Americans), and on Aden on October 12, 2000 (killing 17 Americans).

11. The interview with Atwan appeared in *Al-Quds al-Arabi,* November 1996. Fisk interviewed Bin Laden in Sudan in December 1993 (this was the first interview Bin Laden had given to a Western journalist) and in Afghanistan in July 1996 and again in 1997.

12. A reference to the pivotal role of Florida and its governor, Jeb Bush, in the 2000 presidential elections.

13. The word "mujahedeen" (literally, those who wage jihad) is used here specifically, as it was throughout the 1980s, to designate the armed Afghan resistance. Today, in the parlance of radical Islamists, it has the more general meaning of militants linked to the jihadist movement.

14. Bin Laden is referring here to accusations directed against the Bush administration, to the effect that it profited from the war in Iraq by opening up new markets for U.S. corporations, especially in the field of construction (Halliburton), oil, and arms sales.

15. The economic consequences of the September 11 attacks aroused considerable interest among jihadists, as evidenced by a forty-page pamphlet titled *Ameri-*

can Losses and published on the Web site of the Islamic Research and Study Center (Markaz al-Dirasat wal-Buhuth al-Islamiyya), widely seen as Al Qaeda's mouthpiece between 2000 and 2003.

16. In September 2003 President Bush asked Congress for an additional $87 billion "for the war on terror in Iraq and Afghanistan."

17. Vice President Dick Cheney was CEO of Halliburton from 1995 to 2000, and is widely believed to have maintained illegal financial links to that corporation.

18. Muhammad Atta was *al-amir al-aam,* or general commander, of the terrorist commandos on September 11.

19. On the morning of September 11 President Bush was visiting an elementary school. When one of his advisers came to inform him that a plane had just crashed into the World Trade Center, he was listening to a story about a goat. Visibly stunned, he did nothing for several minutes, and merely continued to listen to the story. The Arabic contains a play on the words *nat-h* (butting with one's horns) and *natihat al-sahab* (skyscraper).

20. An allusion to a fable in which a goat could not be slaughtered for lack of a knife, but scratched the ground until it uncovered one that was buried.

21. Inaudible passage on the soundtrack.

22. The word used for "state" here in the Arabic, *wilaya,* designates political authority or, in modern administrative parlance, a province or federal state. The United States government, by contrast, should have been designated by the term *dawla.* In the American case, the distinction is a fundamental one, since the United States is a *dawla,* while each of the fifty states is a *wilaya.* Some authors therefore interpreted the choice of terms as implying a threat directed against each of the states individually; according to this interpretation, each of the states might therefore be attacked according to its specific voting results.

Introduction: Abdallah Azzam

1. Quote from the Web site www.azzam.com, now defunct.

2. No serious biography of Abdallah Azzam has been published until now. The best reference on the subject in a Western language is Bernard Rougier's *Everyday Jihad: The Rise of Militant Islam among Palestinians in Lebanon,* trans. Pascale Ghazaleh (Cambridge, Mass.: Harvard University Press, 2007). A certain number of biographies in English, which are short, incomplete, and mediocre, are available on the Internet (see for example "Sheikh Abdallah Azzam," originally on www.azzam.com; "The Striving Sheikh: Abdullah Azzam," in *Nida'ul-Islam* 14 (1996), formerly at www.islam.org.au/articles/14/AZZAM.html; Jonathan Fighel, "Sheikh Abdallah Azzam: Bin Laden's Spiritual Mentor," on www.ict.org.il; Steve Emerson, "Abdullah Assam: The Man before Osama Bin Laden," formerly at

www.iascp.com/itobli3.html; and Chris Suellentrop, "Abdullah Azzam, The God-father of Jihad," April 16, 2002, at www.slate.msn.com/. The best of these bio-graphical sketches is the Wikipedia article titled "Abdullah Yusuf Azzam." Our main source here is a fifty-six-page compilation of articles in Arabic, titled "Sheikh Azzam, from Birth to Martyrdom" *(al-Sheikh Abdallah Azzam, baynal-Milad wal-Istishhad).* It can be found in the online jihadist library Minbar al-Tawhid wal-Jihad (www.tawhed.ws)—which was at one time Al Qaeda's largest online archive. This undated compilation, attributed to a Dr. Abu Mujahid of the Martyr Azzam Communication Center in Peshawar, consists of a series of bio-graphical articles about Abdallah Azzam, originally published in jihadist maga-zines in Peshawar between 1990 and 1992. Written by various authors, among them relatives of Azzam, some are pure hagiographies, while others are more nuanced and perfectly accurate.

3. For the biography of Said Hawa, an important member of the Syrian Muslim Brotherhood, see Abdallah Azzam, "The Defense of Muslim Territories." Muhammad al-Bouti is part of the Syrian religious establishment, and he can even be described as Syria's best-known religious figure. He presents a weekly television program there and has his own Web site (www.bouti.com). He has long been quite close to the Muslim Brotherhood, but has never engaged openly in political activities. He gives regular lectures in Paris, at Da'wa Mosque, rue de Tanger, in the nineteenth arrondissement. Mullah Ramadan is Muhammad al-Bouti's father, but the two men split over the question of what attitude to adopt toward the Syrian regime. Like Sayyid Qutb, Marwan Hadid was a leg-endary figure for the Islamist movement in general and an important leader of the Syrian Islamist movement. He studied in Egypt, where he was close to Sayyid Qutb, before returning to Syria in 1966. In the early 1970s, he became the head of a revolutionary wing of the Muslim Brotherhood in Hama, and he was arrested after the 1973 riots. He died in jail in suspicious circumstances: some al-lege that he was assassinated, whereas others claim he died as a result of a hunger strike.

4. *Al-Hayat,* December 14–16, 2004.

5. See Azzam, "The Defense of Muslim Territories."

6. The others were Ahmad Nawfal, Muhammad Abu Faris, Humam Said, and Ibrahim Khraysat.

7. See Jonathan Randal, *Osama: The Making of a Terrorist* (New York, Knopf, 2004).

8. The source is Azzam's son-in-law, Abdallah Anas, cited in Jonathan Randal's biography.

9. See Azzam, "The Defense of Muslim Territories."

10. Sananiri was later jailed in Egypt and tortured to death, as Ayman al-Zawahiri recounts in *Knights under the Prophet's Banner.*

11. Mishari al-Dhaidi, "Matbakh Bishawar," _Al-Sharq al-Awsat._ See Bin Laden, "The Companions' Den."

12. See Bin Laden, "The Companions' Den."

13. Hekmatyar (born in 1947) and Massoud (1953–2001) were rivals on the Afghan political and military scene, starting in the early 1980s. Between 1992 and 1996, a civil war pitted Hekmatyar and his ally Abdul Rashid Dustum against Massoud and his ally Burhanuddin Rabbani.

14. _Majlis al-tansiq al-islami._ See Gilles Kepel, _Jihad: The Trail of Political Islam_ (Cambridge, Mass.: Harvard University Press, 2002).

15. See Gilles Kepel, _Muslim Extremism in Egypt: The Prophet and Pharaoh,_ 2nd ed. (Berkeley: University of California Press, 2003).

16. Abdallah Azzam, _Basha'ir al-Nasr._

17. "Al-Qaeda al-Sulba," _Al-Jihad_ (April 1988): 41.

18. Abu Hamza al-Masri, a radical Egyptian Islamist who lived in London and was jailed in May 2004, until he could be extradited to the United States, cited in Michael Collins Dunn, "Osama bin Laden: The Nature of the Challenge," _Middle East Policy_ 6, no. 2 (October 1998): 24–25.

The Defense of Muslim Territories

1. On this text, see also http://www.religioscope.com/info/doc/jihad/jihadfile.htm#defence.

2. Abd al-Aziz Bin Baz (1909–1999) was already one of the greatest religious authorities of the Muslim world in Azzam's time. He was born in a small town in Najd, a central region of Saudi Arabia, and went blind at an early age, something that did not prevent him from carrying out his religious studies brilliantly with the most eminent figures of the Wahhabi educational and religious establishment. He went on to head various institutions in the kingdom, especially at the universities of Riyadh and Medina, before reaching the height of his career in 1971, when he was nominated to head the Supreme Council of Ulema, the highest body in the Wahhabi establishment. In 1993 he was officially nominated grand mufti of Saudi Arabia, a function he had already held, albeit unofficially, since 1971.

3. The pilgrimage of September 1984. This excuse leaves it in doubt whether the sheikh really agreed with Azzam's fatwa. In fact, some Saudi analysts now say that Bin Baz never considered jihad in Afghanistan to be an individual duty for all Muslims. He allegedly said it was an individual duty for all Afghans but a collective duty for other Muslims.

4. The term "jihad" literally means effort or striving, implicitly in the name of Islam. Although some exegetes have distinguished the "greater jihad" (waged on oneself, in order to improve oneself morally and religiously) from the "lesser" (carried out against pagans and unbelievers, or those who reject Muslim rule),

since the classical era the term has generally been taken to mean efforts Muslims make to propagate the faith. Even then, however, jihad does not necessarily have a military sense: it can mean "jihad of the tongue" *(al-jihad bil-lisan)*, designating the obligation to "enjoin good and forbid evil": *al-amr bil-ma'ruf wal-nahi 'an al-munkar.* Still, the military sense was preferred even in the medieval period, and contemporary jihadist ideologues, Azzam foremost among them, situate themselves within this tradition. Several mosques in Saudi Arabia bear the name Bin Laden Mosque, since Saudi Binladen Group built them. See Bin Laden, "Interview with Al-Jazeera."

5. Alwan taught at King Abdul Aziz Ibn Saud University in Jidda, where he was Azzam's colleague in 1980–1981. Said Hawa (1935–1989), originally from the Syrian city of Hama, was the main ideologue of the Syrian branch of the Muslim Brotherhood but preserved some Sufi tendencies. Azzam met him in the 1960s, when he was teaching at Damascus University. Azzam may have met al-Muti'i, a member of the Egyptian Muslim Brotherhood, while studying in Cairo. Husayn Hamid Hassan, an Egyptian religious scholar and member of the Muslim Brotherhood, was former president of the Islamic University in Islamabad, where Azzam taught in the early 1980s. Omar Sayf was a member of the Yemeni Council of Ulema.

6. In most editions of this work, Azzam's introduction is followed by a series of faxed manuscript messages, signed by Abdallah Alwan, Said Hawa, Muhammad Najib al-Muti'i, and Omar Sayf. All of them praise the book and endorse his fatwa. Among the five individuals mentioned here, Husayn Hamid Hassan was the only one to abstain from signing, perhaps because of a disagreement.

7. Ibn Uthaymin (1928–2001) was an eminent Saudi religious scholar, and the second religious authority in the country after Bin Baz. Afifi was a member of the Council of Senior Ulema, the highest Saudi religious institution, until his death in 1995. Ayub was a professor at King Abdul Aziz Ibn Saud University in Jidda. Al-Assal was an esteemed Saudi religious scholar, who went on to become vice president at the Islamic University of Islamabad, in Pakistan.

8. These remarks show Azzam's position in Islamist circles in 1984: he frequented the most highly respected religious authorities in the Muslim world and was addressing a prestigious audience in Mina during the pilgrimage. Still, his network was made up mainly of Muslim Brothers, which is not surprising since Azzam himself belonged to the organization until he broke with the Jordanian branch of the Brotherhood in 1984.

9. The head of the Islamic Union of Afghan Mujahedeen, Abdul Rasul Sayyaf was one of the Afghan leaders with the closest ties to Saudi Arabia and international Islamic organizations involved in the jihad against the Soviet Army. He was called Abd Rabb al-Rasul Sayyaf starting in the 1980s, because the name he was given at birth, which meant "worshipper of the Prophet," was seen as blasphe-

mous by the Wahhabi ulema, for no one apart from God should be worshipped in Islam. Abd Rabb al-Rasul means "worshipper of the Prophet's Lord," and the blasphemy was thus averted.

10. Ja'far Sheikh Idris is a Sudanese religious scholar residing in Saudi Arabia. He was particularly known, after the coup d'état carried out by Omar al-Bashir in 1989, for his open opposition to Hassan al-Turabi, the Islamist ideologue for the new regime.

11. References in the original texts have been preserved, even though they might be incorrect or refer to editions that are out of print. Ahmad Ibn Hanbal (780–855), a theologian and traditionist, or expert in hadith studies. He founded the last of the four great Sunni schools of law, Hanbalism. After traveling for his education, especially in Syria and the Hejaz, he became renowned for his opposition (on the question of the "createdness" of the Quran, among other topics) to the Mu'tazila, who were partisans of rationalist theology and whose doctrine had been made state ideology at the time. He was persecuted and imprisoned, but reinstated as a professor when Caliph al-Mutawakkil took power and reestablished Sunni orthodoxy. Ibn Hanbal left a collection of hadith, the *Musnad*. He emphasized literal acceptance of the sacred text, particularly with regard to the thorny question of God's attributes. His followers also upheld the consensus of the Muslim community against sedition. Today, the Hanbali school is dominant in Saudi Arabia and certain Gulf countries and is seen as the strictest and most literalist of the four schools. Abu Qasim al-Tabarani (874–971), a hadith scholar and the author of *al-Mu'jam al-Kabir* (The Great Collection). Nasr al-Din al-Albani (1914–1999) was a Syrian religious scholar of Albanian origin who established his own school, rejecting the four canonical schools of Sunni jurisprudence as well as Wahhabi tradition, which he accused of having introduced reprehensible innovations *(bid'a)* in religious practice and allowed recourse to individual opinion *(ra'y)* in judgments on religious matters. Al-Albani argued that a literal reading of the hadith was a fundamental factor in religious judgment; his approach led him to make original decisions considered absurd by most religious scholars, such as advocating that the Palestinians emigrate en masse from territories occupied by Israel. Al-Albani taught at the University of Medina in the late 1950s but had to resign because of numerous disagreements with Saudi ulema on questions of ritual. He settled in Jordan, where he became an authority on apolitical Salafism but maintained ties to the great Saudi sheikhs Bin Baz and Ibn Uthaymin. There are many Internet sites devoted to his work.

12. The second part of the verse is cited.

13. Only the second part of the verse is cited. The interpretation of these verses by exegete Ibn Kathir (see his biography in Zawahiri, "Loyalty and Separation") is the antithesis of Azzam's, for he reads it: "If God had not defended men against each other." This reading depends on the verb *dafa'a*, which can mean "to push,"

or, when followed by *'an,* "to defend." See *Mukhtasar Tafsir Ibn Kathir* (Beirut: Dar al-Ma'rifa, n.d.), p. 91.

14. Jihad of the self *(al-jihad bil-nafs)* is worthier than jihad using only one's resources *(al-jihad bil-mal).*

15. Quran 9:39.

16. Azzam is alluding to the Prophet here. In the original, the pronoun is followed by the formula "Peace and blessings upon him," which in Muslim tradition is reserved for him.

17. Abu Dawud al-Sijistani (817–889) was a renowned traditionist who gathered 4,800 sayings attributed to the Prophet in his "Book of Traditions" *(Kitab al-Sunan),* one of the six canonical collections of Sunni Islam.

18. Tabarani wrote *Al-Awsat* (The Median). Bayhaqi (d. 1066) was a Persian jurist and traditionist of the Shaf'i school. He was a prolific author, whose best-known work is the "Book of Great Traditions" *(Kitab al-Sunan al-Kubra),* a synthesis of and commentary on the various collections of hadith. He is also the author of one of the oldest and most respected treatises of the Shāf'ī school.

19. In Arabic, *isnad,* the list of names of those who transmitted each hadith from one generation to the next. One of the main tasks of hadith experts *(muhaddith)* is to examine the chain of transmission, and to determine how much credit should be given to the transmitters, in order to judge the authenticity of the hadith. The sayings and deeds attributed to the Prophet, initially transmitted orally, were later collected and examined according to rules that were progressively codified during the first centuries of Islam. A hadith is therefore classified according to three criteria. Each collection of traditions may have its own criteria *(shurut)* to integrate or reject hadith and classify them. Authentic *(sahih)* hadith are subdivided into seven categories: first, those featured in the two most prestigious collections, those of al-Bukhari and Muslim; then those featured only in al-Bukhari; then those which are included only by Muslim. Fourth come hadith that do not appear in either of the two collections but still fulfill the conditions imposed by these two traditionists. In fifth rank are those which fulfill al-Bukhari's conditions, in sixth those which fulfill Muslim's, and last are those which are included in the four other anthologies of hadith that the ulema consider valid. In jihadist texts, one often finds hadith that are not considered absolutely sound (and are therefore only *hasan,* and even sometimes *da'if,* as opposed to *sahih).*

20. This is an allusion to the military campaigns the Prophet launched on a regular basis and from a certain point on, on a purely formal basis. Each year, a summer campaign and a winter campaign took place. Azzam seems to have wanted to start this tradition up again, with periodical military campaigns to be led as one would fulfill a dogmatic prescription.

21. Muhammad Amin Ibn Abdin (1784–1836) was a Hanafi jurist and the author of *Radd al-Muhtar alal-Durr al-Mukhtar,* known as the Commentary. The

land of war *(dar al-harb),* in traditional terms, is the part of the world that Muslims do not govern and where Islamic law does not prevail. *Dar al-islam,* by contrast, is the part of the world where Muslims rule and Islamic law holds sway. *Dar al-sulh* is an intermediate territory where Islamic law is not applied but which has peaceful relations with the Muslims, as the Prophet did with the Christians of Najran, in southern Arabia. Other terms developed at various times: *dar al-ahd* designates those territories with which the Muslims have peace treaties; *dar al-adl* are territories where justice prevails; *dar al-bid'a* is the land of heretical innovation; and *dar al-kufr* is the land of unbelief. According to most contemporary ulema, these duties related to war do not apply as long as no unified caliphate headed by a legitimate imam exists.

22. The poll tax that non-Muslim monotheists (Christians, Jews, Sabians) having accepted Muslim rule (known as *ahl al-dhimma* or protected peoples) paid in return for not serving in the military and for preserving their communal autonomy.

23. *Tuhfat al-Muhtaj alal-Minhaj* means "Precious Stone for Those Who Seek the Way."

24. An individual obligation is one that cannot be delegated to anyone else. In Islamic jurisprudence, there are two types of duties: *fard 'ayn* or individual duties, which each Muslim must carry out (like prayer or fasting); and *fard kifaya* or collective duties, which must be carried out by a sufficient number of Muslims in the name of the whole community.

25. One of Azzam's main ideological contributions was to shift modern discourse about jihad from a revolutionary struggle for power to a military struggle for territory. The list of countries in which Muslim territory was at stake conveys the impression of a global battlefield. In the Philippines, since the late 1970s a separatist uprising, led among others by the Moro Islamic Liberation Front, has been under way on the island of Mindanao, which has a Muslim majority, and in neighboring islands south of the Philippines, where the majority of the population is Christian. Kashmir, a majority Muslim state, was attached to India when partition occurred in 1948. Thereafter, an important separatist movement developed. Its Islamization began in the 1970s and was reinforced in the 1990s by the Pakistani authorities. Chad, which won its independence from France in 1960, experienced three decades of conflict. Foreign Islamists view this situation as a war between Muslims (who make up 60 percent of the population) and others (Christians and animists). Eritrea, which has a Muslim majority, was annexed in 1962 by Ethiopia, which is mainly Christian. A separatist conflict broke out that lasted more than thirty years, for it ended only in 1993 with Eritrea's independence (in other words, several years after Azzam wrote this text).

26. The Hindu Kush is a mountainous region in the east of Afghanistan.

27. Quran 9:40.

28. The Islamic Union of Afghan Mujahedeen was one of the seven main parties in the Afghan resistance during the war, headed by Abdul Rasul Sayyaf and very close to Saudi Arabia.

29. Quran 12:67. The concept of *hakimiyya*, which can be rendered as "sovereignty," was introduced into Islamist discourse by the Pakistani ideologue Abul-Ala al-Mawdudi, then developed by Sayyid Qutb, who made it the central element in his doctrine. Qutb used it to distinguish Islamic from un-Islamic societies. When sovereignty is attributed to someone or something other than God, such as the nation or a political party, society becomes un-Islamic, because this situation grants decision-making and legislative power to authorities other than God alone.

30. Azzam frequently expressed his sadness at the secular, fragmented nature of the Palestinian national movement. When he ended his paramilitary activities in 1970, it was in large part because he disagreed with the PLO's policies.

31. Azzam was exaggerating the strength of the ties between Palestine and the Soviet Union. Several Marxist Palestinian organizations did exist, and some members of the PLO did sympathize with the Soviets, but Yasir Arafat always kept his distance from the Soviet Union, for fear that the U.S. policy might become more radical if he drew too close.

32. An allusion to the Israeli invasion of Lebanon in June 1982. See Bin Laden, "Message to the American People."

33. Political power has a negative connotation by comparison with the sole legitimate power, which derives from God's sovereignty and therefore cannot oppose the implementation of jihad.

34. Azzam may have been thinking of his own experience: he personally participated in the infiltration from Jordanian territory in the late 1960s.

Join the Caravan

1. For this text, see also http://www.islamistwatch.org/texts/azzam/caravan/caravan.html.

In the preface to the second edition, dated December 9, 1988, Azzam's own words bear witness to the impact the book had had on the recruitment of Arab volunteers to go and fight in Afghanistan: "When I wrote this text, it never occurred to me that it would provoke such a revolution, to the extent that our number increased tenfold." The title seems to have been Azzam's idea, but subsequently the expression "to join the caravan" was used by many Islamist authors, like Hamid al-Ali or Abu Musab al-Zarqawi. It refers to a unique opportunity to join the jihad; like a caravan through the desert, such an opportunity passes swiftly, and those who fail to join will be abandoned to their fate.

2. Verses by Ibn Qayyim, a Hanbali jurist from Syria, the student of Ibn Taymiyya, and the author of *I'lam al-Muwaqqi'in* (The Signatories' Information).

Born in Damascus in 1292, he acquired a particularly solid and vast education, despite his humble origins, and adhered to Ibn Taymiyya's ideas while remaining close to Sufi teachings. Indeed, *Madarij al-Salikin* (The Degrees) is a work of mysticism, although it takes its place in the Hanbali tradition. His most ambitious work, however, remains the *I'lam,* a legal treatise in three volumes, synthesizing Ibn Taymiyya's positions on *usul al-fiqh,* the sources of Islamic jurisprudence.

3. This phrase is often used in Islamist literature to designate cowardice. It is taken from this hadith: "One day, nations will besiege you on all sides, like starving guests around a single pot . . . You will be like the torrent's foam, God will make your enemies cease to fear you, and he will insinuate weakness into your hearts." What does this mean, O messenger of God? "Love for this world and aversion toward death."

4. "Tyrants": *taghut,* a Quranic term, in jihadist literature designates the "enemy nearby," meaning oppressive regimes in Muslim countries. *Taghut* in a more general sense means a tyrant. The word's history is useful in explaining the rich connotations associated with it. During the pre-Islamic period, it meant a god, and one of the term's derivatives refers to the idea of excess and hubris. In the Quran the term is used indifferently to designate a demon, a magician, or idols, in the plural *(tawaghit).* In the early Islamic period, the term begins to mean Satan. Later, in the classical period, *taghut* is anything that turns humans away from worshipping God and from *tawhid* (monotheism). The Islamists therefore use this term to describe dictatorial secular authority, both authoritarian and idolatrous in nature (as in the brand of "state-olatry" incarnated by the populist regimes of the twentieth century), concentrating all power in its own hands and denying any legitimacy other than is own. Another translation of *taghut,* therefore, could be Leviathan. "Unbelievers": the term *kafir* (plural *kuffar*) means non-Muslims, but it can also be used to mean a Muslim whom the author considers to be impious or an apostate. In that case, the expression *kafir asli* (original unbeliever) is used to mean non-Muslims in particular. The term has the same root as *takfir,* the practice that consists in designating a Muslim as an apostate.

5. Quran 4:84.

6. The word for duty or obligation *(farida),* when used in contemporary Islamist literature, refers to Abd al-Salam Faraj's seminal pamphlet *Al-Farida al-Gha'iba* (The Absent Imperative), published in Egypt in 1981. It is considered the essential guide to the ideology of the Egyptian organization Al-Jihad and is the document that legitimated the assassination of Egyptian president Anwar Sadat in October 1981. The term *nida* (call) has also been taken up in jihadist literature with specific connotations. Several Islamist publications use the word in their titles: the magazine *Nida'ul-Islam,* published in Australia in the late 1990s, is one; the Web site Al-Nida, based in Saudi Arabia, and which served as Al Qaeda's mouthpiece from 2000 to 2003, is another.

7. The term *al-mustad'afin* (the oppressed), used in the Quran, appears frequently in Islamist literature, but it evokes more particularly the theories of Shiite Islamists like Ayatollah Khomeini and Ali Shariati, who used the word to combine Shiite liberation theology and Marxist ideas of social justice.

8. The notion of martyrdom holds a particularly important place in Azzam's work and has since become a central concept in radical Islamist literature. It has had enormous practical consequences, as everyone knows, now that suicide operations have become the trademark of militant Islamist groups.

9. Quran 8:39.

10. This sentence contains a theme that is central to Azzam's writing: that jihad is an eternal activity and must never cease. The author accuses those of his readers who might disregard him of being unbelievers, spreaders of sedition, and polytheists—the three most derogatory terms in the Islamist lexicon.

11. The *Sahih* is collection of authentic hadith, assembled by Muhammad al-Bukhari (810–870), a specialist in hadith who was originally from Bukhara, in contemporary Uzbekistan. This is considered the most trustworthy of the six canonical collections, and as such is one of the main sources for Islamic jurisprudence. Al-Bukhari reportedly took sixteen years to put together this anthology, which is made up of 97 books, 3,450 chapters, and almost 3,000 hadith (not counting repeats). The *Sahih* has been the subject of several commentaries by prestigious theologians, among them Asqalan. Al-Bukhari is also the author of a *Tarikh*, a biographical dictionary of the men featuring in the *isnad*, or chains of hadith transmitters.

12. Azzam occasionally inserts explanatory notes into his text, as if he were aware that some of his young readers had difficulty reading classical Arabic.

13. The Caliph Omar was the second of the Prophet's successors, and the most prestigious leader of the Muslim community. Under his rule (634–644) many territories were conquered (Syria, Mesopotamia, western Iran, Egypt), and the base of the empire's organization was laid with the creation of administrative branches called *dawawin* (singular *diwan*), the establishment of a salary roll for combatants, the use of the title "commander of the faithful," and the first use of the Islamic calendar. He was killed by a slave after having ruled for ten years.

14. Abu Ubayda Ibn al-Jarrah was one of the Prophet's companions, and then leader in the Muslim conquest of Syria. He was known mainly, though not only, for having killed his father, who persisted in adhering to polytheism. The names of the Prophet's companions are often taken as noms de guerre *(kunya)* by jihadist militants. These names are generally chosen according to the stories and attributes associated with the companions. The name Abu Ubayda became popular in jihadist circles and was adopted by one of Bin Laden's close aides, an Egyptian named Ali al-Rashidi, also known as Abu Ubayda al-Banshiri (see Bin Laden, "The Companions' Den").

15. Azzam is alluding to his role in proselytism and instruction during the Afghan conflict: he seems to have spent much of his time in Peshawar, coordinating efforts and instructing recruits who had come from all over the Islamic world. In his writings, he often complained that those who had come to fight in Afghanistan had received only a rudimentary general education and very elementary religious instruction in their home countries.

16. Quran recitation *(tajwid)* is an art requiring that its practitioners respect well-established rules. Learning them requires time and training.

17. The Arabic word for partisans *(ansar)* has a particular meaning in the Islamic tradition: it designates the inhabitants of Medina who supported the Prophet after he had settled there in 622, when Mecca was governed by the pagan tribe of Quraysh. The move from a land of unbelief to a place where Islam was supported is called *hijra,* the emigration. The *muhajirun,* or emigrants, are those Meccans who had converted to Islam and followed the Prophet when he left Mecca. Together, *muhajirun* and *ansar* make up the *sahaba,* the Prophet's companions. The Battle of Uhud, which took place near Medina in November 625, was a military setback for the first Muslims against the Meccans; several Muslim combatants, including the Prophet's uncle, died in the conflict.

18. Used here specifically to mean the Afghan resistance groups fighting the Soviet occupation in the 1980s. In other cases, Azzam uses it to designate the Arabs fighting in this resistance or, more generally, all those waging jihad.

19. The Hanafi school, one of the four schools of Sunni jurisprudence, developed on the basis of the teachings of Abu Hanifa (700–767). The oldest school, it is also considered the most liberal, because its legal interpretations grant an important place to reason or opinion (as opposed to a literalist reading of the sacred texts), and because it was more tolerant of local customs than was the Hanbali school, for instance. It is also the most prevalent of the four schools, in central and southern Asia, Egypt, in the Levant, and in Turkey. The other schools stipulate that martyrs who fall in battle must be buried in the clothes they were wearing, that their bodies must not be washed, and that no funerary prayers must be pronounced over them, for their salvation is guaranteed. See Azzam, "Morals and Jurisprudence of Jihad."

20. It is difficult to identify all the Afghan Arabs Azzam mentions here, since all we know are their noms de guerre. The first may be a reference to Boudjemma Bounnoua, an Algerian also known as Abdallah Anas, who married one of Abdallah Azzam's daughters and is today a figure on the Islamist scene in London. Abu Dujana is probably Abu Dujana al-Afghani, who appeared on a videotape claiming responsibility for the 2004 Madrid bombings (http://www-tech.mit.edu/ V124/N17/17_long_3.17w.html); Abu Asim may refer to Abu Asim al-Makki (Muhammad Hamdi al-Ahdal, who was detained in 2003: http://www.globalsecurity .org/security/profiles/mohammed_hamdi_al-ahdal.htm); the only "Abu Suhayb"

known in connection with Al Qaeda is an American convert to Islam who also went by the name Adam Pearlman.

21. Probably an Afghan Arab who fought with Ahmed Shah Massoud.

22. Quran 9:39.

23. Ibid., 4:97–99.

24. Ikrima Ibn Khalid was a hadith transmitter from the first century A.H. He died in 723. Ibn Abbas was one of the Prophet's companions.

25. The Battle of Badr, which took place in 624, was Muhammad's first victory over the Meccans. In Muslim tradition, it is a symbol of strength and victory against overwhelming odds. Radical groups today occasionally describe a successful operation as "operation Badr." In early 2004, when radical Saudi Islamists broadcast a videotape describing the November 2003 attack on a compound for foreigners in Riyadh, they titled it "Badr in Riyadh."

26. Azzam is referring to the laws prevailing in some Muslim countries, such as Tunisia or Turkey, where beards and headscarves are banned from certain public spaces because the authorities perceive them as badges of membership in Islamist groups and therefore as signs of political opposition, or as elements that disturb the state's secular character.

27. The term used by Azzam is *jahiliyya*, which refers to the pre-Islamic time of "ignorance." In Sayyid Qutb's lexicon, the term designates the modern period, during which the message of Islam has been ignored and the power of despots who do not govern according to revealed law has been accepted.

28. The *mukhabarat*, or intelligence services, are familiar figures in contemporary Arab regimes: they are responsible for surveillance and repression of the population.

29. Quran 41:97.

30. Allusion to the Quranic verses of which Azzam cites fragments above; this is also a reference to Afghanistan.

31. Azzam thus rejects the arguments of more moderate Muslim thinkers, who argue that references to jihad in the Quran and hadith literature should be situated in a specific historical context: that of the conflict between the first Muslims and the polytheists in Arabia between 620 and 630.

32. *Sunna* means, literally, "way; practice, habit, or norm"; but it refers specifically the words and deeds of the Prophet as related in hadith. Sayyid Qutb (1906–1966) was one of the most important ideologues of the radical Islamist movement. A member of the Egyptian Muslim Brotherhood, he was radicalized during the prison term to which the Nasser regime condemned him. His most famous book, *Ma'alim fil-Tariq* (Signposts, 1964), established the basis for revolutionary Islamism and inspired the various movements that appeared, particularly in Egypt, during the 1970s. *In the Shade of the Quran* is an exegesis by Qutb of the Quran.

33. Abu Hurayra was one of the Prophet's companions. Muslim Ibn Hajjaj (817–875) was a renowned traditionist and hadith compiler who was born in Nishapur, in the northwest of modern Iran. As a young man, he traveled through Syria, the Hejaz, and Egypt, collecting hadith attributed to the Prophet. Out of a total of 300,000 hadith he is said to have collected, he kept only 4,000 in his anthology.

34. Quran 9:41.

35. This passage shows how difficult the Quran was for the first Muslims—not to mention subsequent generations—to understand.

36. Ibn Um Maktum, a companion of the Prophet, was blind.

37. Quran 24:61.

38. He lists here as being in agreement the four main categories of Muslim scholars. It is accurate that, over the centuries, there has been a consensus among the ulema with regard to the need to fight each time Muslim territory is subjected to an attack; however, Muslim jurisprudence gives a vague definition of "Muslim territory." Azzam's maximalist definition ("a land that was once Muslim") is not shared by all ulema, and it leads him to advocate the reconquest of distant territories like southern Spain (al-Andalus).

39. Contrary to the assertions of some analysts, this presentation of the obligation to wage jihad spreading out in concentric circles is typical of classical Islamic jurisprudence.

40. A *mahram*, or a relative who is so closely related that marriage is prohibited. In some Muslim countries today, a male relative (father or brother) must accompany women in public places. On individual obligation *(fard ʿayn)*, see Azzam, "The Defense of Muslim Territories."

41. *Zakah*, one of the five pillars of Islam. Additional, voluntary alms are called *sadaqa*.

42. Taqiyy al-Din Ahmad Ibn Taymiyya (1263–1328) was a renowned Hanbali theologian and jurisconsult. When he was very young, his family fled the Mongol invasion, seeking refuge in Damascus at a time when the Crusaders were still occupying parts of the Levantine coast. This political context structured much of his work. He taught at the great mosque in Damascus and rapidly gained renown thanks to his polemical opinions, notably with regard to "innovations" introduced in the pilgrimage ritual and his opposition to various theological trends, as well as to Shiism, Sufism, and so on. He called on Muslims to wage jihad, and he participated in person in several military expeditions (in 1303 against the Mongols; in 1305 against the Shiites of Kisrawan). The authorities harassed him several times, and he was arrested many times in Damascus, Cairo, and Alexandria. During these periods in jail or under house arrest, he wrote his many works, and especially his *Kitab al-Siyasa al-Sharʾiyya* (Book of Legal Policy). He died in Damascus, under house arrest. In his writing, he developed a conservative,

rigoristic doctrine that emerged from Hanbali tradition, while maintaining a certain distance. In the twentieth century this doctrine regained popularity through Saudi Wahhabism, and exerted a great influence on political Islam. The statement by Ibn Taymiyya quoted here, often cited by Islamist authors, represents a central argument in the point of view that has been expressed since Faraj: jihad is the second most important religious duty, just after faith. In this sentence, however, Ibn Taymiyya used not the word *jihad*, but *daf* (which signifies repelling or defending). See Bin Laden, "World Islamic Front Statement."

43. The battle of al-Muraysi, which took place in 626, pitted the Muslims, who were in Medina, against the men of the tribe of Banu Mustaliq, led by Al-Harith Ibn Dirar. The Muslims emerged victorious and seized their enemies' women and children. The Battle of the Trench (al-Khandaq) took place before Medina: the Muslims, besieged by the Meccans, dug a trench around the town, and the Meccans withdrew after a month. The history of this battle is inextricably tied up with the betrayal of the Jewish tribes: in the midst of the battle, they broke their alliance with the Muslims and went over to the side of the Quraysh. In response to the Jews' betrayal during the Battle of the Trench, the Muslims executed six hundred men from the tribe of Banu Qurayza and divided up the women and children among themselves. Khaybar is an oasis to the north of Medina inhabited by Jewish tribes, against whom the Muslims mounted an expedition in June 628. The conquest of Mecca by the Muslims took place in 630. After they had conquered Mecca, the Muslims fought the Hawazin tribe in the Battle of Hunayn. The battle continued in Taef.

44. The Banu Nadir were a Jewish tribe in Medina, which the Muslims exterminated after it had allied with the Meccans.

45. The Arabic adjective *islami* is used indifferently to convey the same meanings as both "Islamic" and "Islamist" in English. This can give rise to difficulties in interpretation. In this passage, Azzam presents a strategic vision that sets him apart from previous ideologues. He defends the idea that the Islamist movement can no longer exist in the form of secret organizations on the territory of oppressive states, for it requires a territory on which it can establish a military force. He considers Afghanistan to be the "solid base" for this struggle. His inspiration was the model of Medina, which served as the Prophet's territorial base in his battles against the Meccans. In the 1990s Bin Laden and Zawahiri managed to create their global terrorist network by using the strategic concept of "military training on the ground," which Azzam had inspired, in Afghanistan. Azzam's strategic approach was more conventional, focusing on the reconquest of Muslim territory, but the underlying idea was the same: to establish a solid base and use it in providing young Muslims with an "education in jihad." Azzam developed this notion in an article published in *Al-Jihad* magazine (April 1988) and titled "The Solid Base."

46. These figures symbolize the two empires that ruled over the Middle East

before the Muslim conquests: the Persian empire to the northeast of Arabia, represented by Chosroes, the last of the Sassanian emperors, and the Byzantine empire to the northwest, represented by Caesar (the generic name given in Arabic to the Roman, and then the Byzantine, emperors).

47. Saad Ibn Abi Waqqas led the great battles against the Persians, especially those of Qadisiyya and Ctesiphon, then the capital of the Sassanid Empire; the Battle of Qadisiyya is considered to have sealed the fate of the empire. Tulayha Ibn Khuwaylid was an apostate who declared himself to be a prophet. After being defeated by Khalid Ibn al-Walid, he converted to Islam once again and died in battle in Persia in 642.

48. An indirect but clear criticism of the strategy followed by many Islamist groups, especially the Egyptian group Al-Jihad, that believed that an Islamic state could be created through a coup d'état. The expressions "general popular jihad" and "popular jihadist movement" that Azzam uses represented a potentially greater force than the vanguard that Egyptian jihadist groups were attempting to form, taking Sayyid Qutb's writing as their inspiration.

49. It is interesting that Azzam is referring to Islamic society, not an Islamic state. This is one of many indications that the concept of the nation-state was virtually absent from his political thought. This serves to distinguish him from other Islamists, notably in Egypt, who always saw the nation-state as important.

50. Miqdim Ibn Ma'd, a hadith transmitter, was one of the Prophet's companions.

51. The "Inqilab-e Saour" (April revolution) was a communist coup d'état that followed months of disturbances. The presidential palace was attacked, and President Daud was killed, along with several of his close aides. On May 1, Nur Muhammad Taraki was named president of the revolutionary council. For Azzam, this date marked the beginning of a time of tragedy and misery in Afghanistan.

52. Azzam often uses very vivid images to evoke Muslims' suffering at the hands of their enemies. His aim, of course, is to galvanize his readers.

53. The title "imam" can refer to the founders of the schools of jurisprudence, or to the community leader (it is then synonymous with "caliph").

54. Known in the West as Averroes, Ibn Rushd was a great Andalusian scholar, who was born in Córdoba in 1126 and died in Marrakech in 1198. A court physician and philosopher to several of the Almohad caliphs (a deeply rigoristic dynasty), he composed renowned glosses on the work of Aristotle, as well as treatises seeking to reconcile religion and reason. The fact that Azzam cites him should not come as a surprise: although some points of Ibn Rushd's philosophy were criticized, his work as a jurist is squarely in line with orthodox Sunni tradition.

55. Ibn Hajar al-Asqalani, an Egyptian jurist of the fifteenth century (1372–1449), traveled throughout the Middle East and the Arabian Peninsula (particularly Yemen) to study with influential teachers, before returning to Syria for good

in 1400. He was the grand judge of Egypt for two decades, although political circumstances caused him to be dismissed from his position and reinstated several times. Today, he is known principally as a hadith specialist. He wrote a gloss on al-Bukhari's *Sahih* (the work cited here: *Fath al-Bari fi Sharh Sahih al-Bukhari*) and several biographical essays on hadith transmitters; because he synthesized knowledge on this topic, his work is still the principal authoritative reference on it.

56. In Arabic, *ahad al-tabi'in*, the successors, refers to the second and third generations of Muslims, after the Prophet's companions. Ibn Abi Abla (679–769) was a hadith transmitter of the third generation. The time that had passed since the Prophet's death justifies Azzam's great suspicion with regard to the material Ibn Abi Abla transmitted. As for the hadith cited here, it can be found, on the authority of Ibn Abi Abla, in the anthology of al-Nasa'i (d. 915), which does not have the same importance as the works of Muslim and al-Bukhari. In this crucial passage, Azzam seeks to refute the argument often formulated by "moderate" Muslim thinkers in their bid to counter the strictly military interpretation that radicals give of the term "jihad." According to these moderates, there is a difference between a "lesser" and "greater" jihad. This distinction is based on the hadith attributed to the Prophet by Ibn Abi Abla, which gives greater value to the spiritual sense of the term "jihad." Azzam, like Faraj in *The Absent Imperative*, considers this hadith to have been forged.

57. The importance of military training for would-be mujahedeen is the focus of one of the most important works in jihadist literature: *Al-Umda fi I'dad al-Idda* (The Pillar of Preparation for Combat), by Abd al-Qadir, Ibn Abd al-Aziz, the ideologue of Islamic jihad in the late 1980s. In Arabic, *ribat* (borders) refers to manning the outposts on the borders of Muslim territory, and to the mujahedeen's rearguard. The *murabitun*—those who performed *ribat*—formed the Berber dynasty known to the Spaniards as the Almoravids: they reigned over North Africa in the eleventh and twelfth centuries.

58. Junada was a hadith transmitter and the military commander who conquered Rhodes. A hadith that can be traced back to the Prophet *(hadith marfu')*, as opposed to *mawquf*, a hadith that can be traced back to only one of the companions.

59. By "delegated," he means in the sense that it was a collective duty delegated to a few, for this was an attack and not self-defense. Tabuk was Muslim expedition against the Byzantines, to the north of the Hejaz, in 630.

60. Khaybar, an expedition toward Mecca, culminated in a treaty between the Muslims and the Meccans in May 628. The treaty was broken by the conquest of Mecca.

61. In Arabic, there is a clear distinction between *futuhat* ("openings"), a word designating the acquisition of territory for Islam, and words that designate purely military conquests.

62. In Arabic, *amir*. The pledge of allegiance *(bay'a)* and of absolute obedience is a crucial aspect of the paramilitary organization envisioned by Azzam.

63. The important place Afghanistan occupies in the Islamist imagination is owing partly to the fact that it is one of the only Muslim countries—despite its strategic value in the Great Game that pitted the Russians against the British in the nineteenth century—that was never formally colonized. The British occupied it briefly on two occasions, after the Anglo-Afghan wars of 1838 and 1878, but each time were forced to retreat very rapidly.

64. Azzam emphasizes this point several times in his writing; the cause of jihad was in his mind thus far superior to any doctrinal divergences among the various schools.

65. Rulings on this topic are justified by reference to the principle of *jawaz ma la yajuz* (allowing that which is prohibited), which is seen as valid in certain circumstances. These divergences from the norm are typical of the teleological thought characteristic of the Malikis and the Hanbalis (including Ibn Taymiyya).

66. Shams al-Din Abu Abdallah Muhammad Ibn Ahmad al-Dhahabi (d. 1347) is known for his biographical dictionaries devoted to the lives of those who compiled the six canonical anthologies of hadith.

67. In the 1980s, Arab volunteers in Afghanistan were received directly, without the intervention of the security forces. Between 1996 and 2001, when Bin Laden and Al Qaeda were organizing training camps in Afghanistan, things took place in a similar fashion but more discreetly. Volunteers coming from the West would go to Istanbul and call Peshawar to announce their arrival date, then travel on to Peshawar and call another number so that they could be picked up, without ever giving their names.

Morals and Jurisprudence of Jihad

1. In the introduction to this text, Azzam announces: "Here are a few paragraphs on the jurisprudence of jihad, which I wrote when everyone had forgotten jihad, when those of God's verses which call on Muslims to fight the unbelievers were interpreted as exhortations to preach Islam by the word and the pen, and when the concept of fighting had become alien in the eyes of Muslims. I wrote to them in the hope that God would accept this attempt to restore jihad to its natural place, at least in the minds of Muslims and in their way of thinking, even if the practical reality they know is very remote from the practice of jihad and from observance of the revealed law."

2. In current Arabic usage, writing is only partly vocalized, so confusion sometimes arises as to the pronunciation and therefore the meaning of certain terms.

3. Quran 24:53.

4. *Lisan al-Arab* (The Arabs' Tongue), by Iban Manzur, and *Al-Bahr al-Muhit* (The Vast Ocean), by Firuzabadi, are classical Arabic dictionaries dating, respectively, from the thirteenth and fourteenth centuries.

5. Like Bin Laden and Zawahiri, for reasons related to mobilization strategies Azzam sought to present his positions as those reached by the four Sunni legal schools consensually, rather than by one in particular. Once again, Azzam disregards the distinction between the "lesser" and the "greater" jihad, often invoked by jurists to counter the radicals' purely military interpretation of the word.

6. Al-Humam was an Egyptian Hanafi jurist (d. 1457).

7. Kasani too was a Hanafi jurist.

8. Ibn al-Qasim al-Ghazzi was a Shāf'ī commentator of Palestinian origin who died in 1512. He was the author of several glosses and works of synthesis in Shāf'ī law, as well as didactic poetry, typical of the spirit of his era.

9. Azzam was echoing argument as formulated by Sayyid Qutb in *Signposts*, where he described the "material obstacles" raised by current political systems to prevent the establishment of an Islamic society. According to Qutb, these obstacles had to be overcome by force.

10. Killing and fighting *(al-qatl wal-qital):* in Arabic the association and the alliteration are clearer because the two words have the same radical.

11. Quran 8:39.

12. Ali Ibn Abi Talib, the Prophet's cousin and son-in-law, became the fourth caliph.

13. This prohibition is the reason jihadist groups have issued so many declarations of war, letters addressed to the enemy, and ideological explanations. In this way militants are sure that the enemy has been warned and given ample time to repent. See Bin Laden, "Message to the American People," or the letter sent by the GIA (Armed Islamic Group) in Algeria to French president Jacques Chirac, calling on him to convert to Islam.

14. Hence the casuistical declarations issued by jihadist movements to justify attacks on civilians (for example, by declaring that in a democracy any decision taken by the government can be imputed partially to every member of society).

15. Quran 9:4.

16. Sarakhsi was a Hanafi jurist who died in 1090.

17. This is what led some radical Islamists to justify the murder of seven Catholic monks in the monastery of Notre Dame de l'Atlas, in Tibehirine, Algeria. The monks were kidnapped on March 27, 1996, and their heads were discovered on May 30. The GIA was accused of the murder, but later information revealed that the Algerian authorities may have been involved.

18. Anas Ibn Malik (d. 711) was the servant of the Prophet, and one of his companions.

19. Al-Simma was an Arab poet and knight who remained pagan after the rev-

elation of Islam. Abu Amir al-Ash'ari, one of the companions, was commander of Muslim troops in the Battle of Hunayn against the Hawazin tribe. Durayd, who was fighting on the side of the Hawazin, was killed in that battle.

20. In Arabic, *wa-Llahu a'lam*, a formula often used to cite God as the highest authority.

21. In other words, in the holiest sanctuary of Islam. This order was allegedly given after the conquest of Mecca. The women in question were "singing slaves" *(jariya)* who had insulted him in the past.

22. *Shahada*—literally, bearing witness that there is no god but God and Muhammad is his Prophet.

23. Hadith cited by al-Bukhari. The Osama in question was Osama Ibn Zayd Ibn Haritha, whom the Prophet is said to have reproached several times for having executed a prisoner who had converted to Islam.

24. Babrak Karmal (1929–1996) was the president of the pro-Soviet Afghan government from 1979 to 1986. His successor, Muhammad Najibullah (1946–1996) was president from 1986 to 1992. In 1991, Najib told a French journalist: "We were Muslim and we still are. Only Afghanistan's enemies accuse us of being communist." See Michael Barry, *A History of Modern Afghanistan* (New York: Cambridge University Press, 2006).

25. These paragraphs show the centrality of martyrdom to Azzam's thought, in contrast to that of his predecessors among Sunni Islamists.

26. In Arabic—as in Greek—the roots of the words "martyr" and "witness" are the same.

27. Shumayl, like Azhari, was a linguist and hadith expert of Persian origin.

28. Nawawi (d. 1277) was a Shāfiʿī jurist.

29. Ishaq Ibn Rahawayh (d. 851) was a famous hadith expert, and al-Bukhari's teacher.

30. Sufyan al-Thawri al-Kufi (715–778) was a highly respected hadith expert of the second century A.H., who was active before the four law schools were formed.

31. Yamama is a region in central Arabia.

32. Uthman Ibn Affan was the third caliph (644–656); his assassination by supporters of Ali Ibn Abi Talib set off an era of civil war ending with the establishment of the Umayyad dynasty in Damascus. Sunnis therefore consider him a martyr.

33. Abdallah Ibn Omar, was the son of Omar, the second caliph, assassinated in 644.

To the Young Muslims of the United States

1. This article was published in *Al-Jihad* 39 (January–February 1988). The article is especially interesting in that it provides information regarding Azzam's

movements in the United States during the war in Afghanistan. It also shows that *Al-Jihad* had a readership in the United States.

2. Azzam made no secret of his contempt for Western society and what he viewed as its moral decadence. The word he uses here—*fitna*—means both temptation and sedition. The latter sense, which has theological connotations, pertains to what threatens to happen when Muslims ignore revealed law and disobey it.

3. The Islamic tradition considers a series of men, from Adam to Muhammad, as prophets; the latter, in that perspective, is the last, or the "seal," of the prophets. The Quran mentions the names of twenty-five prophets, including the principal figures in the Jewish and Christian traditions.

4. *Al-kalima al-tayyiba* (the good word) is the message of Islam.

5. Quran 29:69.

6. Quran 9:46.

7. The mention of a congress may be a reference to a series of conferences held in Kansas City and organized by the Muslim Arab Youth Association (MAYA) in the late 1980s. Azzam was invited, along with Hamas leaders; the lecture Azzam delivered in Kansas City in 1987 was recorded and distributed. The MAYA bought together several small American Muslim associations. It was close to the Muslim Brotherhood and regularly invited high-ranking Brotherhood members to give lectures in the United States. It was attacked in 1994 after PBS broadcast a report titled "Jihad in America," produced by Steve Emerson. Abdallah Azzam's relations with MAYA dated back to 1983, at least; that year, the organization sent Ahmad Yusuf to Peshawar to deliver funds to Azzam. See *Middle East Quarterly,* January 5, 1998. The Web site www.maya.org is currently down.

8. In Arabic, *abiq* literally refers to a fugitive slave.

9. Azzam's condemnation of Western society is reminiscent of Qutb's; Qutb spent two years in the United States in the late 1940s and in his subsequent writings criticized American society's moral decadence, greed, and racial segregation.

10. The first intifada had just broken out when Azzam wrote these words.

11. Human Concern International (HCI) is a federally registered, non-governmental Canadian charity organization. See http://www.humanconcern.org.

12. This Brooklyn mosque was a gathering spot for the most radical Islamists in the United States. In the early 1990s, it was a base for militants acting inside the country.

13. This passage shows how much legitimacy activities in support of the Afghan jihad enjoyed in the United States in the late 1980s. The U.S. branch of the Service Bureau did not work clandestinely: on the contrary, it made every effort to work in a legal framework. This passage also shows that the New York branch of the Service Bureau was not established at Azzam's initiative but at that of the members of the Al-Faruq Mosque community.

14. With hindsight, especially after the events of September 11, it is interesting

to note that in 1988 Azzam could open a bank account in New York, when he was already famous in Afghanistan and surely known to the U.S. authorities.

15. It is difficult to identify these individuals.

16. *Ma'thurat* is collection of Quranic verses and hadith compiled by Hassan al-Banna, the founder of the Muslim Brotherhood.

17. This recommended reading list brings together classic works of medieval theology and jurisprudence as well as works written by authors close to the Muslim Brotherhood during the twentieth century. They help place Azzam within a doctrinal lineage, and indicate what he advised for those wishing to situate themselves in the same tradition. *Book of Doctrine* is a short introduction to the basic principles of Islam by a Hanafi ulema, Ahmad al-Tahawi (853–933). *Commentary of the Two Jalal al-Dins* is an exegesis written by two Egyptian ulema, Jalal al-Din al-Mahalli (d. 1469) and his student, Jalal al-Din al-Suyuti (d. 1505). *In the Shade of the Quran* is Sayyid Qutb's exegesis. Muhammad al-Ghazali (1917–1996) was an Egyptian ulema close to the Muslim Brotherhood. Sayyid Sabiq (1915–2000), an Egyptian ulema, wrote *Jurisprudence of Sunna,* summarizing the positions of the four legal schools on the issues covered by standard legal works, in the 1940s, allegedly at Hassan al-Banna's request.

The Solid Base

1. This article was published in *Al-Jihad* 41 (April 1988). In it, Azzam developed the concept of a solid base that he had introduced the previous year in "Join the Caravan."

2. The term "vanguard" *(tali'a)* is the same one used by Sayyid Qutb in *Signposts* (1964). Qutb, who took it from Marxist discourse, asserted that the Muslim world needed a vanguard that would be capable of breaking down the material barriers put up by the oppressive regimes of the Arab world to prevent the emergence of an Islamic state. Throughout the 1970s, the concept led radical Islamist groups to adopt a classical revolutionary strategy, by forming small groups that were supposed to seize power through a coup d'état. As mentioned previously, Azzam used the term in another sense: according to him, the vanguard was to follow a purely military—as opposed to revolutionary—strategy.

3. Earthly creeds include all secular ideologies: Marxism, capitalism, and so on.

4. In "Join the Caravan," the expression "solid base" refers to a piece of territory; here, by contrast, it designates a group of individuals, the vanguard fighting to establish Islamic society. Some analysts argue that this was the founding text of Al Qaeda, but this opinion seems unjustified, for Azzam used the same expression later in the article to designate the leaders of the Afghan mujahedeen. It seems, rather, that "solid base" was a sufficiently vague and malleable expression in

Azzam's work, something that did not prevent some Afghan Arabs from adopting the term *qaeda* to describe themselves. For a good critical presentation of the term, see Jason Burke, *Al-Qaeda: Casting a Shadow of Terror* (London: Penguin, 2004).

5. Quran 7:195–196.

6. If this assertion is accurate, it allows us to determine that Azzam arrived in Peshawar between January and April 1981, because he arrived in Pakistan in 1981 and wrote this article before April 1988. The expression "Meccan education" refers to the experience of Muhammad and his supporters before they emigrated to Medina in 622. In Muslim tradition, the Meccan period in Muhammad's life is generally associated with ideological preparation and doctrinal clarification, while the Medina period corresponds to a time of legal implementation and military action.

7. The term used in Arabic for believers is *usba,* which means a small group of individuals. Azzam used it as part of an expression: *al-usba al-mu'mina,* or the small band of the faithful, as a synonym of vanguard. The term is rarely used in the vocabulary of militant groups, with the exception of Usbat al-Ansar, a Lebanese Sunni Islamist group. See Bernard Rougier, *Everyday Jihad: The Rise of Militant Islam among Palestinians in Lebanon,* trans. Pascale Ghazaleh (Cambridge, Mass.: Harvard University Press, 2007). *Isaba,* clan or gang, has the same root as *usba.* It is interesting to note that Azzam's call to arms is not unconditional: he stipulates that a long education must take place first. There is an element of anxiety at the possibility that jihad could become a civil war under the effects of discord, if jihadists are not trained sufficiently.

8. It is difficult to distinguish the "small group of believers" from the "pioneering vanguard." This paragraph is reminiscent of *Signposts,* where Qutb advocates the creation of a "new Quranic generation." See Gilles Kepel, *Muslim Extremism in Egypt: The Prophet and Pharaoh,* 2nd ed. (Berkeley: University of California Press, 2003), chap. 2.

9. Azzam envisaged a training infrastructure headed by an elite, similar to the camps headed by the Service Bureau in Afghanistan. Bin Laden and Zawahiri implemented this organizational approach in a professional and extensive way between 1996 and 2001.

10. Azzam uses two different terms for prayers: *salat,* indicating obligatory prayers, and *nawafil,* supplementary prayers.

11. On *al-wala wal-bara,* see "Ayman al-Zawahiri, Veteran of Jihad" in this book.

12. In the preceding passage, which is not translated here, Azzam gave a detailed description of the education of the first generation of Muslims *(al-tarbiyya al-nabawiyya lil-jil al-awwal).* He cited a long series of hadith describing the situation experienced by Muhammad and his supporters during the Meccan period.

13. Along with Ahmed Shah Massoud, these were the most important leaders of the Afghan resistance during the 1980s. Massoud was assassinated in September 2001, and the others ruled as warlords in Afghanistan after the U.S.-led invasion against the Taliban.

14. Quran 35:44.

15. Azzam was alluding to a slogan that was then current in North Africa: that the Islamists, and not secularist nationalists such as the FLN, had been responsible for liberating countries like Algeria from foreign occupation, but that the secularists had then usurped the original uprising.

16. In this text, which was published in spring 1988, less than a year before the Red Army withdrew from Afghanistan, Azzam expressed his anxiety that the United States would be able to "retrieve" a jihad it had financed and equipped, and that the Muslim world would lose interest in the cause. He emphasized the exemplary behavior of the Islamist resistance leaders, and reminded *Al-Jihad's* readership of the need to support this leadership, whatever the cost. The following year, conflicts within the ranks of the mujahedeen, the withdrawal of U.S. and Arab aid after the Soviet retreat, and Azzam's assassination changed the situation completely. These events opened the way to a global proliferation of jihad in the 1990s, of which Zawahiri was the consummate ideologue.

17. Quran 8:73.

Introduction: Ayman al-Zawahiri

This text was available online, at the Minbar al-Tawhid wal-Jihad Web site (www.tawhed.ws). "Abu Qatada the Palestinian," along with Abu Hamza al-Misri and Omar Bakri, was one of the main figures of "Londonistan," the radical Salafist milieu that sprang up in London in the early 1990s. He was detained at Belmarsh prison in Britain from October 2002 to March 2005.

1. A translation of Zawahiri's writings has recently appeared: see Laura Mansfield, *His Own Words: Translation and Analysis of the Writings of Dr. Ayman Al Zawahiri*, Lulu.com, 2006.

2. Until the 1950s, the few shops in Maadi were owned by Greeks, the Sporting Club was run by the British, and the neighborhood's residents were Germans, Britons, Italians, Syrians, Lebanese, and well-off Egyptians. The presence in Maadi of a mainly Christian population—the neighborhood had more churches than mosques—may have contributed to young Ayman's political awakening.

3. See Gilles Kepel, *The War for Muslim Minds: Islam and the West,* trans. Pascale Ghazaleh (Cambridge, Mass.: Harvard University Press, 2004).

4. On Sayyid Qutb, and more generally Islamist movements in Egypt during this period, see Gilles Kepel, *Muslim Extremism in Egypt: The Prophet and Pharaoh,* 2nd ed. (Berkeley: University of California Press, 2003).

5. Al-Zayyat, a human rights lawyer, is a former member of Jihad who was arrested after Sadat's assassination. When he came out of prison, he defended some of the jihadist militants held in Egyptian jails. In that capacity, he became the spokesman for the initiative to abandon violence begun by jailed leaders of the Islamic Group in 1997. Al-Zayyat, who met Zawahiri in prison, wrote a biographical and polemical work about him titled *Ayman al-Zawahri Kama Araftahu* (Ayman al-Zawahiri as I Knew Him), (Cairo: Dar Misr al-Mahrusa, 2002). The English translation, Montasser al-Zayyat, *The Road to Al-Qaeda: The Story of Bin Laden's Right-Hand Man*, trans. Ahmed Fekry (London: Pluto, 2004), is one of the sources of the present chapter.

6. *Al-Kitab al-Aswad: Qissat Ta'dhib al-Muslimin fi Ahd Hosni Mubarak*, n.d., available on the Web site of Minbar al-Tawhid wal-Jihad, www.tawhed.ws.

7. See www.lawrencewright.com/art-zawahiri.html; and for footage of this speech, www.pbs.org/wgbh/pages/frontline/shows/terrorism/etc/video.html.

8. Al-Zayyat, *The Road to Al-Qaeda*, p. 49.

9. The organization became better known as Islamic Jihad during this period, when Zawahiri assumed leadership.

10. Al-Zayyat, *The Road to Al-Qaeda*, p. 88.

11. Peter Bergen, *The Osama Bin Laden I Know* (New York: Free Press, 2006), p. 81.

12. Ibid., p. 79.

13. Wright, "The Man behind Bin Laden," *New Yorker*, September 16, 2002. For an overview of the theories on Azzam's death, see the introduction to the section devoted to his work.

14. Ibid., p. 124.

15. *Tariq al-Quds Yamurr min al-Qahira*, al-Mujahidun, April 1995. *Al-Mujahidun* was the official publication of Egypt's Islamic Jihad.

16. Wright, "The Man behind Bin Laden."

17. Al-Zayyat, *The Road to Al-Qaeda*, p. 75–77.

18. Wright, "The Man behind Bin Laden."

19. He devoted part of *Knights under the Prophet's Banner* to this question. See also Ayman al-Zawahiri, "Al-Suqut."

20. *Al-Sharq al-Awsat*, August 7, 2006.

21. *Nafi wa takdhib* ["Denial and Rebuttal"], August 31, 2006. http://egyig.com/Public/articles/announce/7/54865426.shtml

22. Muhammad al-Hakayima, *Tarikh al-Harakat al-Jihâdiyya fi Misr—al-Tajarib wal-Ahdath* (History of the Islamist Movements in Egypt: Experiences and Events), at http://altabetoun.110mb.com/news.php?action=view&id=101.

23. *Al-Hakayima . . . Man Yasna'uhu . . . wa Man Yu'wihu?* (Hakayima: Who Created Him? And Who Is Protecting Him?), at http://www.egyig.com/Public/articles/essay/6/64188653.shtml.

24. See for example *Al-Hayat*, August 9, 2006; *Al-Sharq al-Awsat*, November 26, 2006; and http://www.almaqreze.com/bayanat/artclo36.html.

25. See, respectively, http://altabetoun.110mb.com and www.egyig.com.

26. For a detailed analysis of this work, see Kepel, *The War for Muslim Minds*.

27. Ibid.

28. The work in question was Sulayman Ibn Abdallah, *Awthaq Ura al-Iman* (The Strongest Bonds of Faith).

29. Asim Barqawi, *Millat Ibrahim*, published in 1984, made *al-wala wal-bara* central to the Muslim faith. The title refers to the following Quranic verse: "There is for you an excellent example (to follow) in Abraham and those with him, when they said to their people: 'We are clear of you and of whatever you worship besides God. We have rejected you, and there has arisen, between us and you, enmity and hatred for ever, unless you believe in God and Him alone'" (Quran, 60:4).

30. Saud al-Sarhan, *Al-Wala wal-Bara: Al-Aydiyolojiyya al-Jadida lil-Harakat al-Islamiyya* (Loyalty and Separation: the Islamist Movements' New Ideology), (n.p., n.d.).

31. By "devil worshippers," Zawahiri is referring to the Yazidis, a majority of whom live in Iraq. The Yazidis revere a creature, the "Peacock Angel," also called Shaytan, whom some Muslims and Christians equate with the devil.

32. *Qadaya Sakhina ma' al-Sheikh Ayman al-Zawahiri* (Hot Topics with Sheikh Ayman al-Zawahiri), http://www.tawhed.ws/r?i=4151&PHPSESSID=6e7cd3991ebce2b89175bbbacb81ca16.

33. Ayman al-Zawahiri, *Kalima hawla al-Udwan al-Sahyu-Salibi 'ala Ghazza wa Lubnan* (A Word on the Zionist-Crusader Attack on Gaza and Lebanon), http://www.tawhed.ws/r?i=4052.

34. On the muted reaction, see especially Thomas Hegghammer, "Global Jihadism after the Iraq War," *Middle East Journal* 60, 1 (Winter 2006): 27.

35. The director of National Intelligence confirmed the letter's authenticity, but some academics have publicly expressed skepticism that the letter is by Zawahiri. See especially Juan Cole, "Zawahiri Letter to Zarqawi: A Shiite Forgery?" http://www.juancole.com/2005/10/zawahiri-letter-to-zarqawi-shiite.html.

36. Alleged letter from Zawahiri to Zarqawi, dated July 9, 2005.

Bitter Harvest

1. This text was written in 1991–1992, while Zawahiri was in Afghanistan. Hassan al-Banna founded the Brotherhood in Egypt in 1928. It soon had at least half a million members and, by the 1940s, branches in most Arab countries. Banna, born in 1906, was a schoolteacher. He established the Brotherhood in Ismailiyya and in 1933, when he was transferred to Cairo, moved its headquarters to the capital. Starting in 1936, when a new Anglo-Egyptian treaty was signed and

the Palestinian revolt broke out, he expanded his activities throughout the Middle East. He died in 1949, probably assassinated by King Farouk's secret services. These excerpts are taken from the book's conclusion.

2. *Tawhid,* expressed in the declaration of faith (the first part of which is "I testify that there is no god but God"). In the Quran, the sura beginning "Say: He is God, the One and Only" (Quran 112) is called the sura of *tawhid.* Several movements have made oneness the center of faith: the Almohads *(muwahhidun)* in Morocco, and later the *muwahhidun* (more reductively referred to as Wahhabis) in Arabia, made it possible to form states on the basis of this central doctrine. Today, Salafist movements have taken it up, to battle what they see as idolatry, promoted by democracy and its institutions. Zawahiri considers that these institutions go against Islam, since they presume to take over God's leadership of the world.

3. *Al-hukm bi ghayri ma anzala Allah:* this accusation is crucial to the process of delegitimizing ruling regimes that Islamist ideologues have undertaken since Abul-Ala al-Mawdudi and Sayyid Qutb.

4. *La hukma illa lil-Lah:* this statement is the basis of Maudoodi's and Qutb's interpretation of the key principle of *hakimiyya.* The word *hukm,* however, has several meanings: it can be rendered as "power" or "judgment." Some ulema, contrary to Qutb, have preferred the second meaning, and taken the verse to mean "judgment is for none but God."

5. Quran, 12:40, 18:26 (only the end of the verse is cited in each instance).

6. Quran 42:21 (only the beginning of the verse is cited). In monotheism, God has no associates. Pagans or idol worshippers are called *mushrikun* (associationists) in Arabic.

7. Zawahiri rejects the idea of a constitution or of human legislation, first because it implies that human beings have been given a right to legislate that belongs to God, and second because both are Western concepts, and to adopt them would be a manifestation of loyalty to unbelievers. The Muslim Brotherhood's position on these questions is very different from Zawahiri's: they see no contradiction between the implementation of Islamic law and the adoption of "human laws" on matters where God's law is vague enough to leave room for interpretation.

8. Quran 5:80–81.

9. For example, Marwan Hadid, a comrade of Sayyid Qutb's, who returned to Syria from Egypt in 1966 and preached armed insurrection against the Baath Party's "apostasy." In 1973, he was sent to jail, where he died in suspicious circumstances. He was posthumously the main inspiration for the jihad initiated by some of the Syrian Muslim Brothers against the regime starting in 1974; the conflict culminated in the Hama insurrection and its brutal repression in 1982.

10. Hudaybi, Hassan al-Banna's successor, became supreme guide of the Brotherhood in October 1951. In 1969, breaking officially with Sayyid Qutb's thought as developed in *Signposts*, he wrote *Preachers, Not Judges* in response. In this work, he advocated a return to the policy defined by Banna, emphasizing the importance of preaching *(da'wa)*.

11. The Brotherhood's position on this question was never as clear-cut as Zawahiri is implying here. Hassan al-Banna, the movement's founder, expressed his opposition to political pluralism, which in his opinion divided the community. At the same time, it is true that since Banna's time the Brotherhood has never hesitated to run candidates in legislative elections (indeed, Banna himself was a candidate), thereby implicitly recognizing the legitimacy of the existing parliamentary system.

12. This is one of the Islamists' main bones of contention with democracy, which they perceive as fundamentally secular, in the sense that parliament is the sole source of legislation. This is an inaccurate idea, however, since the supreme source of legislation, even in Western democracies, transcends the deputies' decisions: human rights declarations and constitutions, for instance, override parliament. Liberal Islamist movements, and some states, like Iran, used this principle to make the Quran not the source of legislation, but the source of the principles of legislation. Zawahiri's position here is more radical.

13. Farouk, the last king of Egypt, was born in 1921 and ruled from 1936 until the Nasserite coup d'état of July 23, 1952. The main nationalist party in Egypt until the 1952 revolution, the Wafd was created after a delegation (*wafd* in Arabic) of Egyptian nationalists, led by Saad Zaghlul, failed in its mission to negotiate Egypt's independence from Britain after World War I. The subsequent arrest and exile of the delegates triggered the revolution of 1919. The members were then allowed to return, and set up a political party, which recruited members from the new urban bourgeoisie. The declaration of February 21, 1922, whereby Britain gave up its protectorate over Egypt (while defining four points on which Egyptian sovereignty was severely limited), is seen as the work of this party, which led the government several times during the interwar period.

14. The allegation that al-Banna offered the king assistance was never confirmed. The hypothesis was formulated on the grounds of contacts Banna had made at court, at a time when the king was increasingly suspicious of the various political trends on the Egyptian scene (and especially of the Wafd and its allies). In 1942, the British unseated a royalist government (suspected of being sympathetic to the Axis powers) and imposed a Wafd government headed by Mustafa al-Nahas. In 1944 the king, who had increased his authority once again, overturned this pro-British government. After 1943 the Brotherhood was also facing competition from the Communist Party and the left wing of the Wafd. All these would

have provided the palace with motives for drawing closer to the Brotherhood. The defeat of the Arab armies by Israel in late 1948 altered the situation, however. From that point on, most political movements (including the Brotherhood but excluding the Wafd) considered the monarchy as principally responsible for the defeat. Finally, relations between the monarchy and the Brotherhood had already been strong under King Fuad, Farouk's father, in the late 1920s, at the time when Fuad aspired to take over the caliphate, which Mustafa Kemal Ataturk had abolished in 1924. The mention of combating communism is a slight anachronism: as we have seen, it was not only the communist threat that prompted a relative rapprochement between the king and the Brotherhood. Only in the 1960s did communism, the common enemy of the Islamists and the conservative regimes, serve to justify alliances between pro-Western governments and Islamic movements in Saudi Arabia, Egypt, and Jordan.

15. The Brotherhood supported the Free Officers coup of 1952, probably in the hope that the new government would implement the Brotherhood's political program. After the coup, the honeymoon continued and on January 17, 1953, when all political parties were banned and dissolved, the Brotherhood was spared. The Brothers were thus able to continue their activities at universities, in trade unions, and so on. In late 1953, there were rumors of a conspiracy against the Free Officers in the police force and the army. On January 13, 1954, the Brotherhood was dissolved and its leaders were jailed. They were soon freed, however, and were once again granted the right to exist as an association. These abrupt shifts in policy may be attributed by the rivalry between Nasser and Muhammad Naguib, the first Egyptian president. On October 19, 1954, an Anglo-Egyptian treaty was signed, putting an end to the "four points" that had restricted Egyptian sovereignty. The Brotherhood, however, opposed any negotiations with the British, and a week later, on October 26, someone attempted to assassinate Nasser in Alexandria. Nasser accused the Brotherhood and unleashed a wave of arrests in circles close to the organization. Over a thousand Brotherhood members were arrested; the supreme guide, Hudaybi, was condemned to death (the sentence was commuted to life in prison); and six members (among them the writer and lawyer Abd al-Qadir Awda) were executed. The Brotherhood then became the regime's enemy Number 1. In 1965, after an alleged conspiracy by the Brotherhood, which was influenced by Qutb's writing at the time, a new campaign of repression hit the movement. After a yearlong trial, three Brothers, Qutb among them, were hanged in August 1966.

16. When Anwar Sadat took power in 1970, he initiated a change in policy with regard to the Brotherhood. Keen to impose his influence, he sought to "de-Nasserize" Egyptian politics and society and used the Islamist movements (freeing Brotherhood members from prison in 1971) to attack the Left.

17. Muhammad Ma'mun al-Hudaybi (1921–2004) was the sixth supreme guide

of the Brotherhood, from the death of his predecessor, Mustafa Mashhur, in October 2002, until his own, in January 2004. He was the son of Hassan al-Hudaybi, who led the Brotherhood after Hassan al-Banna died.

18. A veritable Arab cold war pitted the "progressive" Arab regimes, led by Nasserite Egypt against the "conservative" Arab regimes, under Saudi leadership, from the late 1950s onward. In this context, King Faisal, who ruled Saudi Arabia from 1964 to 1975, worked to found an "Islamic International" that could fight against secular, socialist, or nationalist regimes. The Muslim Brotherhood faced persecution in Egypt and to a lesser extent in Syria; quite naturally, the Brothers found refuge in Saudi Arabia at the time, and indeed the Saudi government became the Brotherhood's chief ally. Zawahiri, however, condemned both antagonists in this cold war equally.

19. In February 1982, Hafez al-Assad's Baath government carried out a bloody repression of an Islamist uprising led by the Muslim Brothers in their bastion, the city of Hama. During a twenty-seven-day siege, the Syrian forces bombarded and gassed the city, destroying at least a third of Hama's infrastructure and killing around twenty thousand of its inhabitants. See, for instance, Nikolaos van Dam, *The Struggle for Power in Syria: Politics and Society under Asad and the Ba'th Party* (London: Tauris, 1996).

20. Saad al-Din may be considered one of the principal members of the Iraqi Muslim Brotherhood, which he helped structure, since a branch already existed before the Syrian exiles arrived. Hawa was the main ideologue of the Syrian Muslim Brotherhood (see Azzam, "The Defense of Muslim Territories"). He fled Syria for Iraq after the first Hama events, in 1964; this is probably what Zawahiri is referring to here.

21. Rifaat al-Assad, took a line surreptitiously opposed to the policies of his brother Hafez and sought to succeed him as Syrian president. In search of allies, he unsuccessfully courted the Muslim Brothers, while assuming the image of a man who was ready to renegotiate the secular basis of the Syrian state.

22. Mahmud Fahmi al-Nuqrashi, who was prime minister at the time, dissolved the Muslim Brotherhood, confiscating its assets and arresting some of its members as the war against the Zionists was raging in 1948 and the Arab defeat was growing more certain. On December 28, 1948, a Muslim Brother shot him in the street. Banna was assassinated, no doubt in reprisal, a month later.

23. "Letter to the Fifth Congress," in *Correspondence*, Shihab Press, p. 159. This Brotherhood congress was held in January 1939.

24. The schism took place in November 1939, when Brotherhood members condemned Hassan al-Banna's negotiations with the monarchy.

25. This is not entirely accurate: in the 1940s, the movement was divided over the question of which method to employ in reaching power. The creation of an armed wing at that time was a response to the hard line, which sought to over-

throw the regime. Historians see Hassan al-Banna's assassination as the regime's reply to the activities carried out by this militia in the late 1940s (assassinations, attacks, and so on).

26. These are the countries where the Brotherhood followed a legalistic line. The Syrian Brothers, who starting in 1974 chose the path of insurrection, are therefore not included.

27. Perhaps Zawahiri was referring here to Sayyid Qutb, although Qutb's position on armed opposition was not as clear as Zawahiri makes it out to be. True, Qutb's analysis of Egyptian society and the regime was unequivocal, for he advocated "movement" *(al-haraka)* to end the state of *jahiliyya* and impose God's sovereignty. Still, his discourse remained confined to a fairly theoretical level, and he was never as explicit as his intellectual heirs, Zawahiri among them, later were. It is also possible that Zawahiri was thinking of the Islamic Group, many of whose members were linked to the Brotherhood (not the case for Islamic Jihad), but with whom the Brotherhood cut off ties when the Islamic Group chose violent confrontation with the state.

28. The veracity of Zawahiri's assertions has already been discussed. Here, however, he seems to be taking part in the debate over Banna's legacy, which many Islamists claim to be pursuing: partisans of legalism within the Brotherhood and radicals inspired by Qutb all pose as worthy heirs to Banna's memory. Zawahiri, however, is implying that contrary to the radicals' claims there was no continuity between Banna and Qutb, but rather a complete break.

29. Brotherhood historiography often refers to Banna as the renewer of the twentieth century. The concept of renewer *(mujaddid)* refers to a fourteenth-century tradition according to which in every century a descendant of the Prophet is sent by God to restore religious orthodoxy. Various theologians and politicians— among them Ayatollah Khomeini—allowed their disciples to confer this title on them. It often goes hand in hand with that of "religious revivalist" *(muhi al-din)*. In 2002, Faris al-Zahrani, a Saudi jihadist ideologue, used this expression to describe Osama Bin Laden.

30. Muhammad Qutb, Sayyid's brother and comrade, was arrested with him in 1965. Unlike his brother, however, he was not condemned to death, and he was freed in 1971 on Sadat's orders. He then moved to Saudi Arabia, where he taught at the Islamic University in Medina. Since his Saudi exile began, he has written many works in which he pursues Sayyid Qutb's intellectual legacy, faithfully taking up his concepts. He lives in Mecca today.

31. Quran 4:135 (only the first part of the verse is cited).

32. Muhammad al-Ghazali (1917–1996) was an Azharite and member of the Muslim Brotherhood. In the 1980s, he became one of the main figures of liberal Islamism (the *wasatiyya* faction) in Egypt. Shukri Mustafa was born in 1942 in a village in Middle Egypt. As a young Islamist militant close to the Muslim Brother-

hood, he was one of the many seized in the mass arrests of 1965 and was jailed until 1971, thus spending several years in the Islamist melting pot of Nasser's prisons. Qutb's writing influenced him greatly, but he read it in a particular way: according to Mustafa, separation from *jahiliyya* as Qutb preached it was not merely spiritual; it also had to translate into physical isolation. Starting in 1972, along with his first disciples, he undertook to exile himself, withdrawing into the mountains. In 1977, his group (which the press dubbed Excommunication and Exile) kidnapped the minister of pious endowments; Mustafa was arrested and executed as a result. His movement did not survive him.

33. The principle of commanding good and prohibiting evil makes every Muslim responsible for the behavior of his or her co-religionists, who must be advised and even reprimanded when they are tempted to stray. It imposes horizontal control among the community's members, in contrast to a vertical type of control such as might exist in a hierarchical party structure. In Zawahiri's opinion, only the first type of control is truly Islamic, and the adoption of the second by the Brotherhood, leading it to abandon the first, is a violation of dogma.

34. The Muslim Brotherhood, which has a more traditional approach to Islam, interprets monotheism as simply believing in God's oneness and reciting the profession of faith. For the Salafist jihadists, by contrast, who are influenced by Wahhabism, monotheism must be practiced in full: in particular, doing so entails excluding from Islam any unorthodox school of thought, such as Sufism, which the Salafists accuse of polytheism. The main bone of contention between the Wahhabis and the Brotherhood, indeed, is the close relation the Brotherhood maintains with Sufism.

35. The 1960s marked the beginning of the era of oil prosperity for the countries of the Gulf. In Saudi Arabia, the country principally targeted by Zawahiri's assertions, dramatic development of state and nonstate institutions took place during that decade. This process called for skills that could not be found within the kingdom, which therefore called on the Muslim Brothers who had sought refuge in Saudi Arabia, many of whom were university graduates. Muslim Brothers thus ended up at every level of these new institutions, especially those Zawahiri singles out here, such as (Islamic) banks. Initially political refugees, the Brotherhood members rapidly became bourgeois "Saudi technocrats just like the others."

36. Quran 21:35.

37. When war broke out between the newly declared state of Israel and the Arab states in May 1948 (the first round of hostilities lasted until early 1949, with interruptions in July and September 1948), political organizations sent militants to the front to supplement the woefully inadequate Arab national armies. The Muslim Brothers sent a contingent under the command of Muhammad Farghali. Zawahiri is referring here to guerrilla warfare against British troops in the Canal

Zone. The Egyptian resistance was led partly by Yusuf Talaat, especially in Ismailiyya, the town where the Brotherhood was founded, and in other parts of the Canal Zone, where the Brotherhood has been strong since its creation. The acts of attrition, undertaken by political movements without authorization from the regime in Cairo, reflect the deterioration of the monarchy in the period immediately preceding its overthrow.

38. Alongside the Muslim Brotherhood there were independent volunteers, members of Young Egypt, Blue Shirts (the Wafd youth organization), and so forth.

39. Some observers question the alleged attempt on Nasser's life in 1954. They suspect that the government was keen to get rid of the Muslim Brothers and made it a target for popular resentment, thereby also legitimating repression of the movement. No act directed by the Brotherhood against the Nasser regime had any result, and indeed it can be argued that none was undertaken seriously. But it is necessary to take into account Nasser's popularity among the Egyptian people and throughout the Arab world, and therefore the risk incurred by the Brotherhood of alienating the population by attacking the individual who was then seen as the symbol of Arab dignity.

40. Quran 9:123. In Zawahiri's conceptual framework, during this period, priority was given to the enemy near at hand, as Abd al-Salam Faraj had proposed in 1981. Zawahiri changed the strategy later, as is clear in *Knights under the Prophet's Banner*. He differentiates between apostates, Muslims who associated with the enemies of Islam (these he condemned, as had Sayyid Qutb), and "original unbelievers" *(kuffar asliyyin)*, who came second in the hierarchy of enemies.

41. Ibid., 24:63. Only the end of the verse is cited.

42. Ibid., 2:160.

43. This is an early mention of the word "crusader" *(salibi)* in jihadist literature. It would later become a key to describing Western enemies.

44. Quran 60:4. This verse, often cited in radical Islamist literature, is interpreted by Islamists as an injunction to declare others to be apostates *(takfir)*.

45. Ibid., 2:256.

46. The Salafists condemn blind imitation *(taqlid)* of Islamic jurisprudence and advocate systematic recourse to the Quran and the sunna of the Prophet and the first generation of Muslims. The opinion Zawahiri was expressing here may be understood in this context.

47. Quran 3:110.

48. Ibid., 5:78–79.

49. Ibid., 29:6.

50. Ibid., 35:15–17.

51. Ibid., 6:89.

52. Ibid., 9:38–40.

Advice to Reject the Fatwa of Sheikh Bin Baz

1. The expression *zallat alim,* the error committed by a religious scholar, is often used to attack the arguments of an antagonist and, in Islamist literature, to discredit those described as court ulema. For the biography of the Saudi scholar Bin Baz, see Azzam, "The Defense of Muslim Territories." This text, posted on the Web site of Minbar al-Tawhid wal-Jihad (www.tawhed.ws), bears no publication date and may have been transcribed from a recorded speech. It was probably published in the early 1990s, when Saudi Islamists were increasingly criticizing Bin Baz. The text must be placed within that dynamic. Its value lies in the fact that Zawahiri, by daring to question a legal opinion by a scholar who was still considered (even by his detractors) one of the greatest figures of Sunni Wahhabi Islam, sought to present himself as a religious scholar in his own right. He hoped that his movement's legitimacy would benefit greatly from this quality. The text also has a political dimension, since it constitutes a veritable declaration of war against the Saudi regime's main instrument of legitimation.

2. One of the publications linked to the Brotherhood. Zawahiri was suggesting that Bin Baz might have been forced to issue his opinion—in particular, by the Saudi regime. The same argument was used after Bin Baz approved the call for Western troops to protect the Saudi kingdom: part of the Islamist opposition refused to believe that Bin Baz, who was so highly respected, could have betrayed principles he had always upheld until then.

3. Quran 5:38, 2:179.

4. The word for corruption is a polysemic term in Arabic, which is always difficult to translate, for it implies corruption, alteration, rotting, perversion, waste, oppression, and violence. In any case, it designates something that should be rejected absolutely. Corruption here refers to the immoral character of a situation that prevails in Muslim countries, according to Zawahiri, and to the rupture of the pact between rulers and ruled, whereby rulers must govern according to God's law.

5. Quran, 67:14.

6. Zawahiri may have been referring to Egypt, among others: in 1875, a "mixed code" was adopted, heavily inspired by the Napoleonic Code that served as the foundation for national code of 1883. French law thus supplanted Islamic law and its associated executive rulings as the principal source of Egyptian law.

7. Zawahiri's theory of neocolonialism presents independent governments in formerly colonized countries in the post–World War II period as simply the beginning of a new stage of imperialism. In this period, native authorities manage the exploitation and domination of former colonies in the service of the former colonial powers: Muslim governments are thus the heirs of the European powers.

One finds the same conceptual framework used by Islamist movements in Algeria, which accuse the FLN (National Liberation Front) and the generals of belonging to the "French party" *(hizb Faransa)* and of having inherited the colonizers' interests in their struggle against the Muslim Algerian people. Usury is defined as excessively exploitative interest rates (and as not interest in any form, as some Islamic banks and Orientalist scholars have claimed).

8. Unlike Bin Laden, Zawahiri did not hesitate to declare nominal Muslims apostates.

9. Quran 5:45. The term Zawahiri uses for apostates here is *murtadd*, designating a Muslim who has forsaken Islam and its laws.

10. Al-Suyuti (1445–1505) was an Egyptian religious scholar of Persian origin. A follower of the Shāf'ī school, he wrote hundreds of books in all the fields of knowledge that existed during his lifetime. Being aware of his talents as a polymath, he frequently opposed contemporary scholars as well as the Mamluks who then ruled Egypt. He refused to associate with Sultan Qaytbay or his successor, al-Ghuri, justifying his position in a famous epistle, where he argued that the first Muslims had prohibited frequenting temporal authorities.

11. Ibn Hajar al-Asqalani was an Egyptian jurist of the fifteenth century. Ismail Ibn Ishaq (815–896) was an Iraqi Maliki jurist. He speaks of the apparent meaning of the verses, as opposed to their esoteric meaning. This argument has particular strength for Zawahiri, as a literalist.

12. Quran 109:6. "Way" is the literal meaning of *sharia.*

13. Another ideologue of the Salafist jihadist movement, Abu Muhammad al-Maqdisi, titled one of his pamphlets against democracy *Al-Dimuqratiyya Din* (Democracy Is a Religion).

14. "Making the people into gods" is an allusion to the principle of popular sovereignty. In Zawahiri's view, this makes the majority the source of legislation.

15. Quran 12:40.

16. Mawdudi was an Islamist thinker (1903–1979) who was born in India and founded the Islamist party Jamaat-i-Islami. Initially opposed to the division of India and the creation of Pakistan, this party then resigned itself to becoming a player on the Pakistani political scene. Mawdudi's writings, translated into Arabic, greatly influenced Sayyid Qutb.

17. It is interesting that Zawahiri is more critical of the democratic principles enunciated in the constitution than of the regime's dictatorial practices; moreover, he does not question whether these democratic principles are actually applied. The English translation of the constitution appears on an Egyptian government Web site.

18. Quran 42:21.

19. Ibid., 109:6.

20. Ibid., 3:64.

21. Ibid. 9:31. Hatim was a companion of the Prophet (d. 687).

22. Ahmad Ibn Hanbal (see Azzam, "The Defense of Muslim Territories") and Muhammad Ibn Isa al-Tirmidhi (824–892), a renowned compiler of hadith.

23. Mahmud Shihab al-Din al-Alusi (1802–1854), an Iraqi religious scholar and the author of an exegesis titled *Ruh al-Ma'ani*. The scion of a family of ulema originally from Alus, a town near Ramadi, west of the Euphrates, he was the mufti of Baghdad. He wrote, apart from his works of grammar and exegesis, polemical tracts aimed at the Shiites.

24. Quran 3:64.

25. Ibid., 21:22.

26. Ibid., 79:24.

27. "People of the book" is used to designate adherents of the scriptural religions—principally Christianity and Judaism—which benefited from a privileged status and were authorized, under Muslim rule, to preserve their communal autonomy in return for paying a poll tax, the *jizya*.

28. Quran 3:64.

29. A reference to idol worship, common in pre-Islamic Arabia.

30. God's creatures are designated as his slaves or those who worship him: the two ideas share the same radical *('-b-d)*.

31. Islam recognizes many prophets, among them Moses, Abraham, and Jesus. They are distinguished from Muhammad, however, who is the only messenger of God.

32. "Desires" here in Arabic is *hawa*, a term that may have connotations of passion, whim, and earthly desire.

33. Quran, 4:59, 42:10.

34. Zawahiri was probably referring to the referendum organized in Pakistan in December 1984 by Zia ul-Haq, regarding the policy of Islamization he had begun to implement when he took power in 1977. He won the referendum, but there were accusations of fraud.

35. Several Arab countries declare that they are democracies and have Islam as the state religion.

36. Musaylima was an unfortunate rival of the Prophet Muhammad, and a symbol of false prophethood in Muslim sources. He was often described as *al-kadhdhab,* "the liar." The leader of a tribe from the Yamama region, east of the Hejaz, he refused to pay allegiance to the new Muslim state in Medina; after the Prophet's death in 632, Musaylima led an uprising in the wake of the *ridda* wars (wars of apostasy). He died in 633 during the bloody battle of Aqraba, when Muslim troops led by Khalid Ibn al-Walid defeated the seditious tribes.

37. Quran 12:106.

38. Ibid., 5:3.

39. Ibid., 29:47.

40. Ibid., 109:1, 6. Interestingly, whereas some modernists interpret this verse as a call to tolerance and mutual respect, Zawahiri reads it as absolute rejection of the non-Muslim Other.

41. Ibid., 39:2–3.

42. Even the most radical Islamists, like Zawahiri, accept the principle of *shura*, or consultation in decision making. Interpreted in a more general way, the same principle is what allows the Muslim Brothers to participate in political life and have representatives in parliament. Zawahiri, however, is arguing that the distinction does not apply: entering parliament, according to him, means implicitly recognizing the legitimacy of a regime he has condemned for apostasy. Worse still, it means admitting that the majority might be able to make a decision even if that decision contravenes God's laws.

43. Law 33 (1978) was promulgated to protect the "internal front" and preserve social peace in society. Article 3 raised many obstacles to participation in elections for local councils, cooperative societies, or syndicates. Opponents of government policies were thus barred from taking part in the elections of their organizations or institutions. After much litigation, this law was determined to be unconstitutional and was abolished in 1979. See Implementation of the International Covenant on Economic, Social and Cultural Rights in Egypt, Parallel NGO Report by the Land Center for Human Rights (LCHR).

44. Talmasani (1904–1986) was originally of North African ancestry (hence his family name, signifying "from Tlemcen). He was the third supreme guide of the Brotherhood, after Hassan al-Hudaybi died in 1976.

45. The implicit accusation of not being in touch with reality, which young Islamists often direct at the older generation of Azharites or the Wahhabi establishment, allows Zawahiri to criticize a figure he continues to respect.

46. The debate over sharia as the principal source of legislation has lasted since the 1970s, pitting some Azharites and the Islamists against some elements in the government.

47. Darimi was a renowned hadith compiler. Al-Albani (see also Azzam, "The Defense of Muslim Territories") not only was a writer, but also verified the validity of hadith cited by other compilers.

48. Using the same logic, in September 1992 Saudi Islamists presented King Fahd with a petition calling for reform, titled "Memorandum of Good Counsel."

49. Al-Ash'ari was a companion of the Prophet, born around 614. Originally from Yemen, he apparently joined the Muslims in Khaybar in 628. He was initially the Prophet's lieutenant, then second-in-command to the first caliph in Yemen. He went on to govern Basra, then Kufa, before undertaking the conquest of Persia in 638: at the battle of Bayrudh, he reduced several Kurdish tribes.

Knights under the Prophet's Banner

1. Various complete translations of this text are available online. See, for example, http://web.archive.org/web/20040629224951/http://www.fas.org/irp/world/para/ayman_bk.html. This text was published starting on December 2, 2001, in *Al-Sharq al-Awsat.* Zawahiri's original text, however, was interspersed with comments added by the editors (indeed, the text itself may have been rewritten, at least in part), and it is often difficult to know whether a given sentence or subheading was written by Zawahiri or by a journalist. In the introduction, the newspaper simply noted that the original text had been passed on by an Egyptian jihadist militant named A. S., who was close to Zawahiri and who had obtained it from him in a cave near Kandahar. A. S. carried the document to Peshawar, and from there it was sent to London. See Gilles Kepel, *The War for Muslim Minds* (Cambridge, Mass.: Harvard University Press, 2004).

2. Al Qaeda's ideologues seem to consider the control of information, or at least its subversion (through terrorism and monopoly of prime-time news), as a central goal of their strategy.

3. The term used here for "fundamentalist" is *usuli,* the adjective derived from *usul,* bases or foundations. The neologism, often used by the media to designate the Islamists, is rarely used by Islamists themselves. Perhaps the journalist was paraphrasing Zawahiri.

4. What was once the heart of the Muslim world is now located on its periphery, or rather in the frontline states. This geographical shift in the representative center of the Muslim world, from the Middle East to the peripheral zones where jihad is being waged, must be seen in relation to the theoretical shift that places jihad at the center of Islam.

5. Eastern Turkistan is the traditional name of Xinjiang, the westernmost region of China, populated by Muslims. In the 1940s, an independent republic was briefly declared there, before Beijing reduced it once again.

6. There were many reports of Islamists leaving their families—parents or wives and children—to join the jihad.

7. After the FIS won the municipal elections of June 1990, and before its expected victory in the second round of legislative elections, scheduled for January 1992, the elections were suspended on the generals' orders and the authorities challenged the legality of the FIS. This situation led to a military takeover and the beginning of a long civil war. Zawahiri implies here that the FIS was partly responsible for this failure, given that it had agreed to participate in elections. Most Western nations, France among them, supported the Algerian military coup of 1992, to the great distress of Islamist parties and movements, which saw in this support a flagrant betrayal of the democratic intentions expressed by Western powers after the fall of the Berlin Wall.

8. By "French party" he alludes to the Francophone elites that have ruled since 1962.

9. Arabic proverb.

10. Quran 3:200.

11. At the time when he was writing this book, in autumn of 2001, Zawahiri was aware of the upheaval that U.S. invasion of Afghanistan would entail for Al Qaeda. He may also have been aware that some in Bin Laden's entourage were unhappy with the leadership's decision to attack New York and Washington, for this ultimately led to the loss of the "solid base" in Afghanistan. In 2004, a member of Al Qaeda in Afghanistan who was close to Bin Laden and Zawahiri wrote: "The last months of Al Qaeda provide the tragic example of a very poorly managed Islamic movement. Everyone knew that their leader was leading them toward the abyss, indeed that he was leading the entire country to its destruction, but they continued to carry out his orders" (*Al-Sharq al-Awsat,* December 9, 2004).

12. Zawahiri seems to be criticizing the coup d'état strategy adopted by his own organization, Al-Jihad.

13. For movements often deprived of access to the political arena, philanthropy—based on Quranic injunctions to give charitably—has been an important means of recruiting and constituting a popular base. This is especially true of the Muslim Brotherhood and Hamas.

14. "For a decade": Zawahiri is referring here to the presence of U.S. troops in Saudi Arabia since the Gulf War, seen as an occupation.

15. If these are indeed Zawahiri's words, he seems to be admitting that certain national liberation struggles were for strategic reasons presented as the expression of a global conflict between Islam and unbelief.

16. Armistice agreements putting an end to the first Arab-Israeli war were signed between Israel and four Arab countries (Egypt, Lebanon, Jordan, and Syria) on the island of Rhodes between February and July 1949. The corresponding peace treaties, however, were never signed.

17. Zawahiri may be tacitly acknowledging the criticism directed against the jihadist movement, especially after the Al-Aqsa intifada, accusing Bin Laden and Al Qaeda of putting the struggle against Israel second.

18. Zawahiri is referring to two entities: first, the secular Arab states (Egypt under Nasser and Sadat and to a lesser extent Baathist Syria, which did not open direct negotiations with Israel but showed its readiness to open negotiations under certain circumstances), and second, left-wing and Arab nationalist liberation movements (like the Popular Front for the Liberation of Palestine [PFLP], and the Democratic Front for the Liberation of Palestine [DFLP]). The PLO, and the Palestinian Authority after the Oslo agreements, belong to both categories at once. According to Zawahiri, the secular factions' recognition of Israel constitutes re-

vealing their true nature, since these groups and regimes had based their legitimacy on defending Palestine.

19. These references to Arab identity, distinct from Islam, seem surprising coming from Zawahiri.

20. Such attacks occurred several times after 2001—for example, when U.S. diplomat Laurence Foley was murdered in Amman in October 2002. A wave of targeted assassinations followed in Saudi Arabia between May and September 2004, and the cinematographer Theo Van Gogh was murdered in Amsterdam in November of the same year.

21. "Ulema of jihad" is a new expression, which appears in counterpoint to that of the "palace ulema" (who legitimate every decision made by the authorities). Many of the "ulema of jihad"—whose function was to guide radical Islamist groups and legitimate their actions—were arrested or silenced after September 11, 2001: Abu Qatada al-Falastini was jailed between October 2002 and March 2005 in Britain, and Nasir al-Fahd and Ali al-Khudayr have been in a Saudi prison since June 2003.

22. Zawahiri is echoing Qutb's idea that no Muslim state currently exists. Mustafa Kemal Ataturk abolished the caliphate in 1924, six months after the end of the Ottoman Empire. Zawahiri, however, is not referring to the Ottoman caliphate, but to the time of the Rightly Guided Caliphs, the first four successors to the Prophet as rulers of the Muslim community.

23. Al Qaeda's ideologues rarely mention the matter of the caliphate—not because they do not aspire to restore it, but because they consider it a distant goal. Zawahiri is therefore marking a break with the movement's discourse and vague political project in a manner more reminiscent of Hizb al-Tahrir, a group that describes itself as nonviolent and makes the restoration of the caliphate the first of its priorities.

24. Zanki was a Seljuk emir who led the battle against the Latin Kingdom of Jerusalem from his kingdom in northern Syria. In tandem, Nur al-Din launched a major movement of intellectual renewal in Sunnism, carried on by Salah al-Din (Saladin), by founding many madrassas (religious academies) in the cities of the Levant, partly in a bid to counter Shiite influence. Salah al-Din, Nur al-Din's Kurdish vassal, led expeditions against the Crusaders to protect Egypt, then overthrew the Shiite Fatimid imamate and declared himself sultan of Egypt in 1171, of Syria in 1174, and of northern Mesopotamia in 1186. He beat the Crusaders at Hattin and took Jerusalem (1187), before dying in Damascus in 1193. He remains a model for the liberation and unification of the Middle East, but he is also known for having encouraged the spread of Sunnism in previously Fatimid lands. *Munafiqun* (hypocrites) is the term used in the Quran to designate Muhammad's opponents among new converts to Islam. Here Zawahiri is referring to Muslim dynasties that allied themselves with the Crusaders.

25. The Crusaders' presence on the Syrian-Palestinian coast ended only a century after Hattin, with the fall of Acre in 1291. Zawahiri is implying that final victories do not immediately follow initial strategic victories.

26. Zawahiri may have been thinking of his own experience in Islamic Jihad, an organization that was on the brink of annihilation several times through repression by the Egyptian authorities: after Sadat's assassination, and in 1995, after the attempted assassination of President Mubarak. But Zawahiri may also be aware of problems linked with the loss of many members of the jihadist movement in the wave of repression following the attacks of September 11.

27. This is the strategy currently followed by Al Qaeda, since Bin Laden and Zawahiri seem to be in a safe place, perhaps in tribal territory between Pakistan and Afghanistan, where they can ensure the movement's survival without taking part in operations on the ground. It is the media, however, that provide the safest place of all, as a sanctuary ruled only by audience ratings.

28. Once again, Zawahiri indicates that one of the motives behind Al Qaeda's actions should be to emphasize the implicit but total break between regimes and populations in the Middle East. This reality appears only when governments are forced to choose between their Western allies and the interests or will of their own people.

29. Zawahiri knew that this was an extreme solution: Ibn Taymiyya, a source of inspiration for many Islamists, noted: "Nothing is more important, after faith, than repelling an aggressive enemy . . . but there is a difference between repelling an unbelieving aggressor and confronting him on his own territory." Despite the importance of the war in Chechnya, Russia is rarely cited in Islamist discourse as an enemy of the same caliber as the United States and Israel.

30. This desire to simplify the fight and emphasize its dualism often recurs in Zawahiri's and Bin Laden's discourse: according to them, tactics and alliances are of no use as long as friends and enemies have not emerged clearly in the eyes of the Muslim people. Hence, once again, the importance of the media, which play a role in this pedagogical endeavor to raise the awareness of the masses.

31. This sentence marks the conclusion of the strategic analysis leading to the September 11th attacks.

32. He speaks particularly of their presence in Saudi Arabia since August 1990.

33. Politically, the Salafist-jihadist movement needed to transcend minor differences to gather as many supporters as possible; but as Abu Musab al-Zarqawi's anti-Shiite brutality showed, such a project proved difficult in practice, since the movement's beliefs reject any other form of Islam.

34. Both, however, were lost to the jihadists after September 11, 2001.

35. This is why the jihad movement saw the U.S. invasion of Iraq as an unhoped-for opportunity to bring jihad into the heart of the Arab and Muslim world.

36. Quran 65:2–3.

37. The formula "martyrdom operations" *(amaliyyat istishhadiyya)* was first used at the time of Hezbollah's operations in the early 1980s and became common when Hamas began to carry out suicide operations in 1995. The distinction between the two expressions ("suicide attacks" and "martyrdom operations") is, of course, extremely politicized. The combination of mystical and operational registers in the second expression is highly representative of contemporary jihadist culture, whose discursive and political excesses cannot conceal an industrial and profoundly disenchanted essence.

38. The media front is seen as having as much importance as the military front. One wonders whether Zawahiri saw the media battle as a metastruggle encompassing military action, since the purpose of violence is in part to break the monopoly on information; the military front thus becomes part of the Islamist media campaign.

Loyalty and Separation

1. This invocation, which precedes every sura in the Quran except for Repentance (9), is used to begin texts of many sorts, including private correspondence or documents. This text was published in *Al-Quds al-Arabi* in December 2002, and could be found until recently on the Web site of Minbar al-Tawhid wal-Jihad. Apart from a declaration recorded in October 2002, Zawahiri had been silent since the war in Afghanistan in late 2001, and the publication of *Knights under the Prophet's Banner*.

2. In one of his more unfortunate turns of phrase, on September 17, 2001, President Bush pledged to launch a "crusade . . . to rid the world of evil-doers." The word triggered an uproar, and the next day, he issued an apology: White House spokesman Ari Fleischer explained that the president had used the word only to mean "an important cause." Jihadists, however, took this as irrefutable evidence that the U.S. administration's war on terror was nothing more than a new crusade against the Muslims and Islam. "Blessed raids" in Arabic is *ghazwa mubaraka*. *Ghazwa* is a raid or expedition that breaks a truce, and this may be the meaning Zawahiri had in mind, if the attacks were aimed at laying bare the state of war that existed between the United States and the Muslim world. More specifically, the term *ghazwa* refers to the battles waged by the Prophet. The adjective "blessed" implies that the acts were sanctioned by God and crowned with success.

3. The threat constituted by the Western media, and by the Western powers' monopoly on information, constitutes a recurring theme in the writings of Al Qaeda's ideologues, especially Bin Laden, who elaborated on his apprehensions in several passages of "Tactical Recommendations."

4. The *murji'a* advocated "referring" or "delaying" *(irja')* judgment on the ac-

tions of humans. The doctrine emerged in Kufa, at the time of the civil war pitting the supporters of Ali Ibn Abi Talib, the fourth caliph, against those of Mu'awiya, later the founder of the Umayyad dynasty, in the 650s. The *murji'a* adopted a neutral stance and refused to pass judgment on human behavior, which in this case resulted in their taking a conciliatory line with Mu'awiya. The *murji'a* define human beings according to their faith, not their actions or their manifest observance of religious rituals. The term became a polemical slur used by contemporary radical Islamists, who use it to delegitimate those they refer to as palace ulema. For instance, Safar al-Hawali, one of the most influential Islamists in Saudi Arabia, wrote his doctoral dissertation on "the phenomenon of *irja'* in Islamic thought," and argued that *irja'* was a contemporary reality, incarnated—as he implied—in the Saudi religious, academic, and legal establishment.

5. In general, radical Salafists refuse to work for the government, and argue that to do so is tantamount to recognizing the regime's legitimacy.

6. "Noblest of dynasties" is an allusion to the Saudi royal family, Zawahiri's opinion of which is well known.

7. The United States used the Northern Alliance, led by Commander Massoud until he was killed on September 9, 2001, to take Kabul in the offensive of October 2001. The lesser and the greater pilgrimages are, respectively, the *umra* and the hajj. The first is a visit that can be made to Mecca at any time during the year and is not compulsory; the second, which is incumbent on any Muslim who can perform it at least once in a lifetime, takes place at a specific time of the Muslim calendar and involves a series of rituals. "Impious imams" may be a reference to the ulema at Al-Azhar University, some of whom approved various Egyptian constitutions, as well as the peace agreement reached with Israel in 1979, or to those in the Saudi religious establishment, who were forced to accept a body of positive law adopted to supplement the sharia, as well as accept the possibility of a peace treaty with Israel.

8. In this polemical passage, Ibn Taymiyya described the way the Mongols, as new converts to Islam, imposed their own laws on their Muslim subjects while claiming to act according to Islam. Zawahiri, having undergone torture himself in Egyptian prisons in the early 1980s, frequently evokes the cruelty of Arab regimes in his writing.

9. Quran 9:46–47.

10. Ibid., 33:12–13. Yathrib was renamed Medina (the Prophet's city) after the Hijra.

11. Zawahiri operated a shift here from an emphasis inspired by Qutb and characteristic of his political opposition to the Egyptian regime, on the violation of dogma as the main problem of our time, to a focus on "loyalty and separation" as the central issue.

12. Quran 9:88.

13. Quran 3:28. Zawahiri cites this verse in reference to the pro-U.S. policies of Middle Eastern regimes like the Egyptian and Saudi governments.

14. Abu Ja'far Muhammad al-Tabari (838–923) was a renowned Muslim polymath and prolific author of Persian origin, best known for his exegesis of the Quran, but also for his *History*, which Ibn al-Athir and Ibn Khaldun cited extensively.

15. Quran, 4:138–139, 144.

16. Ibid.

17. Ibid., 5:51–58. These are the verses most commonly cited to denounce relations between Middle Eastern regimes and Western governments.

18. Emphasis is Zawahiri's.

19. On the groups that take such injunctions as justification for shunning society as a whole when they consider it un-Islamic, see notes to Zawahiri, "Bitter Harvest."

20. Quran, 5:80–81.

21. Ibid., 9:23–24. For many Islamists their interpretation of this verse has provided a justification cutting off all ties with their families.

22. Imad al-Din Isma'il Ibn Omar Ibn Kathir (c. 1300–1373) was a leading intellectual figure of fourteenth-century Syria, was a judge, a master scholar of hadith, and a Quran commentator. Bayhaqi was a *hafiz*—someone who has memorized the entire Quran, and in Bayhaqi's case numerous hadith—and a jurist and hadith compiler who died in 1066.

23. Quran 3:118.

24. Verses from a collection of Abid Ibn al-Abras, one of the most famous poets of the pre-Islamic period.

25. Ibn Masud was one of the Prophet's closest companions and one of the main hadith narrators.

26. The passage on the prohibition against placing unbelievers in important positions appears to be a direct reference to foreign experts employed by Arab regimes. Commander of the faithful *(emir al-mu'minin)* is the title taken by the caliph starting under Omar (r. 634–644).

27. Hira was the capital of the Lakhmid kingdom, allied with the Sassanians in the pre-Islamic period, in Iraq. The region was an important intellectual center in pre-Islamic times.

28. *Dhimmi* (protected peoples) was a status granted to "people of the book" under Muslim rule, who were protected in exchange for payment of tribute *(jizya)*.

29. *Kharaj* is a term that designated taxes in general before the rise of Islam. Later, it acquired the more specific sense of land tax, and was distinguished from the *ushr*, a form of tithe. Abu Talib, the paternal uncle of the Prophet, brought him up and protected him in the early years following revelation. Abu Talib died

in 619, possibly without having converted to Islam. He is still considered a model in Islamic apologetics, contrary to other notables among the Quraysh.

30. Abu Bakr, the first of the Prophet's successors, was called al-Siddiq (the Righteous). One of the earliest converts, he accompanied the Prophet on the Hijra. His caliphate lasted for two years, during the early Muslim expansion into Syria and Iraq, the establishment of control over the Hejaz, and the repression of tribes that had seceded after the Prophet's death.

31. The Sheikh al-Islam is Ibn Taymiyya, a major source for Salafists. Emphasis is Zawahiri's in the quotation that follows.

32. Quran 47:25–26.

33. Ibid., 5:51.

34. Ibid., 41.

35. Ibid., 9:47.

36. Quran 5:51–53. The heading "On the prohibition against helping them against the Muslims" is a clear reference to states in the Middle East that participated directly or indirectly in U.S.-led wars in the region: for instance, the invasion of Afghanistan in October 2601, led from U.S. bases in Qatar and Bahrain. At the time Zawahiri was writing, in late 2002, the war on Iraq seemed both inevitable and imminent, and the question of how the states of the region were going to react was arising. The repetition of certain verses ad nauseam indicates that the aim of this text is indoctrination, in the literal sense.

37. Emphasis is Zawahiri's.

38. Quran 9:71. Abu Muhammad Ibn Hazm (994–1064) was a great Andalusian man of letters and theologian who lived during the troubled times of the "party kings" (petty rulers who had divided among themselves the cities and provinces of the declining Umayyad caliphate in Spain). He retired from public life to devote himself to scholarship; his *Ring of the Dove* (or *Necklace of Love*) is a literary classic, renowned for its psychological subtlety.

39. One of the consequences of declaring a man an apostate is the immediate annulment of his marriage, since a non-Muslim man cannot marry a Muslim woman. In 1995 a religious tribunal in Cairo thus dissolved the marriage of Nasr Hamid Abu Zayd, a Quran scholar and professor of literature at Cairo University, on the basis of accusations that he was an apostate. He chose to leave Egypt and settle in the Netherlands with his wife. The case embarrassed the Egyptian regime by undermining its image as the guarantor of "moderate Islam."

40. Sind is the valley and delta of the Indus River; today, one of the provinces that make up Pakistan.

41. General headquarters for the U.S. Central Command (CENTCOM) in the Middle East is located in Qatar; the Fifth Fleet is based in Bahrain.

42. Pakistani President Pervez Musharraf, who took power in a military coup

in 1999, has been one of Washington's most faithful allies since the September 11 attacks.

43. "Gulf states": the port of Aden has been an important stop for Western ships traveling between Europe, Africa, and Asia. In mentioning Egypt in this context, Zawahiri was probably referring to the Suez Canal, the passage for Western ships on their way between the Middle East and Europe.

44. On November 3, 2002, an alleged Al Qaeda operative, Abu Ali al-Harithi, suspected of having helped plan the attack on the USS *Cole*, was killed along with five others near Marib, two hundred kilometers from Sanaa, by a missile fired from an unmanned Predator operated by the CIA. The Yemeni government tacitly supported the operation.

45. *Hurma* may be rendered as "honor" or "personal integrity" but also refers to private space, which must not be violated: the root encompasses various meanings, including forbidden, sacred, and taboo.

46. Emphasis is Zawahiri's. Ibn Taymiyya's distinction highlights the difference between Bin Laden and Zawahiri.

47. Before the late 1990s, this was the most important form of jihad, in Zawahiri's opinion. As one can see here, he still believes that it is important, but he now places it second on his list of priorities.

48. Quran 5:65. Once again, Zawahiri uses the Quran as a conclusive argument.

49. Shāfʿī was one of the founders of the four main legal schools of Sunni Islam. He was born in 767 into a family descended from the Prophet and studied with Malik Ibn Anas. He was persecuted for a time for having supported rivals of the Abbasids (r. 750–1258). Refusing all official posts thereafter, he ended his life in Egypt, where he taught at a mosque in Fustat. Some Malikis and Hanbalis accused him of a lack of rigor in his narration of hadith; the fact that Zawahiri cites him here is evidence, once again, that Zawahiri relied on a variety of traditions rather than a specific school to give his positions legitimacy.

50. Quran 4:59, 64, 80, 65.

51. Ibid., 24:63.

52. Emphasis is Zawahiri's.

53. Quran 5:50.

54. Emphasis is Zawahiri's. Zawahiri probably intends to highlight the point that minor and major matters are considered equivalent for this purpose.

55. Quran 66:9.

56. In this passage, as in most of this text, the cumulative weight of quotations has the effect of making the text as impersonal as possible. Commentaries, no matter how vehement, are situated in a tradition of classical authorship, the better to demonstrate their orthodox, unassailable character. Zawahiri showed an almost

compulsive concern for citing his sources scrupulously, which many traditional ulema, who are confident of their erudition, do not do. Perhaps this was a way for Zawahiri to compensate for his lack of formal religious training and consequent potential lack of legitimacy.

57. Quran 5:51–53.

58. Ibid., 8:72–75.

59. Ibn al-Arabi, a Muslim mystic (1165–1240), was one of the greatest metaphysical thinkers and the author, among other works, of the *Futhat Makkiyya* (Meccan Conquests).

60. A *dirham* was a unit of medieval currency.

61. The danger represented by the Arab regimes, according to Zawahiri, also derives from their control of the educational and cultural establishments in the Middle East, promoting what the Islamists view as un-Islamic policies.

62. Zawahiri's review of the international system born after World War II presents decolonization and the creation of the United Nations as the continuation of Western domination over the Muslim countries, established through the creation of artificial and arbitrary borders, support for pro-Western regimes, and the imposition of international law in violation of Islamic principles. Furthermore, the veto power granted the five permanent members of the Security Council enables them to impose their respective policies on the council's decisions—in the eyes of many in the Middle East the main reason that resolutions condemning Israel have so rarely been passed by the council. Beyond their legal position with regard to the United Nations, radical Islamists have shown intense dislike for the institution: in May 2004, for example, Bin Laden offered ten kilograms of gold to whoever was able to kill Kofi Annan.

63. At the Arab League summit held in Beirut in 2002, the Arab states accepted a proposal put forth by then crown prince Abdullah of Saudi Arabia for general peace with Israel in return for its withdrawal to the 1967 borders. The proposal had been formulated in April 2002, when the crown prince visited the United States.

64. Quran 4:75.

65. The first "world summit against terrorism" (restricted to its Islamist form) was held in Sharm al-Sheikh, Egypt, in March 2002.

66. Especially the Pakistani government is meant, which Al Qaeda has condemned repeatedly for its strategic alliance with the United States.

67. *Ahl al-sunna wal-jama'a* designates the consensus of Muslim scholars, past and present, and adherence to that body of opinion.

68. The Kharijites were initially allied with Ali Ibn Abi Talib, the fourth caliph, but turned against him, one of them going so far as to assassinate him (in 661 C.E.). They advocated leadership by the best of the Muslims, applying extremely stringent criteria in this regard, and frequently condemned as apostates those who

did not conform. The accusation is most generally directed by official Islamic institutions against jihadist groups; here, Zawahiri turned it against them, thereby condemning them in one fell swoop for a conciliatory attitude toward the political establishment and an intransigent, highly rigoristic attitude toward fellow Muslims.

69. Al-Azhar blessed the agreement on the basis of *maslaha,* or public interest, a principle of jurisprudence whose application in this case was justified, according to him, by the benefits that would accrue from the treaty.

70. Zawahiri is referring to Bin Baz's approval of the Saudi authorities' request that U.S.-led military force protect the kingdom against a possible Iraqi attack in August 1990.

71. In August 1990 Bin Laden offered Sultan Ibn Abd al-Aziz, Saudi Arabia's minister of defense, Afghan Arabs to defend Saudi Arabia and free Kuwait. His proposal was turned down, on the pretext that the terrain was not amenable to an Afghan-type guerrilla war. This was the first major disagreement between Bin Laden and the Saudi authorities, and led to a split a few months later.

72. Resolution 687 required that Iraq accept inspections of its nuclear facilities, carried out by teams from the International Atomic Energy Agency. Among the conditions of the cease-fire imposed by the U.N. in March 1991 was the payment of compensation for war damages, most of which Saddam Hussein's government owed Kuwait.

73. This is a reference to threats made by some members of Congress after September 11 against Saudi Arabia, which they accused of supporting and financing terrorism. The most virulent remarks were made by Laurent Murawiec, an analyst at the Rand Corporation, in July 2002, when he described Saudi Arabia to the Defense Policy Board as U.S. public enemy Number 1, and called for military intervention aimed at dividing it into three separate parts: in the west, the province of the Hejaz, where the sanctuaries are located; in the east, in the region inhabited by the country's Shiite majority, a vast "Petrolistan"; and in the center, the Najd, left to its own devices.

74. Quran 5:51.

75. Ibid., 2:256.

76. Ibid., 4:60.

77. Ibid., 9:47.

78. Ibid., 2:149.

79. Ibid., 63:4.

80. Ibid., 4:143.

81. Ibid., 9:10.

82. The metaphor refers to preoccupation with mundane affairs to the detriment of jihad.

83. Ibid., 61:10–13.

84. In late March 2002, Israeli forces launched their largest offensive in the West Bank since they had occupied it in 1967, targeting civilians, government buildings and records, historical sites, and urban infrastructure. The operation included a massive incursion into Jenin refugee camp, carrying out wide-scale destruction and preventing humanitarian workers from entering the camp for eleven days. See, for example, http://news.bbc.co.uk/1/hi/world/middle_east/1937387.stm.

85. Emphasis is Zawahiri's.

86. Quran 3:200.

87. Ibid., 18:21.

Introduction: Abu Musab al-Zarqawi

1. Jean-Pierre Milelli, "Une lettre d'Al-Zawahiri à Al-Zarqawi" [A Letter from al-Zawahiri to al-Zarqawi], *Maghreb-Machrek* 186 (winter 2005–2006).

2. His name, like the noms de guerre of many Islamists, was a construct using two traditional Arabic forms: the *kunya* (Abu, or "the father of," usually followed by the name of the man's son, or, as in Zarqawi's case, by the name of a figure he admired) and the *nisba,* denoting geographical origin, for example (in this instance, al-Zarqawi signifies "from the city of Zarqa"). See Annemarie Schimmel, *Islamic Names* (Edinburgh: Edinburgh University Press, 1990).

3. He used this *kunya* even before the birth of his eldest son by his first wife, who bore him three other sons and daughters; today they live with their mother in Zarqa. He also had an eighteen-month-old son by a second wife. Both were killed with him in Iraq.

4. The Circassians were a people from northern Caucasia, who fled as the Russian army advanced through Asia in 1864. They found employment in the Ottoman Empire, many of them in the cavalry, where they were employed to put down nationalist uprisings.

5. Reference to a Quranic verse (46:31).

6. Maan is a town in southern Jordan where clashes between the inhabitants and government forces broke out at least four times between 1989 and 2004. In October 2002 one particularly violent confrontation was triggered by investigations carried out among local Islamists after the U.S. diplomat Laurence Foley was assassinated.

7. "Al-Zarqawi's Tribe Cables King Abdallah Pledging Allegiance," *Al-Ra'y al-'Am,* May 29, 2004.

8. The Popular Front for the Liberation of Palestine, a left-wing organization headed by George Habash.

9. Described as "the most influential living Jihadi Theorist": http://www.army.mil/professionalwriting/volumes/volume5/january_2007/1_07_3.html.

10. For his biography, see Jean-Charles Brisard, *Zarqawi: The New Face of Al-Qaeda* (New York: Other Press, 2005).

11. *Al-Bunyan al-Marsus* (The Ranks) is named after a verse in the Quran (61:4).

12. Autonomous since 1991, by virtue of U.N. resolution 687, enforced by "Operation Restore Hope."

13. The American businessman was executed in May 2004. According to Human Rights Watch, in the decapitation video Berg's captors explicitly noted that they were killing him because the U.S. authorities had rebuffed their requests for an exchange of prisoners. The administration denied any knowledge of such claims.

14. See also http://www.uga.edu/islam/zarqawi.html. The reference to exchange of prisoners is far terser: "As for you, mothers and wives of the American soldiers, we say to you that we offered the American Administration the chance to exchange this prisoner for some of the prisoners in Abu-Ghraib, but they refused."

15. *Al-Zarqawi: Munasara wa Munasaha,* formerly on www.tawhed.ws.

16. Al-Maqdisi was released in June 2005, after having been acquitted of having planned attacks on American targets in Jordan, but was arrested once again after giving an interview to Al-Jazeera. He is currently in Jordanian custody.

17. They had three children, among them a son named Anas and another named Malik, probably in homage to Malik Ibn Anas.

18. The attacker said to have carried out the operation, however, was Yasin Jarrar, a Palestinian from Zarqa, and the father of Zarqawi's second wife, according to the investigation carried out in Jordan by Hazim al-Amin and published in *Al-Hayat* on December 14, 15, and 16, 2004.

19. *Al-Ra'y al-'Am,* September 20, 2004.

20. Qa'idat al-Jihad fi Bilad al-Rafidayn.

21. The Arabic original may be found at http://www.cpa-iraq.org/arabic/transcripts/20040212_zarqawi_full-arabic.html.

22. See http://www.cpa-iraq.org/transcripts/20040212_zarqawi_full.html.

23. See http://www.cpa-iraq.org/transcripts/20040212_zarqawi_full.html.

24. "Our Legal Position on the Karzai Government of Iraq," published after Iyad Alawi's government was appointed. The title is reminiscent of a sentence used by Bin Laden in his "Tactical Recommendations": "The crusaders gave power to the Karzai of Kabul and the Karzai of Pakistan, the Karzai of Kuwait, the Karzai of Bahrain, and the Karzai of Qatar."

Letter to Bin Laden and Zawahiri

1. The author's name does not appear in the text, but it is possible to guess that the two recipients (the dual grammatical form is used) are Bin Laden and

Zawahiri: the "summits" and "mountains" clearly refer to Afghanistan, and at the end of the text a phrase makes it clear that this is an offer to collaborate with Bin Laden and Zawahiri in Iraq. See also http://www.cpa-iraq.org/transcripts/20040212_zarqawi_full.html.

2. The entire text is in the traditional rhythmic prose form called *saj'*.

3. After the U.S. invasion of Iraq in March 2003, jihadists have frequently described the American presence as a wonderful opportunity. On December 16, 2004, for instance, Bin Laden declared: "A strike against the United States in Iraq, in terms of the economy and the loss of life, would be a golden opportunity." Zarqawi avoids recognizing Iraq's legitimacy, and prefers to designate it as a geographical entity. In the same manner, Saudi Arabia is usually referred to in this literature as the land of the two sanctuaries.

4. A reference to Evangelical Christians, especially those who support the Bush administration.

5. "With all its allies" is a sarcastic reference to the coalition that the United States had difficulty cobbling together, which included microstates in the Pacific and a few small states in Central America.

6. While Zarqawi depreciates this term, coined by the Western media in the aftermath of the invasion of Iraq, the "triangle" already existed under Saddam as a territorial unit characterized by its inhabitants' renowned loyalty to the regime.

7. This may be a reference to the Shiites' bid to obtain representation proportionate to their demographic weight (60 percent of the population). The term *rafida* (rejectionists) can be traced back to a hadith in which the Prophet is said to have warned: "There will be a group of people that call themselves rejectionists. If you meet them, kill them, for they are polytheists."

8. For Zarqawi, the point is not to eradicate these differences but to prevent power from slipping from the Sunnis' grasp. His remarks are in keeping with the very pragmatic, realistic general tone of the "analysis" he presents here. Ibn Abihi was governor of Kufa, then Basra, under the first Umayyad caliph. He died in 673.

9. Massoud Barzani, the son of Mustafa Barzani, a legendary figure in the Iraqi Kurdish independence movement, headed the Kurdistan Democratic Party (KDP); Jalal Talabani was head of the Patriotic Union of Kurdistan (PUK), which split from the KDP in 1974. Barzani controlled northern Iraqi Kurdistan, on the border with Turkey, and Talabani controlled the southern part, on the border with Iran. On April 6, 2005, the Iraqi National Assembly nominated Talabani president of Iraq.

10. The two main Kurdish parties are secularist. The Islamic Movement of Kurdistan, which was created in the 1980s as a local branch of the Muslim Brotherhood, never caught on among the Kurds. In December 2001 an Islamist group named Ansar al-Islam was created, but it had a marginal position, especially after it was radicalized in 2002.

11. Turning the widespread view of the Kurdish situation on its head, Zarqawi is implying that the Kurdish zones' self-declared secularism was the result not of autonomy in these regions, but rather of the Baath project's success among the Kurds.

12. This view of the Shiites as cunning and dishonest, practicing religious dissimulation *(taqiyya; kitman)*, is common in Sunni jihadist literature of Wahhabi inspiration.

13. Quran 63:4. The verse cannot designate the Shiites, who appeared several decades after revelation; rather, as the sura's title indicates, it refers to hypocrites.

14. Shiites consider that the leaders of the community should be descendants of Ali Ibn Abi Talib and Fatima, the Prophet's daughter. "Tomb worship" is a reference to the practice, common among Shiites, of visiting the tombs of pious figures. Jihadist Salafism, by contrast, views such expressions of faith as a form of polytheism. "Mothers of the believers" refers to the wives of the Prophet, especially Aisha, who took sides against Ali Ibn Abi Talib in the first civil war that broke out after the Prophet's death. Sunnis, on the contrary, see her as one of the most reliable sources of hadith. The most radical Shiites are highly critical of the first three caliphs and of some of the Prophet's companions, whom they accuse of having kept Ali Ibn Abi Talib away from the caliphate, when it was he, according to them, who should have been the Prophet's first successor. Ritual excoriation of the caliphs was long an integral part of the Shiite Friday sermon. Shiites believe that the imams are the only ones capable of knowing the true meaning of the sacred texts.

15. *Nawasib* is a pejorative term by which Shiites designate the Sunnis.

16. Zarqawi pretends not to know about the oppression of the Shiite population in Iraq under Saddam Hussein's regime. Tikrit and Anbar are Sunni strongholds; Tikrit is Saddam Hussein's birthplace.

17. According to Zarqawi's analysis, that the majority of the Shiite community, under the leadership of Ayatollah Sistani, has refrained from rebelling is proof of a strategy of infiltration aimed at seizing power silently.

18. Zarqawi presents the Iraqi conflict as one pitting Iraq's Shiites against the Sunni community worldwide, reflecting his belief that the Shiites seek to undermine the unity of Islam and act only according to their group interests.

19. See the introduction to this section. The Badr Brigade was named after the Battle of Badr. The American forces did withdraw from several areas and allow previously trained units to take over. For Zarqawi, these units are treacherous for two reasons: because they are collaborating with the enemy, and because they are Shiites, and therefore by definition motivated by their desire to take power away from the Sunnis. In an audio recording broadcast on July 4, 2005, Zarqawi announced that the Omar Brigade had been created to "eliminate the symbols and factions of the perfidious Badr Brigade."

20. A few pages later, Zarqawi contradicts himself, stating that the Americans did not go to Iraq only to leave, and predicting that they will not pull out.

21. Zarqawi is alluding to the numerous assassinations that followed the U.S. invasion and that were possibly motivated by a desire to settle scores with former regime cadres—hence the high number of Sunni victims.

22. In August 2004, during the second uprising of Muqtada al-Sadr's supporters, a mysterious Zulfiqar Army (named after Ali Ibn Abi Talib's sword) came to prominence by assassinating insurgents. This anti-insurgent group may well be made up of Shiite tribal elements, mobilized by the United States to combat the resistance from within.

23. Zarqawi is echoing a classical theme in Iraqi propaganda of the late 1980s, at the time when the country was at war with Iran and felt threatened by the Alawite ruling class (tenuously linked to the Shiites) in Syria, allied with Tehran. The theme of the "Shiite axis" was used as a bogeyman to evoke the potential creation of a Shiite federation extending from Lebanon to Iran, and even Pakistan (the Shiite Bhutto family was still powerful, and intermittently controlled the government).

24. The Safavid dynasty that ruled Persia from 1501 to 1736 was Shiite. The army of Shah Abbas I pushed back the Ottoman troops and took Baghdad in January 1624, massacring part of the Sunni population. The Ottomans reconquered Baghdad only in 1638. The Ottomans had besieged Vienna once in 1529, unsuccessfully, and failed again in 1683.

25. Genghis Khan was the Mongol leader (1167–1227) who unified the main tribes of the Mongolian steppe, waged devastating military campaigns, and conquered China and Persia. His sons carried on his legacy. For the imperial civilizations that he conquered, he remains the symbol of the brutal barbarian. Genghis Khan's grandson Hulagu (1217–1265), who ruled Iran, conquered Baghdad in 1258, and executed the last Abbasid caliph, among others. Hulagu went on to conquer Syria, before the Mamluks in Egypt halted his onslaught in 1260. He founded the Ilkhanid dynasty in Persia. In February 1260 the Mongols, led by Hulagu, massacred the Muslim population of Aleppo.

26. Ibn al-Alqami, a Shiite, was the last vizir of the last Abbasid caliph, a Sunni. Aleppo fell to the Mongols in February 1260. Many Shiites, Christians, and followers of heterodox faiths served them.

27. By Ibn Taymiyya. The long quotation creates a telescopic effect between the thirteenth century and the present.

28. The two first caliphs and the Prophet's favorite wife, whom Ali Ibn Abi Talib's supporters opposed.

29. Abu Bakr al-Khallal (d. 923) was a disciple of Ahmad Ibn Hanbal who devoted his life to writing down his teacher's opinions.

30. Faryabi was one of the first hadith compilers (d. 827).

31. The Shiites claim that verses announcing that Ali Ibn Abi Talib was to be the Prophet's successor were expunged by his opponents.

32. Ibn Taymiyya presented battle against "deviant" Muslim groups as a virtual obligation for Sunnis. On the Kharijites, see Zawahiri, "Loyalty and Separation."

33. Jihadists see Muslim dissidents as having a special status. Whereas the members of other monotheistic religions enjoy a status regulated by the Quran, those who are not identified explicitly by sharia are surrounded by a "legal vacuum." According to the jihadists, the only solution is to kill them as apostates.

34. Saying attributed to Ali Ibn Abi Talib, who classified people into three categories: spiritual masters, their disciples, and the mob.

35. Salafist jihadists, and Wahhabis in general, see the ceremonies associated with Sufism as heretical behavior.

36. This expression illustrates Zarqawi's autodidactic culture, cobbled together from various different intellectual movements.

37. A reference to the story of Joseph in the Quran, and his brothers' assertion to their father that a wolf had devoured him.

38. The Iraqi branch of the Muslim Brotherhood, Al-Hizb al-Islami, was established in the 1950s.

39. Paradoxically, Zarqawi is admitting that funds for jihad were provided partially by the Muslim Brothers, although the Brotherhood had refused to fight.

40. "Events in Syria" is an allusion to the Hama uprising from 1974 to 1982 against the Syrian regime.

41. Loss of life, therefore, was not only a hazard of war, in Zawahiri's opinion: it was also a means to an end.

42. This observation confirms estimates made by intelligence services and published by the media: foreign jihadists in Iraq, numbering a few thousand at best, have played a minor military role in the resistance. See for example "CIA Studies Provide Glimpse of Insurgents in Iraq," *Washington Post*, February 6, 2005.

43. By "declaring a general mobilization," he means making jihad an individual obligation.

44. Phrase attributed to the Prophet's companions during the Khaybar expedition, in a desperate situation, before divine intervention produced a miracle. The hadith says: "The enemy is at our heels and the river is before us." This passage shows astonishing realism and objectivity, typical of a relatively recent genre in jihadist literature that offers rational, realistic analysis of the strategic situation. See Brynjar Lia and Thomas Hegghammer, "Jihadi Strategic Studies," *Studies in Conflict and Terrorism*, May 27, 2004.

45. This passage echoes Bin Laden's theories on the critical mass of mujahedeen that must be reached before mobilization can be suspended. In his "Tactical Recommendations," Bin Laden noted that too many unarmed and untrained volunteers could constitute more of a burden than an advantage.

46. The only difference between Saddam's regime and the occupation, then, is that taking up arms has become possible under the occupation.

47. A frequent theme in jihad literature, which presents the U.S. use of unmanned aircraft and heavily armored vehicles as proof of cowardice.

48. This is a particularly interesting remark, given that Zarqawi was making it in January 2004, at a time when no foreign hostages had been taken in Iraq. The wave of kidnappings began suddenly in April 2004, during the first siege of Falluja. The first Americans were kidnapped on April 9. Zarqawi's group took its first hostage, Nicholas Berg, on the 10th. This text shows that Zarqawi had been envisaging such operations for a while.

49. Indeed, in February 2004 the number of suicide attacks against the Iraqi security forces escalated sharply, with a concomitant drop in the number of attacks on Western targets.

50. "Sabeans" is a reference to Abdallah Ibn Saba, who appears in anti-Shiite Islamist literature as a Jew who created Shiism in order to destroy Islam from within.

51. In Zarqawi's lexicon, the heretics are the Shiites, and the unbelievers the non-Muslims (that is, the U.S. forces).

52. For Zarqawi, it is the Shiites, not the regime, who are the "nearby enemy," and they must therefore be targeted first.

53. The Governing Council was the interim structure set up by the U.S. forces before an Iraqi government was elected. Critics of the invasion saw it as a puppet regime.

54. Zarqawi's sensitivity to public opinion is particularly surprising, given that his group was one of the most violent in the Iraqi resistance.

55. A saying attributed to the poet al-Farazdaq (641–730), who was leaving Iraq for Medina while al-Husayn, Ali Ibn Abi Talib's son, was traveling toward Iraq, where he was killed by the Umayyad caliph's men in October 680. According to Tabari's *History*, al-Husayn is said to have asked Farazdaq for news of those he had left behind; the poet replied: "You have asked the right person: men's hearts are with you, and their swords with the Umayyads. The decision will come from heaven, for God does what he will." *Tarikh al-Umam wal-Muluk* (Beirut: Dar al-Kutub al-Ilmiyya, 1997), 3:296. Whether or not the story is apocryphal, Muawiya the Umayyad caliph, and his son, Yazid, went down in history as symbols of harsh political realism. The mention of suffocation and wearing down the roads appears to be a reference to the jihadists' continual search for a new arena.

56. Quran 85:4. The verse refers to Christian martyrs persecuted in 530 by Abu Nuwas, the Jewish ruler of Yemen. Nawawi, a hadith expert, died in 1277. The reference is to his *Commentary* on Muslim's compilation.

57. *Husayniyyas* are Shiite places of worship, named after Husayn, the son of Ali Ibn Abi Talib.

58. An interim "Iraqi government" (nominated by the United States) was initially meant to take power on June 30. It gained sovereignty two days ahead of schedule.

59. Zarqawi seems to be questioning the recipients of his message about the Shiite issue, for Bin Laden—unlike the Iraqi jihadists—never dealt with the matter directly or made it a central problem. Rather, different local offshoots of Al Qaeda introduced their particular preoccupations into the general system.

60. A pledge of allegiance did follow, and it was accepted by Bin Laden, on December 27, 2004. Does this mean that Bin Laden accepted the strategy as well?

INDEX